D1239332

The Design of
Social Welfare

THE DESIGN OF SOCIAL WELFARE

David Macarov

Paul Baerwald School of Social Work
The Hebrew University of Jerusalem

Holt, Rinehart and Winston

New York   Chicago   San Francisco   Dallas
Montreal   Toronto   London   Sydney

Copyright © 1978 by Holt, Rinehart and Winston

Library of Congress Cataloging in Publication Data

Macarov, David.
  The Design of social welfare.

  Bibliography: p. 259.
  Includes index.
  1. Social service. 2. Public welfare. I. Title.
HV40.M128   361   76-50864
ISBN 0-03-029346-4

Printed in the United States of America

   1   038   9 8 7 6 5 4

Preface

This book is a direct outcome of many years of introducing students to various phases of social welfare: as a faculty member of the Hebrew University of Jerusalem and as a visiting faculty member at Haifa University, Boston University, the University of Pennsylvania, Adelphi University, and the University of Melbourne; conducting seminars at Virginia Commonwealth University and the University of Michigan; and as a lecturer in a variety of settings. The questions and comments of students, suggestions by colleagues, and the shared experiences of many social workers have shaped my views concerning the reasons for, and the influences upon, social welfare that determine its present shape.

The bulk of the writing for this book was done while I was in residence at the Adelphi University School of Social Work, and I should like to record my appreciation for the many kindnesses extended to me during that period by the entire faculty and staff, and especially by Dean Joseph L. Vigilante and Associate Dean Beulah Rothman. I am equally grateful to the Director of the Paul Baerwald School of Social Work of the Hebrew University of Jerusalem—Professor Jona M. Rosenfeld—who made possible my extended leave.

A number of friends and colleagues have read various drafts of the manuscript, in whole or in part, and all of them have been generous with their help. These include Professors Risha Levinson, Louise Skolnik, Richard Skolnik, Naarayan Viswanathan, and Sophie Wojciechowski, as well as Dean Joseph L. Vigilante. Dr. Katherine Kendall of the International Association of Schools of Social Work made extensive comments on one proposed chapter. I am grateful to them all.

Nevertheless, as Florian might have put it: "Advice is what, if you have to take it, it ain't." Consequently, all lacks, failings, and errors in this book should be attributed to my failure to accept some of the advice offered. I alone am responsible.

I am also grateful to the many authors whose work I have drawn upon and cited. Without the enormous amount of investment each of them made, not only would this book not have been possible, but social work practice and life itself would be immeasurably impoverished. Truly, "we may be pygmies, but we sit on the shoulders of giants."

Finally, despite the burden of her own work and studies, my wife, Frieda, eased the process of writing in her own inimitable way, and I am truly appreciative.

D.M.

Contents

PART I

MEETING HUMAN NEEDS

Introduction

Social welfare has become an enormous, varied, and complex institution. When changes in welfare policies and programs take place, they affect millions of people, and even experts have difficulty comprehending the widespread ramifications of what may at first seem to be relatively minor shifts in goals, methods, or activities. In the United States, federal-state-local relationships regarding social welfare have become a field of expertise in themselves, as has each area of service, type of problem, and category of client. Consequently, the traditional methods of studying social welfare—description, history, and partialization— require supplementation in order that an adequate understanding of this immense, complicated, and ever-changing institution be conveyed. Those people interested or involved in social-welfare policy, programs, and practice find it necessary to understand, describe, and define the essence, boundaries, and dynamics of social welfare. If they are not to be mere functionaries or dilettantes, they need to be able to predict future developments, prescribe desirable steps, and take effective action.

For such purposes, an outline of policies, a listing of programs, or a description of practice is neither possible nor sufficient. Understanding the totality of social welfare requires the use of organizing concepts that inform the various parts. By comprehending the underlying motivations that lead individuals, organizations, and governments to engage in social-welfare activities, and by understanding the deep-seated societal attitudes that support and constrain these motivations as they are put into practice, one can understand the strengths exhibited by some programs and the weaknesses of others; the gaps between policies and practice that result from conflicts between, or ambivalences regarding, motivations and attitudes; the changes in direction that have occurred and that can be anticipated; and the areas in which improvements can most successfully be sought.

Education for social work, in particular, must attempt to instill in students an understanding of the basic concepts that mold social-welfare policy and practice if ι e graduates are to be prepared to grapple effectively with important issues in the real world. Unless this is done, practice will continue to be ahead of education, as it so often has been in the past. For example, the emergence of new roles for social workers, such as advocates, brokers, and mediators, arose not from laws or administrative regulations that mandated training or retraining of social workers for these new tasks, but as a result of a dialectic between changing societal forces, and from new views regarding the nature of these forces and their interfaces. It is the ability to view such changes in conceptual terms that will allow social-work educators to remain abreast of the social-welfare scene, and that will allow students to deal with important issues instead of minutiae.

This increasing dependence on conceptual thinking has its roots in the quiet revolution that has been taking place within American society for the last several decades. The revolution consists of an inexorable shift from the production of goods to the production of services. For many years the United States acquired and maintained its reputation as a world leader through manufacturing and distributing goods that assured its population of a high standard of living and permitted it to export goods. Economic theory, the structure of the market, manpower policies, the educational system, and social welfare were all based on, and conditioned by, the need for production of goods, which became both means and goal for the society. People viewed themselves, and were viewed by others, in terms of their relationship to the productive sector.

However, the service field—both the indirect sector, including transportation, wholesaling, retailing, and banking, and the direct sector, including doctors, dentists, hairdressers, teachers, and social workers—has been slowly growing in proportion to the production of material goods. In 1929, service employment was about 40 percent of total employment;[1] in 1950, the United States edged into what has been described as the "post-industrial" world when service employment reached 51 percent.[2] By 1967, it had reached 55 percent.[3] It has been estimated that by 1980 the service sector will be more than double the size of the productive sector.[4]

The results of this change are obvious in many areas and will have continuing and growing impact. Between 1973 and 1983, expenditures for education alone will have increased by almost 30 percent in dollars held constant, and by a good deal more than that in inflationary terms. During that period there will have been a 5 percent increase in bachelor's degrees granted, an 18 percent increase in master's degrees, and a 32 percent increase in doctorates.[5]

Social welfare, too, has been and will continue to be an important component of this growth in the service sector. No matter how it is measured, social-welfare growth is almost exponential. For example, in 1928–29, state and federal social-welfare services (omitting voluntary and private services) cost almost $4 billion, and in 1967–68, this had increased twenty-eightfold to $112 billion. The latter sum made up 40 percent of all government expenditures and was well over half the total expenditures of many states.[6] If cash benefits alone are considered, these grew from $4 billion in 1940 to more than $125 billion in 1975;[7] and it is estimated that by 1980 cash income-maintenance programs, helping people buy essentials, and aid for social programs will increase by 40–50 percent, to something more than $200 billion.[8] Finally, whereas the cost of total social-welfare expenditures in the United States, including those of voluntary agencies, was 13.5 percent of the Gross National Product in 1968,[9] it had risen to 23 percent by 1971.[10] In Australia, the "Federal sphere welfare expenditure grew by 91.94 percent" from 1974 to 1976.[11]

This sheer growth in expenditures has been accompanied by a commensurate increase in social-welfare services and by their increasing complexity and complicated interrelationships.[12] The major breakthrough insofar as proliferation of government services on the national level is concerned took place in 1935 with the passage of the Social Security Act. Since that time, new programs have been undertaken and new agencies to carry them out have spun off with bewildering rapidity. A complete diagram of the Department of Health, Education, and Welfare and the relationships between its various departments, sections, and agencies resembles nothing so much as a wiring diagram for a new type of space capsule—and that omits state, county, and local services. In the voluntary sector, it was estimated as long ago as 1961 that there were 100,000 voluntary health and welfare agencies in the United States, to which must be added another 100,000 fraternal, civic, veterans', and related organizations that sponsor some health and welfare activities, as well as many of the 300,000 churches, which offer similar programs.[13] In 1975, using a slightly different method of defining such organizations, it was estimated that "counting local chapters of regional or national groups, there may be as many as six million private voluntary organizations in the United States." There are 37,000 human-service organizations in the "core group" of traditional philanthropic organizations. New York City alone has around 6,000 block associations.[14]

The growth in social welfare as an institution has been paralleled by
an increase in the number of social workers undertaking professional
training. In 1952, there were about 4,000 full-time students enrolled in
master's programs in social work. In 1974, there were not only more
than 16,000 such students, but there were also almost 30,000 full-time
undergraduate students studying social work, and another 14,000 students in other concentrations taking social-work courses.[15] In 1940
about 70,000 people were employed as social workers, and by 1974 this
had risen to 300,000. It is estimated that there will be more than
400,000 social workers by 1980, and that 200,000 of them will need
professional training.[16]

Nor is rapid growth the only hallmark of modern social welfare.
Changes in policies and programs sometimes occur virtually overnight.
The sudden adoption of Supplementary Security Income (SSI) to replace Aid to the Blind, the Aged, and the Disabled was a move from
decentralized to centralized services and required such immediate administrative changes, with no opportunity to plan the new system or to
try it out, that the result has been estimated as 25–50 percent errors in
payments. Title XX of the Federal Social Security Act requires that
states develop and implement comprehensive new plans for the provision of social services such as day care, foster care, homemaking assistance, and family counseling—a requirement that will result in massive
changes in present programs.

Further, new agencies continually develop in response to newly recognized needs. One of the most recent is an organization concerned
with Sudden Infant Death Syndrome (SIDS). The multiplicity of agencies is attested by the handbook for Long Island social workers, published in 1977, which includes—among others—BOCES, VEEB, CASA,
WIN, DSS, CLAC, and FISH. Most of these agencies did not exist as
recently as five years earlier, and since publication of the handbook
there have appeared CAIR, AID, and SHARE.[17]

The future promises equal, if not faster, changes. We can expect new
kinds of sex therapy, abortion counseling, clinics for insomniacs, services for the dying, lifetime education, new forms of interpersonal
recreation, women's groups, men's groups, new parareligious mind-
expanding programs, and more.[18] The work week will probably continue to contract, with a consequent increase in leisure.[19] Each of these
developments will create individual and societal stresses and tensions
that will require new responses, including social-welfare services. The
very move from a productive to a service economy will create changes
in job statuses, training, salaries, and self-images, each of which may
result in a need for social-welfare services, or changes in such services.[20]

Together with this growth in sheer size and kinds of social-welfare
services, there has been and will continue to be increasing complexity

within services and among them. Larger services will require specialized subsystems to perform specific functions,[21] and the relationships between the subsystems will become increasingly intricate. Organizations will need to distinguish between direct services and access services,[22] or core services, component services, and linked services,[23] and allocate resources accordingly. Establishment of information and referral services will require new means of communication between agencies,[24] and differentiation between competition, cooperation, coordination, and collaboration.[25]

The total effect of this continuing and faster growth, change, and complexity is that social welfare is becoming more difficult to comprehend through the traditional explanatory methods mentioned previously—description, history, and partialization. In order to describe welfare, it has been found necessary to group certain of its attributes, such as fields of service, into units like

> family agencies
> services to children
> school social work
> services in health care
> services in psychiatric settings
> correctional services
> services for the aging[26]

and to discuss each one separately. Or social welfare may be described in terms of types of services, as

> adjunctive social services
> advocacy and legal services
> vocational rehabilitation
> homemaker and home-help services
> community-center, settlement, and group services
> family planning
> job placement and training
> participation[27]

Again, social welfare may be grouped according to broader headings —justice, education, health, and urban families.[28] Kamerman and Kahn list as the five basic social programs income maintenance, health, education, housing, and employment, and make a plea for recognition of a sixth area, which they term "personal" or "general" social services.[29]

There are also attempts to portray the totality of social welfare by describing the methods used in its implementation: social casework, social group work, community organization, social policy and planning, social administration, and research.[30] Finally, there are many combinations of these various approaches, usually emphasizing one over the other. Each of these is an attempt to *describe* social welfare—to present a snapshot or portrait, as it were, of social welfare.

Another approach is the historical treatment, which, owing to the complexity of social welfare, must perforce limit itself to only one strand of social welfare, such as institutionalization,[31] or the community-development movement,[32] or one period in history, such as the past half century[33] or century.[34] Even the history may focus on only one problem or program, such as the War on Poverty[35] or the Family Assistance Plan.[36]

Finally, it is sometimes deemed more feasible to partialize social welfare, paying attention mostly to poverty,[37] or to mental health,[38] child care,[39] policy,[40] planning,[41] or education for the social services.[42] There are also international and transnational perspectives,[43] as well as studies of single concepts that are implicit in or affect social welfare, such as work incentives[44] or religious motivations.[45] And, of course, there are attempts to include several of these approaches or to synthesize them.

Each of these views of social welfare plays a part in presenting it from a specific viewpoint, and each is helpful in complementing the others. What is needed, in addition, is a conceptual framework that will allow these various approaches to be seen as parts of a coherent whole—in short, a functional analytic base that will lead to in-depth understanding of the dynamics of social welfare, which permeates every service and affects every agency.

In recognition of this need, some of the most recent writing on social welfare has proceeded from just such an analytic base. Gilbert and Specht, for example, use a paradigm consisting of allocation, provision, delivery, and finance, acted upon by values, theories, and alternatives.[46] Kahn analyzes some of the underlying issues in terms of policies, programs, and practice systems.[47] Galper, writing from a self-styled radical position, begins his analysis "at the broader level and works down."[48] The approach of each of these writers indicates that, in view of the myriad changes taking place in social welfare on an increasingly rapid scale, adequate understanding of the totality cannot be acquired through lists, descriptions, history as such, or concentration on small parts, but rather through an understanding of the basic concepts that underlie and affect the entire social-welfare establishment. The use of concepts is an indication of critical thinking, and it is critical thinking, not mere technical ability, that will mark the competent social worker of the future. This has been termed "a basic quality which needs to be developed by all who plan to become social work professionals. Those unable to think critically (and creatively) . . . tend to become mere technicians."[49]

Consequently, it is the thesis of this book that understanding of social welfare requires familiarity with the determinants of social-welfare policy and practice. These have been postulated as situations, events, structures, attitudes, and processes,[50] but, for purposes of simplification, they will be discussed here in terms of some of the major motivations that give rise to social welfare, and some of the major intellectual and ideological influences that, interacting with those motivations, shape social welfare into the policies and services now existing.

Clearly, this is not meant to imply that there are only a few basic concepts that, once mastered, offer a key to complete understanding. On the contrary, the concepts are numerous, global, complex, and often conflicting. Wilensky and Lebeaux, for example, describe the impact of industrialization on society and on social welfare;[51] Thoenes approaches it from the point of view of the "elite";[52] Galper views it as an attempt to retain and strengthen capitalism;[53] and others explicate different concepts. Nor do the views and influences of the individuals chosen for inclusion in this book exhaust the universe of such concepts.

However, an understanding of the conceptual base of social welfare as exemplified by the concepts and individuals discussed here seems to offer at least a beginning understanding of the importance of such an approach, in terms of generalizability, transferability, prediction, and prescription concerning social welfare.

Chapter 2 deals with some of the problems of arriving at an operational definition of "social welfare," and some of the insights inherent in the attempt. Each of the next five chapters deals with one of the motivations that bring social welfare into being and maintain it. The succeeding five chapters analyze the impact of seven social philosophies upon the social-welfare policies, programs, and activities created because of the motivations—sometimes supporting them, sometimes opposing them, sometimes subverting and distorting them—thus shaping, in large part, the institution of social welfare as it exists today. The final chapter is a summary and a conclusion.

A word on terminology. This book deals with social welfare as an *institution,* including money, manpower, and material; planning, policy-making, programs, and performance; roles, ranks, and relationships—among other attributes. For example, public assistance that gives money to those poor who meet certain requirements is a social-welfare institution. Provisions for the care of the mentally retarded, including custodial care when needed, educational activities, training, recreation, counseling of parents and siblings, help in the home, and so forth, are part of the social-welfare institution. Provisions for the elderly are another part of the social-welfare institution.

Most of the references in this book, however, are to social-welfare *policies,* which are deliberate attempts to achieve goals determined by those designated as policy-makers.[54] Policies, in turn, may be of two kinds: There are those that designate the end to be sought and those that dictate—at least in part—the method to be used. For example, the goal policy of the Aid to Families with Dependent Children program is to make it possible for children to grow up without being crippled physically, emotionally, or socially by lack of money. The method policy indicates that the assisted child must be in the home of a relative. Similarly, the goal policy of Unemployment Compensation is to protect working people from penury during temporary periods of worklessness. The method policy dictates that they should not receive as grants as much as they would receive as salaries if they were working.

Policies, in turn, are effectuated through social-welfare *programs*, which are attempts to carry out the policies (that is, to reach the goals) through activities. Although, as will be discussed in the next chapter, it is difficult to define programs as purely social-welfare programs, programs with some elements of social welfare in them, or nonsocial-welfare programs, such programs are generally conceded to include—or to be part of—income maintenance, housing, education, health, employment, and a more general category sometimes called the "personal" social services, which includes child care and placement, services for the elderly, family welfare and planning, services for the disabled, and help to disadvantaged groups, among other services.

A full description of all, or even the major, social-welfare programs in the United States is beyond the scope of this book, which is devoted to formative influences, rather than to descriptions. Nevertheless, some idea of the programs under discussion, as well as their scope, is necessary. The outline that follows includes government programs only.

I. **Financial programs**
    These are programs that distribute money as their major activity, though other kinds of services may also be offered.

    A. INSURANCE-TYPE PROGRAMS
        These are programs into which payment is made for purposes of acquiring eligibility.

        1. *Old Age, Survivors' and Disability Insurance (OASDI)*, commonly referred to as *Social Security*
            This arose during the Great Depression and has been extended in coverage and amounts several times. A federal-government program to pay retired workers, their survivors, and dependents, it is funded by a tax on salaries. At the end of 1976, more than 33 million people were receiving more than $6.4 billion in monthly benefits; almost 12 million of these people were younger than age sixty-five and were disabled workers, survivors, or dependents.[55]

2. *Unemployment Insurance*

This is a state program. Each state determines its own rates and time limits. Funds are raised by a tax on employers; workers do not pay into this fund but become eligible through time engaged in work. It is intended to tide people over from job to job, and often requires proof that one is actively looking for work. Monthly payments in 1976 ranged from about $650 million to more than $1 billion, and in 1975, almost 4 million people, amounting to 6 percent of those in covered employment, collected unemployment compensation.[56]

3. *Workmen's Compensation*

States require employers to insure employees against accidents, and this is usually done through a private insurance company. Not all workers are covered, and a judgment is made in each case as to whether the injury is temporary or permanent, partial or total. Total benefits in 1975 were almost $4.5 billion.[57]

B. GRANT PROGRAMS

These are programs in which money is distributed because of recipients' situations or conditions. Prior payment by the recipient is not a condition.

1. *Supplemental Security Income (SSI)*

This is a federal program superseding the original state-federal-local programs for Old Age Assistance (OAA), Aid to the Permanently and Totally Disabled (APTD), and Aid to the Blind (AB). Amounts are paid out of general revenue to bring the income of these categories of people up to a predetermined level. In December 1976, more than 4 million people received $507 million. Some states also pay income supplements to the aged, the blind, and the disabled. However, in October 1976, this amounted to only $283,300.[58]

2. *Aid to Families with Dependent Children (AFDC)*

This was part of the Social Security Act of 1935, but the title has been changed several times since. The purpose is to allow children to grow up in their own homes with their basic needs met. This is a federal-state-local program, with provisions that vary widely from state to state. Generally speaking, benefits are lower in AFDC than in other public-assistance programs. However, this is one of the largest grant programs. In 1975, more than 3.5 million families, amounting to more than 11 million recipients, received a total of more than $9 billion.[59] This program is discussed in detail in Chapter 3.

3. *General Assistance (Home Relief)*
    This is a state and local program. Hence, there are wide varia-
    tions in eligibility conditions and benefits. It is a residual pro-
    gram for those who do not fit into the other programs, or whose
    benefits from them are inadequate. It is usually poorly funded
    and erratically administered.

II. In-kind programs

These programs distribute material items other than money or
distribute money earmarked for specific items.

A. INSURANCE-TYPE PROGRAMS

1. *Medicare*
    This provides medical assistance for the aged and operates as
    an insurance program under the aegis of the Social Security
    Administration. The hospitalization portion is available to those
    covered by Social Security, while the medical portion—requir-
    ing monthly fees and stipulating a deductible amount—is op-
    tional. From July to December 1976, 45 million medical bills
    were paid, amounting to $2.3 billion.[60]

B. GRANT PROGRAMS

1. *Medicaid*
    This offers medical care to the needy, who are defined as wel-
    fare recipients in most states, though some other low-income
    people may be eligible. Medicaid is state-administered but
    heavily subsidized by the federal government. In 1973, 23.5
    million people made use of Medicaid.[61]

2. *Public housing*
    Intended to make adequate housing available to all who need
    it through federal contributions for capital costs and through
    local tax exemptions, this program usually has waiting lists of
    several hundred thousand families.

3. *Rent supplements*
    These are intended to pay landlords the differences between
    the low rents that tenants can afford and the costs of mainte-
    nance.

4. *Urban renewal, rural housing, leased housing*
    Programs with various amounts of federal, state, and local fund-
    ing and administration, these are intended to build or lease
    housing for low-income people.

5. *Food-provision programs*
Including commodity distribution, food stamps, school lunches, and special milk programs, these are discussed in more detail in Chapter 6.

III. **Social-service programs**
These are "organized activity that aims at helping toward a mutual adjustment of individuals and their social environment."[62]

1. *Social services in public assistance*
As noted earlier, some of the insurance-type and grant programs also offer services. At one time payments and services were offered at a single source; lately there has been a separation of the two functions—a development discussed in Chapter 11.

2. *Child welfare*
This includes foster-home care, adoptions, protective services, day care, and services to unmarried mothers. Of the children receiving such services in 1967, 48 percent were in their own or relatives' homes, 34 percent in foster homes, 10 percent in institutions, and 7 percent in adoptive homes.

3. *Neighborhood service centers*
This is a relatively new service to bring about coordination and decentralization. Chapters 3 and 7 discuss it in more detail. A variation consists of neighborhood health centers, where the primary services offered are aimed at meeting the health needs of mothers, children (in some cases, crippled children), and other community or neighborhood residents.

4. *Vocational rehabilitation* and *manpower development and training*
Both programs are intended to prepare people for entry or re-entry into the job market. Many different kinds of programs are included in this area, ranging from sheltered workshops to on-the-job-training plans. Some of these programs are linked to employment programs.

5. *Employment services*
Although the major function of these is to provide employment information and counseling, and to administer Unemployment Insurance claims, there are also actual employment programs such as the Job Corps, the Neighborhood Youth Corps, the work-incentive portions of the AFDC program, and others.[63]

The enormous scope of social welfare should be obvious from this merely partial list of government services. In addition, there are government programs not listed above—social-welfare programs in government, including veterans', hospitals; in the schools; in the armed forces; and others. To all of this must be added the services of the nongovernmental public sector and the private sector. The scope of such services, with some examples, is discussed in Chapters 3 and 4. Generally speaking, these can be categorized as those that provide resources—free meals, small sums of money; those that provide counseling—marital, family, travelers'; those that provide recreation and informal education—community centers and settlement houses; those that provide rehabilitation—Alcoholics Anonymous, Synanon, the Salvation Army; and those that deal with special groups—Jewish immigrants, orphan children, "native Americans" (Indians). Listed by functions, these services have been categorized under:

adoption	prisoners
alcoholism	protective services for children
casework	psychiatry, counseling
elderly persons	referral
family services	rehabilitation
foster-home placement	residential homes
group work	sheltered employment
homemaker services	shelters
immigration, naturalization	transients
information	unmarried mothers
legal services	vocational guidance
medical services	volunteer services[64]
mental patients	

In addition to agencies serving these needs on the local level, there are also national organizations under secular and sectarian auspices. One compilation lists ninety-four such national organizations. Some of those under secular auspices include

American Cancer Society
American Diabetes Association
American Foundation for the Blind
American Heart Foundation
American National Red Cross
Arthritis Foundation
Big Brothers
Boy and Girl Scouts
Child Welfare League

Family Service Association of America
National Council for Homemaker-Home Health Aide Services
National Council on Aging[65]

Sectarian organizations include

B'nai B'rith Youth Organization
National Catholic Community Service Inc.
National Conference of Catholic Charities
National Council of Jewish Women
National Jewish Welfare Board
United Church of Christ Board of Homeland Ministries Health
    and Welfare Division
United Presbyterian Health, Education and Welfare Association[66]

These programs are carried out by *social workers*, though the definition of a social worker may vary. To professionals in the United States, this has traditionally meant a trained person with a master's degree in social work, and sometimes only a person with this degree who is a member of the National Association of Social Workers (NASW). The advent and proliferation of bachelor of social work programs, however, brought about acceptance of their graduates into the NASW, and they are also generally referred to as social workers now. Many agencies, on the other hand, have used graduates of other fields, or nongraduates, to staff their services, and have referred to these employees as social workers.[67] Clients, who tend to be less aware of the professional qualifications of those helping them, are apt to refer to "my social worker" or "the social worker," without drawing such distinctions.

In other countries too, social-welfare functions may be performed by people trained in other disciplines. In the Soviet Union, for example, marital problems are usually dealt with by a judge. Australia uses "welfare officers" in addition to social workers. Similarly, agricultural extension workers in some areas handle problems usually thought of as social problems, or even as social-welfare problems. Then, the increasing use of paraprofessionals by social-welfare agencies further confuses the term. At one time, Israel legally defined "social workers" as those who had been holding jobs, themselves legally defined as "social work," for three years or more. This resulted in a "blanketing-in" of relatively untrained workers with those with various degrees of training. For the purposes of this book, therefore, a broad definition of "social worker" will be used, consisting of anyone carrying out a social-welfare program.

Thus, in summary, a *policy* to help the indigent may lead to a *program* such as the AFDC or General Assistance, administered by *social workers*, the whole being part of the social-welfare *institution*.

It is difficult to exaggerate the size or importance of the social-welfare institution within modern society. In the United States, for example, literally millions of people depend upon some facet of the social-welfare system for survival. In fiscal terms, it should be noted that the federal-budget expenditures for income security alone exceed expenditures for defense. In most states, such expenditures constitute from one-third to well over one-half of all state-government expenditures. In light of these facts, it is clear that calls for reduction in welfare expenditures do not necessarily arise from the malevolence of those issuing the calls, or from the relative weakness of those benefiting from social welfare, but, rather, from the very size of the expenditures in comparison with those for other activities—a situation that invites concern and misunderstanding. Were the same attention paid to the number of the poor, rather than to the costs of welfare, policies and programs might well take entirely different forms.

Inasmuch as the historical developments in social welfare will be dealt with in this book in terms of the motivations and influences that shaped them, it might be well to offer a capsule history of some of the salient events in social welfare.

Government social welfare is usually considered to have formally begun with the Elizabethan Poor Laws of 1601. Although statutes of 1531 and 1536 dealt with the aged and the destitute, the statutes of 1601 codified the state's responsibility for dependent people. These statutes were intended to repress begging, use work as the major vehicle for overcoming need, help children and the handicapped, and punish the idle poor. They also assigned responsibility to local parishes. Although many changes and amendments that represented evolving thinking about society and social welfare were made in these laws, they have remained until this day the basis for much government social-welfare policy. The concepts of deserving and undeserving poor, less eligibility, residency requirements, and relatives' responsibility—to name but a few—continue to operate in many parts of the world.

The next major government involvement in social welfare took place in the 1880s, when Bismarck introduced several pieces of legislation that amounted to social insurance—an innovation that soon spread to many other countries. The Great Depression of the 1930s brought about massive changes in social-welfare programs throughout the world, mostly in the form of increased government responsibility, in the face of the inability of individuals or private agencies to deal with the massive problems.

World War II resulted in the concept of the "welfare state," with social welfare being considered one of the permanent and desirable government activities, rather than an emergency or residual response. In the United States the 1960s brought with them the War on Poverty, and a great deal more responsiveness to the needs of various minority groups—blacks, Chicanos, Hispanics, native Americans, women—as well as concern for poverty in general. At the time of this writing, some sort of welfare reform, probably in the nature of guaranteed minimum income, seems in the offing.

The beginning of institutionalized public, nongovernmental social welfare is usually thought of in terms of the creation of the Charity Organization Society in England in 1869. As its name implies, the basic idea of the COS was coordination of the many charities—estimated at 640 in London alone—that operated individually, and sometimes in competition with each other.[68] From such coordination grew planning, exchange of information, and research. This tradition has spread and carried over into today's United Fund drives, federations of agencies, and information and referral services.

At almost the same time, the Young Men's Hebrew Associations (YMHAs) began in the United States, in Baltimore, in 1854, and Toynbee Hall, the prototype of settlement houses, was established in London in 1884. Whereas the COS dealt primarily with relieving poverty, the settlement houses involved themselves in education, recreation, employment, intergroup relations, and counseling. And, to a much greater extent than did the COS workers, settlement-house workers engaged in social action (usually referred to as "social reform") and encouraged their members to do likewise.

The impact of the Great Depression was to cause government activities to overshadow the work of all voluntary and public organizations, because only the national government had the resources and the structure to attack the widespread problems. The voluntary groups then attempted to be innovative in a manner in which the government bureaucracy could not be; to serve special groups, such as religiously identified bodies or new immigrants, for which the government had no special apparatus; and to help those who fell through the cracks between government services. The problems of the relationship between government and voluntary public services are considered in Chapters 4, 5, and 7, in terms of religion, politics, and organized philanthropy.

Taken together, government and voluntary public services make up such a large part of societal activity that no one volume can do justice to the diversity, the intricacy, and the implications of the totality. Consequently, readers of this book—especially students—are referred to the notes at the end of each chapter, not only for the sources used herein but also for clues as to where to begin searches for the deeper and wider understanding that it is hoped they will undertake. For such purposes, an effort has been made to provide copious documentation of the facts cited, as well as references to other, more specialized, sources. In the course of such investigations, readers will undoubtedly make their own judgments concerning the relative impacts of the motivations and influences discussed here, and of others not taken into account. It is to be hoped that those judgments will lead to empirical investigations that will test and perhaps carry forward the inferences contained in this book.

NOTES

1. · C. Gersuny and W. R. Rosengren, *The Service Society* (Cambridge, Mass.: Schenkman, 1973).
2. A. Gartner and F. Riessman, *The Service Society and the Consumer Vanguard* (New York: Harper & Row, 1974).
3. Gersuny and Rosengren, *op. cit.*
4. Gartner and Riessman, *op. cit.*
5. K. A. Simon and M. M. Frankel, *Projections of Educational Statistics to 1983–84* (Washington, D.C.: Department of Health, Education, and Welfare, 1974).
6. M. S. March and E. Newman, "Financing Social Welfare: Governmental Allocation Procedures," in *Encyclopedia of Social Work* (New York: National Association of Social Workers, 1971), p. 426.
7. "Current Operating Statistics," *Social Security Bulletin,* 39 (March 1976): 35.
8. B. M. Blechman, E. M. Gramlich, and R. W. Hartman, *Setting National Priorities: The 1975 Budget* (Washington, D.C.: The Brookings Institution, 1974).
9. March and Newman, *op. cit.*
10. J. H. Galper, *The Politics of Social Services* (Englewood Cliffs, N.J.: Prentice-Hall, 1975); A. J. Kahn, *Social Policy and Social Services* (New York: Random House, 1973).
11. A. Graycar, *Social Policy: An Australian Introduction* (Melbourne: Macmillan, 1976).
12. M. Shapira, "Reflections on the Preparation of Social Workers for Executive Positions," *Journal of Education for Social Work,* 7 (Winter 1971): 55–68.
13. R. H. Hamlin, *Voluntary Health and Welfare Agencies in the United States* (New York: Schoolmaster Press, 1961).
14. *Giving in America: Toward a Stronger Voluntary Sector* (Washington, D.C.: Commission on Private Philanthropy and Public Needs, 1975), p. 36.
15. L. Ripple, *Statistics on Social Work Education in the United States: 1974* (New York: Council on Social Work Education, 1975).
16. S. Siegel, *Social Service Manpower Needs: An Overview to 1980* (New York: Council on Social Work Education, 1975).
17. BOCES=Board of Co-operative Educational Services; VEEB=Vocational, Educational and Extension Board; CASA=Co-ordinating Agency for Spanish Americans; WIN=Work Incentive Program; DSS=Depart-

ment of Social Services; CLAC=Community Legal Assistance Corporation; FISH=Friends Interested in Service and Help; CAIR=Client Advocacy, Information and Referral; AID=Aged in Distress; SHARE= Senior Housing at Reduced Expense; from L. R. Skolnik, *Public Assistance and Your Client: A Handbook* (Garden City, N.Y.: Adelphi University School of Social Work, 1977), and personal communication.

18. Gartner and Riessman, *op. cit.*

19. M. Kaplan, *Leisure: Theory and Policy* (New York: Wiley, 1975).

20. See, for example, E. R. Lowenstein, "Social Work in Postindustrial Society," *Social Work*, 18 (November 1973):40–47.

21. Shapira, *op. cit.*

22. J. L. Vigilante, "Back to the Old Neighborhood," *Social Service Review*, 50 (June 1976):194.

23. Abt Associates, Inc., *A Study of the Neighborhood Center Pilot Program*, Vol. 3: *The Neighborhood Services Program Model* (Washington, D.C.: Executive Office of the President, Bureau of the Budget, 1969).

24. R. W. Levinson, "Access to Health Care: An Information and Referral Approach," *Proceedings of the Information and Referral Roundtable 1975* (Phoenix, Ariz.: Alliance of Information and Referral Services, 1976).

25. Z. Feine *et al.*, *Interagency Collaboration in Drug Rehabilitation* (Richmond, Va.: Department of Mental Health and Mental Retardation, 1974).

26. A. E. Fink, *The Field of Social Work* (New York: Holt, Rinehart & Winston, 1974).

27. Kahn, *op. cit.*

28. *Bulletin: 1975–76* (Philadelphia: University of Pennsylvania School of Social Work, 1974).

29. S. B. Kamerman and A. J. Kahn, *Social Services in the United States: Policies and Programs* (Philadelphia: Temple University Press, 1976).

30. D. Brieland *et al.*, *Contemporary Social Work* (New York: McGraw-Hill, 1975).

31. D. J. Rothman, *The Discovery of the Asylum: Social Order and Disorder in the New Republic* (Boston: Little, Brown, 1971).

32. C. Hampden-Turner, *From Poverty to Dignity* (Garden City, N.Y.: Anchor, 1975).

33. R. Lubove, *The Professional Altruist: The Emergence of Social Work as a Career: 1880–1930* (New York: Atheneum, 1973).

34. C. A. Chambers (ed.), *A Century of Concern: 1873–1973* (Columbus, Ohio: National Conference on Social Welfare, 1974).

35. D. P. Moynihan, *Maximum Feasible Misunderstanding* (New York: Free Press, 1969).

36. D. P. Moynihan, *The Politics of a Guaranteed Income: The Nixon Administration and the Family Assistance Plan* (New York: Vintage, 1973).

37. P. Roby (ed.), *The Poverty Establishment* (Englewood-Cliffs, N.J.: Prentice-Hall, 1974).

38. S. Feldman, *The Administration of Mental Health Services* (Springfield, Ill.: Charles C. Thomas, 1973).

39. A. Kadushin, *Child Welfare Services* (New York: Macmillan, 1974).

40. R. M. Titmuss, *Social Policy: An Introduction* (New York: Pantheon, 1974).
41. R. Morris and R. H. Binstock, *Feasible Planning for Social Change* (New York: Columbia University Press, 1966).
42. F. W. Kaslow, *Issues in Human Services* (San Francisco: Jossey-Bass, 1972).
43. D. Thursz and J. L. Vigilante (eds.), *Meeting Human Needs*, Vol. 1: *An Overview of Nine Countries* (Beverly Hills, Calif.: Sage, 1975), Vol. 2: *Additional Perspectives from Thirteen Countries* (Beverly Hills, Calif.: Sage, 1976).
44. D. Macarov, *Incentives to Work* (San Francisco: Jossey-Bass, 1970).
45. G. C. Chakerian, "Religious Sponsorship," in *Encyclopedia of Social Work* (New York: National Association of Social Workers, 1965).
46. N. Gilbert and H. Specht, *Dimensions of Social Welfare Policy* (Englewood Cliffs, N.J.: Prentice-Hall, 1974).
47. Kahn, *op. cit.*
48. Galper, *op. cit.*
49. F. M. Loewenberg and R. Dolgoff (eds.), "Preface," in *The Practice of Social Intervention: Goals, Roles, and Strategies* (Itasca, Ill.: Peacock, 1972), p. 1.
50. D. Macarov, *How Function Follows Form: The Relationship of Social Welfare Services to Societal Structure* (paper presented at the Annual Spring Meeting, School of Social Work, Adelphi University, Garden City, N.Y., May 20, 1976).
51. H. L. Wilensky and C. N. Lebeaux, *Industrial Society and Social Welfare* (New York: Free Press, 1958).
52. P. Thoenes, *The Elite in the Welfare State* (New York: Free Press, 1966).
53. Galper, *op. cit.*
54. Policy may be made by legislative bodies, by the courts, by program administrators, and by the public, not excluding clients and workers.
55. "Program Operations," *Social Security Bulletin*, 40 (April 1977):1.
56. "Current Operating Statistics," *Social Security Bulletin*, 40 (April 1977): 58, 87.
57. *Ibid.*
58. "Program Operations," *op. cit.*, p. 2; see also *Supplemental Security Income for the Aged, Blind, and Disabled*, SSA 74-11000 (Washington, D.C.: Department of Health, Education, and Welfare, 1973).
59. "Current Operating Statistics," *op. cit.*, p. 84.
60. "Program Operations," *op. cit.*, p. 2.
61. R. Stevens and R. Stevens, *Welfare Medicine in America: A Case Study of Medicaid* (New York: Free Press, 1974), p. 369.
62. *The Development of National Social Service Programmes* (New York: United Nations Social Commission, 1959), p. 6; quoted in *President's Commission on Income Maintenance Programs: Background Papers* (Washington, D.C.: Government Printing Office, 1970), p. 299.
63. Most of the information, as well as the basic form, of the outline, unless otherwise noted, is from R. C. Federico, *The Social Welfare Institution: An Introduction* (Lexington, Mass.: Heath, 1973), pp. 182–208.

64. H. B. Croner, *National Directory of Private Social Agencies 1975–1976* (Queens Village, N.Y.: Croner, 1969) (updated monthly).
65. *Service Directory of National Voluntary Health and Social Welfare Organizations* (New York: National Assembly of National Voluntary Health and Social Welfare Organizations, 1974).
66. *Ibid.*
67. For a good discussion of the paucity of trained social workers in public assistance, see G. Y. Steiner, *Social Insecurity: The Politics of Welfare* (Chicago: Rand McNally, 1966), p. 184.
68. K. Woodroofe, *From Charity to Social Work in England and the United States* (Toronto: University of Toronto Press, 1962), p. 23.

2

The Scope of
Social Welfare

ON DEFINITIONS

Social welfare is not an easy concept to define. For one thing, it is beset, as are all definitions, with the problem of infinite regression—every word in the definition is itself subject to further definition, as is every word in that definition, and so on, ad infinitum. Thus, the word "social" can refer to everything that affects people[1]—practically all of living—while the Constitution of the United States makes promotion of the "general welfare" the responsibility and reason for being of the entire government endeavor and apparatus.

Consequently, arriving at a definition of "social welfare" that is exclusive (fitting no other activity) and inclusive (encompassing every social-welfare activity) is not easy. Such a definition as "a system that embodies a multifaceted approach to social and economic problems, reflecting social values and using the expertise of interrelated disciplines for the collective good"[2] would apply equally to education, political science, and futuramics, among other things. On the other hand, the definition neglects intrapsychic problems and physical problems such as disablement.

Definitional problems arise both because social welfare actually overlaps with the activities of many other institutions and because the activities of social welfare itself are so varied. There is overlap between social welfare and medicine, for example, in the areas of preventive medicine, teaching of personal hygiene, community health, sanitation, and sex (or "family life") education, each of which might be sanctioned by a health or a social-welfare policy or agency. In hospital settings in the

United States, the nurse may take blood pressures or give shots while the social worker does not, and the social worker may make a home visit to the patient's family for purposes of providing a homemaker or emergency financial aid, or even speaking to the children's teacher, which the hospital nurse does not do; but both the social worker and the nurse counsel the patient, seek to relieve anxieties, explain the import of the condition, offer moral support, and so forth. In France, where social work grew up through the nursing profession and where social workers were, at one time, required to have prior nursing training, the concept of the "social nurse" blurs these lines of demarcation.[3] Both teachers and social workers try to help schoolchildren with problems; there is an overlap between social workers and manpower agencies in the field of employment help and counseling; and so forth. It is in this sense that Kahn distinguishes between these social services that become so elaborate and extensive as to achieve independent identity—such as education, medical care, and public housing—and social welfare as such.[4] The fact that an American cabinet division is called the Department of Health, Education, and Welfare is, however, an acknowledgment of the necessity for continued close linkages among these three areas of concern.

Nor is it easy to summarize all of the activities that are subsumed under the rubric "social welfare," even narrowly defined. These range from meeting urgent here-and-now needs to engaging in long-term social planning, from helping individuals to engaging in community-wide—or even national—endeavors. In some places, emphasis is on one-to-one relationships;[5] in others, it is said to be changing from "a purely therapeutic 'micro' level to the community or societal or 'macro' level of concerned action";[6] while in still others, social welfare is equated with efforts toward national development.[7] The goals, as well as the methods, may vary greatly. In Poland, "social welfare" is defined as help to individuals as compensation for consequences of great categories of risk, such as suffering in war, and those consequences are largely defined as inability to work.[8] In Australia, social welfare is seen as a public right, contributing to the well-being of the total community through a comprehensive range of services benefiting all members of society.[9] One of the goals of social welfare in Sweden is to redistribute income more evenly among different kinds of people and during different periods in a person's life,[10] while in Iran aims include improving the quality of the work force and encouraging people to save.[11] In the Netherlands a distinction is made between social work, which is equated with grants, and social services, which are equated with counseling and advice,[12] while one American definition speaks of the goal as a more humane and creatively stimulating social environment.[13] There is also the view of social welfare as being engaged in a social mission—a view said to be more prevalent in Britain than in the United States.[14] The "mission" aspect is discernible in a number of places where social-welfare policy is beginning to be concerned with the quality of life in general, rather than individual problems exclusively.

Not only do methods and goals differ, but specific programs also show great variety. Among the more exotic are "wet-time" insurance in Ireland;[15] pensions for reindeer-herding Lapps in Norway;[16] a special retirement fund for bank employees in Uruguay;[17] juvenile probation services in Jordan, which deal with offenses such as "falsehood" and "dispraise";[18] special services for salt workers and the establishment of fisherman's homes abroad by the Republic of China (Taiwan).[19]

Owing to such differences, definitions of "social welfare" are highly culture-bound[20] and even the terms "social services," "social welfare," and "social work" tend to take on somewhat different meanings in different political and cultural contexts. In some countries, the generic term is "social administration," and increasingly the terms "human services" and "human-service administration" are being used.[21] One factor making for differential use of terms seems to be the stage of a country's economic development.[22] However, in no country has terminology been standardized enough to make possible the assignment of precise meanings to these various terms,[23] and therefore transnational usage becomes increasingly confused.

These problems in defining "social welfare" tend to lead to longer and more elaborate definitions, including aims, values, auspices, populations, and methods,[24] with the result that descriptions replace definitions and, conversely, descriptions and discussions of social welfare make no attempt to define the term.[25] Because definitions are, in the final analysis, attempts by one person or group to describe certain aspects of reality, they cannot be correct in an absolute sense, or better than others, or more complete, except insofar as other people or groups judge them to be so. Therefore, in many cases it suffices if the subject being discussed is understood in a rather general way. When, however, certain items seem to appear in all definitions, they indicate at least a partial consensus.

ON HUMAN NEED

One constant that seems to run through many, if not all, definitions and descriptions of social welfare seems to be that it deals with human need. The goal may be to prevent new categories of need from arising or to prevent recognized categories of need from affecting hitherto untouched individuals or groups, it may be to maintain people or groups at their present state of need fulfillment, or it may be to help those with unsatisfied needs. These categories are often spoken of as the preventive, maintenance, and rehabilitative functions of social welfare, respectively.

The aid itself may be given by the agency applied to, or the applicant may be referred to a more appropriate source. (Improvement in the latter method is the goal of newly emerging "information and referral" services.) There may also be a cooperative effort among a number of agencies in an attempt to solve the problem. Further, the aid may be direct, as is a financial grant; semidirect, as is training in work habits for successful job placement; or indirect, as is engaging in social action to have needs met through establishing a new agency or making changes either in existing ones or in society as a whole.

The needs that social welfare attempts to meet can be categorized in a number of ways. There are those common human needs that affect everyone at some time in his or her life,[26] special human needs that affect only certain groups or individuals, and those needs that arise from, or are created by, the very structure of society.

Common Human Needs

Although it is possible to distinguish among different types of common human needs—for example, between physiological or biological, psychological or emotional, and sociological or relational needs—the close links between various kinds of needs are becoming increasingly apparent with growing knowledge in the field of psychosomatic medicine, including biofeedback, and in related areas. To put this more concretely, the extremely tall adolescent girl may have trouble finding dancing partners or dates (a social problem), may develop a negative self-image or think of herself as a freak (an emotional problem), and may develop back pains from walking hunched over to minimize her height (a physical problem). Similarly, the mother who deprives herself of food so that her child can be well dressed, the soldier who volunteers for a dangerous mission because of patriotism or loyalty to his fellows, the person who assumes guilt in order to spare someone else shame—each of these is an example of the way in which the demands of one need may be subordinated to the satisfaction of another.

In this connection, Maslow's approach to human need (or to need satisfaction as motivation) is an interesting one.[27] He postulates a hierarchy of human needs, with each becoming potent as the previous need is relatively well satisfied. In Maslow's formulation, the most basic needs are physiological, and until they achieve reasonable satisfaction, other needs are not felt. With satisfaction of physiological needs, security needs become potent, followed by the need for love and the need for self-esteem. The highest, or final, level of need in Maslow's view is the need for self-actualization—the need to become everything one is capable of becoming, to use all of one's powers and abilities to the utmost. The common human needs with which social welfare deals can be viewed through the Maslow paradigm with some profit.

Special Human Needs

In addition to the common needs with which social welfare deals, there are needs that affect only certain individuals or groups, or that affect many individuals occasionally.[28] It might be useful to view these in five categories:

The incapable are people who cannot fend for themselves, at least not completely, owing to some characteristic that puts them at a disadvantage. Included are children, the aged, the mentally ill and the mentally handicapped, and the physically handicapped.

The unprepared are capable, but not prepared, individuals or groups, including the illiterate, the uneducated, those with few or no usable skills, and those who have not learned social skills or behaviors. Included, too, are those who are not prepared for the normal tasks and vicissitudes of life. For those unprepared for marriage, there are premarital counseling services; for expectant parents, "prospective parents" groups. There are also programs to prepare people for retirement from employment, though not many to help people prepare for old age generally. There are increasing numbers of books, articles, and discussions about death and dying,[29] though what seems to be a deep-seated belief in, and fear of, the "evil eye"—if you mention something it will happen—militates against preparation for widowhood or widowerhood. Because most people do not participate in efforts to prepare themselves for these "transformations of identity,"[30] many of the needs that are served by social welfare in such cases are ex post facto; that is, they arise after the transformation because people were unprepared.

Disaster victims are those who are capable and prepared for the normal exigencies of life but are struck by catastrophes, or undergo crises, for which they need at least temporary help. Crises have been classified as those caused by (1) natural disasters such as floods and earthquakes, (2) environmental situations such as air or water pollution, and (3) civil disturbances such as riots.[31] To these may be added crises caused by (1) removal of a person, for example, a loved one or a charismatic or authoritarian leader, (2) economic upheavals such as the stock-market crash of 1929, and (3) social dislocations such as mass migrations. Each of these can be scaled down to the individual level—a home burned out, rats running loose, a sudden arrest, runaway children, job loss, or a move to a new neighborhood.

The unconforming are also those who seem capable, prepared, and spared from disaster but who nevertheless violate the norms of society.

Included in this group are juvenile delinquents, prisoners, and all of those who are generally subsumed under the heading of deviants.[32] Although increasing understanding of the power of environmental and societal considerations in creating deviance has led to a view of much deviance as not only uncontrollable on the part of the so-called deviant but even a functional reaction to his situation, in the public view the distinction between pathology and deviance lies in the ability of the deviant to control his behavior. Consequently, people seen as ill are related to differently than are people seen as deviant,[33] and the methods of meeting the needs they exhibit are dissimilar.

The unmotivated: Although lack of motivation can be seen as a condition that could affect each of the other four categories, it is generally seen by enough people as responsible for a large enough share of social problems to deserve separate mention. In some cases, the lack of motivation is viewed more or less benevolently, and a search is made for the best method of creating motivation—to study, to relate to other people, to be concerned about personal appearance or behavior, or to join in some endeavor. In other cases, the lack of motivation is viewed malevolently as unwillingness to work, to work hard, or to take care of one's parents or children. In these cases, negative sanctions are more apt to be used than positive ones. The purported lack of motivation is one of the most salient parts of descriptions of the "culture of poverty,"[34] and a strong controlling factor, under the guise of fear of work disincentives, in determining welfare rates and benefits[35]—a factor that will be examined at greater length later in this book.

Societally Caused Needs

In addition to common and special human needs, there are also needs that affect the total society or flow from difficulties or gaps in the society itself. In Chapter 1, mention was made of needs caused or exacerbated by the shift from a goods-producing economy to a service-producing economy. In the same manner, countries that are moving from an agricultural to an industrial economy are affected by lack of suitably trained workmen, housing shortages, and sometimes abandoned land. In societies with officially sanctioned discrimination, needs flow from being discriminated against; in those with discrimination despite official bans, such as the remaining effects of the caste system in India, the needs are no less great. Countries that "import" foreign workers thereby create a whole array of needs,[36] while countries that maintain —and occasionally call into service—large reserve armies bring about dislocations that require services.[37]

Dramatic examples of social problems flowing from societal structure are the decisions made by the governments of Tanzania and Upper Volta immediately after obtaining their independence. Lacking the

resources to provide public education for all of the school-age population, they made quite different decisions. In Tanzania, it was decided
to provide school facilities for one-half of the country's children, with
subsequent arrangements for continuation into high school and university for some of them. In this manner, Tanzania opted for a small cadre
of university graduates, a larger number of high school graduates, and
still more elementary-school graduates, while relegating half the population to no formal schooling at all. This decision traded off the existence
of an educated elite against the possibility of subsequent intercommu-
nal jealousy, feelings of discrimination, and unrest.[38] Upper Volta, on
the other hand, faced with the same problem, decided to give three
years of primary schooling to every child between the ages of eleven
and fourteen, thus ensuring equality of educational opportunity among
the population and a base for further self-development efforts, at the
cost of absence of groups with higher education.[39] These are cruel
choices that, though resolved in dissimilar ways, almost certainly resulted in social problems in both cases.

There are societally caused problems in countries with chronic unemployment. Although an official unemployment rate of 5 percent has
long been considered optimal for the United States by economists,
other industrial countries such as Japan and West Germany have
achieved lower rates, and even in Israel the unemployment rate is
usually less than 1 percent. In any case, unemployment and underemployment are usually conceded to be the results of government policies,
rather than individuals' actions.

It is possible, of course, to categorize and analyze human needs in
ways different from the above. Rein, for example, speaks of needs as
arising from resource deficiency, individual deficiency, and institutional
deficiency—categories that are almost self-explanatory.[40]

ON NEED DETECTION AND MEASUREMENT

It is not sufficient for the emergence of social welfare that needs exist.
"Social intervention generally occurs in response to someone identifying a condition as problematic or faulty . . . unless a condition becomes
identified as a problem, it will not receive attention and will not become
the object of any social intervention activity."[41]

Need Detection

Problem detection is more advanced and formalized in medicine
than it is in social welfare. Physicians are required by law to report cases
of certain contagious diseases, and may report interesting, baffling, or

novel cases to the local health authority.[42] There is almost no mandatory reporting of types of cases in social work, though agencies and government departments may require certain statistics. The social worker becoming aware of a new problem, or intensification of an existing problem, usually has no formal channels through which to report on it, and such individual instances rarely reach a central body or unit charged with correlating such reports and making an assessment of need. Reporting in social work tends to take place within the context of professional supervision, and little machinery has been established to allow for, or to demand, data that would result in action.

One exception to this is the case of the battered child, which, in the United States, must be reported by anyone aware of its existence—doctors, nurses, policemen, social workers, and others.[43] There is, in some places, a growing movement toward mandatory reporting of battered wives and rape. As a general rule, however, new services do not arise within social-welfare agencies as much from the reports of social workers as from other sources.

This does not mean that social-welfare agencies are not willing, or even anxious, to find people needing their services, or to set up new services. "Case-finding" is an important part of some agencies' functions. Nevertheless, lack of resources often deters some agencies from seeking new clients, and may even cause them to discourage clients who seek to apply. However, the major problem in need detection seems to be a structural one—few agencies have a unit, a group, or a person charged with detecting changes in kinds or amounts of need. In fact, clients usually turn to agencies because of the services they are known to offer, rather than for new services. In Israel, the lack of services for girl friends and engaged women whose men were lost in the Yom Kippur War was not reported—if detected—by the social-service agencies but, rather, by university-based researchers who were gathering information about problems.[44]

The lack of formal methods of problem-detecting within welfare agencies has led to attempts to identify existing and potential problems through the observance of factors felt to exemplify the presence of problems. Such "social indicators"[45] have been the focus of considerable interest. In some places density of population, or crowdedness of dwelling places, is seen as an indicator of the presence of such problems as physical and mental illness and crime. In Israel, a high correlation has been found between large families—defined as more than six people—and certain problems, such as dropping out of school, juvenile delinquency, and poverty, though crowdedness and recent immigration are intervening variables. Unemployment and pockets of high unemployment are often seen in the United States not only as problems in themselves but as indicators of a high incidence of related problems. The search for reliable social indicators continues, more as an intellectual or academic exercise than as a function of social-welfare agencies or institutions.

As it happens, some of the most dramatic and influential exposures of social problems have taken place outside the social-welfare establishment. For example, a widely read and commented-on essay by Mac-Donald, in the *New Yorker,* entitled "Our Invisible Poor,"[46] almost coincided with the publication of Harrington's seminal book *The Other America.*[47] This concatenation has been termed the "discovery of poverty" in America, because it focused public attention on what had been an obscure problem, and it was a forerunner of and immediate impetus for the War on Poverty programs. Both MacDonald and Harrington were journalists, not social workers.

Problems are sometimes dramatized and publicized by well-known or charismatic figures. Franklin D. Roosevelt's own problem with polio focused attention on the organizations active in that problem area, and John F. Kennedy's interest in mental retardation gave impetus to organizations engaged with that problem. In her day, Dorothea Dix did the same thing for the incarcerated mentally ill, as did Margaret Sanger for birth control.[48]

One of the traditional methods by which voluntary organizations come into being is through the shared concerns of victims of a situation, or their relatives. An organization new at the time of this writing, concerned about the problem known as sudden infant death syndrome (SIDS)—commonly called crib death—has been organized by parents who have suffered this kind of loss, and who want both to extend comfort to other bereaved parents and to sponsor research into the problem.

Public demand for services is not limited to small groups of sufferers, however. Widespread agitation—voiced in letters to newspapers and officials, in rallies and advertisements, or in protest marches and riots —is a potent factor in calling attention to a problem and demanding action. The burning of Watts may have had little long-term effect in solving the problem of that particular area, but it was an important incident in that it set in motion a chain reaction, not only of services but of modified attitudes as well.

Need Measurement for Societal Problems

Whether a detected need is considered to have reached the proportion of a problem depends on its extent and intensity as compared with some norm. Hence, it is necessary to measure needs. Conventionally, such measurements have been either relative, normative, or absolute.[49]

Relative Need. A relative need is one that is considered to exist as compared to some nonneed situation. Statistics are often used in this manner. Poverty may be defined as the economic condition of people within the lowest tenth, or quintile, or some other percentage of the income distribution. The educationally disadvantaged or deprived may be considered those achieving the lowest scores on national achievement tests. Relative need can also be determined longitudinally—the amount of crime, drug abuse, or mental illness as compared to the amount at some other time. The comparison can also be made with some other place: Per capita income in India as compared to Israel might indicate the relative affluence of Israelis while comparing Israelis to Americans might indicate relative poverty in Israel. Similarly, the infant-mortality rate in America is seen as a problem when it is compared to the lower mortality rates in other, less developed countries.

In addition to statistical methods of comparison, there are also comparisons of life-styles. Poverty, for example, can be defined as absence of indoor toilets, inability to plan ahead, lack of motivation, or people who are "immoral, uncivilized, promiscuous, lazy, obscene, dirty, and loud."[50] Similarly, swaddling infants, or binding feet as was once practiced widely in the Orient, or setting the aged adrift on ice floes, or isolating sufferers from Hansen's disease (previously called leprosy)— each might be seen as constituting a social problem when compared to customs in societies that do not engage in these practices.

Finally, definitions may be relative to some norm or reference group that once existed, exists, or is hoped for or fantasized. Financial inequality, of whatever degree, may be seen as a problem by those who envision or desire a society of complete equality. Lack of mutual aid, neighborliness, or viable and meaningful neighborhoods may be defined as a problem in relation to a viewpoint that regards these as attributes of the past or desiderata for the future. Even lack of happiness may be relative to the presumed happiness among primitives of the past or among citizens of future utopias. In these cases, the existence of a problem is seen as relative to some other group, situation, time, or place.

Normative Need. There are some needs that are considered normative, in that they are expected to exist. For example, poverty is not only seen as inevitable by some people; it is considered necessary, for a number of economic and social reasons.[51] That the aged should also be ill is considered normal, to the point that their problem is viewed as age, not illness.[52] It is generally assumed that people in institutions—homes for the aged, hospitals for the mentally ill, homes for disturbed children, and the like—are living in poverty, though both reflection and logic indicate little basis for this belief.

The normative view also operates to obscure problems: If all blacks were seen as suffering from sickle-cell anemia, there would be no need to deal with black poverty, ghettoization, discrimination, and so forth, because these would be "mere symptoms," caused by the "real problem"—a medical condition. Again, if the members of communes are seen as immoral, antisocial, or disturbed, by virtue of their joining such groups, there is no reason to deal with these problems, which could be solved by outlawing communes.

Absolute Need.   In addition to relative measures and normative views in measuring problems, there are also absolute measures. Thus, the poverty level in the United States at the time of this writing is $5,500 for an urban family of four. This is an absolute measure of poverty, in contradistinction to relative and normative measures. Illness is also usually determined by absolute measures—the number of hospital admissions, office visits to doctors, house calls, and so forth. Infant-mortality rates, longevity and life expectancy, deaths due to starvation or various diseases, and many other measures of the extent and intensity of social problems are determined with reference to absolute scales.

In the same manner, there are legal definitions of blindness, based upon amount of various kinds of sight; of deafness; and of disability. Both Workmen's Compensation and Veterans' Administration staffs spend time and effort determining not only the existence of disability but also its degree. The difference between a 10 percent hearing loss and a 20 percent hearing loss incurred in military service is not only statistical; compensation varies with the amount of loss. There is even a 0 percent disability classification, which entitles the veteran to some benefits but no compensation.

Need Measurement for Individual Problems

In addition to detecting and measuring societal problems, there is also the question of determining the extent to which individuals' needs are defined as problems. Again, the method may involve relative, normative, or absolute measures. Poverty usually involves measurement of income and sometimes of assets. The degree of mental retardation is often determined by a series of verbal, written, and motor tests. Individual health measures almost invariably begin with thermometer, stethoscope, and sphygmomanometer, and the ascertained fever, heart rate, and blood pressure are determinants of whether further tests are necessary. Juvenile delinquency is determined with reference to a "guilty" or "not guilty" verdict, as are adult crimes. These, and others like them, are absolute measures.

When a Mongoloid child is assumed to be mentally retarded, or when a widow or widower is assumed to be sad and lonely, or when a drug addict is assumed to be desperate for the next "fix," these are normative measures applied to individual cases.

The question of how much marital discord constitutes a problem; or whether mental illness is present; or whether social isolation is healthy independence or neurotic withdrawal; indeed, the difference between normal, neurotic, and psychotic behavior—all of these are generally resolved by comparison with some other group, all the rest of society, or some norm or standard determined as a nonproblem.

Different kinds of needs are amenable to or require various methods of measurement to determine whether they constitute an individual or societal problem. On the other hand, it should be obvious that the distinction between relative, normative, and absolute measures is useful, but not complete. Absolute measures are ultimately derived from relative standards: For example, the number of calories deemed minimal in America is far more than the majority of people have in some other countries, and the standard is based on a view as to how healthy, strong, or long-lived an American is expected to be. Relative standards, too, are sometimes based on norms of society: to misbehave, or even to commit a crime, may mean to violate the norms of society, but the behavior may be no different from that of others, or even of the majority.[53] Nevertheless, these three kinds of measures are used variously for different needs, and identify different problems.

Social-Welfare Programs

As noted in the previous chapter, programs through which help is offered can be categorized variously: those that give financial aid, those that give goods other than money (often referred to as "in-kind" programs), and those that offer intangible services. Financial-aid programs, in turn, can be divided between (1) the insurance-type programs that require vestedness of would-be recipients in terms of having paid into the program a sufficient amount, or over a sufficient period—as for American Social Security—or of someone else having paid premiums for them, as in the case of Unemployment Insurance or Workmen's Compensation, and (2) grant programs, which require no prior participation.

The former are referred to here as insurance-type programs rather than as insurance because they are not insurance in the classical sense: The insured holds no written policy; has no control over changes in premiums and benefits, which are changed arbitrarily; and has no choice as to coverage. As a matter of historical record, the Social Security Act of 1935 was not passed as an insurance program. The sponsors of this legislation were afraid of its annulment by the Supreme Court as government engagement in private business, as well as of congressional opposition. Hence, the Act included, among other things, a separate title instituting a payroll tax and a separate title establishing old-age benefits. The intention was "to get away from an insurance plan altogether, but to establish the equivalent of such a plan without resorting to a definite insurance scheme."[54]

Regardless of such intricacies, the purposes of programs that at least appear to be insurance are not only to provide a source of revenue for the program but also to create the feeling among recipients that they are entitled to the benefits because of their own previous performance, and hence to obviate the stigma felt to be attached to noncontributory social-welfare programs. That the desired goal is generally attained is evidenced by the lack of stigma associated with unemployment compensation, though workers do not contribute to this program—it is entirely employer-financed (which means, ultimately, consumer-financed).

Grant programs, on the other hand, do not rest on prior performance or payment but are based on demonstrated need coupled with absence of sufficient resources. The determination of need and resources is usually referred to as a "means test," and it is almost axiomatic in most social-welfare thinking that being subjected to a means test is inherently degrading and that participation in means-tested programs is stigmatizing. Harry Hopkins once testified before Congress in this respect: "The pain and suffering ... involved when a man and his wife have to apply for relief [are] beyond description, and tens of thousands will not do it."[55]

So ingrained is this feeling that one of the first proposals for a guaranteed minimum income was intended as, and entitled, a "way to end the means test."[56] During the 1960s, an attempt was made to simplify the means test and to accept applicants' simple declarations of income, with little attempt to investigate further, except for spot checks. In the 1970s, an agency verification model had come back into general use.[57]

In addition to insurance programs and grant programs, there are a few programs that give grants without requiring a means test or prior contributions. They are, however, often based on some sort of prior performance. Such programs were veterans' bonuses and the GI Bill of Rights. The entire Veterans' Administration congeries of programs can be seen in the same way.

Programs that give material goods sometimes offer the goods directly —food, clothing, toys for Christmas, or the like. Meals on Wheels for the elderly and hot lunches for schoolchildren are also of this type of in-kind benefits. Perhaps the most widespread in-kind benefit in the United

States today, however, is the Food Stamp Program, which sells stamps that can be used to buy more food than the stamps cost. There has also been some experimentation with the use of vouchers for educational costs, and vouchers are often used to pay rent or other bills of welfare clients. When vouchers are usable at a number of places or for a number of items, they can be viewed as a liberating device, freeing recipients to seek the best buys and providing them with bargaining power. Indeed, this is the strongest rationale among those who favor vouchers instead of goods or services. When vouchers can be used at only one place or for only one purpose, they have a controlling effect, and the rationale is to make sure that the grant is used for the purpose for which it was given.

Another way of labeling programs is universal vis-à-vis categorical or selective. In the former, programs are designed for, or open to, everyone within the population designated—every family, every family with children, or everyone over a certain age. Selective programs are for people in certain circumstances—the poor, ghetto dwellers, or refugees, for example.

It is obvious that this division of programs is not clear-cut—the universal programs deal with categories, albeit large ones, and the selective programs are for everyone in a certain category and are, hence, somewhat universal. The issues of universality and selectivity are dealt with in greater detail in Chapter 8, using children's allowances as a case in point.

CHANGING NEEDS

As society changes and societal norms and behaviors evolve and become transmuted, situations that were once considered problems are no longer so thought of, while situations once considered normal become identified as problems. Homosexuality was once seen as both a societal and an individual problem, but in America today it is increasingly being viewed as a condition, a situation, or one of a variety of acceptable behaviors. Pornography grows and recedes as a problem in accordance with varying court rulings. Both sex discrimination and racial discrimination are moving from being defined as problems to being defined as crimes. The incidence of unwed mothers appears to be in inverse ratio to the spread of birth-control pills, with consequent reduction in the area of adoptions. The constant change in human needs defines the problems with which social welfare deals and in turn, adds to the difficulty of arriving at an inclusive, exclusive, stable definition of "social welfare."[58]

NOTES

1. For a thorough discussion of the meaning and possible consequences of use of the word "social" in a definition, see R. M. Titmuss, *Social Policy: An Introduction* (New York: Pantheon, 1974), pp. 24–25; for a similar discussion of "welfare," see N. Rescher, *Welfare: The Social Issues in Philosophical Perspective* (Pittsburgh: University of Pittsburgh Press, 1972).
2. H. M. Crampton and K. K. Keiser, *Social Welfare: Institution and Process* (New York: Random House, 1970).
3. Public-health nurses in New Zealand have been described as "all purpose social workers," despite lack of social-work training. J. H. Robb, "Family Structure and Agency Coordination: Decentralization and the Citizen," in M. N. Zald (ed.), *Social Welfare Institutions* (New York: Wiley, 1965), p. 383.
4. A. J. Kahn, *Social Policy and Social Services* (New York: Random House, 1973), p. 19.
5. I. M. Agouba, *Social Realities and the Response of Social Work Education in Africa* (paper presented at the Eighteenth International Conference of Schools of Social Work, San Juan, Puerto Rico, July 13–17, 1976).
6. A. C. Almanzor, and E. C. Viloria, *Social Realities and the Response of Social Work Education in Asia* (paper presented at the Eighteenth International Conference of Schools of Social Work, San Juan, Puerto Rico, July 13–17, 1976), p. 28.
7. "Social Realities and the Social Work Response: Report from the English-speaking Caribbean." (Paper presented at the Eighteenth International Conference of Schools of Social Work, San Juan, Puerto Rico, July 13–17, 1976).
8. R. Brzozowski, *et al.*, *Social Welfare and the Lines of Its Development in the Polish People's Republic* (Warsaw: Polish Medical Publishers, n.d.), p. 20.
9. *Social Security: 1974* (Canberra: Australian Government Printing Service, 1974), p. 4.
10. "Social Welfare: Ends and Means," in *Current Sweden*, No. 54 (Stockholm: Swedish Institute, 1974).
11. C. J. Prigmore, *Social Work in Iran Since the White Revolution* (University: University of Alabama Press, 1976), p. 33.
12. *The Kingdom of the Netherlands: Facts and Figures* (The Hague: Government Printing Office, 1971).
13. K. M. Wiltse, "The Field of Social Work: An Overview," in A. E. Fink, *The Field of Social Work* (New York: Holt, Rinehart and Winston, 1974), p. 7.
14. J. L. Vigilante, "Between Values and Science: Education for the Profession During a Moral Crisis or, Is Proof Truth?" *Journal of Education for Social Work*, 10 (Fall 1974): 107–15.
15. "Wet-time" is time lost from gainful employment at outdoor jobs, such as house-painting, owing to bad weather. *Guide to the Social Services* (Dublin: Stationery Office, 1974).

16. *Social Insurance in Norway* (Oslo: National Insurance Institute, 1973), p. 45.
17. *Labor and Social Legislation in Uruguay* (New York: Consulate of Uruguay, n.d.), p. 165.
18. *Annual Report: Ministry of Social Affairs and Labour* (Amman: Hashemite Kingdom of Jordan, 1974).
19. *China Yearbook 1976* (Taipei: Republic of China, 1976).
20. F. M. Loewenberg, "Social Work, Social Welfare, and Social Intervention," in F. M. Loewenberg and R. Dolgoff (eds.), *The Practice of Social Intervention: Goals, Roles, and Strategies* (Itasca, Ill.: Peacock, 1972), p. 4.
21. For example, in G. T. Horton, *Readings on Human Services Planning* (Arlington, Va.: Human Services Institute for Children and Families, 1975).
22. Kahn, *op. cit.*, p. 11.
23. Loewenberg, *op. cit.*, p. 3.
24. See, for example, H. L. Wilensky and C. N. Lebeaux, *Industrial Society and Social Welfare* (New York: Free Press, 1958), pp. 138–47.
25. For example, J. Axinn and H. Levin, *Social Welfare: A History of the American Response to Need* (New York: Dodd, Mead, 1975).
26. C. Towle, *Common Human Needs* (New York: National Association of Social Workers, 1965).
27. A. H. Maslow, *Motivation and Personality* (New York: Harper Bros., 1954).
28. For a partial listing and a description of such needs, see N. E. Cohen (ed.), *Social Work and Social Problems* (New York: National Association of Social Workers, 1964).
29. E. Kubler-Ross, *On Death and Dying* (New York: Macmillan, 1969); R. G. Dumont and D. C. Foss, *The American View of Death: Acceptance or Denial* (Cambridge, Mass.: Schenkman, 1972); E. S. Sheidman (ed.), *Death: Current Perspectives* (Palo Alto, Calif.: Mayfield, 1976).
30. A. Strauss, "Transformations of Identity," in A. M. Rose (ed.), *Human Behavior and Social Processes* (Boston: Houghton Mifflin, 1962), pp. 63–85.
31. R. A. Stallings, "The Community Context of Crisis Management," *American Behavioral Scientist,* 16 (January-February 1973):312.
32. See H. S. Becker, *Outsiders: Studies in the Sociology of Deviance* (New York: Free Press, 1963), and C. H. McCaghy, *Deviant Behavior: Crime, Conflict and Interest Groups* (New York: Macmillan, 1976).
33. D. Macarov, *Incentives to Work* (San Francisco: Jossey-Bass, 1970), pp. 27–29.
34. There are many descriptions and studies of the "culture of poverty." Perhaps the most seminal is O. Lewis, "The Culture of Poverty," *Scientific American,* 215 (October 1966):19; see also Macarov, *op. cit.,* pp. 109–22.
35. Macarov, *op. cit.*
36. A. Saxer, *Social Security in Switzerland* (Berne: Paul Haupt, 1965), pp.

105–6; *The Federal Republic of Germany at a Glance* (Wiesbaden, West Germany: Franz Steiner, 1974), pp. 67–68.

37. D. Horowitz and B. Kimmerling, "Some Social Implications of Military Service and the Reserves System in Israel," *Archives of European Sociology*, 15 (1974):77–91; D. Macarov and U. Yannai, *A Study of Centers for Discharged Reservists* (Jerusalem: Ministry of Labour, 1974) (in Hebrew).

38. A. Z. N. Swai, "Developmental Planning Related to Needs of Children in Tanganyika," in H. D. Stein (ed.), *Planning for the Needs of Children in Developing Countries* (New York: UNICEF, 1964), p. 102.

39. *Family, Child and Youth Welfare Services in Africa* (New York: United Nations, 1966) II.K.7,E/CN14/SWSA/5, p. 29.

40. M. Rein, *Social Policy: Issues of Choice and Change* (New York: Random House, 1970).

41. "Social Geography," in Loewenberg and Dolgoff, *op. cit.*, p. 13.

42. For some fascinating cases of medical detection, see B. Roueche, *Eleven Blue Men* (New York: Berkeley, 1965).

43. R. E. Helfer and C. H. Kemps, *The Battered Child* (Chicago: University of Chicago Press, 1974); *Guidelines on Reporting Child Abuse and Maltreatment* (Hauppage, N.Y.: Suffolk County Department of Social Services, 1974).

44. D. Macarov, "The Israeli Community Center During the Yom Kippur War," *Journal of Jewish Communal Service*, 51 (Summer 1975):340.

45. R. A. Bauer (ed.), *Social Indicators* (Cambridge, Mass.: MIT Press, 1966); E. B. Sheldon and W. Moore (eds.), *Indicators of Social Change: Concepts and Measurements* (New York: Sage, 1968); A. Shonfield and S. Shaw, *Social Indicators and Social Policy* (London: Heinemann, 1972); F. M. Andrews and S. B. Withey, *Social Indicators of Well-Being: Americans' Perceptions of Life Quality* (New York: Plenum, 1976); W. J. Cohen, "Social Indicators," in Loewenberg and Dolgoff, *op. cit.*, pp. 98–99.

46. D. MacDonald, "Our Invisible Poor," *New Yorker*, January 19, 1963.

47. M. Harrington, *The Other America* (New York: Macmillan, 1963).

48. H. E. Marshall, *Dorothea Dix: Forgotten Samaritan* (Chapel Hill: University of North Carolina Press, 1937); D. M. Kennedy, *Birth Control in America: The Career of Margaret Sanger* (New Haven, Conn.: Yale University Press, 1970).

49. Macarov, *Incentives to Work, op. cit.*, pp. 18–41.

50. H. Rodman, "On Understanding Lower Class Behavior," *Social and Economic Studies*, 8 (1959):441.

51. On the necessity and desirability of poverty, see Macarov, *Incentives to Work*, op. cit., pp. 32–33; H. Gans, "Income Grants and 'Dirty Work,'" *The Public Interest*, 6 (1967):110; and D. Horowitz and R. Erlich, "Proving Poverty Pays: Big Brother as a Holding Company," in P. Roby (ed.), *The Poverty Establishment* (Englewood Cliffs, N.J.: Prentice-Hall, 1974), pp. 141–56.

52. See "A Child's View of Old Age," *New York Times*, October 10, 1976, p. 6E.

53. For a discussion of the tension between norms and behaviors, see Macarov, *Incentives to Work, op. cit.*, p. 106.

54. E. W. Witte, *The Development of the Social Security Act* (Madison: University of Wisconsin Press, 1962), pp. 146–47.

55. H. L. Hopkins, *Hearings before the Subcommittee of the House Committee on Appropriations on H. R. 7527, Federal Emergency and Civil Works Program*, Washington, D.C., Seventy-third Congress, Second Session, House of Representatives, January 20, 1934, p. 20; quoted in J. Charnow, *Work Relief Experience in the United States* (Washington, D.C.: Social Science Research Council, 1943), p. 10.

56. E. E. Schwartz, "A Way to End the Means Test," *Social Work*, 4 (1963):3.

57. M. Cunningham, "Eligibility Procedures for AFDC," *Social Work*, 22 (January 1977):21–26; see also *Evaluation of the Welfare Declaration: Eligibility Simplification for Public Assistance* (New York: City University of New York, 1969), and J. Anderson and E. Lourey, *Issues in the Development, Implementation and Evaluation of Simplified Eligibility Methods for Public Assistance* (Minneapolis: American Rehabilitation Foundation, 1969).

58. Which Graycar refers to as the "chimera of a neat definition." A. Graycar, *Social Policy: An Australian Introduction* (Melbourne: Macmillan, 1976), p. 1.

PART II

THE MAJOR MOTIVATIONS FOR SOCIAL WELFARE

3

Mutual Aid

The determination to help meet human needs, which, as discussed in the previous chapter, is a theme running through all definitions of "social welfare," may arise from a number of motivations. This and the next four chapters will discuss these major motivations for social welfare: (1) mutual aid; (2) religious commandments; (3) the desire for political advantage; (4) economic considerations; and (5) ideological factors.

These motivations coexist and intermingle; one may strengthen another, weaken it, or have little relationship to it. Most social-welfare policies arise from more than one motivation, and it is only in order to clarify them and their relationships to one another that they are presented here as separate entities.

One of the oldest and most ubiquitous motivations for meeting human needs is the desire or the necessity to engage in mutual aid. There have been times in the past, and there are still places today, in which social welfare consists almost entirely of mutual-aid activities. In addition, many programs arising primarily from other motivations contain elements of mutual aid or are affected by it. Voluntary social-welfare organizations, in particular, often originate as "a happy sharing of small resources"[1] with mutual aid as one of the mainsprings. Finally, there are social-welfare programs designed to enlarge mutual-aid activities in families, neighborhoods, and other settings. Mutual aid, in short, is one of the basic motivations for social-welfare policies and programs, and one can comprehend these in their entirety, or in depth, only by understanding the influence of mutual aid in their development and existence.

THE ROOTS OF MUTUAL AID

The roots of mutual aid lie in the prehistory of the human race. Just as aggression,[2] territoriality,[3] and the hunting need,[4] which humans share with other animals, serve to emphasize the continuing existence of certain traits that date back to the prehuman period, so mutual aid goes back to a time when people were unable to withstand alone the vicissitudes of nature and banded together in herds, or tribes, in order to survive. Societies, bands, or tribes were the most primitive forms of organization of mankind and its earliest ancestors.[5] In this phase of society, individual survival was not important; the continuation of the tribe was paramount, and all else was subordinated to it. Mutual aid was thus neither purposefully willed nor consciously undertaken; it was a normative condition, the only way that life could be lived. Kropotkin's seminal study of mutual aid in animals and humans leads to the conclusion that the species that have survived throughout evolution have not been those most able to dominate or destroy others but those most able to cooperate with one another.[6]

When people lived as undifferentiated parts of a tribe, they all shared the same thoughts and emotions, and thereby developed a "collective unconscious," which is said to be present to this day, as well as the ability to share thoughts with little, if any, verbal or nonverbal communication. Consequently, it is from this phase of human development that the collective unconscious—a "timeless and universal psyche"—and the archetypes, which are central to Jung's psychoanalytic theories, arise,[7] as well as the empathic communication that is central to some conceptions of social-work practice.[8]

It is not surprising, then, that in recapitulation theory, which holds that individuals repeat during their own development the stages through which their species evolved, the need to become a member of a group is seen as programed into the human phylogeny of mankind.[9] Others, who do not necessarily accept the theory of recapitulation, nevertheless emphasize that the individual "self" cannot emerge as a distinct entity without constant reference to other selves in the human community who, by their reactions, mold the individual: "He is what he is insofar as he is a member of this community, and the raw materials out of which this particular individual is born would not be a self but for his relationship to others in the community."[10] The dependence of individuals upon mutual aid is nowhere more dramatically illustrated than in the universal experience of birth. Here is "the special, unique case in which the loved one really was once a spatial, corporeal 'part' of the one who loves"[11] and is completely dependent upon the latter for life maintenance. Nor is this a one-way relationship, for, as the folk saying has it, "More than the calf wants to suck, the cow wants to suckle." Mutual aid, then, is the very essence of human relationships, as well as the basis for individual and societal existence. Consequently, one way of comprehending social welfare is as *"that patterning of relationships which develops in society to carry out mutual-support functions."*[12]

Although mutual aid has its roots in the distant past, and new forms of living have since emerged, this does not mean that the mutual aid that once made life possible in herds, tribes, or similar groups does not exist today. Among Bedouin in the Near East, American Indians, and Gypsies in Europe, and in many parts of Africa, in the South Pacific islands,[13] and in other parts of the world, the basic structure of society continues to be based on tribes that command the primary allegiance of their members. In these places, social welfare, to be successful, must take into account the tribal structure of society and the patterns of mutual aid that this entails, in the same way that other cultural differences must be given deep consideration in determining the role of social welfare.[14]

THE FAMILY: PRIMARY LOCUS OF MUTUAL AID

Over time, the tribal structure may evolve into clans; locality, ethnic, and language groups; and other kinds of associations. However, none of these is as universal or influential as the family. Mutual-aid activities were not only taken over by this new type of group as it emerged, but the very definition of a family often includes the extent to which mutual aid can be expected to obtain. As families developed, in turn, differences in family structure also came into being.

The "traditional" family is usually an extended family including cousins, in-laws, and several generations, customarily living under one roof or in close proximity to one another, sometimes on communally owned land. In the Near East this is called, in Arabic, the *hamula,* and it includes some aspects of a feudal society in that the patriarch usually receives all income, dispenses all funds, and makes all decisions regarding the family as a whole and each individual member.[15] Mutual aid is built into the structure of the extended family to the point that it has been termed a source of security more time-honored than any social security system.[16] In Pakistan, for example,

> Families generally are extended family systems. The role of each family member is clearly defined and each is dependent on the other. Strong family ties exist and there is little privacy in most homes. Sharing of family matters with outside people, however, is considered an act of great irresponsibility, warranting censure. Family quarrels, plans, and economic

circumstances, illness of social consequence, are all matters to be carefully safeguarded from public knowledge. Thus, if a social worker wants to talk to a junior member of the family, he often must get permission and acceptance from the head of the family. Many times initial contact is made in the presence of the head of the family.[17]

A different version of the extended family is found in Japan:

The distinguishing feature of the Japanese family system is the importance of the House as distinct from a less well defined group of blood relations, usually referred to as the family. The House has been described as "a legal entity originally founded upon ancestor-worship," and consists of the Head of the House and its members, who are subject to his authority. The House is in fact a name group and not a group related by blood, as it may include persons, both male and female, who are not blood relations of the Head of the House but have entered it with his consent.[18]

It should not be assumed that because the extended family is basically undemocratic, mutual aid is unnecessary. On the contrary, mutual aid is an important aspect of the extended family, and many essential activities—house-building, sowing, reaping, and so forth—are based upon every member of the extended family pitching in to help. So important is the mutual-aid aspect of the extended family that where the extended family system is strong, the role of the state in social welfare has been found to be weak:[19] The extended family takes care of its own, reducing the need for outside help.

In many places, particularly in the industrialized West, the extended family is in the process of being replaced by the modern, or nuclear, or conjugal, family, consisting of parents and unmarried children living at home.[20] Although the nuclear family is more prevalent than the extended family in most developed countries, even within these areas there still remain substantial segments of the population who cling to the older tradition. Social problems, such as anomie, alienation, intrafamily discord, and intergeneration problems often arise from the interface of the traditional and modern types of family structures.[21]

Problems that stem from the conflict between extended and nuclear family structures and processes are particularly acute in countries that are in the process of developing, moving from a traditional agricultural socio-economic system to a modern industrialized one. The conflict of values between parents and children is one part of this problem, leading to familial tension. Another touches the claims of the extended family on the income of its members, as opposed to the individual-success ethic of "getting ahead."

Countries that receive immigrants from societies with a differing family structure also face this problem. The usual pattern is for immigrants from a traditional society to be bewildered and resentful of the values (or, to them, loss of values) in the nuclear family structure. In Israel, for example, immigrants from Russian Georgia resisted the modern, one-family apartments made available to them, because they did not offer the communal kitchen, joint dining room, and other central facilities that helped maintain the cohesion of the traditional family.

The same problem is found within countries in which there is a migration from rural areas or small towns with an extended family tradition to the large cities, most of which are characterized by an atomistic and anonymous existence. Hence, the new arrivals search for relatives.

These are not only problems with which social welfare must be concerned in terms of seeking solutions: Social-welfare policies and practice themselves may cause or contribute to these problems. Some social workers, for example, have been accused of creating or aggravating family problems by seeing the extended family as encouraging immature dependence patterns on the part of its members, and by seeing health as lying in the direction of breaking kinship ties and establishing closed nuclear families.[22] Policies that weaken or eliminate mutual dependence of parents and children, or encourage removing one of them from the home, or inculcate values in children that are at variance with parents' values—all exacerbate the situation.

Some families are neither extended nor nuclear: A number of other variants have been identified: dyadic-nuclear families, dual-work families, single-parent families, three-generational families, middle-aged or old-aged couples, kin networks, second-career families, institutional families, and others.[23] Throughout all these patterns, however, runs the common thread of familial mutual aid. Whenever a person is in trouble or in need, he or she naturally turns to the family first. The family is seen as the first line of defense for its members both by society and by family members, and all needs that can be satisfied within the family are generally expected to be handled in this fashion. That "blood is thicker than water" is a widely accepted axiom, and throughout society the family is considered to be one of the major sources of need satisfaction.[24]

SOCIAL WELFARE AND FAMILIES

In addition to mutual aid, there are many other functions that families are expected to carry out, such as socialization, control, and continuity. Nor is the family the only element charged with these responsibilities. The "mix" considered desirable of government, voluntary services, the market, and the family varies from time to time and location to location as regards responsibility for religious beliefs and practices, education, health, deportment, inculcation of values, and career choices, among other things. There have been societies in which education was the family's responsibility, religion that of the Church, and defense that of the government. Others have entrusted religion to the family, education to the state, and health to voluntary organizations. Transnational studies indicate a number of additional permutations.[25]

The same situation obtains for social welfare. However, with mutual aid one of the most distinguishing characteristics of families, and with the family the basic unit in most societies, it is inevitable that social-welfare policy is affected by the extent to which families engage in mutual aid, and that the amount of mutual aid in which families engage is conditioned by the extent and type of social welfare. For example, mutual aid within families may reduce the need for institutions, whereas unavailability of institutions may increase mutual aid within families.

Policies, including those of social welfare, that are designed to strengthen families arise from a number of motivations. There is the desire to maintain strong family structure so that the family can carry out the normative activities mentioned above—education, training in deportment, and so forth. There is also the desire to provide a healthy environment for growing and living, which will avoid or minimize psychic and interrelationship problems. Then there is the instrumental goal of avoiding social-welfare costs and activities by increasing the amount of mutual aid that families extend to their members.

Consequently, there are two main thrusts in social-welfare policies regarding families. One is an attempt to affect families—to strengthen, enlarge, or limit families as such.[26] The second goal is to use, exploit, or rely on families in carrying out social-welfare activities. Obviously, those who would like to see families carry more of society's need-fulfilling activities can be expected to take steps to maintain or strengthen families, while those who see strong families as a social good might see the necessity for families to undertake more mutual-aid activities as an instrumental device for strengthening the family. In short, both healthier families and mutual aid may be either means or end. Nevertheless, it is possible to separate these two aspects of social welfare for heuristic purposes.[27]

Policies Designed to Affect Families

The amount of importance a society ascribes to families as such, attempts to affect families, and the means by which such attempts are made vary from place to place. Most Western countries, however, at least profess to see the family as a social good. For example, a report

from West Germany speaks of "the Bund's solicitude to base social
policy more strongly on family promotion,"[28] while "the ideology upon
which socialism is being built in Poland considers the family, not the
individual, as the basic social unit."[29] In France, social welfare is clearly
directed toward families. Thirty-five percent of French social-security
benefits are in the form of family allowances. Schorr points out that "a
substantial French consensus views the family, *as a unit*, as the ultimate
beneficiary of Government policy."[30] The French attitude toward the
family has direct impact on social-welfare policies:

> The people have been unwilling to accept health and welfare services
> such as medical protection, school lunches, and vacation camps for chil-
> dren as a supplement to their family allowances, as has been done in
> Great Britain. The French tend to consider the provision of regimented
> services for the family or children as an infringement upon the personal
> liberty of the parents, and particularly an affront to the prestige of the
> father.[31]

In Europe, a number of firms began adjusting salaries to family size
at the end of the nineteenth century, and this practice spread widely
after World War I. After World War II, this tended to become a government activity, and by now a majority of the countries in the world, and
all of the industrialized West, except the United States, have either a
children's allowance or a family allowance.[32] In Israel, emphasis on
families is indicated by the facts that salaries of employees are geared
to the sizes of their families and that there is also a universal children's
allowance.[33]

In India, on the other hand, the major preoccupation is limiting the
size of families, with some sort of enforced sterilization under consideration at the time of this writing. Conversely, insofar as concerns for
family structure or helping with family problems are concerned, there
are reported to be only a few family agencies in India, located in certain
urban areas. "Not more than a tiny fraction of the population knows of
their existence, however."[34] In Thailand, the family is considered so
important that a problem has been identified in finding foster homes
for children: So many families have taken the children of relatives or
servants into their own homes that they have no room to receive
other children.[35]

The history of social welfare in both England and the United States
is replete with references to the importance of the family. For example,
one of the pioneer social reformers who lived at the beginning of the
nineteenth century saw the "kindness of relatives" as one of the essential founts from which flowed beneficial work,[36] and the Charity Organization Society in England early adopted as a firm tenet the position

that the family was to be considered as a whole.[37] Consequently, it is possible to view charity, reform, and welfare work as being family- and child-oriented since their inception.[38] The very names of the Family Service Association and the Jewish Family Service bespeak the concern of voluntary agencies for families. Nor is this concern confined to voluntary organizations: When the Secretary of Health, Education, and Welfare appointed an ad hoc committee on public welfare in 1961, its recommendations were "designed to reinforce and support family life through rehabilitation, prevention, and protection,"[39] and in the 1974 Code of Federal Regulations dealing with social welfare, there is a clear provision concerning the goal of strengthening family life.[40]

Despite these pronouncements and even without examining the content or the results of the policies thus enunciated, it is nevertheless possible to question the validity of the belief that families have always been at the center of social-welfare concern. Axinn and Levin point out that despite the Charity Organization Society's stated concern with families,

> Not until 1919 . . . did the Association's name include the word "family" . . . not until 1930 . . . did the title suggest an aggressive force for the welfare of families. This slow evolution from charity organization to social work organization to family welfare can be traced through a . . . perusal of the *Proceedings of the National Conference of Charities and Corrections.* . . . There is limited concern with the family as a unit or with the interaction between family life and social institutions.[41]

The difficulty in determining America's "real" concern for families lies in the fact that almost every area of social services involves families in some way:[42] Rehabilitation of a disabled person might enable him or her to play a better family role as child, sibling, spouse, or parent; cash grants to an aged parent relieve the children of some financial responsibility; and so forth. Consequently, it is possible for the same social-work leader to say in 1964 that American society is noteworthy for its emphasis on the family[43] and in 1967 that "individual fulfillment, not family continuity or group solidarity, is the salient emphasis of much American family life, in sharp contrast to family and child-rearing values in many parts of the world."[44] The bulk of opinion, however, at least among those who have held important policy-making positions in America, is succinctly expressed by a former commissioner in the Department of Health, Education, and Welfare: "The United States has no explicit national policy with respect to family life."[45] A former commissioner of Social Security details this charge:

> Although . . . programs of the Federal government are significant in the lives of American families, the principal changes in the American family

over the past fifty years have not been influenced directly by the economic programs of government . . . they have been the results of urbanization, industrialization, and other broad economic and social
movements. It is surprising how little attention has been given to a "family policy" by the United States government. This is in contradistinction
to the family policy goals of other countries. Some nations have formally
enunciated policies encouraging large families through rewards of various kinds, for example, the Soviet Union . . . others have established goals
to reduce family size—Japan and India—some have clearly established
policies of financial assistance to large families to help in lessening the
economic burden of children through a system of family allowances, and
others have set forth family goals in their constitutions or in a variety of
programs.[46]

As a matter of record, American social-welfare programs usually begin with individuals, and only later take into account the fact that
individuals are parts of families.[47] To some, this lack of policy regarding
families is so disturbing that a proposal has been made to establish a U.S.
Department of Marriage and the Family on a par with other cabinet
posts.[48] This neglect of legislative concern for the family as an institution is not accidental but, rather, a conscious and deliberate form of
"benign neglect." Moynihan holds that it arose from a fear of "great"
families, on the one hand, and, on the other, a laissez-faire attitude that
defined families as inviolate and private. This avoidance was reinforced
by immigration containing diverse family patterns.[49] Recently, however, there has been growing concern for American families, occasioned by the rising rate of divorce, which now ends one in three
American marriages—the highest proportion in the world.

However, not all observers are as pessimistic about the present status
or future of the family. Using empirical methods to examine the myth
of selfish children and lonely parents, Schorr found that only 15 percent
of aged parents live farther than a short ride from some child; about half
live within walking distance or a short ride; the remainder are in the
same dwelling with a child. More than two out of three aged parents
see their children at least weekly, and when there are no visits, they
keep in touch by telephone.[50] Some people go even farther and predict
a counterrevolution in which family structure and authority will be
renewed.[51]

In summary, it seems clear that though there are belief in and desire
for whole, healthy, functioning families, few U.S. government policies
have as their result the enhancement of healthy family functioning.

Despite this lack of policies, there are organizations and programs
specifically designed to help families. Among voluntary agencies, the
names previously mentioned—Jewish Family Service, Family Service
Association, and others—speak for themselves. There are specific pro-

grams, too, including government programs, that are at least nominally aimed at strengthening families, for example, Aid to Families with Dependent Children and the proposed Family Assistance Plan.[52] Generally speaking, however, most early social workers—governmental and voluntary alike—were concerned with the environment and the social action necessary to change it. Hence, while speaking of the integrity of the family, they did not hesitate to break up families, especially those of the poor and the dependent,[53] by sending them to live with "more suitable" families. Institutions began to replace foster homes early in the nineteenth century and became the preferred loci of treatment in many cases, continuing the breakup of natural families. Orphan homes, for example, accepted children whose parents were alive but poor or "morally . . . inadequate to their task."[54] Home care began to be looked upon more favorably early in the twentieth century, as evidenced by President Theodore Roosevelt's address to the 1909 White House Conference on Child Dependency, which extolled the virtues of home life and urged that children not be deprived of it.[55] But simultaneous with the renewed interest in home care came the "psychiatric deluge,"[56] which focused attention on the individual rather than the environment—often to the exclusion of the current family. Family therapy has emerged as important only during the last few decades, and then almost exclusively within voluntary family-service agencies, which numbered about 340 in 1973 and gave help to only 150,000 families,[57] a minute proportion of the total of 4,000,000 families helped by social welfare. Consequently, although dependence on mutual aid—as epitomized in families—is widely accepted conceptually and receives much public approbation, it is actually not the common social-service practice[58] to try to strengthen families.

The Case of AFDC.   The major exception to the government's neglect of families in social welfare is the program originally called Aid to Dependent Children (ADC). This program, mounted in a deliberate effort to keep families together and to ease their lot, had some interesting precursors. In 1898, the New York State legislature passed a bill to allow any child in an institution to be released to his parents, and directed city comptrollers to pay to the parents the same amount that the city had been paying the institution for the upkeep of the child. The bill was vetoed as "pauperizing" recipients by paying parents to take care of their own children.[59] But New York City (which dealt with the bulk of such cases) agreed to refer applications for commitment of dependent children to voluntary agencies, which would "assist in keeping homes together by granting relief to as many families as possible."[60] From such experiences grew the "mothers' aid" laws, first adopted by Illinois in 1911, which spread rapidly to the other states.[61]

When the states proved unable to cope with welfare needs during the Great Depression,[62] the federal government took over such programs through the Social Security Act of 1935. The aim of the Aid to Dependent Children program, as later amended, became

> To enable each state to furnish financial assistance, rehabilitation, and other services in order to encourage the care of dependent children in their own homes or in the homes of relatives with whom they are living, to help such parents or relatives to attain or retain the ability for self-support, and to help maintain and strengthen family life.[63]

It can justifiably be argued that when this bill was first operationalized into a program, it was aimed exclusively at one-parent families, and that no program for "whole" families was ever attempted. It was, however, at least directed toward families rather than individuals, and at a later date in its metamorphosis it also included families with both parents, if the breadwinner was unemployed. In its history, the program underwent a number of changes, some of which are reflected in the changes in title that have taken place: Aid to Dependent Children (ADC); Aid to Families with Dependent Children (AFDC); Aid and Services to Needy Families with Children; Aid to Families of Dependent Children—Unemployed Parent (AFDC-UP); and others.[64] The avowed original intent of this law was to allow and encourage mothers to stay home and take care of their children. The public image that lay behind the original law was of the genteel, middle-class, white widow —perhaps a preacher's widow—unable to sustain herself and her children by giving piano lessons at home, forced to leave the children every day in order to go out and work. Everyone saw her as deserving of help, and her children as precious assets entitled to the best of education and other opportunities. Hence, the AFDC program.

The AFDC program, in its various forms, has grown into the largest noninsurance welfare program in the United States. When it began as part of Social Security in 1936, 162,000 families received $49.7 million in benefits. In 1975, more than 3.5 million families received assistance amounting to more than $9 billion.[65] The phenomenal growth in AFDC recipients and costs came to be seen by the general public and legislators alike not as an indication of the depth and breadth of poverty in America but as evidence of the mendacity of the poor. Either as cause or as effect, the public image behind AFDC changed to that of a black, unmarried teenager having children in order to receive more money.[66]

As a result, AFDC uses a number of devices today to force mothers to go to work—on pain of withholding payments—and is responsible in great part for the current proliferation of child-care programs that are generally not established as educational or family-welfare programs but as baby-sitting or holding operations that remove the excuse of child-care duties from mothers viewed as basically lazy. With the adoption of the Work Incentive Program (WIN) in 1967, which required applicants to accept any job available or undergo training, a double standard for families was established. "While white middle-class women are insisting on equal pay and equal opportunities, women in welfare families are expected to take any job, at any pay."[67] In its history, AFDC has used a number of other devices that are basically antifamily. Because married couples living together were not eligible for AFDC at one point, regardless of income, desertion was rewarded. Further, if the mother was presumed to know the whereabouts of her husband, she was required to notify law-enforcement officers (known in welfare jargon as NOLEO—notice to law-enforcement officers). In any case, she was legally required to name the father to be eligible for help. Midnight raids on welfare households to detect signs of a man in the house—a hat, a cigar—were common.[68] In fact,

> Justification of relatives' liability laws is based in part on the claim that such laws encourage mutual support within kinship systems, thereby strengthening family bonds . . . this is a shallow assumption that quickly bottoms out when put into practice. In order to qualify for aid in many states, public assistance applicants may be required to sue their legally liable relatives . . . or they may be required to allow the assistance agency to sue their relatives as a condition for eligibility. In either case, it has been observed that these sanctions against uncooperative or irresponsible relatives are "strangely at odds with the stated purpose of increasing family cohesion."[69]

Although there is little empirical evidence available as to the actual effect of AFDC on families, and particularly as to whether it does, in fact, encourage desertions, the fact that this could be a result of the program raises the value question as to whether policies should attempt to maintain "intact families" through lack of economic alternatives or should be designed to allow men and women the freedom to make marital choices on grounds other than economic necessity.[70]

Thus, despite rhetoric concerning the importance of the family in American society, most social-welfare policy is designed without regard to its impact on families or with effects that are actually hostile toward them, while programs designed to strengthen families often have the opposite effect, with the exception of some programs sponsored by voluntary agencies, which affect only a minute proportion of the population.

Policies Designed to Utilize Families

Turning now to the second thrust of social welfare regarding families
—those policies and programs that rather than attempting to affect
families and their mutual-aid functions, attempt to use, exploit, or build
on family relationships and mutual aid—the most prominent and widespread example has to do with relatives' responsibility.

Relatives'Responsibility Laws   That families should be responsible for
their own members seems to be taken for granted in most societies of
which families are important components. And, as noted previously,
where mutual aid in families is strong, outside social-welfare measures
are correspondingly weak. As such outside measures come into being
—through church, voluntary agencies, or governments—the desires to
reduce costs, on one hand, and not to weaken the structure of the family
or the "moral fiber" of the individual, on the other, combine to transform family mutual aid from a desideratum into a responsibility. The
law then foists upon families responsibility for their members or, conversely, denies help to persons with families that could help them.[71]

Few pretend that relatives' responsibility (or family responsibility, as
it is sometimes called) laws originally stemmed from a desire to
strengthen families. Rather, they clearly were a response to rising
social-welfare costs at the time of the enactment of the Elizabethan
Poor Laws in 1597 and 1601.[72] And because the law reinforced public
attitudes, at least insofar as parents' supporting children was concerned,[73] the responsibility of family members for each other was insisted on, even if it meant breaking up the family. The Charity
Organization Society, for example, ruled that if possible, a husband
should be forced to support his family, and if he disappeared the family
should be broken up and its members placed in public institutions.[74]

Nor were family members' actual resources the only criterion: Potential resources were also considered. An agent of the Boston Associated
Charities in 1898 reported turning down a request from a young
woman for money to help pay the rent, claiming that the applicant was
one of a family of six, only one of whom was willing to work.[75]

There were times when moral judgments combined with administrative and fiscal considerations to result in policies intended to dissolve
families in some cases and to neglect individuals in the family, in the
name of family solidarity, in others. Thus, the wife of a drunkard was
required to leave him to obtain help for herself and her family, and she
was thenceforth treated for social-welfare purposes as a widow. But if
a husband deserted his wife, she would not be given a widow's benefits,
for if she were, other men would presumably be induced to desert their

families.[76] The records do not reveal how many men arranged to have themselves termed "drunkards," rather than "deserters," so their families could receive benefits. Such policy-induced choices have not been eroded by history. A 1965 Wisconsin law stipulates that a woman deserted by her husband must file *criminal* charges of abandonment against him as a condition of eligibility for AFDC.[77] And in Egypt today aged persons can apply to a residential institution only if they have *no* relatives; and this is confined to urban areas—in rural areas, it is simply assumed that the aged will be taken care of by members of the family.[78]

The definition of a responsible relative differs radically between those who are eligible to receive support for a child and those who are responsible for his support. The former include father, mother, grandfather, grandmother, sister, stepfather, stepmother, stepbrother, stepsister, uncle, aunt, first cousin, nephew, and niece (including such relatives of half-blood, preceding generations as denoted by the prefixes "grand-," "great-," or "great-great-," and people who legally adopted the child or his parents).[79] In New York State, however, the law discriminates against natural parents, paying to foster parents more for child upkeep than to relatives. Definitions of "child" also vary. In the original Social Security Act the maximum age was sixteen; Wisconsin ruled in 1965 that the maximum age was eighteen; today the maximum age varies from ten to twenty-one years.[80]

Insofar as contributing to support, rather than receiving it, is concerned, colonial law specified that parents, grandparents, and children were responsible for each other, but by 1836 most states had added grandchildren, and many states later added brothers and sisters.[81] New Hampshire held maternal grandmothers liable for the support of needy illegitimate grandchildren.[82] In other countries, responsibility is spread much wider. In Israel, for example, a person is responsible for his and his spouse's parents, his adult children and their spouses, his grandchildren, his and his spouse's grandparents, and his and his spouse's brothers and sisters.[83] In New York State, this responsibility is not a light one. In 1966, public-welfare officials had the power to subpoena relatives, compel their appearance, take their testimony under oath, and examine their books and other records.[84]

In recent years, however, there has been a redefinition of the concept of family responsibility. As the extended family has been replaced by the nuclear family, the Poor Law inheritance concerning relatives' responsibility has been successively limited.[85] This movement may be attributable to new views about, and definitions of, individual liberty and rights. For example, courts have ruled that selecting certain relatives as liable for others deprives them of equal protection under the law because family membership is an unreasonable classification for separating the liable from the nonliable.[86]

In contrast with the widespread responsibility in force previously, recent definitions have tended to be narrow. As long ago as 1965, Medicaid law limited responsibility to spouse for spouse and parent for minor or disabled child.[87] The 1974 Code of Federal Regulations regarding public welfare says, "In family groups living together, income of the spouse is considered available for his spouse and income of a parent is considered available for children under 21."[88] In New York State in 1976, primary responsibility was placed on husbands and fathers: Relatives' responsibility was defined as husband for wife, husband for child up to twenty-one, mother for child up to twenty-one if father died, wife for husband if husband is incapacitated, and natural parents for illegitimate child.[89]

The amount of legal coercion necessary for obtaining family support has been found to differ along several dimensions. There is more of a tradition of mutual aid among lower-class families—particularly women—than in the middle class.[90] Responsibility in all classes tends to flow more in the direction of parents for children than the reverse.[91]

Despite the legal narrowing of relatives' responsibility, the practical effect on recipients often remains unchanged.[92] Although laws may designate the categories of relatives who are to be considered responsible, administrators of programs in some states expand on legislative intent by instructing staff to seek out additional categories of relatives (and even friends) as potential "financial resources,"[93] and any relative, whatever the degree of relationship, may be considered a potential resource for public-assistance clients.[94]

In social-work jargon, this is referred to as the concept of "past management." Although such questions are actually illegal in New York State, clients who apply for assistance are asked how they managed previously, and unless they can prove some drastic change in their situation, are instructed to continue in the same way, even if this involves depending on a nonresponsible relative. This arises because many policies are not supported with sufficient appropriations. Hence, the invocation of relatives' responsibility or past management is not necessarily due to malevolence on the part of program administrators or practitioners but is a measure to stretch the resources available to cover the largest number of needy clients[95]—a process that has been termed "rationing services."[96]

On the other hand, narrowing the concept of relatives' responsibility leads to methods of exploiting the social-welfare system in ways probably neither foreseen nor intended by the legislators. For example, limiting responsibility to "family groups living together," as the Code of Federal Regulations does, means that any person moving away from his or her family becomes eligible for welfare help, regardless of the income or resources of the family. Thus, students who live away from home at college, even youngsters sent to expensive private high schools, and young people setting up their own household—all are technically the financial responsibility of the government, rather than of their families. Couples who postpone or reject marriage formalities, although living together, are also technically two individuals not living in their family group.

From one point of view, this situation can be seen as reflecting the attitude of the times, perhaps sprung from the "youth revolt" of the 1960s, according to which individual choice and freedom from dependence on older people became an accepted value among large sectors of the population. The term in use for a young person living away from home is "emancipated minor," with all of the positive valence that emancipation contains. And, indeed, for many such young people, being no longer financially dependent on their parents probably has sound psychological results.

On the other hand, dependence has simply been shifted from parents to taxpayers, and despite the greater ease and sense of freedom that this may give the recipients, there are questions as to both the justice of such arrangements and the extent to which the public will continue to condone them. In 1976, for example, there were eleven thousand cases of emancipated minors on the relief rolls in New York State. In order to limit the growing expense in this area, it was ruled that eligibility would henceforth depend on family-court orders, which in essence declare the emancipation necessary or desirable; or the minors' petitions asking their parents for support—evidence of attempts to invoke relatives' responsibility.[97]

In summary, the institutionalization of mutual aid into relatives' responsibility laws and practice proceeds from two bases: One is the rationalization that supporting one's family is good therapy, that failure to require such support leads to "catastrophic consequences for family cohesion and morality,"[98] and that, therefore, relatives' responsibility laws enhance families and their functioning by placing responsibility upon them. The second is that such laws remove from the government, the taxpayers, or the contributors to voluntary organizations burdens that rightfully belong on families.

The weight of the empirical evidence, however, insofar as the first contention is concerned, is that responsibility imposed from without tends to destroy rather than enhance families. Insofar as the second contention is concerned, it is true that case loads tend to rise when relatives' responsibility laws are repealed and that vigorous collection methods addressed to responsible relatives result in increased income to the state. However, less is known concerning the effect of the law on the financial situation of relatives. To the extent that relatives of poor people tend to be poor, relatives' responsibility laws may save money at the cost of family cohesion and interrelationships,[99] which may create other costly problems.

OTHER MUTUAL-AID INSTITUTIONS

Although the family is the major vehicle through which mutual aid is manifested in society, and although in technologically underdeveloped countries mutual-support activities are carried out primarily by the family, as societies have become more complex, other groups, organizations, and agencies have developed that carry out mutual-support activities.[100]

Guilds, Unions, and Mutual-Aid Societies

One example of extrafamily mutual aid was the medieval guild. Guilds were either social-, craft-, or merchant-based, but they all tended to be small closed groups that emphasized brotherhood among members and, consequently, cooperative self-help.[101] Guild members were required to help each other in time of need, but such help was confined to the members of the guild. From the guild flowed the concept of labor unions, and in the original small unions mutual aid was a primary concept: Members spoke of the organization as a brotherhood, and belonging to the same union created a bond of which mutual aid was one of the results.[102] As unions began to grow in size, their social-welfare activities became institutionalized, with results that will be discussed below. In some cases, the social-welfare benefits of unions outstripped those of both governmental and voluntary agencies. The railroad union in the United States was known from its inception for its munificent social-welfare benefits, and when the Social Security Act was passed, railroad workers were not originally covered by it; their benefits from union funds were greater than those promised by the new law.[103] The social-welfare demands of unions have become a major factor in bargaining negotiations, having outstripped salary demands in many cases. A growing number of unions, including most of the large ones, employ social workers, and the element of mutuality—that this is "our" service, and benefits are a right rather than a privilege—is an important aspect of such services.

Mutual-aid societies are, as their name implies, another vehicle for the expression of people's concern for one another. Most of these societies are based on some commonality between members—place of origin, religion, neighborhood, political affiliation or belief. With the growth of government and voluntary social-welfare agencies, the need for such mutual-aid societies diminished, but a surprising number still exist. Fraternal orders are usually larger than mutual-aid societies, and some of these—Benevolent Protective Order of Elks, International Order of Oddfellows, etc.—are nationwide and even international. They offer free-loan funds, sickness funds, funeral benefits, and other help, in addition to their social events. Mutual-aid societies and the local chapters of fraternal orders usually start as small groups, because one of the requirements of mutual aid is a continuing interaction among the members.

Small Groups

An even smaller mutual-aid element in society is the myriad groups to which every person belongs all his or her life. Social-welfare activities —usually in the form of improving interrelationships, mental health, citizenship education, leisure, and rehabilitation—include work with or through groups. This is the method in social-work practice known as social group work.[104] In contradistinction to other types of group leadership, in which task completion is paramount, the role of the social worker dealing with groups is to strengthen each group as a whole so that the members can be enabled to help one another. That the help in the group flows from peers, rather than only from the worker, is fundamental to social group work, and has been emphasized even more in certain approaches to group work whose practitioners speak of the "group-work group" as one in which members consciously contract to seek a common goal by helping each other.[105] All group work, however, recognizes the importance of "we feeling"—the recognition by members that they are bound together by virtue of their membership in the group.

A current phenomenon flowing directly from mutual-aid philosophies and not confined to the social-welfare sphere is the proliferation of various kinds of encounter groups. This movement stems from the work of the National Training Laboratory in Maine, which began with efforts to make groups more effective through leadership training, via so-called T-groups. This has since spilled over into various other types of groups, under many auspices, which can generally be categorized as T-groups, laboratory method, human-relations training, sensitivity training, personal growth experiences, basic encounter, and intensive group experiences.[106] Around the fringes of these basic types of groups, as it were, have grown up more esoteric groups—primal scream, marathon encounters, and what are referred to vulgarly as "touchie-feelie" groups. There is little agreement concerning the ethics, methods, results, and side effects of such groups, as well as the motivations of some "group-entrepreneurs."[107] However, for better or for worse, these groups are rooted squarely in the philosophy that members get aid from one another and that only group members can give such aid.

The belief that people need one another and—given the proper circumstances—can help one another finds dramatic expression in the "self-help" groups, which focus on specific problems.[108] Whether the problem is obvious and acute, as drug addiction or alcoholism is, or nagging and chronic, as obesity is, the basis of such groups as Synanon (for drug addicts), Alcoholics Anonymous, and Weight Watchers is that only people who suffer from the same problem can help others and, in doing so, be helped themselves.[109] The other members of the group, and not a group leader or anyone outside the group, are seen as the source of help.

Communities and Neighborhoods

The collaborative approach also characterizes at least one school of thought that uses the social-work method known as community organization. Although some see the proper role of the worker as coordinating services and agencies for the benefit of clients, identifying gaps in services, and initiating new services, others are more deeply committed to cooperation among people in solving their own problems. This approach can be divided between (1) those who see the end result in terms of roads built, garbage collected, or problems solved and (2) those who see the desired result as self-images improved, attitudes changed, and relationships strengthened.[110] The latter school of thought may view mutual aid as either a goal or an instrument, but even when community-organization efforts are directed toward agencies and organizations, rather than toward individuals, collaboration—that is, working together for mutual benefit—is usually preferred to either cooperation or coordination.[111]

Focus on communities is subject to various definitions, and in some cases the community is almost synonymous with a neighborhood. Organized concern with neighborhoods or communities can be traced back to the work of Canon Barnett and others like him,[112] culminating (or beginning) with the establishment of Toynbee Hall in London in 1884,[113] and, as noted previously, the YMHA in Baltimore, which was established even earlier, in 1854.[114] From these separate beginnings grew the settlement-house (or neighborhood-community center) movement. In 1970, more than three thousand neighborhood multiservice centers alone were identified in the United States,[115] and to these must be added the Jewish community centers, YM&WCAs, and settlement houses—in all, a vast network of social-welfare agencies, all flowing from the concept of neighborhood or community.

Since medieval times, at least, neighbors have been considered an

important source of help.[116] In the eighteenth century this was institutionalized to the point that when a poor person was without relations,
or sick or feeble, a neighbor was reimbursed for assuming the responsibility for his or her care.[117]

Societal changes have taken away from local neighborhoods many of
their former functions.[118] Mobility, expressed in number of cars, ease
of car ownership, and proliferation of highways; changing residential
patterns, mainly through suburbanization; centralized services, as represented by huge shopping malls; the anonymity of metropolitan living
—all have reduced the amount of "neighboring" that goes on in many
areas of modern living. In order to overcome some of the problems
flowing from urbanization, and in light of recognition that mutual-aid
activities flourish better in small or contiguous settings, there has been
a movement to return services to local units[119]—to states through revenue sharing of national income, to cities through Model Cities and
similar programs, and to neighborhoods through multiservice centers
and client-participative structures. This movement received considerable impetus during the 1960s and the War on Poverty, followed by
concurrent black and student revolts. As a consequence, services were
required to offer local residents "maximum feasible participation."[120]
This resulted in a plethora of local groups designed to take control of
certain aspects of social-welfare activities and policy.[121] Neighborhood
cooperative nursery schools and credit unions are examples of this type
of locally based mutual aid.

As local units found themselves restricted by outside controls, including earmarked grants or other funds with strings attached, moves for
more autonomy resulted in free-standing agencies and in such legal
bodies as the Community Development Corporations,[122] in which
groups of local residents incorporate themselves into a legal structure
in order to acquire funds to carry out the activities they consider important. In France, for example, social security is administered by mutual-
aid societies, which are independent institutions with a legal status in
private law.[123]

Cooperatives, Collectives, and Communes

There have also been attempts to go beyond mere communities to
cooperatives and collectives. The early charities in America were cooperatives—not gifts of the rich to the poor. "The cooperative aspect
faded away in the nineteenth century. Whereas the cooperatives were
concerned with *us*, the nineteenth century agencies were concerned
with *them*, the poor and the sinful."[124] Now the traditional communes
in the United States and Canada—the Hutterians,[125] Amish, and others[126]—and the newer forms of kibbutzim and moshavim that have

been created in Israel[127] have been joined by hundreds of communes, most of them associated with the so-called counterculture.[128] In each of these, mutual aid is an important element of living, and in many cases the groups were formed in order to permit mutual aid, which is seen as a value in itself, to take place. Consequently, there are calls to try to build all large decision-making structures of society on the strongest possible collective units at the local level—units in which people "come together around a range of common concerns and build their lives with each other."[129]

This reliance on mutual aid has not only resulted in new or renewed structures, it has also been the basis for some reformulations of social workers' roles. The role of mediator, for example, presumes a common bond between people and is rooted in the belief that conflict is a sign that at least one party to the encounter has lost sight of the need each has for the other.[130] The task of the social worker as mediator is then to bring this need back into focus for both of the parties.

In social welfare, a common theme running through group work, self-help groups, community organization, and communes is belief in the efficacy of smallness.[131] In economics, this has been termed the "small is beautiful" philosophy.[132] Part of the return to the community or neighborhood movement is based on patterns of ethnicity that continue,[133] but part seems to be a nostalgic attempt to re-create a past remembered as more enjoyable. The need to examine the supports and constraints that neighborhoods contain, and to take decisions on the basis of objective factors rather than sentiment, has been emphasized by a number of writers.[134]

Residency Requirements. Another theme in the neighborhood, community, village, or small-town approach is proximity—the fact that this approach is locally based. That only people who live close to one another are responsible for one another on a more than one-time or indirect basis has been codified in social-welfare policy and law, and is referred to as residency requirements.

In ancient and medieval times hospitality to the traveler was enjoined.[135] This was not mutual aid, however, as the traveler rarely had help to give to the resident, other than news from afar and a break in routine. Aid that was extended over time from one person to another was confined to small groups. Consequently, the codification of mutual aid into law brought with it limits as to who should be aided, and these were usually only those within the group or the locality. Athenians were "jealous about restricting citizenship to a narrowly limited body. . . . In 451 B.C. it is required that both his parents must be Athenians if he is to be a citizen."[136] The first English law of settlement was promulgated in 1388: "Able-bodied beggars were subject to punishment; those unable to work were permitted to beg, but only at their current place of residence or their birthplace."[137] The Poor Laws of 1601 not only relieved a locality of the burden of supporting people from other localities, it also protected those who lived there against strangers,[138] guaranteed a supply of labor by not allowing people to leave freely, and reduced the number of vagrants, who often became criminals.[139] The Law of Settlement and Removal of 1662 went farther and made it possible to "eject persons and families from the parish who, in the opinion of the local authorities, might in the future become dependent."[140]

Residency laws remain in force to varying degrees in different places. Social welfare in Switzerland, for example, is governed by a grandfather clause: One is entitled to help only from the parish in which one's grandfather lived. In Israel, residence is defined as the last place in which the applicant lived on two consecutive March 31s.[141] In 1939, in the United States, residency laws varied from six months to five years and were applied by jurisdictions as varied as states, counties, and townships.[142]

The purpose of residency laws is to dissuade poor people from leaving areas offering parsimonious benefits for localities where benefits are higher and thus constituting a "strain drain" from some communities at the expense of others. As it became clear, however, that people left poor areas because of the total situation, or for personal reasons, rather than mendaciously, application of residency laws relaxed in some areas. In Wisconsin, for example, it sufficed for an applicant to declare an intention to live there.[143] The erosion of residency requirements in the United States reached its legal culmination in 1969, when the Supreme Court declared them unconstitutional.[144] However, the consequent specter of hordes of indigents migrating into Arizona, for example, gave politicians in that state an excuse for reducing benefit payments to AFDC recipients.[145] So strongly were residency requirements embedded in tradition and emotions that New York State attempted to evade the court decision by withholding welfare from newcomers who had not managed to find standard housing,[146] by threatening to give them only emergency relief and a ticket back to where they had come from,[147] and by imposing a one-year residency requirement despite the Supreme Court ruling—a requirement that was again declared unconstitutional.[148] Remnants of residency requirements continue to exist in the state, however, as in the preference for public housing given persons who have lived in the state for at least two years.

Social welfare for migrant workers is a continuing problem, even where there are no residency laws, because local populations feel little responsibility for temporary residents. Approximately a million Americans move with their families from place to place to meet seasonal labor demands.[149] Mexican labor is used in parts of the American West, while Canadian Indians are imported to Maine to pick potatoes every year. In countries dependent upon foreign labor, the difference between social-welfare benefits for residents and those for nonresidents may be striking. Until recently, a hundred thousand African workers entered Rhodesia every year, the men being separated from their families for long periods.[150] Switzerland receives every Monday morning a quarter of a million Italian workers who will leave again on Friday afternoon. They are not allowed to bring their families with them into Switzerland until they have worked in this manner for five years. In the meantime, they spend the work week in barracks-like accommodations, with the consequent effects on themselves and on their families. The best social-welfare arrangements in such cases can only be palliatives. Kuwait, on the other hand, extends its social-welfare services to visitors as well as to residents,[151] as do England and the Netherlands, among other countries.

THE INSTITUTIONALIZATION OF MUTUAL AID

Despite the widespread existence of mutual-aid functions in families, groups, neighborhoods, and collectives, the activity is subject to various forms of decay, many of which lead to the institutionalization of mutual aid, and consequent departure from its basic nature.

One form of decay arises when there is inequality of necessary or desired resources within the group. Some members then become constant givers, while others become permanent receivers. These roles usually lead to a series of rules and regulations that govern the kind and amount of help, and the procedures to be followed to obtain it. This does not necessarily mean that the givers insist on such structures, though they often do. It also happens that the recipients of help, in their desire for equality, resent and resist their roles and demand different methods of being helped. In short, although the rich uncle may get real pleasure from helping members of his family, they may prefer other forms of help to being dependent on their uncle.

The type of help needed, or its quality, can also contribute to the decay of mutual aid. When members of a group are incapable of providing the skills or resources needed and outside professionals are called in, the mutual-aid function begins to change form.

Mutual aid is sometimes spoiled by success. When a small group is successful in helping its members, it is understandable that other people would want to join such a group, and large size is one of the variables that make mutual aid difficult, if not impossible. This is precisely the path followed by some mutual-aid societies that began as small groups of neighbors, compatriots, or workers but are today huge, institutional- ized mutual building and loan associations or international fraternal bodies like those mentioned previously.

Finally, members of a group may change their attitudes toward mu- tual aid for a number of reasons. When aid comes to be based on a "put in, take out" psychology and judgments are made as to whether one has contributed enough to others to deserve their help, a difference has been established between helping another by inclination and helping as a result of reasoning,[152] and the latter is no longer mutual aid. In Whyte's study of factory workers, for example, those who contributed too little to the group's objectives—the goldbricks—and those who went beyond the work quota set by the group for its members—the rate-busters—were not seen as helpful by the others.[153]

It should be pointed out that mutual aid is not an "all or nothing" phenomenon. There may be some elements of mutual aid in many other types of undertakings, while mutual aid itself may benefit one party more than another. For example, in cases where schoolchildren help younger children with their homework, or the needy or disabled help those even more needy or more seriously disabled, the "helper therapy" principle may apply: The helper benefits at least as much as the person helped. One could, in fact, make a pedantic argument that even in a professional relationship elements of mutual aid are present: The doctor learns from dealing with patients; social cases make possible social-work jobs;[154] and so forth. However, this is stretching the mean- ing of "mutual aid" very thin.

THE FUTURE OF MUTUAL AID

Perhaps because of the complexity of modern living, the growth in welfare programs, seemingly intractable social problems, and the changed structure of society, some discussions of social welfare assume that mutual aid no longer takes place or decry the decrease they as- sume. Some such thinking seems based on a nostalgic view of an ideal- ized past. Whether there is less mutual aid today than there was at some given point in history is subject to empirical investigation, but that there still exists considerable mutual aid in families, groups, and neigh- borhoods—among other places—seems irrefutable. Given the gaps in social welfare alone, and the levels at which help is given, many people would not be able to survive if they could not call upon relatives, friends, or neighbors. There are no reliable studies as to the amount of neighboring that goes on in American communities, but there are some indications that it is greater among inhabitants of slums and ghettos than among more affluent people.[155]

Either in a desire to increase this activity or in ignorance of it, some movements in social welfare today are aimed at reviving neighborhoods by decentralizing services and giving decision-making over to local groups or, in some cases, thrusting it upon them. There are, indeed, functions that local groups can perform better than centralized services,[156] and others that they have a right to perform regardless of outcome. These functions and rights need to be clearly explicated, however, and based upon manifest criteria, and should not be undertaken in an attempt to re-create a situation for which the necessary requirements no longer exist, or exist in a greatly altered form. In short, as the "return to the old neighborhood" thrust meets the "you can't go home again" phenomenon, the result is likely to be a new synthesis for both neighborhoods and mutual aid.

Although it seems that in crisis situations the amount of mutual aid always increases,[157] and that this is true whether the crisis arose from a natural disaster, an environmental situation, or a civil disturbance;[158] in fact, the type of event will dictate whether it unites the community, defeats it, or causes controversy and conflict.[159] Reduction of social-welfare services as occasioned by New York City's financial crisis of 1975, for example, might have resulted in an upsurge of neighboring in lieu of suspended services. It would be hazardous, however, to use the concept of past management in this context, deciding that because people managed somehow through help from their families and friends, social welfare should be frozen at the new, lower levels. Crisis-induced mutual aid does not tend to become either permanent or institutionalized. Even in Homer's time it was pointed out that one's neighbors "can be expected to contribute once or twice, but not forever."[160] Consequently, mutual aid—as one of the important motivations for, and methods of, social welfare—should be seen as an element to be identified in, and contributed to, the mix of motivations and methods that constitute good social-welfare systems.

SUMMARY

In summary, mutual aid is one of the strong motivations for filling needs, and thus of social welfare. Because mutual aid is considered normative in families, social-welfare policy may be designed to strengthen families so that they can better engage in mutual help, or make use of the mutual aid that does exist. In practice, however, most social policy ignores families, and social-welfare policies intended to affect families positively often, as a result of other and conflicting motivations, do not achieve their stated goals. The Aid to Families with Dependent Children program is a particularly clear example of this.

Those policies that attempt to exploit families for positive purposes often end up as restrictive, as in the case of relatives' responsibility and residency laws. Both of these have been considerably mitigated in recent years, however, though for reasons other than their effects on families. Finally, the desire to return to, or engage in, mutual aid is a current motivation for the development of communes, self-help groups, and a trend toward a return to neighborhood services and autonomy.

NOTES

1. K. D. Hardwick, "As Long as Charity Shall Be a Virtue," in P. Smith (ed.), *Boston Private Charities from 1657 to 1800* (privately printed pamphlet, 1962), quoted in H. D. Stein, "Observations on Determinants of Social Work Education in the United States," in *An Intercultural Exploration: Universals and Differences in Social Work Values, Functions, and Practice* (New York: Council on Social Work Education, 1967).
2. K. Lorenz, *On Aggression* (New York: Bantam, 1971).
3. R. Ardrey, *The Territorial Imperative* (New York: Delta, 1966).
4. R. Ardrey, *The Hunting Hypothesis* (New York: Atheneum, 1976).
5. P. Kropotkin, *Mutual Aid: A Factor of Evolution* (New York: Knopf, 1925).
6. *Ibid.*
7. J. Campbell (ed.), *The Portable Jung* (New York: Viking, 1971).
8. G. Rossbach, "Caseworkers' Use of the 'Third Ear,'" *Smith College Studies in Social Work*, 36 (October 1965):127; T. Keefe, "Empathy and Social Work Education: A Study," *Journal of Education for Social Work*, 11 (Fall 1975):69; D. Macarov, "The Concept of Empathy and the Educational Process," *Applied Social Studies*, 2 (1970):107.
9. Lorenz, *op. cit.*, p. 256.
10. A. Strauss, *George Herbert Mead on Social Psychology* (Chicago: University of Chicago Press, 1956).
11. M. F. Scheler, *The Nature of Sympathy* (London: Routledge & Kegan Paul, 1954).
12. N. Gilbert and H. Specht, *Dimensions of Social Welfare Policy* (Englewood Cliffs, N.J.: Prentice-Hall, 1974), p. 5. (Emphasis in original.)
13. Lorenz, *op. cit.*, pp. 242–43.
14. For example, see D. Macarov and G. Fradkin, *The Short Course in Development Activities* (Ramat Gan, Israel: Massada Press, 1973); M. O'Collins, "Introducing Social Work Education at the University of Papua New Guinea," *International Social Work*, 16 (1973):20; and D. Macarov *et al.*, "Consultants and Consultees: The View from Within," *Social Service Review*, 43 (September 1967):283.
15. For a description of the *hamula*, see Y. Ben David, *Agricultural Planning and Village Community in Israel* (New York: UNESCO, 1964).

16. H. H. Aptekar, "The Values, Functions and Methods of Social Work," in *An Intercultural Exploration . . . , op. cit.,* p. 27.
17. R. Rashid, "Social Work Practice in West Pakistan," in *An Intercultural Exploration . . . , op. cit.,* p. 150.
18. A. B. Sansom, *The Western World and Japan* (New York: Knopf, 1958).
19. Stein, *op. cit.,* p. 161.
20. T. H. Walz, "The Family, the Family Agency, and Postindustrial Society," *Social Casework,* 56 (January 1975):13–20.
21. H. L. Wilensky and C. N. Lebeaux, *Industrial Society and Social Welfare* (New York: Free Press, 1958), p. 69; R. L. Birdwhistell, "The Idealized Model of the American Family," *Social Casework,* 51 (1970):195.
22. J. H. Galper, *The Politics of Social Services* (Englewood Cliffs, N.J.: Prentice-Hall, 1975), p. 54. These findings are based on a study of worker orientations in a Jewish family-service agency. See H. Leichter and W. Mitchell, *Kinship and Casework* (New York: Sage, 1967).
23. A. J. Kahn, *Social Policy and Social Services* (New York: Random House, 1973), p. 15; M. B. Sussman, "Family," in *Encyclopedia of Social Work* (New York: National Association of Social Workers, 1971), p. 329.
24. Wilensky and Lebeaux, *op. cit.,* p. 139.
25. D. Thursz and J. L. Vigilante (eds.), *Meeting Human Needs,* Vol. 1: *An Overview of Nine Countries* (Beverly Hills, Calif.: Sage, 1975) and Vol. 2: *Additional Perspectives from Thirteen Countries* (Beverly Hills, Calif.: Sage, 1976).
26. K. A. Kendall, *Population Dynamics and Family Planning: A New Responsibility for Social Work Education* (New York: Council on Social Work Education, 1971).
27. J. T. D. Bandler, "Family Issues in Social Policy: An Analysis of Social Security," Ph. D. diss., Columbia University School of Socail Work, New York, 1975. R. A. Feldman, "Family Theory, Family Development and the Future of American Social Work," *International Social Work,* 16 (2/3, 1973):61.
28. *Social Conditions and Social Security: Germany Reports* (Bonn: Press and Information Office, Federal Government of Germany, 1964).
29. S. Wojiechowski, "Poland's New Priority: Human Welfare," in Thursz and Vigilante, Vol. 1, *op. cit.,* p. 169.
30. A. L. Schorr, *Social Security and Social Services in France* (Washington, D.C.: Government Printing Office, 1965), p. 3. (Emphasis in original.)
31. W. A. Friedlander, *Individualism and Social Welfare* (New York: Free Press, 1962).
32. A. L. Schorr, *Poor Kids* (New York: Basic Books, 1966).
33. D. Macarov, "Israel's Social Services: Historical Roots and Current Situation," in Thursz and Vigilante, Vol. 1, *op. cit.,* p. 130.
34. Aptekar, *op. cit.*
35. *Social Welfare in Thailand* (Bangkok: Department of Public Welfare, Ministry of the Interior, 1962).
36. K. Woodroofe, *From Charity to Social Work in England and the United States* (Toronto: University of Toronto Press, 1962), p. 46.
37. *Ibid.,* p. 33.

38. T. K. Hareven, "Societal Problems," in C. A. Chambers (ed.), *A Century of Concern: 1873–1973* (Columbus, Ohio: National Conference on Social Welfare, 1974), p. 72.
39. J. Axinn and H. Levin, *Social Welfare: A History of the American Response to Need* (New York: Dodd, Mead, 1975), p. 240.
40. *Code of Federal Regulations: Public Welfare, Parts 200 to 499* (Washington, D.C.: Office of the Federal Register, General Services Administration, 1974).
41. Axinn and Levin, *op. cit.*, p. 244.
42. A. E. Fink, *The Field of Social Work* (New York: Holt, Rinehart and Winston, 1974), p. 140.
43. H. D. Stein (ed.), *Planning for the Needs of Children in Developing Countries* (New York: UNICEF, 1964).
44. Stein, "Observations . . .," *op. cit.*, p. 161.
45. E. Winston, "A National Policy on the Family," *Public Welfare*, 27 (January 1969):54.
46. C. I. Schottland, *The Social Security Program in the United States* (New York: Appleton-Century-Crofts, 1963), p. 121.
47. A. L. Schorr quoted without citation in N. Glazer, "A Sociologist's View of Poverty," in M. S. Gordon (ed.), *Poverty in America* (San Francisco: Chandler, 1965), p. 19.
48. V. M. Rue, "A U.S. Department of Marriage and the Family," *Journal of Marriage and the Family*, 35 (1973):89–99.
49. D. P. Moynihan, *The Politics of a Guaranteed Income: The Nixon Administration and the Family Assistance Plan* (New York: Vintage, 1973), p. 21.
50. A. L. Schorr, "On Selfish Children and Lonely Parents," *The Public Interest*, 4 (Summer 1966):8.
51. C. Z. Zimmerman, "The Future of the Family in America," *Journal of Marriage and the Family*, 34 (May 1972):323.
52. Moynihan has written the most detailed account of the futile attempt to have this program adopted *(op. cit.)*.
53. Hareven, *op. cit.*, p. 72.
54. D. J. Rothman, *The Discovery of the Asylum: Social Order and Disorder in the New Republic* (Boston: Little, Brown, 1971), p. 207.
55. Axinn and Levin, *op. cit.*, p. 133.
56. Woodroofe, *op. cit.*, p. 129.
57. Kahn, *op. cit.*, p. 43.
58. *Ibid.*, p. 21.
59. B. D. Coll, *Perspectives in Public Welfare* (Washington, D.C.: Department of Health, Education, and Welfare, 1969), p. 77.
60. *Ibid.*
61. Axinn and Levin, *op. cit.*, p. 134.
62. C. Bird, *The Invisible Scar* (New York: Pocket Books, 1966).
63. M. C. Barth, G. J. Carcagno, and J. L. Palmer, *Toward an Effective Income Support System: Problems, Prospects, and Choices* (Madison: Institute for Research on Poverty, University of Wisconsin, 1974), p. 15.

64. D. Macarov, *Incentives to Work* (San Francisco: Jossey-Bass, 1970), p. 154; Axinn and Levin, *op. cit.*, p. 244.
65. "Current Operating Statistics," *Social Security Bulletin*, 40 (April 1977): 83–84.
66. On welfare stereotypes, see Macarov, *Incentives to Work, op. cit.*, pp. 109–22, 224.
67. Hareven, *op. cit.*, p. 62.
68. For a detailed account of the impact of AFDC on recipients, see J. F. Handler and E. J. Hollingsworth, *The "Deserving Poor": A Study of Welfare Administration* (New York: Academic Press, 1971).
69. Gilbert and Specht, *op. cit.*, p. 72.
70. Barth, Carcagno, and Palmer, *op. cit.*, p. 167.
71. For a full, if somewhat dated, description of the polar and intermediate positions regarding relatives' responsibility, see H. M. Leyendecker, *Problems and Policy in Public Assistance* (New York: Harper Bros., 1955).
72. On the economic basis of relatives' responsibility laws, see A. L. Schorr, *Filial Responsibility in the Modern American Family* (Washington, D.C.: Government Printing Office, 1960); W. Bell, "Relatives' Responsibility: A Problem in Social Policy," *Social Work*, 12 (January 1967):39; and Axinn and Levin, *op. cit.*, p. 10.
73. Schorr holds that common law and public attitudes prior to the Elizabethan Poor Laws never held children to be responsible for their parents. Schorr, *Filial Responsibility . . . , op. cit.*
74. Coll, *op. cit.*, p. 55.
75. R. Lubove, *The Professional Altruist: The Emergence of Social Work as a Career: 1880–1930* (New York: Atheneum, 1973).
76. Coll, *op. cit.*, p. 54.
77. Handler and Hollingsworth, *op. cit.*, p. 74.
78. H. Badran, "Egypt's Social Service System: New Ideology, New Approaches," in Thursz and Vigilante, Vol. 1, *op. cit.*, p. 63.
79. *Findings of the 1973 AFDC Study—Part I: Demographic and Program Characteristics* (Washington, D.C.: Department of Health, Education, and Welfare, 1973), p. 91.
80. W. Bell, "Relatives' Responsibility: A Problem in Social Policy," *Social Work*, 12 (January 1967):34.
81. Coll, *op. cit.*, p. 21; *McKinney's Consolidated Laws of New York: Social Welfare Laws* (Brooklyn, N.Y.: Thompson, 1966), p. xvii.
82. Bell, *op. cit.*, p. 34.
83. *Amendment to Family Law (Support), 1959* (Jerusalem: Government of Israel, 1959) (in Hebrew).
84. *McKinney's Consolidated Laws . . . , op. cit.*, pp. 225–26.
85. C. I. Schottland, "The Changing Roles of Government and Family," in P. E. Weinberger (ed.), *Perspectives on Social Welfare: An Introductory Anthology* (New York: Macmillan, 1974), pp. 120–21; N. E. Cohen, "Changing Perspectives on United States Social Services," in Thursz and Vigilante, Vol. 1, *op. cit.*, p. 223.

86. E. Eagle, "Charges for Care and Maintenance in State Institutions for the Mentally Retarded," *American Journal of Mental Deficiency*, 65 (September 1960):199.

87. Coll, *op. cit.*, pp. 89–90.

88. *Code of Federal Regulations . . . , op. cit.*, p. 95.

89. *Judiciary—Court Acts—29A Part I: New York State Family Court Act; Family Court Rules and Forms* Sections 413–416 (Albany: State of New York).

90. Wilensky and Lebeaux, *op. cit.*, p. 83.

91. Schorr, *Filial Responsibility . . . , op. cit.*, p. 7.

92. K. de Schweinitz, *England's Road to Social Security* (Philadelphia: University of Pennsylvania Press, 1943), pp. 223–24.

93. R. A. Cloward and R. M. Elman, "Social Justice for the Poor," in L. A. Ferman, J. L. Kornbluh, and A. Haber (eds.), *Poverty in America* (Ann Arbor: University of Michigan Press, 1972), p. 326.

94. Handler and Hollingsworth, *op. cit.*, p. 76. In 1977 the Social Services Department of Nassau County, New York, offered a service, for a fee of $20, called "Services to Locate Absent Parent." Of course, relatives are not the only potential resource. In New York State an applicant must sell his or her car and use the proceeds before being eligible. Exceptions are only for health, health of a child, and absolute inability to get to work by public transportation. Each of these is investigated with great severity.

95. D. Macarov and N. Golan, "Goals in Social Work Practice: A Longitudinal Study," *International Social Work*, 16 (2/3, 1973):2.

96. H. Glennerster, *Social Service Budgets and Social Policy: British and American Experience* (New York: Barnes & Noble, 1975).

97. *New York Times*, May 11, 1976.

98. Bell, *op. cit.*, p. 34.

99. *Ibid.*, p. 39. Whether it is economic to enforce collections has also been questioned. New York State spent $26 million in fiscal 1976 to collect $6 million. A. L. Schorr, "Enforcing Child-Support," *New York Times*, October 8, 1976, p. 29. Steiner points out that when relief was terminated in Clermont County, Ohio, in 1961, "clients did not magically become self-sufficient nor did responsible relations come out of the woodwork. . . . Instead, the burden of support was shifted . . . to landlords, grocers, physicians, churches, schools, and other civic groups." G. Y. Steiner, *Social Insecurity: The Politics of Welfare* (Chicago: Rand McNally, 1966).

100. Gilbert and Specht, *op. cit.*, p. 5.

101. Schweinitz, *op. cit.*, p. 15.

102. Kropotkin, *op. cit.*, p. 262.

103. Schottland, *The Social Security Program . . . , op. cit.*, pp. 34–35.

104. There are many excellent books on the principles and practice of social group work. Although old, the classic remains G. Wilson and G. Ryland, *Social Group Work Practice* (Cambridge, Mass.: Houghton Mifflin, 1949).

105. E. Tropp, "A Humanistic View of Social Group Work: Worker and Member on a Common Human Level," in E. Tropp (ed.), *A Humanistic Foundation for Group Work Practice* (New York: Selected Academic Readings, 1969).

106. C. P. Papell, "Sensitivity Training: Relevance for Social Work Education," *Journal of Education for Social Work*, 8 (Winter 1972):42.
107. A. Burton (ed.), *Encounter* (San Francisco: Jossey-Bass, 1969).
108. A. H. Katz and E. I. Bender, *The Strength in Us: Self-Help Groups in the Modern World* (New York: New Viewpoints, 1976).
109. A guide to self-help groups in the New York City area lists sixty-four such organizations (many with chapters or branches) divided into groups dealing with disabilities, "exceptional" people, emotional problems, facing death, surgical trauma, chronic illness, abusers and phobics, special situations, and couples. B. Claflin and P. Thaler, "Banding Together: The Best Way to Cope," *New York Magazine*, 5 (February 28, 1977):41–48.
110. Macarov and Fradkin, *op. cit.*, p. 210.
111. Z. Feine, *et al.*, *Interagency Collaboration in Drug Rehabilitation* (Richmond, Va.: Department of Mental Health and Retardation, 1974).
112. S. A. Barnett, *Canon Barnett: His Life, Work, and Friends* (London: Murray, 1921).
113. J. A. R. Pimlott, *Toynbee Hall* (London: Dent, 1935).
114. L. Kraft and C. J. Bernheimer, *Aspects of the Jewish Community Center* (New York: National Association of Jewish Center Workers, 1954).
115. E. J. O'Donnell and O. M. Reid, "The Multiservice Neighborhood Center: Preliminary Findings from a National Survey," *Welfare in Review*, 9 (May/June 1971):1.
116. Coll, *op. cit.*, p. 3.
117. Rothman, *op. cit.*, p. 33.
118. See, for example, J. A. Trolander, *Settlement Houses and the Great Depression* (Detroit: Wayne State University Press, 1975).
119. D. Morris and K. Hess, *Neighborhood Power: The New Localism* (Boston: Beacon Press, 1975).
120. D. P. Moynihan, *Maximum Feasible Misunderstanding* (New York: Free Press, 1969).
121. H. W. Hallman, *Neighborhood Control of Public Programs: Case Studies of Community Corporations and Neighborhood Boards* (New York: Praeger, 1970).
122. C. Hampden-Turner, *From Poverty to Dignity* (Garden City, N.Y.: Anchor, 1975); E. S. Cahn and J. C. Cahn, "Maximum Feasible Participation: A General Overview," in E. S. Cahn and B. A. Passett (eds.), *Citizen Participation: Effecting Community Change* (New York: Praeger, 1971).
123. W. Peterson, *The Welfare State in France* (Omaha: University of Nebraska Press, 1960), pp. 18–19.
124. Hardwick, *op. cit.* (emphasis in original).
125. V. Peters, *All Things Common: The Hutterian Way of Life* (New York: Harper & Row, 1965).
126. B. Zablocki, *The Joyful Community* (Baltimore: Penguin, 1971).
127. M. Weingarten, *Life in a Kibbutz* (New York: Reconstructionist Press, 1955); Y. Talmon, *Family and Community in the Kibbutz* (Cambridge, Mass.: Harvard University Press, 1972); D. Macarov, "Work Without Pay: Work Incentives and Patterns in a Salaryless Environment," *International Journal of Social Economics*, 2 (Summer 1975):106.

128. K. Melville, *Communes in the Counter Culture: Origins, Theories, Styles of Life* (New York: Morrow, 1972).

129. Galper, *op. cit.*, p. 146.

130. R. R. Middleman and G. Goldberg, *Social Service Delivery: A Structural Approach to Social Work Practice* (New York: Columbia University Press, 1974), p. 59.

131. J. Leiby, "Provision and Management of Social Services," in C. A. Chambers (ed.), *A Century of Concern: 1873–1973* (Columbus, Ohio: National Conference on Social Welfare, 1974), pp. 54–55.

132. E. F. Schumacher, *Small Is Beautiful: Economics as if People Mattered* (New York: Harper & Row, 1973).

133. J. L. Vigilante, "Back to the Old Neighborhood," *Social Service Review*, 50 (June 1976):194.

134. A. J. Naperstek and K. Kollias, "The Ethnic and Class Dimensions in Neighborhoods: A Means for the Reorganization of Human Service Delivery Systems," *Journal of Sociology and Social Welfare*, 2 (Spring 1975):406; and A. J. Naperstek, *Neighborhood Decentralization: An Option for Urban Policy* (Washington, D.C.: National Center for Urban Ethnic Affairs, 1976).

135. Coll, *op. cit.*, p. 3.

136. A. W. Gouldner, *The Hellenic World: A Sociological Analysis* (New York: Harper & Row, 1969), p. 138.

137. Coll, *op. cit.*, p. 4.

138. Axinn and Levin, *op. cit.*, p. 15.

139. Schweinitz, *op. cit.*

140. Coll, *op. cit.*, p. 7.

141. *Social Welfare Law, 1958: Regulations Concerning Helping the Needy* (Jerusalem: Government of Israel) (in Hebrew).

142. Schweinitz, *op. cit.*, p. 147.

143. Handler and Hollingsworth, *op. cit.*, p. 74.

144. *Shapiro* v. *Thompson*, 394 U.S. 618 (1969); see also M. K. Rosenheim, "*Shapiro* v. *Thompson:* 'The Beggars Are Coming to Town,'" *1969 Supreme Court Review 303.*

145. J. J. Graham, *The Enemies of the Poor* (New York: Random House, 1970), p. 286.

146. Axinn and Levin, *op. cit.*, p. 278.

147. "New York City had applied a state law to a family of eleven which it was judged had come from Mississippi for the purpose of collecting welfare. The city bought them a ticket home." Moynihan, *The Politics . . . , op. cit.*, p. 97.

148. *Ibid.*, p. 33.

149. J. Ramos, "Migrant Farmworkers," in *Encyclopedia of Social Work* (New York: National Association of Social Workers, 1971), p. 829.

150. *Social Reconstruction in the Newly Independent Countries of East Africa* (New York: United Nations, 1965), p. 91.

151. *The Arab World* (New York: Arab Information Center, 1965).

152. Lorenz, *op. cit.*, p. 244.

153. W. F. Whyte, *Money and Motivation* (New York: Harper Bros., 1955).

154. For a discussion of mutual-aid elements in poverty and in antipoverty programs, see Macarov, *Incentives to Work, op. cit.*, pp. 32–33, and H. J. Gans, *More Equality* (New York: Vintage, 1968), pp. 102–26.
155. See, for example, C. B. Stack, *All Our Kin: Strategies for Survival in a Black Community* (New York: Harper & Row, 1974), and A. Billingsley, *Black Families in White America* (Englewood Cliffs, N.J.: Prentice-Hall, 1968).
156. Hallman, *op. cit.;* A. J. Kahn, "Service Delivery at the Neighborhood Level: Experience, Theory, and Facts," *Social Service Review*, 50 (March 1976):23–56.
157. D. Macarov, "The Israeli Community Center During the Yom Kippur War," *Journal of Jewish Communal Service*, 51 (Summer 1975):340.
158. R. A. Stallings, "The Community Context of Crisis Management," *American Behavioral Scientist*, 16 (January-February 1973):312.
159. J. S. Coleman, *Community Conflict* (New York: Free Press, 1959).
160. D. Constantelos, *Byzantine Philanthropy and Social Welfare* (New Brunswick, N.J.: Rutgers University Press, 1968).

4
Religion

Almost all religions have obligated their followers to engage in acts of charity, either to coreligionists or to everyone in need. The Egyptian Book of the Dead, which antedates the Bible, records acts of charity. The Old Testament explicates the responsibilities of Jews toward others. Vanished religiocivilizations, such as the Sumerians, planned and organized aid for their helpless citizens. Gautama Buddha established the foundations of Buddhism, with its interpretation of poverty and the relief of poverty, about 500 B.C.[1] Prince Asoka of India, a Hindu, endowed hospitals and shelters for both people and animals three hundred years before the beginning of Christianity. Only in the Greek world before Christ did no underlying and widespread spirit of *philanthropia* prevail,[2] and that was due to the fact that, though the Athenians could be said to live off the state, they were not living off a dole, because the nature of the society was such that the citizens *were* the state.[3] With the advent of Christianity, both the Eastern and the Roman branches of that church engaged in charity. Indeed, it has been said that the "Byzantines [were] a nation . . . characterized by its many works of practical philanthropy . . . a virtue not only of the rich and prominent, but of all organizations and classes of people."[4]

Among the first organized social-welfare institutions of the Roman Catholics was the hospital opened in Rome for sick slaves, and this type of activity grew so that between the years 500 and 1500 the early Christian hospitals sheltered the homeless and orphans, as well as the sick. In Arab countries, hospitals were magnificently built and equipped as early as the twelfth century, while in Europe the needs of Crusaders on their way to the Holy Land resulted in many kinds of help. Catholic social work was first conceptualized along modern lines by Vives (1492–1540),[5] and Saint Vincent de Paul (1581–1660) established voluntary local groups for those in need,[6] which became institutionalized in the Ladies of Charity in 1617 and in the Society of Saint Vincent de Paul in 1833.[7]

The emergence of Protestantism did not bring a renewal of, or an addition to, social-welfare activities. Indeed, in some respects, the "Protestant Ethic" was inimical to charity because hope of salvation depended more on faith than on good works.[8] Nevertheless, there did arise a congeries of social services, such as the YM&WCA, and institutions of various Protestant groups, such as Lutheran Children's Homes, either to serve group members or to evangelize among recipients.

None of the more recent religious or pseudo-religious groups—the Black Muslims, the Hare Krishna movement, the Unification Church, and others—have yet evidenced strong trends toward charity or social welfare.

RELIGIOUS MANIFESTATIONS OF SOCIAL WELFARE

The religious motivation in social welfare may manifest itself in the behavior of the individual, or it may be delegated to some institution or agency.

Personal Behavior

When religious beliefs are demonstrated in individual behavior regarding charity, this is usually the result of carrying out a commandment or a requirement of the religion, and the deed is done with no ulterior motive. In other words, acts that arise from a desire to gain friendship, companionship, prestige, material advantage, or any recompense other than carrying out the will or instruction of God or the gods are not, strictly speaking, purely results of religious motivation.

It was in this sense that Sir Thomas Browne said, "I give no alms to satisfy the hunger of my brother, but to fulfill and accomplish the will and command of my God; I draw not my purse for his sake that demands it, but his that enjoined it."[9]

Such desires to engage personally in charity may result in individual behavior patterns, such as never passing a beggar without giving alms, never refusing a request to contribute for philanthropic purposes, or volunteering to help in a social-welfare agency or institution. The motive may also manifest itself in structured ways. Buddhists undertook to become—rather than help—beggars, because begging was considered a breeding ground for many virtues, and made possible a life of contemplation, which was considered the only justification of human existence.[10] In Europe, many monastic orders took vows of poverty and maintained themselves by begging.[11] And because obeying the command to help the needy required the existence of the latter, the desire to obey the command undermined measures to alleviate or abolish poverty, and furnished a rationale (or a rationalization) for countenancing demonstrated need.

The previously noted absence of philanthropy in the ancient Greek world may have arisen from a lack of religious commandments concerning charity. A concept of gods who competed with people, manipulated people, and behaved like people did not lend itself to divine commandments concerning peoples' actions. Thus, Socrates, Plato, and Aristotle did not include charity in their lists of the "natural virtues": prudence, temperance, fortitude, and justice. Indeed, according to Plato's *Republic*, the aged and the handicapped were to be done away with.

In Judaism, however, prior to and coexistent with ancient Greece, the concept of a transcendental monotheistic God resulted in commandments as to how people should behave: Regardless of aberrations and transgressions, repentance, prayer, and charity would avert the evil decree that was imminent once a year, on the Day of Atonement. The decree itself, incidentally, concerned earthly torments—flood, fire, plague, and death: There is no concept of salvation or damnation in Jewish thought, and life after death is rather hazily drawn. Hence, charity was as necessary as prayer and repentance to achieve a year of the good life, and the requirement was renewed annually.

As a matter of fact, the word "charity" is a mistranslation. The Hebrew *tzaddakah* actually means righteousness. It is derived from the etymological root meaning "justice." Giving charity, then, meant simply being just or righteous, or as one was required to be. There was to be no special effort or conscious behavior denoted as being charitable.[12] The medieval Jewish philosopher Maimonides outlined eight degrees of charity. The first, and lowest, level is to

Give, but with reluctance and regret. This is the gift of the hand, but not of the heart.

The second is to give cheerfully, but not proportionately to the distress of the sufferer.

The third is to give cheerfully and proportionately, but not until we are solicited.

The fourth is to give cheerfully, proportionately, and even unsolicited; but to put it in the poor man's hand, thereby exciting in him the painful emotion of shame.

The fifth is to give charity in such a way that the distressed may receive the bounty and know their benefactor, without being known to him.

The sixth, which rises still higher, is to know the objects of our bounty, but remain unknown to them.

The seventh is still more meritorious, namely, to bestow charity in such a way that the benefactor may not know the relieved persons, nor they the name of their benefactor.

Lastly, the eighth and most meritorious of all, is to anticipate charity by preventing poverty; i.e., to assist a reduced person so that he may earn an honest livelihood and not be forced to the dreadful alternative of holding up his hand for charity.[13]

Christianity emphasized the heavenly, or postlife, rewards for enjoined behavior on earth. Whereas *philanthropia* in the ancient Greek world was mostly anthropocentric, in Christianity it became eminently theocratic. "The principle of philanthropy was the love of God rather than the love of man."[14] The "theological virtues" were set forth as faith, hope, and charity, the greatest being charity. A person's behavior was to be rewarded in heaven, and good works on earth were a prerequisite. In the Eastern Church, too, "forgiveness of sins after death as a philosophic motive for philanthropic action was maintained."[15]

Institutionalization

Inevitably, in almost every religion, personal giving or participation in charity came to be supplanted or paralleled by religiously sponsored institutions and agencies. Help was no longer given directly by the individual to the needy person but was channeled to the church or a church-sponsored or church-related group, which, in turn, dispensed it. Even individual behavior became, in large part, institutionalized, including that of beggars and monks:

In the course of time ... the practice of begging was discontinued [by Buddhist monks]. The reasons for the abrogation of the ancient poverty are very noble and altruistic; they are, at present, heard frequently among well-to-do Christians. ... Monks may possess wealth and property, even gold, silver, and silken clothes, because their possessions allow them to be more useful to others and to help them.[16]

The monasteries in Europe, too, accumulated wealth in order to help the indigent. In England, for example, "Their hospitality was beyond compare ... they kept most bountiful houses."[17]

An important aspect of the institutionalization of charity was the custom of tithing—contributing part of one's income to the church. At one time, the tithes were used mainly or entirely for the upkeep of the church and its functionaries. Gradually, however, such monies came to be used for the needy. In 1014, King Ethelred II decreed that the tithe should be divided three ways for the reparation of the church, for religious functionaries, and for the poor.[18] Some churches went further and basically divested themselves of social-welfare functions, initiating and encouraging religious orders to undertake those activities.

As institutionalization took place, methodology became codified. The Jewish community was enjoined that if a man became needy and asked for aid, he was to be aided to continue his customary style of life. Specifically, if a man accustomed to riding a horse with an attendant preceding him could no longer afford to do so, it was the duty of the community to provide him with a horse and an attendant.[19] Inherent in this interpretation are the ideas that stigmatization may be worse than poverty itself and that cosmetic and psychological measures may be as necessary as economic ones. Flowing from this interpretation, and obviously arising from the agricultural economy and simple society of these days, is the idea that poverty is a transient, recurring phenomenon due to chance elements—wind, rain, natural disasters—that affect everyone periodically. Consequently, it will be necessary to furnish the horse and attendant for a short time only, as luck will change and the temporarily poor will again be self-sustaining.

The institutionalization of social welfare not only dealt with methodology and amounts but also began to establish the concept of eligibility. Whereas individuals might have given to, or otherwise aided, anyone needing help, agencies established criteria that often carried moral overtones: "The orphan, the widow, and the stranger deserve every assistance, but not the hypocritical and the lazy. To give to those who do not deserve it is to deprive those who merit it."[20]

The sanctions that religion gave to philanthropy can be summarized as follows:

1. The inspiration of casual relief
2. Establishing the principle that relief of distress is good for the giver, good for the recipient, and good for the community
3. Giving dignity to poverty and creating social acceptance of the poor, as being necessary for others' salvation
4. Giving poverty the status of a way of grace because it made possible the meritorious deed of alms-giving[21]

The institutionalization of religiously motivated social welfare has not been easily or completely achieved. In every group, there are some who prefer to be personally involved. In some cases, this is because they do not see, or trust, that the contributions are used exclusively for social welfare, or for the programs that they favor. Some question the amount of necessary overhead, and consequent diminution of help, that institutionalization inevitably involves. Others feel, perhaps irrationally, that the merit in giving comes from personal involvement. In Israel, for example, despite laws against begging, ingrained custom dictates that one who is so reduced as to beg should be helped directly. A religious Minister of Justice, charged with suppressing begging, confessed that he could not pass a beggar without contributing.

In addition to such attitudes, the institutionalization of the religious value of charity has created an underlying feeling in some places that poverty and need are not only inevitable but, in a certain sense, desirable. This is due not only to the needs of institutions as such (to be discussed in more detail in Chapter 7) but also the feeling that—to reverse Lincoln's comment—if God hadn't wanted poverty to exist, He wouldn't let people become poor. Countenancing the continued existence of poverty and other problems is thus given a pseudo-religious basis.

Defining Recipients

One of the questions adherents of all religions have been called upon to face is that of the extent to which charity is to be extended to members of the same faith, to nonbelievers, and to those who profess other faiths.

In the instances in ancient Greece where philanthropy was practiced, it was mostly directed toward civilized Hellenes. "The 'love of man for man' found its actual outlet in application to relatives, friends, fellow citizens, and allies."[22] Jewish law, on the other hand, specifically included the stranger with the fatherless and the widow as deserving help, if he had no land or sustenance of his own.[23] Not until the fourth century, however, was Christian philanthropy extended to believers and nonbelievers alike.[24]

Despite the right to extend services to nonbelievers, most sectarian agencies have continued to render the bulk of their services to coreligionists. Until recently, many of the Jewish agencies have limited their services to Jews, while Catholic services have tended to provide few services to non-Catholics. Protestant denominations have been more willing to extend services outside their own groups, primarily to other Protestants, however, possibly because the criteria for membership in the various groups are less clear-cut than among Catholics and Jews.[25]

The inclination to render service only to members of the religious group has a second, parallel root, and that is the desire of members to receive help only from their coreligionists. This feeling is compounded of attitudes that contributions of members should only be used for members (an important aspect of the previously discussed mutual aid), that only fellow members can understand the need, that it is shameful to expose one's needs to members of other groups, and—sometimes—that other groups have refused to aid nonmembers.

Although since the earliest immigration to America, concern has been expressed by members of various religious groups for the welfare of people—and this "was true of Protestants, of Catholics, of Jews, and of members of the Society of Friends from the first day they set foot on American soil"[26]—the bulk of such help has gone to coreligionists. It was natural for the Catholic Church to be concerned about the needs of Catholic immigrants, just as Jewish institutions have catered to Jewish immigrants. For a Jew to have turned to a Catholic institution, or vice versa, would, in the view of the public, have tarred these institutions as being uncaring or unable to help, and the recipient as a renegade.

Perhaps the most clear-cut case of religious xenophobia due to outside pressures dates back to the arrival of the first Jews in New Amsterdam in 1654. Refused admission by Peter Stuyvesant, who was subsequently ordered by the Dutch West Indian Company to admit them, they were admitted on the condition that they always be responsible for one another and never become public charges.[27] The so-called Stuyvesant Pledge has been held to account for a great part of the autonomy—or separateness—that has characterized Jewish communal and social-welfare institutions in the United States.[28]

CHURCH AND STATE

With the advent of the nation-state, the relative roles of the church and the state concerning social welfare came into focus. When religious and secular authority were one, the intermingling of authority and activity was relatively unimportant. In Byzantium, for example, a sharp line of differentiation between the church and the state, the monastery, or the individual, as we know this differentiation today, could not be clearly made.[29] As separation of functions began to take place in some areas, social welfare was seen as the proper responsibility of religion, rather than of government. Thus, church wardens played a major role in the provision of care for the poor in England,[30] and in Victorian times need was traditionally relieved by families, the churches, the religious orders, and neighbors. "It was only in a supplementary way, to coordinate or to provide special types of service, that the public authorities stepped in."[31] Even when governments moved more massively into social-welfare activities, they often did so through use of church structure and personnel. In the sixteenth century, the government in England turned to the established church organization for the administration of relief.[32] Little conflict was seen between church and state functions, because the church not only was the established church but had become, in effect, a government institution supported by taxes.[33] In a modified way, the same situation holds true today in Israel. Separation of church and state is not complete. Religious functionaries in Israel are civil servants, and religious courts—Jewish, Catholic, Eastern Orthodox, Armenian, Druze, Muslim, and others—have jurisdiction over matters of personal status, defined as marriage, divorce, adoption, and inheritance. Although social welfare is a government function, the Ministry of Social Welfare has been assigned to the religious parties in the governing coalition almost without exception since the inception of the state.

The manner in which church-state relations have evolved will have an influence on the relative roles of both institutions in social welfare. Where the church has been the traditional dispenser of charity, there still may be areas reserved, by law or by popular consent, to religious authorities, despite secular control. When, however, the position of the church has been diminished or eradicated by revolution or civil reform, any social-welfare activities undertaken by the church may be seen as competing with the state, or attempting to strengthen religion. States undergoing communist revolutions often display this syndrome, at least in the early years. If a church or a particular religion is seen as an incipient or past oppressor, or is identified with a colonial power, there may be limits to the extent to which it can engage in social welfare. The social-welfare activities of certain Christian missionaries in India, immediately after independence, gave rise to accusations that they were trying to establish separatist Christian states—in Assam, for example.

In countries where church and state are completely separated, social welfare may be assigned exclusively to religious bodies, may be the exclusive responsibility of the government, may be administered by parallel systems that—in turn—may or may not divide up the areas of action between them, or may be handled cooperatively by government and religious bodies. For example, the following has been said about the United States:

> Separation of church and state has made the church's efforts distinctly private. Churches developed institutions for orphans and for the aged in their congregations. They also collected alms for the poor and provided food, clothing, and shelter to the needy. Adoption and foster care were added later. Counseling was seen basically as pastoral advice, but the clergy often found that problems required expert help.[34]

The proper relative roles of government and religious bodies in social welfare have been one of the most difficult philosophic and practical problems—obviously in those countries in which separation of functions is seen as desirable. The problem is intensified because various religions have differing views.

In America, the traditional stance of the Protestant church has been that it is religion's function to be concerned with man's soul, and because salvation rests primarily on faith, concern with good works is a diversion of energy. Noted Protestant thinkers have reiterated the position that the church has no role in social welfare.[35] In addition to this view, there is also the view, promulgated by Protestant theologians, that the church has a pioneering role, which should be relinquished as the government recognizes its responsibility. This was enunciated by Niebuhr as follows: "It is the business of the church . . . to pioneer in the field of social work and to discover obligations which society, as such, has not yet recognized, but to yield these to society as soon as there is a general recognition of society's responsibility thereof."[36]

There is also the third view, more evident in practice than in theory, that though churches or religious bodies as such should not engage in welfare activities, secular Protestant organizations, so to speak, should be concerned with the state of the world and of humanity. This helps to explain the establishment and growth of such organizations as the Salvation Army, Volunteers of America, Baptist hospitals, Lutheran homes for the aged, and Methodist Fresh-Air Funds. For example, though Lutheran agencies are likely to be church-owned, the majority of such organizations, by and large, are not owned or controlled by churches as such but by organizations of church members.[37] Coughlin presents a convincing argument as to why Protestant groups in America have not engaged in social welfare under their own auspices to the extent that Catholics and Jews have:

> A majority group, however, does not need . . . a bulwark to assure the preservation of its way of life, since its values are reflected in the patterns and policies of the larger society. At one time American society was practically identical with Protestant society. Social institutions reflected Protestant values, and in the field of welfare agencies, staffs and boards of directors were frequently also lay trustees of Protestant churches. Nonsectarian social work was therefore bound to reflect Protestant values, and it was easy for Protestants to adjust to secularization in social welfare.[38]

The Catholic view of the church-state relationship in social welfare differs greatly from the Protestant views outlined above. Good works as a requisite to salvation make it imperative that the opportunity to engage in social welfare not be taken out of the hands of church groups and individuals.[39] Consequently, Catholics have enunciated the principle of "subsidiarity," which means that smaller units and those closer to individuals should perform, and be allowed to perform, as much as they can, relinquishing to larger and higher units of society only what they cannot accomplish alone:

> The word *subsidiary* means "giving help." Applied to relationships be-tween government and voluntary agencies, the principle prescribes that where a voluntary association is wholly unequal to its task, the agency must relinquish the task. Where, however, the voluntary association can with help fulfill its responsibility and function, government should extend enabling assistance. Applied in this way, the principle is one of self-deter-mination on the societal level. When, however, government chooses not to give enabling assistance and to take to itself unnecessarily the responsi-bility and function of such an association, it not only overburdens itself with functions for which it is not equipped, but it also deprives individuals of their right to and need for voluntary association.[40]

The Jewish view of church-state relations in social welfare has been complicated, if not ambiguous. Usually classified within the "liberal" political camp,[41] Jews have favored government measures against pov-erty, discrimination, and other welfare problems; and fearful of en-croachment by other religions or discrimination by a government dominated by another religion, they have opted for clear lines of divi-sion between church and state. At the same time, they have built up a Jewish welfare establishment paralleling, in many important aspects, that of government. This has included hospitals, employment services, family-counseling agencies, schools, loan funds, neighborhood and com-munity centers, and immigrant-absorption services. One rationale for such services is that they are instruments of Jewish survival at least as important as the synagogue.[42] Another rationale is that they are a leg-acy of the previously mentioned Stuyvesant Pledge to the effect that the Jewish group would take care of its members. Still another possibil-ity is that though Jews as individuals have felt that the government should deal with social problems, the organized Jewish community has feared government intervention as secular. In any case, the separation of church and state in America fostered a large growth of welfare structure under religious auspices, including all three major group-ings.[43]

The question of church-state relationships in social welfare took on new dimensions in the United States with the Great Depression, and the acknowledgment that existing welfare organizations—sectarian and secular—could not cope with the massive need. Government entry into the social-welfare field brought with it a sharpening of previous questions: Would it be better to encourage government action at the expense of weakening voluntary organizations,[44] to seek government funds for sectarian groups at the risk of violating church-state separation, or to establish religious organizations for their own members, allowing the government to take care of nonmembers? Although much discussion and debate accompanied the decision-making from the 1930s through the 1950s, by the time the War on Poverty programs began in the 1960s the role of government as the prime mover in social-welfare programs was well established.

The continued existence of sectarian programs was usually justified in terms of dealing with peculiarly religious aspects (such as Sabbath observance among Jews or anti-Semitism in some businesses, as the rationale for Jewish employment services). In some cases, it is the comfort expressed by clients in being dealt with by "one's own," or in being among coreligionists. As Kahn points out, "There are people to whom religion is so critical a component of daily life that, precisely under circumstances during which they require social services, they wish sectarian services."[45] In other cases, the importance of religious identification was recognized in law, as when adoption was allowed only to parents of the child's religion (a stipulation that has begun to be overridden by specifications based upon the best interest of the child).[46]

However, the professionalization of social work—including that in community centers, youth work, hospitals, and homes for the aged—led to the postulation of a "value-free" agency, and even the sectarian services began to question the extent to which they helped maintain the religious group or the religious tradition—one of their own justifications for existence. This question was sometimes phrased in terms of whether there is a "Jewish," or a "Catholic," or a "Protestant" casework, group-work, or community-organization method.[47] In terms of center work, for example, it was sometimes half seriously asked whether there is Catholic, as opposed to Jewish or Protestant, basketball.[48] The realization that there were Jewish hospitals that did not serve kosher food, and Catholic hospitals in which abortions might be performed, led to further questioning of the rationale that maintained sectarian institutions paralleling secular ones. In this connection, Eckardt studied religious beliefs and social-work practice and found that despite identifiable differences in beliefs, practices tended to remain the same.[49]

Another possible explanation of the growth of government, as opposed to religious, social welfare has been the postulation of an American civil religion. In this view, there has grown up in America a system of myths, beliefs, values, and behaviors that are essentially religious in nature but which transcend the three major religions in the United States. The flag becomes a holy object; the Pledge of Allegiance, a prayer; and "The Star-Spangled Banner," a hymn. ("God Bless America" also requires the audience to rise: Witness its use at the national political conventions of 1976.) This "American" religion and the government are so intertwined that there is no separation between this "church" and the state. Social welfare is thus one manifestation of religious activity, carried on by and through the government structure.

Opposed to this view is the position that the reception and absorption of various immigrant groups in America, via either assimilation or the "melting pot," were never intended to synthesize their religions as they synthesized many other aspects of their heritages.[50] On an empirical basis too, doubt has been thrown on the civil-religion theory.[51]

Another cause for the trend away from sectarian agencies is the differential quality of service provided by government and the various sectarian agencies. It is quite possible that the desire for good service might overcome otherwise strong sectarian identification.[52] Again, the need for funding beyond that available from sectarian sources might lead to acceptance of funds from other, that is, government, sources. This was, for a long time, the sticking point for many sectarian agencies. Although tax-exemption for church property was almost universally seen as proper, exemption for church-run enterprises was less clear, and exemption for fund-raising devices such as bazaars, bingo games, and raffles, even for social-welfare purposes, raises legal and moral questions in some circles.

Actually accepting money from the government was seen as violating the separation between church and state, or as opening the way for secular control of sectarian activity. For a while, some agencies struggled with inadequate budgets while ignoring the availability of relatively massive federal funds, overcoming their scruples only on the grounds that they were doing a disservice to clients by limiting their resources. Nevertheless, agencies attempted to retain their autonomy of operation while accepting outside (either welfare-federation or government) funds. In the United States, this has proved a problem, both in view of the mandating of certain services and methods as a condition for government funding and in view of the accountability such funding usually demands. In Britain, there is much more reliance upon voluntary, and even sectarian, agencies, with government funds being made available to them without specific earmarking, on the basis of the general goals and reputation of the recipient organizations.

In general, however, funding from church or other sectarian bodies is insufficient for the needs of their agencies, and

> ... both participation in federated funding and payments for services from public agencies have become characteristic for sectarian agencies.... Agencies are tending to become less sectarian; their eligibility policies retain priority for their own members, but ... the majority of persons served are often not members of the group sponsoring the agency.[53]

Further, rather than eschewing government funds, sectarian agencies have come to vie for them, and are not above accusing the government of religious discrimination if the grants go to the agencies of another religious group.[54]

The opposite side of the coin—whether the government has the right to fund, help, or buy services from sectarian agencies in societies where church and state are separate—has raised an equal number of difficult questions. However, beginning with court opinions that allowed monies to be spent for the needs of children in sectarian schools—such as lunches, schoolbooks, and supplies—rather than for the schools themselves, the concept of the person rather than the institution or agency as the ultimate recipient has eased the problem in the United States for those who favor government support of sectarian agencies.[55]

In addition to funding questions, there are also questions concerning government inspection and licensing of religiously sponsored social-welfare institutions. Just as the power to tax is the power to destroy, so the power to license is the power to control. That physical facilities must meet certain standards is generally agreed, but the extent to which the government can or should control the content of programs is less clear. In the field of education, for example, the curriculum in Amish schools in the United States or Hutterian schools in Canada has been a bone of contention, while the right of Christian Scientist parents or those who believe in faith healing to withhold medical care from their children is still a passion-arousing question.

In this connection, it is interesting that some religious authorities distinguish between educational programs, which are seen as legitimate opportunities for evangelism, and welfare programs, which are not.[56] Some Africans, for example, decry missionaries "who find it hard to conceive of a school as anything except an instrument for the propagation of the beliefs of a sect."[57] Other religious authorities, however, would accept help for needy people, in the form of purchases of service and capital grants, providing that "such payments do not imperil church control, compromise basic principles, or interfere with their proclamation of the gospel."[58]

It is, indeed, this desire or obligation of religious institutions to proclaim their gospel, or to evangelize among their clients, that impresses upon some people the need for government, that is, nonevangelical, social-welfare agencies, on the one hand, and the need for agencies that support, offer continuity for, or proselytize for different branches, sects, or beliefs, on the other. In the first connection, there is sometimes a need of a minority group to maintain its own institutions with their value orientation as a "bulwark against encroachment of the value system of the majority group."[59] In other cases, there may be competition between groups for members. Distinctions between social-service activities dictated by religious commandments and proselytizing by offering services, and perhaps material goods, are not always easily drawn. What one group views as humanitarian programs may be seen by another as missionary activities,[60] and sometimes with reason. (For instance, during the Great Depression, the New York Tribune Coal and Food Fund was used by Hebrew Christian missionaries to make converts through the distribution of tickets.)[61] Because of this ambivalence, many want such programs to be offered by a secular body, such as the government. Conversely, the group's need to go beyond social welfare and to deal in spiritual welfare is justification for the existence of sectarian groups—for example, a cardinal wrote, "Catholic social science will do all things for the individual that secular social science can do, but it will and must go further and help to save the soul of the one with whom it comes in contact."[62] This viewpoint is the reason for the existence of scout troops and youth movements sponsored by churches and synagogues in the United States, and of Jewish, Arab, Druze, Armenian, and other scout troops in Israel.

In summarizing this discussion of church-state relations in social welfare, it can be said that religious groups maintain their own agencies and services.

1. For fear that other sectarian agencies will attempt to proselytize, missionize, or subvert their members
2. For fear that secular agencies will lessen need or respect for religion
3. In order to garner strength and continuity for the groups by serving members' needs
4. In order to perpetuate their values, beliefs, and customs
5. Because appealing for help outside the group may stigmatize the group as needy, as unable to help its members, or as neglecting them
6. In order not to violate the separation of church and state, as a matter of principle

RELIGIOUSLY INSPIRED INTERNATIONAL SOCIAL WELFARE

Although church-state relationships determine the extent and kind of religiously sponsored social-welfare activities in many countries, the religious motivation to engage in social welfare also operates across national boundaries. In addition to such secular social-welfare agencies as the Red Cross, CARE, International Social Service, the Save-the-Children Foundation, and the United Nations agencies, there are also religious organizations. Perhaps the best-known Catholic international organization for social welfare is Caritas, though the previously mentioned Society of Saint Vincent de Paul also exists in many countries, as do various Catholic orders. Protestants participate through their various denominational organizations, though the YMCA and YWCA movement is broadly supported, and the World Council of Churches also engages in such work. Jewish worldwide social-welfare organizations include the Joint Distribution Committee, the Hebrew Immigrant Aid Society, the Organization for Rehabilitation through Training (ORT), and others. There are also worldwide Jewish organizations whose services are primarily intended for Israel, such as the Women's International Zionist Organization.

RELIGION AND SOCIAL-WORK EDUCATION

Insofar as religious ideals and values are felt to be important components of social-work practice, a need is felt to imbue practitioners with such values, to professionalize work stemming primarily from religious motivations, and to bring into harmony sectarian and secular values. In the United States, for reasons noted previously, little need seems to be felt for purely Protestant schools of social work as such. There are, nevertheless, schools devoted to preparing senior staff for YMCAs, such as Springfield College, and schools sponsored by more fundamentalist groups that include social work in the curriculum.[63] Catholic schools include Catholic University in Washington, D.C.; Boston College School of Social Work; Loyola University; and others. In addition, numerous books and articles discuss social work in the light of Catholic beliefs.[64] A Jewish school of social work that was not organically connected with any of the three major branches of Jewish practice (Orthodox, Conservative, and Reform) was relatively short-lived, lasting only from 1925 to 1940,[65] and the only American school of social work attempting to be specifically Jewish is at Yeshiva University. A number of schools have joint programs with various religious bodies, in which social-work training is given in the secular school and the values and practices of a given religion are subjects of supplementation in a theological seminary or similar setting.

Finally, the International Association of Schools of Social Work is paralleled by a similar association of Catholic schools, while the International Federation of Social Workers also has a parallel in a similar Catholic group.

RELIGION AS A CAUSE OF SOCIAL PROBLEMS

Although it is customary to think of religion and religiously oriented bodies as ameliorating or solving problems, in some cases the religious aspect is irrelevant: "Consider the problem of religion in a culture of overwhelming physical and psychic scarcity. How can one express undying love for a neighbor when there is only one job for the two of you, and you intend to have it?"[66]

In other cases religion is the cause of the problem. Anti-Semitism and anti-Catholicism have engraved their marks on many individuals, with consequent deleterious effects on self-images, motivations, and behaviors. Hope and joy have been occasioned by religious beliefs and experiences, but so have feelings of guilt and anxiety. Consider the effects of excessive religious zeal, not only on groups and mobs but on individuals:

> Medical superintendents [of asylums] were hardly cheered by the state of religion. . . . Psychiatrists distrusted the more successful manifestations of religious enthusiasm in the revival. The subject was not altogether a comfortable one—for belief in God was not supposed to resemble financial or political ambitions, where too much was a dangerous thing. Still, medical superintendents regularly included religious excesses among the causes of insanity. And occasionally, a movement as extreme as the Millerites afforded them the opportunity to denounce "a popular religious error" for having produced "so much excitement in the community and rendered so many insane." The church did little to counterbalance prevailing trends, and at times even stimulated them.[67]

In earlier times, the excesses of the Crusaders as they pillaged their way across Europe, the tragic Children's Crusade, pogroms, and religious wars all played their parts in creating problems, as did the enormous wealth that accrued to some monasteries and other religious establishments.

In a slightly different vein, the attitude of religious groups has an impact on the way social problems are handled, and even as to whether they are defined as problems. Where the dominant church is opposed to the dissemination of birth-control information, or condones begging, or crusades against prostitution, the implications are clear. When the church is a minor influence, its attitudes have less impact on policy and practice. The fact that nothing in the Hindu religion contraindicates family planning makes it possible for the government of India to institute and pursue various methods of birth control, including sterilization. In the Orthodox Jewish religion, regulations against abortion have been deduced, but because this is a police matter in Israel, there is tacit agreement not to enforce the law there except in the event of malpractice. At the moment of writing, there are proposals to amend the Israeli law concerning abortions.

THE FUTURE OF RELIGIOUSLY MOTIVATED
SOCIAL WELFARE

A number of factors point to a future diminution of the role played
by religious motivations for social welfare. One of these is the increasing
complexity of society, which is correlated with the increasing complexity of societal problems. Social-welfare agencies will probably continue to grow in size, scope, and comprehensiveness, thus placing ever
more distance between the giver and the ultimate recipient. Such institutionalization of the religiously motivated act may lessen enthusiasm,
even while increasing donations. Secondly, the missionizing aspect of
certain religious social-welfare activities will probably become clearer
as literacy and sophistication grow, not to mention political awareness,
resulting in a rejection of suspect religious services in favor of secular
ones. Finally, laws that prohibit discrimination on the basis of race, sex,
national origin, or religion will probably continue to be expanded and
enforced, with the result that sectarian agencies will have to deal with
increasing numbers of nonmembers, weakening their reason for being.

On the other hand, the commandments that lead to social welfare
will continue to be seen as immutable by religious adherents, and one
of the major reasons why men and society engage in social welfare will
continue to be—in greater or lesser amount, one way or another—the
desire to do God's will.

NOTES

1. E. Conze, *Buddhism: Its Essence and Development* (New York: Harper
   & Row, 1959).
2. D. Constantelos, *Byzantine Philanthropy and Social Welfare* (New
   Brunswick, N. J.: Rutgers University Press, 1968), p. 11.
3. A. W. Gouldner, *The Hellenic World: A Sociological Analysis* (New York:
   Harper & Row, 1969), p. 138.
4. Constantelos, *op. cit.*, p. 41.
5. S. C. Kohs, *The Roots of Social Work* (New York: Association Press, 1966),
   p. 105.
6. *Ibid.*
7. *Ibid.*, p. 106.
8. E. Faris *et al.*, *Intelligent Philanthropy* (Chicago: University of Chicago
   Press, 1930), pp. 112–13; quoted in *ibid.*, p. 139.
9. Sir Thomas Browne, *Religio Medici* (1643); quoted in K. de Schweinitz,
   England's Road to Social Security (Philadelphia: University of Pennsylvania Press, 1943), p. 14.
10. Conze, *op. cit.*, p. 56.
11. *Ibid.*, p. 55.

12. K. Kohler, "Charity," in I. B. Singer (ed.), *The Jewish Encyclopedia*, Vol. 3 (New York: Funk & Wagnalls, 1903), p. 667.

13. All nouns, verbs, adjectives, and adverbs in Hebrew are either male or female; there is no neuter gender. Hence, "he" is used for generic references, and is so used herein where Hebrew texts are cited. M. Maimonides, *Yad*, "Hilkhot Mattenot Aniyyim," 10:7–12. See *Encyclopedia Judaica*, Vol. 5 (Jerusalem: Keter, 1971), p. 343.

14. Constantelos, *op. cit.*, p. 11.

15. *Ibid.*, p. 23.

16. Conze, *op. cit.*, p. 57.

17. T. Fuller, *The Church History of Britain from the Birth of Jesus Christ until the Year MDCXLVIII*, Book 2 (London: 1655), pp. 289, 299; quoted in Schweinitz, *op. cit.*, p. 18.

18. Schweinitz, *op. cit.*, p. 17.

19. Babylonian Talmud, "Ktuvim," samech zion, p. 2; M. Maimonides, *Mishna Torah*, viii (Seeds), "Giving to the Poor," Chapter 7, Part 3.

20. Constantelos, *op. cit.*, p. 25.

21. Schweinitz, *op. cit.*, pp. 17–19.

22. Constantelos, *op. cit.*, p. 11.

23. Deut. 14:29, 24:19–21.

24. Constantelos, *op. cit.*, pp. 15–16.

25. D. Brieland *et al.*, *Contemporary Social Work* (New York: McGraw-Hill, 1975), p. 49.

26. A. E. Fink, *The Field of Social Work* (New York: Holt, Rinehart & Winston, 1974), p. 35.

27. B. J. Coughlin, *Church and State in Social Welfare* (New York: Columbia University Press, 1965), p. 25.

28. I. M. Rubinow, "What Do We Owe to Peter Stuyvesant?" in R. Morris and M. Freund (eds.), *Trends and Issues in Jewish Social Welfare in the United States, 1899–1952* (Philadelphia: Jewish Publication Society of America, 1966), pp. 288–98. Not everyone agrees concerning the effect or even the existence of the Stuyvesant Pledge: See I. S. Chipkin, "Judaism and Social Welfare," in L. Finkelstein (ed.), *The Jews*, Vol. 2 (Philadelphia: Jewish Publication Society of America, 1949), pp. 713–44.

29. Constantelos, *op. cit.*, p. 65.

30. Brieland *et al.*, *op. cit.*, p. 49.

31. T. H. Marshall, *Social Policy* (London: Hutchinson, 1965).

32. Schweinitz, *op. cit.*, p. 24.

33. *Ibid.*, p. 83.

34. Brieland *et al.*, *op. cit.*, p. 49.

35. H. Miller, "Government's Role in Social Welfare" (address to the Second National Conference on the Churches and Social Welfare, National Council of the Churches of Christ in the U.S.A., Cleveland, 1961); quoted in Coughlin, *op. cit.*, p. 23.

36. R. Niebuhr, *The Contribution of Religion to Social Work* (New York: Columbia University Press, 1932); quoted in Coughlin, *op. cit.*, p. 21.

37. Brieland *et al.*, *op. cit.*, p. 49.

38. Coughlin, *op. cit.*, p. 24.

39.   Kohs, *op. cit.*, p. 109.

40.   Coughlin, *op. cit.*, pp. 31–32.

41.   S. Siegel, "Judaism and Liberalism: A Conservative View," in P. E. Weinberger (ed.), *Perspectives on Social Welfare: An Introductory Anthology* (New York: Macmillan, 1974), pp. 33–39.

42.   P. E. Weinberger and D. Z. Weinberger, "The Jewish Religious Tradition and Social Services," in *ibid.*, pp. 402–11.

43.   H. L. Wilensky and C. N. Lebeaux, *Industrial Society and Social Welfare* (New York: Free Press, 1958), p. 161.

44.   The fight of voluntary organizations against the "encroachment" of government is described in L. H. Feder, *Unemployment Relief in Periods of Depression* (New York: Sage, 1936).

45.   A. J. Kahn, *Social Policy and Social Services* (New York: Random House, 1973), p. 104.

46.   S. L. Gollub, "A Critical Look at Religious Requirements in Adoption," *Public Welfare*, 32 (1974):23–28.

47.   G. B. Bubis, "Professional Education for the Jewish Component in Casework Practice," *Journal of Jewish Communal Service*, 52 (Spring 1976): 270–77.

48.   For a general view of this question, see J. M. Carp, "The Social Work Function of the Jewish Community Center," *Journal of Jewish Communal Service*, 52 (Fall 1975):43–58.

49.   R. W. Eckardt, Jr., "Evangelical Christianity and Professional Social Work: A Study of the Beliefs and Practices of the Social Work Majors of Philadelphia College of the Bible and Temple University," Ph.D. diss., University of Pennsylvania, Philadelphia, 1974.

50.   W. Herberg, *Protestant, Catholic and Jew: An Essay in American Religious Sociology* (Garden City, N.Y.: Doubleday, 1955).

51.   M. C. Thomas and C. C. Flippen, "American Civil Religion: An Empirical Study," *Social Forces*, 51 (1972):218–25.

52.   Weinberger and Weinberger, *op. cit.*, p. 407.

53.   Brieland *et al.*, *op. cit.*, p. 49.

54.   "A move by the Beame administration to a Roman Catholic hospital instead of a Jewish medical college in the Bronx produced a confrontation yesterday marked by ethnic and religious charges." *New York Times*, October 20, 1976, p. 1.

55.   A Kentucky court ruled, for example, that a distinction should be made between the auspices of an institution and its purpose: "A private agency may be utilized as a pipe-line through which a public expenditure is made, the test being not who receives the money, but the use for which it is expended." Coughlin, *op. cit.*, p. 48.

56.   *Ibid.*, p. 53.

57.   *Social Reconstruction in the Newly Independent Countries of East Africa* (New York: United Nations, 1965), p. 53.

58.   Coughlin, *op. cit.*, p. 52.

59.   *Ibid.*, p. 24.

60.   D. Macarov *et al.*, "Consultants and Consultees: The View from Within," *Social Service Review*, 43 (September 1976):285.

61. Feder, *op. cit.*, p. 157.
62. Patrick Cardinal Hayes, in a letter of July 1931 appearing in the Fordham University School of Social Service, *1934–1935 Catalogue,* p. 6; quoted in Kohs, *op. cit.*, p. 110.
63. Eckardt, *op. cit.*
64. M. J. McCormick, *Diagnostic Casework in the Thomistic Pattern* (New York: Columbia University Press, 1954); M. Stock, *Freud: A Thomistic Approach* (Washington, D.C.: Thomist Press, 1963).
65. See G. Berger, "Strengths and Limitations in Present Attempts at Preparing Workers for Jewish Communal Service," in *Innovation by Tradition: Articles on Jewish Communal Life* (New York: Federation of Jewish Philanthropies of New York, 1976), p. 151.
66. C. Hampden-Turner, *From Poverty to Dignity* (Garden City, N.Y.: Anchor, 1975).
67. D. J. Rothman, *The Discovery of the Asylum: Social Order and Disorder in the New Republic* (Boston: Little, Brown, 1971), p. 119.

5
Politics

The separation of church and state led inevitably to the entry of government into the arena of social welfare. The extent to which governments have undertaken responsibility for various facets of social welfare has differed, however, from country to country. There have been and there still are a number of ways in which this responsibility is divided among government, religious bodies, the family, the market, and voluntary groups.

In some places—mainly heavily Catholic countries—the church may have responsibility for education and religion, the family for health, government for material need, the market for employment, and voluntary groups for recreation. In others—such as some developing countries—the government may be responsible for education, the church for religious instruction, voluntary groups (often from abroad) for health care, and the family for recreation. In Israel, the government is responsible for education and material need, voluntary groups (including labor unions) for most health care, recognized religious bodies for religious matters plus matters of personal status (as noted previously, marriage, divorce, adoption, and inheritance), and the family for recreation. Other combinations can undoubtedly be identified. In any case, the current situation in the United States, where the government is basically responsible for education and material need, the family (with some exceptions) for health care, the church for religion, and voluntary groups for recreation and preventive health care, is neither universal nor immutable.

HISTORY

It is difficult to identify an absolute beginning point for the involvement of government with social welfare. Certainly, pre-Biblical and Biblical writings speak of obligations concerning the needy, the widow, and the orphan, but because these obligations lay within historical situations in which it is difficult to distinguish between the people, government, and religion, they are not precisely germane.

Later history also records many charitable acts on the part of rulers and governments. However, during the days of absolute rulers, and especially when kings were felt to rule by divine right, charity usually was dispensed at the whim of the ruler or flowed from his desire to attain salvation (often as he lay dying). When some sort of help was given, it was usually to the ruler's relatives, his immediate retainers, his military leaders, or the church. The essential point is that insofar as the ruler did not need the support, or even the sanction, of the ruled—and insofar as social unrest was an attempt to upset the divine order of things and was therefore heresy rather than revolution—there was little political motivation to engage in social welfare.[1] This situation passed a turning point when the nobles wrested the Magna Charta from King John in 1215, thereby establishing the ruler's dependence on at least some of his subjects.

The process of separating church from state also passed a turning point with Henry VIII's expropriation of the monasteries in 1536 and 1539.[2] Although the newly established religion and the state were still one, the state had in this instance established the religion instead of the reverse, as in the past. It was also during the reign of Henry VIII, in 1531, that the government of England first took responsibility for the relief of economic distress. It is true that Edward III had issued the Statutes of Laborers in 1349, but because this essentially *prohibited* giving to beggars, it is hard to view it as a social-welfare measure. Although the responsibility undertaken in 1531 consisted merely of licensing the right to beg, thereby revising Edward's ruling, its major significance lay in the fact that a type of social-welfare right was conferred by an act of Parliament. Five years later, the right to beg was superseded by government responsibility for stimulating and securing contributions from private citizens for the relief of the needy.[3] These laws continued to be expanded and revised during the reign of Elizabeth I, who succeeded to the throne in 1558 and died in 1603. Because the last important law in this series was passed in 1601, the entire complex is usually referred to as the Elizabethan Poor Laws. These laws dealt with the employment of the able-bodied poor, almshouses for the unemployable, and measures for dependent children. The importance of these laws lay in the fact that "the achievement of a better society came to be no longer looked upon as a task to be undertaken by God, but by man."[4]

The Elizabethan Poor Laws, one of the first enunciations of government responsibility for social welfare, contained a number of features that continue to influence social welfare to this day. The Poor Laws were based upon three principles: the responsibility of the state; limitation of this responsibility to those unable to take care of themselves, in contradistinction to "sturdy beggars"; and administration of social welfare through local units. From these principles and later amendments flowed several important concepts.

One controlling concept in social welfare, flowing from the Poor Laws, is the above-mentioned distinction between those who cannot take care of themselves—the "deserving poor"—and those who are in need presumably because of their own behavior—the "undeserving poor." This distinction was, at one time, based solely upon physical ability, with the healthy poor man, who would not "put himself to labor as a true man ought to do," being assigned to a workhouse or even farmed out to work for another person. One side effect of this system was a distinction between "outdoor relief," which was given to people living outside the workhouse, and "indoor relief"—assignment to workhouses, almshouses, and other institutions. Farming out the poor resulted in so many abuses, such as their exploitation and actual mistreatment, that it was eliminated. Indoor relief, however, continued to be preferred to outdoor relief for the undeserving poor, thus adding a certain punitive element to the aid given the undeserving. Similarly, the present-day requirement that AFDC mothers take any job offered, with only minor guarantees concerning payment or conditions, can be seen as a form of farming out, as can the requirement that home-relief (General Assistance) clients in New York State enroll in public-works programs.

The Poor Laws also established the concept of residency requirements, which were discussed in Chapter 3. Poor people not only were entitled to aid exclusively in their home parishes but were required to return there. The law contained provisions for returning the aged and the infirm to their places of residence on horseback or in carts, while the able-bodied were required to walk home—at least ten miles a day —and they could receive one meal and one night's lodging at each stop.[5]

Relatives' responsibility, too, stems from the Poor Laws, with the Act of 1601 adding grandparents to the mutual obligation of support that previously extended to parents and children.[6]

After the days of the Poor Laws, Britain hesitantly moved into the area of government responsibility, taking a tentative step in 1802 with the Health and Morals of Apprentices Act. "From this tentative, almost surreptitious beginning, the State . . . gradually extended its sphere of operation."[7]

Although the first compulsory social-insurance system was adopted by Austria in 1854, the next benchmark in the history of government social welfare is usually considered to be when Bismarck, the Iron Chancellor of Germany, introduced comprehensive plans for social insurance between 1882 and 1889, including compulsory insurance against illness, accident, and old age.[8] Social security spread throughout Europe, but the next important date in the United States is 1935, when Franklin D. Roosevelt, as part of his New Deal, persuaded Congress to pass the Social Security Act.[9] Finally, modern social welfare should mark the year 1942, which was the date of the submission of the Beveridge Report in Britain, which led to what has come to be called the welfare state. In a negative way, perhaps 1970 should also be noted as the year in which the Family Assistance Plan—actually a proposal for a guaranteed minimum income—failed in the U.S. Congress.[10]

POLITICAL MOTIVATIONS FOR SOCIAL WELFARE

The major motivations that have brought governments into the social-welfare arena can be categorized under three interrelated headings: the acquisition of political power, the avoidance of social unrest, and social welfare as a side effect of the political process itself.

Acquisition of Political Power

With the waning of the divine right of kings, and with the growth of governments dependent on the sanction, if not the support, of the populace, many devices were used by rulers to gain such sanction and support. These included feasts, holidays, the release of debtors from prison, territorial acquisition, military adventures, and—of a quite different nature—repression of opposition. Social-welfare benefits also have been used to gain support for rulers or political parties.

Bismarck's introduction of social-security measures in 1882 in no way stemmed from humanitarian motives. Bismarck opposed limited working hours for women and children in factories and was against state interference in agriculture and industry. However, because social insurance was being advocated by an opposition political party, it was adopted by the government solely "to make German social democracy less attractive to the working man."[11]

One of the prime motivations for the adoption of Social Security in the United States was quite analogous to Bismarck's. As a result of the Great Depression, a number of politicians and would-be politicians began to attract political followings because of their proposals to over-come the effects of the economic situation. The most powerful of these was Francis E. Townsend, a retired California physician, who devised a plan to relieve the poverty of the aged while contributing to the economic recovery of the country. The Townsend Plan called for monthly payments of $200 to every person over sixty, provided that the money was spent within thirty days. The plan was to be financed by a sales tax. Thus, the poor would have sufficient disposable income, the demand for consumer goods would rise sufficiently to provide jobs for all, ahd in return for the proposed prosperity, the sales tax would be a small price to pay. The Townsend Plan gained widespread support among the aged, gaining an estimated 10 million adherents at one time.[12] Townsend clubs—which were, incidentally, interracial—grew up in almost every city. There were twelve hundred clubs by the end of 1934.[13] The *Townsend National Weekly* had a circulation exceeding two hundred thousand.[14]

There is little question but that one of the taproots of the Social Security Act was a desire to defuse the Townsend movement before it became too powerful politically, as it was both endorsing candidates and nominating its own. As Altmeyer notes, "The political motivation was particularly strong in old age assistance because of the strength of the Townsend movement,"[15] and "the President was concerned about the Townsend plan."[16] Even on the state level, the plight of the aged became a political issue because of the Townsend movement. When-ever there was an increase in old-age assistance, governors would write letters to recipients taking credit for the increase,[17] rather than have it credited to the Townsend movement. Even after the adoption of Social Security, the Townsend forces had to be reckoned with when changes and amendments were discussed. A proposal to require uni-form payments by the states was scrapped for fear of fanning the flames of the Townsend movement, which reached "the peak of intensity during the 1938 Congressional elections."[18] As late as 1939, in discuss-ing an amendment, "the strength of the Townsend movement was demonstrated by the fact that more than fifty congressmen and two senators testified in support of it."[19]

Nor were the votes of the aged the only prize at issue during those days. Senator Huey Long of Louisiana gained national prominence with his "Share the Wealth" plan, which was intended to make "Every Man a King."[20] The details of Long's program were vague, but his personal-ity created a following that might have taken enough votes away from the Democratic Party to have resulted in a Republican victory in 1936. The President "was even more concerned about the Long threat than that of Townsend."[21] In California, Upton Sinclair promoted a political platform called EPIC (End Poverty in California) and also became a power to be reckoned with.[22] Consequently, there is little question but that one of the motivations for Social Security in the United States was a desire to weaken the appeal of competing programs.

There have been other instances in American history where the potential political power of a bloc or group resulted in "preventive" or "anesthetizing" social-welfare programs. The potential political power of veterans, for example, resulted in a bonus payment to veterans in 1937[23] and the GI Bill of Rights after World War II. No other status group was as well rewarded as veterans after the war.[24] Although veterans' benefits were not explicitly a social-welfare program, the results were the same as if they had been.[25] They represented, in fact, one of the most remarkably successful instances of social welfare without socialism.[26] Demonstrations of "black power," however, have rarely resulted in legislative acts; yet the slow, quiet, continuous registration of black voters, particularly in the south, is credited by some with making possible Jimmy Carter's election victory, and may yet be used to demand changes in social-welfare programs. Consequently, one of the political motivations for social-welfare measures is the desire to attain or maintain political position, making for "the fundamental political nature of [many] social-welfare measures—spawned in the first place to maintain a political leadership, and then continuously adapted to a changing political environment."[27]

Avoidance of Social Unrest

A second political motivation for social-welfare programs, though related to the first, is somewhat different. It is the desire to avoid social unrest, even if those creating the unrest neither pose a political threat nor aspire to political power. For example:

> The whole congregation of the children of Israel murmured against Moses and Aaron in the wilderness . . . ye have brought us forth into this wilderness, to kill this whole assembly with hunger. . . . And Moses said . . . The Lord shall give you in the evening flesh to eat, and in the morning bread to the full.[28]

In the same vein, one of the major motivations for the Poor Laws was to reduce the threat from roving bands of beggars who often turned to robbery or pillage. "Poor relief, far from being designed to afford a modicum of social security, was conceived of as a police measure which, by preventing the despair of starvation, would diminish the potential danger of desperate action and the ensuing disturbance to society."[29] Victorian society too "was shot through with the fear that one day the masses would overthrow the existing order,"[30] and in the nineteenth century:

That a good deal of the charity of this period was inspired more by fear than love can hardly be denied, the fear of revolution inherited from those who saw the French Revolution was present to their minds, and in every agitation for better conditions they saw the red terror raising its head in their own country. The provision of soup was a method of keeping the poor quiet.[31]

Responses to social-action efforts vary with the times. The veterans who made up the bonus marchers to Washington in 1932 were gassed, dispersed by force, and hustled through state after state.[32] In 1933, the same maneuver resulted in housing in an army camp and three solid meals a day. "The U.S. Navy band played for the veterans, and Army doctors ministered to their ills. . . . Most of the members of the second Bonus Expeditionary Force were enrolled in the Civilian Conservation Corps."[33]

The distinction between measures designed to gain political power and those designed to minimize social unrest is clear when the history of the 1960s in the United States is examined. The rioting in ghettos, student riots, civil disobedience, antiwar demonstrations, and draft evasion were not seen as attempts by a political body or party to gain power —perhaps because the participants were seen as essentially powerless from a political point of view. They belonged to and formed no parties; backed no candidates; were divided into many small, squabbling groups; often rejected the entire political process and hence did not vote; and were therefore viewed as outside the political spectrum. Rather, these activities were seen as threats to internal peace and security, and perhaps to the position of groups that were not necessarily political in nature. In any society, "those in a position of dominance lay particularly heavy stress upon preventing the disaffected from raising issues that are threatening to the former's preferred position,"[34] and this seems to be what happened in America in the 1960s.

Of course, not all threats to internal security are met by adopting welfare measures. The responses range from attempting to reason with and convert the disaffected, through compromises, bribes, chicanery, promises, threats, bargains, and confrontation, to conflict—and at various times and in differing situations, any of these might be seen as the response of choice.[35] One method of dealing with social threat is to co-opt the leaders of the threatening group by bringing them into the influential bodies of the threatened controlling group. Seen benevolently, this is an attempt to give power to such leaders, to make them cognizant of the wider picture, and to take their views into account. Viewed critically, this is intended to buy off the leaders with jobs or prestige, create distance between themselves and their constituencies, and bury their views in those of a larger group.

Another method has been termed "nondecision making," in which latent or manifest challenges are suppressed or thwarted before they become threats.[36] Still another method is the use of "pseudo-democracy,"[37] in which people are given the feeling that they have participated in reaching a decision, when in reality they have not. A method used by Congress (and not unknown in other countries) is to respond to the pressure of interest groups by passing requested legislation but not appropriating enough resources to implement it. In this connection, it has become commonplace in the United States for vast pressure to be brought to bear through letters, telegrams, visits to representatives, marches on Washington, and so forth, resulting in the passage of a bill. However, because appropriation of funds is a separate procedure that often comes later, it is virtually impossible to remount the whole campaign a second time, and the appropriation is made, if at all, after the appearance of only a few witnesses.

Most often, the method of meeting unrest has been attempted suppression.[38] There are times, however, when adoption of new programs, or changes in old programs, is the result. Perhaps the most famous recent instance was the Family Assistance Plan proposed to Congress by President Nixon. Arising as a result of welfare scandals, public backlash, and increasing resentment toward the welfare system on the part of recipients and nonrecipients alike, "the proposal was made . . . as part of an over-riding *short term* strategy to bring down the level of internal violence."[39] That the proposal did not pass was a result of conflicting views concerning the basis of the unrest and its solution, as well as the political process, with its trade-offs and logrolling.

As pointed out previously, absolute monarchs need neither the sanction nor the support of their subjects, but democracies often respond to the wishes and pressures of their populations with social-welfare measures, among other things. It should logically follow that the more representative the government, the better the social-welfare process. This was the hypothesis of Cutright, who studied seventy-six nations in 1965. He found that when economic development is controlled for, the more representative governments had older and more numerous social-insurance programs.[40] That this is not simply a difference in economic systems is indicated by another study, which found no such differences between Communist and capitalist countries,[41] as such.

Social Welfare as a Political Side Effect

In addition to the desire to attain or maintain power, and the desire to avoid social unrest, there is a third aspect to the political motivation for social welfare. In many instances social-welfare programs arise as a side effect of other or previous policies. One type of side effect is referred to as a "decisionless decision." Such decisions "simply 'happen,' in the sense that certain steps are taken that are necessary but preliminary to a decision and the sequence of steps acquires ... a life of its own."[42] That is to say, each step requires another, perhaps beginning with the question as to whether a decision will have to be made at all —the answer to which is itself a decision.[43] This is a variation of what is referred to as "incremental" decision-making,[44] or the "tree-branch" model. The ultimate result of such processes may be welfare programs that were not intended, such as subsidies to farmers. A further result of "incrementalism" (and not, in this case, incremental decisions) is the organic growth of welfare programs. Once a program is established, it tends to encompass more and more participants, and to offer larger and larger benefits. This is why, in a transnational study of welfare programs, Wilensky finds that the single most powerful predictor of coverage is the age of the program under study.[45] There seems to be almost no chance, therefore, of government's stepping out of welfare programs, or even reducing its participation.

Another type of decisionless decision is the social-welfare program that becomes necessary because of other government activities—social welfare as a by-product, as it were. America's entry into World War II led to the construction of munitions plants, which in turn required housing for workers, which necessitated schools, clinics, and welfare services.[46] Similarly, the adoption of WIN (the Work Incentive Program), which required welfare applicants to undergo vocational training or take available jobs, necessitated the establishment of day-care programs for children so that mothers could go to work. It should not be surprising that many such programs, as mentioned previously, have no educational or developmental goals: They are basically artifacts created by other programs. In the same way, pensions for the aged inevitably require establishment of recreational and leisure-time facilities, again without clear goals or purposes. Full-employment bills similarly usually require vocational training and other educational programs, which in turn may require scholarships or subsidies while participants are in training. Further, budget-cutting in relation to institutions results in inmates' being returned to the larger community, requiring housing, counseling, and various kinds of care. (Because such care is often unavailable, this can be termed returning people to community care in a community that doesn't care.)

In addition, government sometimes enters the social-welfare field because the size and complexity of the problem simply remove it from the power of other institutions. Income deductions for children are a type of family subsidy, and only the government collects income tax. Controlling agriculture, stimulating the economy, or ensuring a reasonable margin of profit so that industries won't collapse and cause unemployment[47]—each of these requires government intervention, and each such intervention brings in its train the necessity to engage in subsidiary activities, some of which have social-welfare implications.

Once government enters an area of social welfare, the goals and methods of its programs become legitimate targets in the political process.[48] Political parties become identified with various approaches, and, as noted previously, the programs are used to gain support for parties.

There is another aspect of the political process, however, that bears scrutiny. In order for a policy or a program to be adopted, it must acquire the support—or, at least, avoid the opposition—of large segments of the electorate. Consequently, one of the arguments advanced for "universal" as opposed to "categorical" or "selective" programs (as mentioned in Chapter 2) is that when the benefits are available to, if not received by, everyone, there is a much greater chance that the program will be approved.

The political structure, as well as the process, can affect the shape of social welfare. When President Franklin Pierce, in 1854, vetoed the proposal made by Dorothea Dix and passed by Congress to allocate 10 million acres of land to take care of the blind, the deaf, and the insane, he did so on the basis of "states' rights," claiming that it was not proper for the federal government to enter into social-welfare activities, though he urged that the individual states do so. The "federalization" of social welfare is one of the most talked-about possible reforms in the United States today, and "revenue-sharing," intended to give the states more autonomy in welfare and other questions, was one of the chief accomplishments of the Nixon Administration. The necessity to negotiate federal-state-local relationships in the acquisition of grants, matching funds, and so forth, owing to the "three-tiered" system of government in the United States, has given rise to a new area of expertise regarding this process.

Israel, on the other hand, has a "two-tiered" system. There, no legal or government divisions, areas, regions, or states intervene between the national and local levels. Administratively, this structure is much simpler, and presumably more efficient. Whether it results in more or less individual involvement and program variety is debatable.

THE FUTURE OF POLITICALLY MOTIVATED SOCIAL WELFARE

The political motivations for engaging in social welfare have been confined here to three: the desire to attain or maintain political power, the desire to avoid social unrest, and social welfare as a side effect of the political process itself. These are not the only reasons why governments engage in social-welfare activities. They may do so for humanitarian purposes, for economic reasons, because of religious beliefs and commitments (especially in those countries with near-monolithic religions), in order to deal with population problems, or as a result of another motivation.

However, insofar as the motivations are political in the sense discussed above, the growing size and complexity of the social-welfare establishment will probably dictate more political attention, rather than less. As social welfare throughout the world begins to use more and more of national budgets, benefits, costs, recipients, and policies will become much more significant as political issues. The shares that states, regions, or localities require and receive will have repercussions on those levels. Schools of social work will need to add more content concerning social-welfare politics to their curricula, and professional associations will need study groups and pressure groups such as the Task Force on Social Legislation of the National Association of Social Workers, in the United States. Such groups will be required to study the impact of political trends on social-welfare questions, such as the trend to shift power from the executive branch to the legislative branch, which is currently under way in the United States.

At the same time, there may be attempts to return as much as possible of the activity to smaller and more local units. Decisions will be made as to those things that, by their nature, must be done on a national level, and those things that can be done as well or better on the local level. For example, one of the aims of revenue-sharing, or the "new federalism," is to return resources to the states so that problems can be dealt with at the state or local level.

This move from centralization to decentralization is not without its doubters, as well as opponents. There is said to be more corruption on the local level, more prejudices that penalize some groups, and unfair lack of uniformity in eligibility and benefits from state to state. Some states, for example, have such ineffective standards for social welfare that they respond to public opinion locally, and largely through the "law of anticipated reaction."[49]

The centralization-decentralization decision is also made pragmatically in some cases: immediately after Cyprus acquired independence, decision-making was highly centralized down to the point of practically telling every farmer what he should plant. The result was highly successful. Over time, however, the system became decentralized. Inquiry as to why a successful method was abandoned indicated that immediately after independence, the major problems were clear and the solutions obvious. As these problems were solved, however, the proper priority to be given to the remaining problems became more blurred: Many seemed of the same intensity, and the solutions were no longer so obvious. At that point the government decided it needed to know from local units and individuals how the problems compared and what solutions might work—hence, decentralization.

Although the future will see continued tension between the proponents of a "return to the neighborhood"[50] and those favoring centralization within government, the role of government relative to any other sponsor of social welfare will remain enormous.

NOTES

1. P. Thoenes, *The Elite in the Welfare State* (New York: Free Press, 1966), p. 11.
2. K. de Schweinitz, *England's Road to Social Security* (Philadelphia: University of Pennsylvania Press, 1943), p. 19.
3. The continuing evolution of the separation of church and state is evident in the fact that payments to the indigent, though required by government, were secured mainly through church collections and paid out through the church wardens of local parishes.
4. Thoenes, *op. cit.*, p. 32.
5. Compare New York State's 1971 attempts to give migrants from other states one meal and a ticket home, mentioned in Chapter 3.
6. For extensive discussion of the provisions of the various Poor Laws, see Schweinitz, *op. cit.*, pp. 20-29; A. E. Fink, *The Field of Social Work* (New York: Holt, Rinehart and Winston, 1974), pp. 20-21; and W. I. Trattner, *From Poor Law to Welfare State: A History of Social Welfare in America* (New York: Free Press, 1974), pp. 1-12.
7. K. Woodroofe, *From Charity to Social Work in England and the United States* (Toronto: University of Toronto Press, 1962), pp. 14-17.
8. C. I. Schottland, "The Changing Roles of Government and Family," in P. E. Weinberger (ed.), *Perspectives on Social Welfare: An Introductory Anthology* (New York: Macmillan, 1974), p. 129
9. Comprehensive accounts of the beginnings of the Social Security Act are found in E. W. Witte, *The Development of the Social Security Act* (Madison: University of Wisconsin Press, 1962); and in A. J. Altmeyer, *The Formative Years of Social Security* (Madison: University of Wisconsin Press, 1966).
10. D. P. Moynihan, *The Politics of a Guaranteed Income: The Nixon Administration and the Family Assistance Plan* (New York: Vintage, 1973).
11. A. Briggs, "The Welfare State in Historical Perspective," in M. N. Zald (ed.), *Social Welfare Institutions* (New York: Wiley, 1965).
12. W. Manchester, *The Glory and the Dream: A Narrative History of America, 1932-1972* (Boston: Little, Brown, 1973), p. 111.
13. W. E. Leuchtenberg, *Franklin D. Roosevelt and the New Deal* (New York: Harper & Row, 1963). For a full description of the Townsend movement, see A. Holtzman, *The Townsend Movement* (New York: Bookman, 1963).

14. R. Goldston, *The Great Depression: The United States in the Thirties* (Greenwich, Conn.: Fawcett, 1968), p. 151.
15. Altmeyer, *op. cit.*, p. 75.
16. *Ibid.*, p. 10.
17. *Ibid.*, p. 75.
18. *Ibid.*, p. 61.
19. *Ibid.*, p. 99.
20. Goldston, *op. cit.*, pp. 152–56. Technically, it was termed "Share Our Wealth," but it was usually referred to as "Share the Wealth."
21. Altmeyer, *op. cit.*, p. 10.
22. *Ibid.*, p. 12; Goldston, *op. cit.*, p. 157.
23. J. Axinn and H. Levin, *Social Welfare: A History of the American Response to Need* (New York: Dodd, Mead, 1975).
24. G. Perrett, *Days of Sadness, Years of Triumph: The American People 1939–1945* (Baltimore: Penguin, 1973), p. 342.
25. *Ibid.*, p. 341.
26. *Ibid.*
27. F. F. Piven, "Federal Interventions in the Cities: The New Urban Programs as a Political Strategy," in E. O. Smigel (ed.), *Handbook on the Study of Social Problems* (Chicago: Rand McNally, 1971).
28. Exod., 16:3, 8.
29. *Introduction to Social Security: A Workers' Education Manual* (Geneva: International Labor Organization, 1970), p. 3.
30. Woodroofe, *op. cit.*, p. 12.
31. C. R. Attlee, *The Social Worker* (London: Bell, 1920), p. 162.
32. Manchester, *op. cit.*, pp. 10–19.
33. Goldston, *op. cit.*, p. 124.
34. P. Bachrach and M. S. Baratz, *Power and Poverty: Theory and Practice* (New York: Oxford University Press, 1970), p. 105.
35. For example, see L. A. Coser, *The Functions of Social Conflict* (New York: Free Press, 1954), and L. A. Coser, *Continuities in the Study of Social Conflict* (New York: Free Press, 1967).
36. Bachrach and Baratz, *op. cit.*, p. 44.
37. S. Verba, *Small Groups and Political Behavior* (Princeton, N.J.: Princeton University Press, 1961), pp. 206–43.
38. "Although it has generally been recognized that riots are motivated in part by legitimate grievances, the ensuing political response clearly reveals that order has been given priority over justice [and that] control recommendations [are] implemented without concomitant implementation of social reform measures." J. H. Skolnick, *The Politics of Protest: A Task Force Report Submitted to the National Commission on the Causes and Prevention of Violence* (New York: Simon & Schuster, 1969), p. 343.
39. Moynihan, *op. cit.*, p. 12. (Emphasis in original.)
40. P. Cutright, "Political Structure, Economic Development, and National Social Security Programs," *American Journal of Sociology*, 70 (March 1965):537. This is not an absolute: Kuwait, which is hardly a democracy, the Amir being absolute ruler and required to be a descendant of Mubarak al-Sabah, spends $240 annually per person on health, education, and

welfare, compared to $210 spent by England. There is no income tax in Kuwait, and telephone service is free. "Not only is education free in Kuwait from the kindergarten to the university level, but each student is provided with free transportation, free books and stationery, free school uniforms, a daily well-rounded hot meal and afternoon snacks." *The Arab World,* Vol. 40, No. 3 (New York: Arab Information Center, 1965).

41. H. L. Pryor, *Public Expenditures in Communist and Capitalist Nations* (Homewood, Ill.: Irwin, 1968).
42. Bachrach and Baratz, *op. cit.,* p. 42.
43. For an excellent description of this process, albeit in another context, see D. Halberstam, *The Best and the Brightest* (New York: Random House, 1972).
44. C. E. Lindblom, "The Science of 'Muddling Through,' " *Public Administration Review,* 19 (1959):79–88; also D. Braybrooke and C. E. Lindblom, *A Strategy of Decision: Policy Evaluation as a Social Process* (New York: Free Press, 1963).
45. H. L. Wilensky, *The Welfare State and Equality: Structural and Ideological Roots of Public Expenditures* (Berkeley: University of California Press, 1975); this finding has been questioned, however; see L. S. Miller, "The Structural Determinants of the Social Welfare Effort: A Critique and a Contribution," *Social Service Review,* 50 (March 1976):57–79.
46. Perrett, *op. cit.,* pp. 84–86.
47. Thoenes, *op. cit.,* p. 129.
48. For the working out of the political process as it affects social welfare, see G. Y. Steiner, *Social Insecurity: The Politics of Welfare* (Chicago: Rand McNally, 1966), especially Chapter 8.
49. C. E. Gilbert, "Policy Making in Public Welfare," *Political Science Quarterly,* 81 (June 1966):197–98.
50. J. L. Vigilante, "Back to the Old Neighborhood," *Social Service Review,* 50 (June 1976): 194.

6

Economics

There is no social-welfare program without an economic aspect, if for no other reason than that programs cost money. The economic *motivation* for social welfare, however, arises either from a desire to reduce the cost of social problems or because sufferers from such problems hurt the economy in various ways.

THE COST OF SOCIAL PROBLEMS

Social problems are expensive, and it is the avowed goal of some social-welfare programs to reduce expenses to society by alleviating or eliminating a problem. This is a very compelling motivation for social-welfare programs, and many are approved either because they submit cost-benefit analyses proving that the economic benefits of the program outweigh its costs[1] or because there is a general consensus that the program will reduce the cost of social problems. Counseling services, for example, are generally understood to reduce the costs associated with mental illness and marital problems. Further, some programs are approved because they are expected to bring the same benefits as existing programs but at less cost.[2] For example, probation has been urged over incarceration because the former costs 38 cents a day, and the latter, $5.24.[3] Finally, there are even programs that are intended to show a profit: Vocational-rehabilitation programs have been proposed and defended because, "for every federal dollar spent in their rehabilitation, the rehabilitated employed person pays from $7 to $10 in federal income taxes each year for the remainder of his working life."[4]

The total cost of social problems—both direct and indirect—is difficult to determine exactly.[5] However, the cost of mental illness in the United States, as "conservatively" measured in 1971, was $26.2 billion.[6] Given a population of approximately 200 million at that time, mental illness put a burden of $131 on each American, or considering about one in four to be taxpayers, an average cost of more than $500 per taxpayer.

Programs to reduce crime and juvenile delinquency, such as neighborhood and community centers, street-corner workers, youth movements, and other leisure-time and character-building efforts are sometimes justified in terms of property damage avoided and crimes not committed. Nevertheless, though the cost of crime to the nation has been described as staggering—each year losses of $20 billion to $25 billion burden American society,[7] and these are just the direct property losses: institutionalization alone costs more than $800 million annually[8] —this does not mean that a program to prevent juvenile delinquency and crime costing, let us say, $15 billion would be approved, despite the $5 billion to $10 billion saving that might ensue. For reasons to be discussed later, there are limits to the amount of money society is willing to spend for social welfare, regardless of savings. Further, insofar as crime is concerned, there is the view that the cost of eliminating, or almost eliminating, crime would be greater than the losses from criminal activity. Therefore, from a purely economic point of view, "the money spent on crime ... may actually be a bargain for society."[9]

Despite such caveats, the fact remains that programs that promise to cut the costs of social problems stand better chances of acceptance than those that do not. For example, total expenditures for health and medical care in 1972 reached $76.5 billion,[10] and a social-welfare program that could prove, by demonstration, that $10 spent on counseling patients would save $100 in Medicare or Medicaid payments would be presenting a strong case for sponsorship. However, to gain acceptance the promised savings would have to be immediate and result from a causal chain of no more than one step. To illustrate this problem: Arbitrarily assume that 5 percent of medical costs are somehow rooted in economic distress—insufficient or improper food, bad sanitary conditions, crowdedness, poor housing, insufficient clothing, untreated minor symptoms, and so forth.[11] Relieving this economic distress would save the country, in medical costs, $3.8 billion. This is precisely three times the estimated cost of the defeated Family Assistance Plan,[12] or, to put it differently, the income guarantee promised under that plan could have been three times more generous. Logically, this might have removed the objections of those who were opposed to the plan because of low benefits. However, this argument, even if supported by appropriate evidence, would probably not have influenced the vote on the plan, because the distance from higher income among the poor to generally lower health costs involves too many hard-to-discern steps.

   Although the economic motivation for social welfare is not the only one, it is strong for a number of reasons. Savings, like mother love, are hard to oppose, particularly in societies where those who must approve the program must also bear the cost. By contrast, political motivations are usually hidden: People who support a program do not usually admit that their reason is to add to their own political power, or that they believe it will co-opt, and thus control, the disaffected. Religious motivations may also be suspect in secular societies and those with church-state separation. And mutual aid, of course, does not require approval of programs. Thus, economic (and, as will be seen, ideological) considerations are the most overt and socially approved motivations.

   Economic considerations are used in many places to justify various kinds of welfare programs. For example, the "workfare" program (WIN) proposed by President Richard M. Nixon has been placed in judgment on purely economic grounds: "What would be the cost of this kind of program . . . would it be cheaper than simply maintaining families on public assistance?"[13] Family planning in Egypt has been justified on the basis that the economic benefit of preventing a birth is estimated to be 2.5 to 8.7 times as great as the cost.[14]

   In addition to those direct costs of social problems that social-welfare programs are mounted to reduce, there is also the cost of social welfare itself to consider. Measures that would reduce the number of people on welfare—whether receiving cash, in-kind benefits, or services—also result in savings. One method of reducing costs, then—even if it solves no problem—is to make eligibility for relief more restrictive. This might be through an income limitation, and in such cases the means test is a device to determine eligibility. Another method of reducing costs, however, is to maintain existing income limitations but to make the means test itself, as well as other procedures, so slow, cumbersome, and demeaning that eligible people are deterred from applying.[15] Still another way is to hedge the law with restrictions. For example, in New York State, work-related expenses are deductible from income for purposes of determining eligibility for relief. However, the amount of such expenses is limited to $80 per month. Families whose work expenses are more than $80, and that would be eligible for relief were they allowed to deduct the full amount of their actual work expenses, are barred from such help.[16]

   In addition to the direct costs of social problems, such as property loss, the costs of institutions and services, and payments, there is also a whole congeries of indirect costs, hard to quantify, but present nevertheless. Deterioration of housing leads to tax losses; incarceration of prisoners may lead to child neglect or breakup of families; lack of perceived opportunity may lead to drug abuse. As Harrington points out, "Poverty is expensive to maintain. . . . In some cities a quarter of the annual funds are devoted to taking care of the special fire, police, and health problems created by the slums."[17] It is not surprising, then, that social-welfare programs often seek to justify themselves in terms of the money they save rather than the money they spend.

EFFECTS ON THE ECONOMY

Production

One must take into consideration, in addition to the direct and indirect costs of social problems, their other effects on the economy.[18] One such effect is the impact of problem-ridden people on production. In all industrialized countries, there is heavy emphasis on production. The production of goods and services makes possible employment, which in turn distributes the resources of society. People who do not or cannot work—or whose work is not sufficiently productive—are a drag on the economy. Hence, there is a strong pressure within all social-welfare programs to prepare people for, or return them to, productive employment.

The view that social-welfare measures are good for the economy dates back to the earliest social-welfare legislation. The Statute of Laborers of 1349 was concerned about beggars not as a problem of destitution but, rather, as a seepage from the supply of labor[19] that reduced production. Its modern application has been clearly enunciated:

> From the experience of developed nations it is proved that welfare policies contribute to increased production over time, and also ensure better balance between different sectors of the economy. Price support policies, agricultural subsidies, unemployment insurance are examples. . . . Welfare is not a leakage of national resources but a contribution to productive capacity.[20]

In Rumania, for instance, it is the express purpose of social welfare that "all individuals, groups, and communities shall produce material and cultural goods."[21]

This view is often the major motivation for social-welfare programs in rehabilitation, vocational training or retraining, education, child welfare, community centers, and employment. A clear expression of this view is that of Kershaw: "Increasing welfare payments . . . frequently is the factor that will permit a child to stay in school or a mother to work or become literate, and hence will have a payoff in increased productivity of labor."[22] The "investment in welfare" approach has also been applied to education: "Funds devoted to pre-schools and schools in . . .

low-income areas are sound investments and will result in increased employment and productivity and reduced welfare expenditures."[23] Thus, social welfare is looked upon as an investment, and its justification becomes the anticipated return in productivity.[24]

One of the major methods of attempting to increase the productivity of welfare recipients is to establish training or retraining programs intended to inculcate job habits and skills.[25] Such programs are beset with many problems, and have been since their beginnings.[26] The most obvious problem is the necessity to train for jobs that are needed, that is, to be reasonably certain that graduates will be able to get jobs in the fields for which they prepare. The job market changes rapidly, however, with the result that only very short courses can be easily matched with job opportunities;[27] and the skills learned in very short courses are mostly for poor-paying, dead-end jobs[28] or the types of jobs for which training courses are virtually unnecessary—night watchmen, motel maids, and so forth.[29] Insofar as long-term job opportunities are concerned, the lag between identifying the need and including the material in formal educational structures may be as long as fifty years.[30] It is no surprise, therefore, that "course offerings have no relationship with the current labor market and, indeed, often run as though oblivious of it."[31] Even when the emphasis is not upon specific skills but upon basic traits, "The core of the matter is that the world of work is not served by institutions or budgets which provide fundamentals, adaptiveness, and skill flexibility."[32]

A further problem is the need for prerequisite basic skills, such as reading and writing at a high school level, which many applicants do not have. Then there is the need for concurrent counseling and advice, concerning external problems that might cause the trainee to drop out, or problems within the course itself. In many cases, a subsidy payment during the training period is necessary. Finally, even when the trainees graduate and get jobs for which they were trained, they are dismissed because of personal characteristics: They have poor health, poor personalities, or poor dispositions; they talk too much or are careless, untidy, intemperate, or unreliable.[33]

As for the disadvantaged, job training is even more questionable as a method of relieving their problems. Successful trainees do increase their incomes, and at an even greater rate than others do. "Nevertheless, the average disadvantaged enrollee was not raised out of poverty ... the trend was simply from deep in the depths of poverty to near its upper ranges.... The Joint Economic Commission found in this fact reason to doubt the usefulness of manpower training programs."[34] Further, if an overall reduction in unemployment is the goal, it has been found that there is little that a remedial program can do to reduce the general level of unemployment in the short run.[35] Some training programs, in fact, have been found to have negative effects. Black female welfare recipients who fail in courses or in the work world tend to become more dependent on welfare and unwilling to try again.[36]

The desire to increase the productive capacity of the country by returning those afflicted with problems to the labor market, despite the demonstrated limited usefulness of such attempts, is matched by the desire to reduce the cost of social welfare by shifting recipients from welfare rolls to payrolls or to school rolls. At one point during the 1960s, "street gangs were being bribed with federal grants for 'job training.' "[37]

The futility of this approach is illustrated in the experience of the previously described WIN program, which requires welfare recipients receiving Aid to Families with Dependent Children to register for work or for work training:

> [Of] about 1.6 million welfare cases eligible for the WIN program . . . only about 10 percent . . . were considered suitable for enrollment. . . . Of all those who had been terminated from WIN by April 1, 1970, only about 20 percent had jobs. Hence, the WIN program was successful in getting jobs for only about 2 percent of the total eligible welfare population.[38]

Returning people to the labor market is not the only way in which social welfare is used to help the economy. Keeping certain people out of the labor force is also a goal. Mass unemployment, which attended the Great Depression in the United States, made provision of jobs an imperative. There is little question, therefore, that one of the major motivations for the old-age portion of the Social Security Act—Old-Age, Survivors' and Disability Insurance (OASDI)—was a desire to remove millions of older people from the labor force, thus making jobs for younger workers.[39] And, in fact, what began as a program that made it possible for a person to retire if he wished to, on reaching the specified age, was quickly transmuted by restrictive provisions[40] and by public custom into forced retirement.

The situation of the aged in the United States is a good illustration of the strength of economic motivations in social welfare. The mandatory age for receiving old-age benefits was set in 1935 at sixty-five, probably because this was the conventional age in use in European programs. At that time, the average life expectancy at birth in the United States was about fifty-five years.[41] By 1972, life expectancy had risen to almost seventy years.[42] Logically, one would expect the mandatory retirement age—or even the age at which pensions begin—to have risen proportionately. Indeed, there is a close correlation between life expectancy at birth and the date at which old-age pensions begin, viewed nationally.[43] Typically, developing countries with short life expectancies, particularly those in Africa, begin their pension plans at age fifty-five, and some even at age fifty. Mali, for example, with an average life expectancy of thirty-three years,[44] begins old-age grants at age fifty-five, with the possibility of retiring on a smaller pension at fifty.[45] Sweden, with the world's highest life expectancy (72.12 years),[46] begins pensions at sixty-seven and does not require retirement from work to collect.[47]

Despite this general correlation of life expectancy with eligibility for old-age pensions, there is very little chance that the retirement age will be raised in the United States with increasing longevity. Although it is likely that increased longevity results from better health (despite a proportion of what has been called "medicated survival"), and that therefore people can work productively for a longer period, there is every likelihood that the age for eligibility will be lowered, rather than raised, for this is one of the simplest ways to ensure job openings for younger people.[48] In 1972, about one-fourth of family heads over age sixty-five were in the labor force, but this is expected to decline to one-fifth by 1980, "as involuntary retirement becomes institutionalized throughout the economy, making way for the very large pool of young job entrants born between 1949 and 1957. Indeed, it is likely that the age of involuntary retirement will be lowered in response to this population pressure, and that of a recession economy."[49] One serious proposal to this effect was made in New York City in 1974, when budget-cutting required a number of layoffs. It was proposed to lower the mandatory retirement age to sixty-three, thus getting rid of workers who could, presumably, live on their pensions, and preserving the jobs of younger workers.[50]

There are other inequalities in the Social Security program in the United States—for example, the fact that "nonwhites, on the average, can expect to live fewer years than is true of whites,"[51] but nevertheless begin their pensions at the same age—but these arise from noneconomic considerations to be discussed later.

The aged are not the only group that social policy attempts to keep out of the labor force. Because an increase in the minimum wage would lift many of the working poor out of their present positions, and would not affect those making more than the minimum, such a move is regularly suggested. The response is as regularly given: that raising the minimum wage would require industry and services to pay marginally productive people the same as productive people, thus raising the cost of manufacturing or service, and contributing to inflation; or, contrariwise, that it would cause management to release the marginally productive workers, thus contributing to unemployment. In short, it is deemed better to allow less productive people to work and earn less, and have the difference made up by social welfare, than to have higher unemployment figures. This type of underemployment, incidentally, consisting of people employed only seasonally or part-time who would like to work more regularly or longer hours than they do, is an important factor in the "masking" of the true extent of unemployment.

Because the minimum wage in the United States at the time of this writing is $2.30 per hour, anyone working a forty-hour week at the minimum rate will make $4,784 a year. Since the official poverty line in the United States is $5,400 for an urban family of four, the minimum wage offers no relief to such families if they are poor.

In this manner, welfare subsidizes the work of supposedly marginally productive people, who are paid less than subsistence wages. A histori-cal parallel to this situation occurred in 1795 when some justices and clergymen in Berkshire, England, meeting in Speenhamland, guaran-teed a wage supplement to workers whenever wages dropped below a "floor" based upon the cost of bread and family size. The experiment was disastrous, because employers promptly dropped wages, thereby increasing their profits, while the government made up the wage differ-ence to workmen. The government was thus paying profits to owners while attempting to help workers.[52] The parallel to this situation in modern Medicaid and Medicare, where government subsidies in-tended to allow the poor and the aged to obtain medical care are exploited by the care-providers for their own profit, is clear.

The pressure to keep people out of the labor force is usually stronger during times of, and in countries with, high unemployment. Israel, as a labor-short economy, for example, begins retirement pensions at age seventy. In the United States, an official unemployment rate of about 5 percent has been considered acceptable—if not actually desirable—for many decades.[53] A rate higher than 5 percent is considered reces-sionary—too many people can't consume enough. A rate lower than 5 percent, however, is considered inflationary—too many marginally pro-ductive people are employed, which drives prices up. Were the unem-ployment rate to drop drastically, creating a labor shortage, one might witness changes in the Social Security regulations designed to draw the aged back into the labor force—by ignoring unearned income, for ex-ample. If high unemployment remains despite all measures, or even continues to grow, a result will be pressure to lower the retirement age. In either case, the economic motivation for social welfare is clearly present.

Consumption

Social welfare to increase production is but one side of the coin. The other is the effect of policies on consumption. An economy based on production requires, in exactly equal amounts, the ability to consume. A society suffers if it cannot consume all that it produces or cannot export the surplus. Indeed, the Great Depression in the United States is usually said to have been caused by overproduction in relation to consumption, and not by underproduction. In this sense, then, people who do not consume sufficiently are also a drag on the economy. Consequently, an important part of America's economic system is based upon advertising, which is basically an attempt to induce people to purchase, that is, to consume. That more than 9 million new automobiles were sold in the United States during 1976, though they represented relatively minor modifications of existing models, was not only a triumph of advertising and the consumer psychology it created but also evidence of the need for continued consumption to maintain the economy.

Because poor people do not have enough money to spend, their condition is a deterrent to the country's prosperity. A publication of the Department of Health, Education, and Welfare makes this clear:

> It is basic to the good health of a market-oriented economy that consumption keep pace with production. . . . Industrial societies have thus learned to place a high value on the role of social welfare programs in helping to maintain a stable and progressive growth in the total economy.[54]

The importance of poor people as consumers is emphasized by the fact that the poor spend a greater proportion of their income on consumable items than do the more affluent: Food, clothes, transportation, fuel, and so forth make up a large part of the budget of the poor, while the more affluent are able to save, invest, buy capital goods, and in general spend on nonconsumable items.

One way of increasing consumption by the poor is, obviously, to put money into their hands, and this is what most insurance and grant programs do. However, it is also possible to force consumption on the poor, as it were, by giving them all or part of their relief in food or other material items. Food has been distributed directly to the poor for many years through many programs, antedating cash relief in the United States, which did not begin under government auspices until the 1930s.[55] Christmas and Thanksgiving baskets are still traditional in some voluntary organizations. "Soup kitchens" and "bread lines" are operated continuously in some areas, and in times of economic distress in others.[56] Giving out surplus farm commodities began during the Great Depression, and to prevent recipients from selling the products rather than eating them, a number of devices were used, including dyeing potatoes a deep blue. From the actual distribution of food, the program moved to giving out stamps to be exchanged for food and selling stamps for less than their redeemable value in food. At present, there are four large federal programs—the Food Stamp, Commodity Distribution, Special Milk, and School Lunch programs—and several smaller and local programs, such as Meals-on-Wheels for the aged and disabled and playground lunches.

As discussed previously, food stamps serve both a liberating function, in allowing recipients to choose the food that they want and its purveyor, and a control function, in assuring that the help given is used for food and nothing else.[57] The economic motivation for this program is most clearly evident, however, in connection with food stamps and agricultural surpluses. The major purpose of giving food stamps instead of money is to aid in the distribution of agricultural surpluses, thus keeping retail prices at a level that would benefit farmers.[58] In fact, the Food Stamp Act of 1964, as adopted, begins, "AN ACT TO strengthen the agricultural economy. . . ."[59] Further, the chairman of the Senate Agricultural Committee stated in 1966 that "the Special Milk Program was for the producer, rather than a program to assist children."[60] The continuation of this motivation is seen in the fact that the Food Stamp Program continues to be lodged in the Department of Agriculture, rather than the Department of Health, Education, and Welfare. Reports on the efficacy and efficiency of the program are available in publications of the former, and it is this department that reports on the program to Congress.[61] A further indication of the influence of agricultural and economic considerations in this program is in the restrictions it contains. Food stamps may not be used to purchase imported foods, cleaning materials, paper goods, or—for other reasons—cigarettes, beer, or other alcoholic beverages. They may be used only for products that directly aid the American farmer.[62]

From the recipients' point of view, food stamps are a distinct addition to income, and the opportunity to buy more with stamps than would be possible with cash alone is a not inconsiderable gain for many poor families. On the other hand, the requirement that stamps be purchased in advance creates an insurmountable difficulty for families living from hand to mouth. There are also problems of transportation—to get the stamps, to get to a store that will accept stamps (many do not), and to get home with the packages. The program is also felt by some to be stigmatizing, and some store owners have been accused of discriminating against food-stamp users by not allowing them "specials" or unusual bargains. For these reasons, among others, for every additional 100 welfare recipients, there are only 53 more Food Stamp Program participants; whereas for every additional 100 unemployed, there are 95 more Food Stamp Program participants. Evidently, the recently unemployed are not in as dire straits as those who go on welfare.[63] The connection between production and consumption is clearly demonstrated by a little-known requirement that food-stamp recipients, with the exception of those in certain categories, must register for work.[64]

Although the Food Stamp Program is a case in point, the totality of programs, and even the very terminology, of social welfare reflects "a central concern in American life—economics. Production, distribution, exchange, and consumption occupy at least half the time of those in the mainstream. A consumer psychology orders our view of life."[65] It is therefore no accident that economic considerations are paramount in many conceptions of social welfare.

Social welfare affects the economy, but the economy also affects social welfare, and perhaps even more profoundly. In Cutright's study of seventy-six countries, mentioned in Chapter 5, political representativeness was found to be the strongest indicator of coverage of social-insurance programs, but only if economic differences are held constant. More important than political differences was the impact of economics. In summary, Cutright found that social-insurance coverage is highly correlated with economic affluence: "The level of economic development has a power role in determining the level of social-insurance development . . . the level of economic development is related to social-insurance program experience."[66] In other words, the more affluent a country, the more likely it is to have good social-insurance coverage.

From this flows the attitude that policy measures that lead to higher and higher Gross National Products are of the most importance, and social security and social welfare should be geared to guarantee ever higher GNPs. This has been termed the "trickle down" theory, which says, in effect, that the richer the country, the better off the poor will be. Increasing the Gross National Product thus becomes a talismanic incantation, while social welfare is presumed to occur almost automatically—or, in any event, without too much extra thought or effort. On an international level, this has been expressed as a belief that when welfare grows out of economic development, that is sound, but if welfare considerations precede development plans, they may inhibit economic growth and be an obstacle to economic development. The effects of social welfare and affluence may also be seen as reciprocal—the more that social welfare helps the economy, the better the social-welfare program will be, which will, in turn, be helpful to the economy, and so on.

SOCIAL WELFARE AS AN ECONOMIC SIDE EFFECT

Finally, just as the political process has side effects that result in social-welfare programs, so are there spin-offs from the economic process. For one thing, once programs are embedded in the economy, they are never phased out and never disappear. For example, it was assumed at the beginning of Social Security that when pensions to the aged began to be paid, there would be no further need for direct assistance to the aged. In his account of the beginnings of Social Security, Alt-meyer recalls:

> I well remember the November 27 meeting when the staff exhibited a wall chart which illustrated how the plan would work. It showed two lines: one declining year by year, which represented the declining num-ber of old age assistance recipients, the other rising year by year, which represented the number of old age insurance beneficiaries. The two lines eventually crossed, demonstrating how the old age insurance system would gradually liquidate the old age assistance system.[67]

That was in 1935. In 1974, 1.82 million people were still receiving old-age assistance,[68] and though the program has been combined with others as Supplemental Security Income, there is no reason to believe that the number of recipients has declined or will decline.

In fact, welfare programs almost invariably grow over time.[69] Benefits become larger, and more people are blanketed in. Consequently, a study done by Wilensky, covering sixty-four countries, found a strong correlation between the age of social-welfare programs and their cost and coverage.[70] Wilensky argues that both the age of the population (another strong indicator of the amount of coverage) and the age of the program are linked to the affluence of the country.

Further, not only is the cost of a program a strong factor in determin-ing whether or not it will be approved, but safeguards against excessive costs become important parts of program planning, and arouse more discussion than do the benefits the program is designed to impart.

There is a further economic aspect to consider: Owing to federal-state funding arrangements in the United States, a locality might mount a social-welfare program in order to qualify for grants. A publication of the State of New York reads, in part:

> Did You Know?
> Hundreds of thousands of New York State residents are eligible for Food Stamps but are not using them.
> If every eligible person used Food Stamps, it could mean many millions of dollars in new Federal money for the State economy.
> New Federal money means hundreds of new jobs for New Yorkers.
> The Food Stamp Program is paid for by Federal funds. No municipal or county taxes pay for the Food Stamp Program.[71]

Another example of social welfare as a by-product[72] of the economic system, arising from federal-state financial arrangements, is contained in the experiment mentioned in Chapter 2 in which simple declarations of need were used in place of very complicated application forms. Although the ineligibility rate revealed with the use of simplified forms, through spot checks, was no higher than that found with the use of conventional forms, the simple forms were never widely adopted. One reason seems to be that the Social Security amendments of 1962 guaranteed to states 75 percent repayment of the cost of social services, with no limit as to amounts. Accordingly, it became financially important to states to have their social-welfare activities defined as "services" rather than as "payments"—the former being a definition that both simple declarations and separation of services from payments made it difficult to make and to defend.

Perhaps the most salient feature of the economic impact on social welfare, however, is summed up in this wry epigram: "When we can afford it, we don't need it. When we need it, we can't afford it."

NOTES

1. This is easier said than done. For a description of some of the problems in using cost-benefit analyses for social services, and the differences between cost-benefit and cost-effectiveness analyses, see A. M. Gross, *Is Cost Benefit Analysis Beneficial? Is Cost Effectiveness Analysis Effective?* (Waltham, Mass.: Heller School, Brandeis University, 1976) (mimeographed).

2. One of the arguments advanced for Nixon's Family Assistance Plan was that a saving would ensue. "A guaranteed income could be had for $1.3 billion. This was no more than the cost of the proposed changes in the food-stamp program. . . . Service programs were just as expensive, however partial their coverage, and in many instances considerably more expensive." D. P. Moynihan, *The Politics of a Guaranteed Income: The Nixon Administration and the Family Assistance Plan* (New York: Free Press, 1969), p. 143. (Emphasis in original.) See also a comparison of day-care and Head Start costs, ranging from $640 to $5,380 per child, in J. E. Bedger, "Cost Analysis in Day Care and Head Start," *Child Welfare*, 53 (1974):514–23.

3. "Crime in America," in A. Birenbaum and E. Sagarin, *Social Problems: Private Troubles and Public Issues* (New York: Scribner's, 1972), pp. 429–54.

4. B. J. Black, "Vocational Rehabilitation," in *Encyclopedia of Social Work* (New York: National Association of Social Workers, 1965), pp. 819–20. Rehabilitation of the mentally retarded has also been urged because "it is good economics . . . rehabilitation is a profitable undertaking." J. F. Garrett and B. W. Griffis, "The Economic Benefits of Rehabilitation of the Mentally Retarded," *Welfare in Review*, 9 (March–April 1971):1–7.

5. On the difficulty of determining social costs, see R. M. Titmuss, *Social Policy: An Introduction* (New York: Pantheon, 1974), p. 60.

6. E. J. Lieberman (ed.), *Mental Health: The Public Health Challenge* (Washington, D.C.: American Public Health Association, 1975).

7. R. S. Benson and H. Wolman (eds.), *Counterbudget: A Blueprint for Changing National Priorities 1971–76* (New York: Praeger, 1971), p. 218.

8. E. Studt, "Crime and Delinquency: Institutions," in *Encyclopedia of Social Work* (New York: National Association of Social Workers, 1971), p. 186.

9. R. Quinney, "The Future of Crime," in J. A. Inciardi and H. A. Siegel (eds.), *Emerging Social Issues: A Sociological Perspective* (New York: Praeger, 1975), p. 198.

10. S. B. Kamerman and A. J. Kahn, *Social Services in the United States: Policies and Programs* (Philadelphia: Temple University Press, 1976), p. 543.

11. Physical defects due to hunger alone are estimated to affect 10 million Americans. C. Hampden-Turner, *From Poverty to Dignity* (Garden City, N.Y.: Anchor, 1975), p. 91; Bremner says, "Sickness struck the poor more frequently than the well-to-do . . . their bad housing, improper diet, strenuous labor in adverse surroundings, and inability to acquire regular medical attention made the poorer classes more susceptible to the attacks of disease." R. H. Bremner, *From the Depths: The Discovery of Poverty in the United States* (New York: New York University Press, 1956), p. 258.

12. Moynihan, *op. cit.*, p. 143.

13. R. D. Husby, "Child Day Care for Welfare Mothers," *Social Work*, 19 (July 1974):420–26.

14. G. C. Zaidan, *The Costs and Benefits of Family Planning Programs* (Baltimore: Johns Hopkins Press, 1971), p. 2.

15. Glennerster discusses a number of such ways to ration service. H. Glennerster, *Social Service Budgets and Social Policy: British and American Experience* (New York: Barnes and Noble, 1975), p. 39.

16. *Roundtree, Folsom, and Pelligrino* v. *New York State Department of Social Services,* Memorandum and Order, and Dissenting Opinion, 75-C-1052, U.S. District Court, Eastern District of New York. The dissent held that insofar as the expenses were legitimately work-related, it was discrimination to grant relief to people with few such expenses and withhold it from those with many expenses, because the amount of expenses is not under the control of the worker.

17. M. Harrington, *The Other America* (New York: Macmillan, 1963), p. 133.

18. See E. Winston, "The Contribution of Social Welfare to Economic Growth," *Social Welfare Forum 1966* (New York: Columbia University Press, 1966), pp. 3–24.

19. K. de Schweinitz, *England's Road to Social Security* (Philadelphia: University of Pennsylvania Press, 1943), p. 6.

20. S. L. Parmar, "What Good Is Economic Betterment . . .," *CERES,* 3 (1970):21.

21. *Organization and Administration of Social Welfare Programs: Romania* (New York: United Nations, 1967), p. 4.

22. J. A. Kershaw, "The Attack on Poverty," in M. S. Gordon (ed.), *Poverty in America* (San Francisco: Chandler, 1965), p. 56.

23. M. B. Folsom, "Measures to Reduce Poverty," in Gordon, *op. cit.,* p. 67.

24. Such statements run throughout discussions of social-welfare policy; for

example: "Society needs the productive effort of every person, and it is good business to help handicapped individuals to be maximally productive." E. B. Whitten, "Disability and Physical Handicap: Vocational Rehabilitation," in *Encyclopedia of Social Work, op. cit.*, p. 236; also J. A. Schofield, "The Economic Return to Preventive Social Work," *International Journal of Social Economics*, 3 (1976):167–78.

25. About $2.8 billion was invested in manpower programs of various kinds during 1971. S. A. Levitan, "Manpower Programs Under New Management: Some Lessons Learned and Their Applications," in G. F. Rohrlich (ed.), *Social Economics for the 1970's: Programs for Social Security, Health, and Manpower* (New York: Dunellen, 1970), p. 143.

26. Welfare recipients, in particular, are expected to take jobs not covered by minimum-wage laws, or to work for less than the minimum wage. In 1970, the Secretary of Health, Education, and Welfare insisted that they work for $1.20 per hour, because $1.60 jobs were all filled. L. Goodwin, *Do the Poor Want to Work? A Social-Psychological Study of Work Orientations* (Washington, D.C.: The Brookings Institution, 1972), p. 172.

27. D. Macarov and G. Fradkin, *The Short Course in Development Activities* (Ramat Gan, Israel: Massada Press, 1973).

28. In 1942, one-quarter to one-half of youth trained in such programs failed to profit from them. S. C. Menefee, *Vocational Training and Employment of Youth* (New York: Da Capo Press, 1971). (Reprint of 1942 report.)

29. Hoos calls such jobs "disguised unemployment." T. R. Hoos, *Retraining the Work Force: An Analysis of Current Experience* (Berkeley: University of California Press, 1969), p. 192.

30. S. P. Marland, Jr., *Career Education: A Proposal for Reform* (New York: McGraw-Hill, 1974), p. 3.

31. Hoos, *op. cit.*, p. 258.

32. H. E. Striner, *1984 and Beyond: The World of Work* (Kalamazoo, Mich.: Upjohn, 1967), p. 6.

33. K. McFarland, "Why Men and Women Get Fired," *Personnel Journal*, 25 (1957):307.

34. G. L. Mangum and J. Walsh, *A Decade of Manpower Development and Training* (Salt Lake City: Olympus, 1973), pp. 34–35.

35. *Ibid.*, p. 140.

36. Goodwin, *op. cit.*, p. 113.

37. A. W. Green, *Social Problems: Arena of Conflict* (New York: McGraw-Hill, 1975), p. 16.

38. Goodwin, *op. cit.*, p. 114. The overall placement of WIN as of February 1971 was still only 20 percent.

39. A. Pincus and V. Wood, "Retirement," in *Encyclopedia of Social Work, op. cit.*, p. 1126.

40. The payment is reduced $1 for every $2 earned above $2,520 a year until age seventy-two. *Social Security Programs Throughout the World, 1975* (Washington, D.C.: Department of Health, Education, and Welfare, 1975), p. 236.

41. J. Agate, *The Practice of Geriatrics* (London: Heinemann, 1970), p. 2.

42. To 67.4 for men and 75.1 for women. *Demographic Yearbook 1974* (New York: United Nations, 1975), p. 1016.

43. There is a correlation of .95 between the latest life-expectancy figures reported in *ibid.*, and the age at which government old-age pensions begin, according to *Social Security Programs Throughout the World, op. cit.*, for the 104 countries reporting both figures.

44. The lowest life expectancy of countries reporting 1970 data. *Demographic Yearbook, op. cit.*, p. 1008.

45. *Social Security Programs Throughout the World, op. cit.*, p. 102.

46. *Demographic Yearbook, op. cit.*, p. 1032.

47. *Social Security Programs Throughout the World, op. cit.*, p. 212.

48. "Since one of the main purposes of the OASDI legislation was to remove older persons from the labor market, the legal definition of old age was based more on economic considerations than on biological, social, or psychological grounds. The age for retirement might well have been set higher if unemployment rates were lower." Pincus and Wood, *op. cit.*, p. 1127.

49. B. B. Hess, "America's Aged: Who, What, When, and Where?" in B. B. Hess (ed.), *Growing Old in America* (New Brunswick, N.J.: Transaction, 1976).

50. *Ibid.*

51. J. J. Jackson, "Aged Blacks: A Potpourri in the Direction of the Reduction of Inequality," in *ibid.*, p. 408.

52. S. Webb and B. Webb, *The Prevention of Destitution* (London: National Committee for the Prevention of Destitution, 1911). Not everyone agrees with their analysis. For a dissenting view, see M. Blaug, "The Myth of the Old Poor Law and the Making of the New," *Journal of Economic History*, 23 (June 1963):151.

53. The unemployment rate is subject to many definitional artifacts. Consequently, fluctuations from an alleged 4 percent in 1956, to 6.8 percent in 1958, to 4 percent in 1967, to 3.6 percent in 1968 represent differences in measurement as well as real differences. An average of 5 percent for the normal economic period is generally accepted as normative, however. The figures above are from Striner, *op. cit.*, and R. Munts and I. Garfinkel, *The Work Disincentive Effects of Unemployment Insurance* (Kalamazoo, Mich.: Upjohn, 1974).

54. E. Wickenden, *Social Welfare in a Changing World: The Place of Social Welfare in the Process of Development* (Washington, D.C.: Department of Health, Education, and Welfare, 1965).

55. J. Colcord, *Cash Relief* (New York: Sage, 1936), p. 32.

56. R. Goldston, *The Great Depression: The United States in the Thirties* (Greenwich, Conn.: Fawcett, 1968), pp. 49–50.

57. In short, that the poor would spend their resources wisely, rather than widely. Moynihan, *op. cit.*, p. 117.

58. *Ibid.*

59. Select Committee on Nutrition and Human Need, U.S. Senate, *Who Gets Food Stamps?* (Washington, D.C.: Government Printing Office, 1975), p. 29.

60. N. Kotz, *Let Them Eat Promises* (Garden City, N.Y.: Doubleday, 1971), p. 45.
61. Select Committee on Nutrition and Human Needs, U.S. Senate, *op. cit.*
62. Despite such documentation, the Department of Agriculture presents the program as "aimed at providing an adequate diet for the poor." B. K. Fishbein, *Social Welfare Abroad: Comparative Data on the Social Insurance and Public Assistance Programs of Selected Industrialized Democracies* (White Plains, N.Y.: Institute for Socioeconomic Studies, 1975).
63. F. K. Hines, *Factors Related to Participation in the Food Stamp Program* (Washington, D.C.: Department of Agriculture, 1975), p. 5.
64. S. A. Levitan, *Programs in Aid of the Poor in the 1970s* (Baltimore: Johns Hopkins Press, 1973); J. Richardson, *Food Stamp Program Reform: 94th Congress* (Washington, D.C.: Library of Congress, 1976).
65. R. R. Middleman and G. Goldberg, *Social Service Delivery: A Structural Approach to Social Work Practice* (New York: Columbia University Press, 1974), p. 3.
66. P. Cutright, "Political Structure, Economic Development, and National Social Security Programs," *American Journal of Sociology,* 70 (March 1965):537.
67. A. J. Altmeyer, *The Formative Years of Social Security* (Madison: University of Wisconsin Press, 1966), p. 26.
68. "Current Operating Statistics," *Social Security Bulletin,* 39 (March 1976): 59.
69. For examples of growth through mere existence, see M. Derthick, *Uncontrollable Spending for Social Service Grants* (Washington, D. C.: The Brookings Institution, 1975).
70. H. L. Wilensky, *The Welfare State and Equality: Structural and Ideological Roots of Public Expenditures* (Berkeley: University of California, 1975).
71. *How I Found a Way to Eat Better for Less Money* (Albany: New York State Department of Social Services, 1976).
72. D. Macarov, "Social Welfare as a By-Product: The Effect of Neo-mercantilism," *Journal of Sociology and Social Welfare* (forthcoming).

7
Ideology

ALTRUISM AND HUMANITARIANISM

One of the strongest and most widely held motivations for social welfare is the belief, feeling, attitude, or ideology that one should or must help other people. This is not the same thing as mutual aid, which is predicated upon helping and being helped; nor does it necessarily include a concept of divine commandment. Although it may coincide with political or economic motivations, it may as easily clash with them. On an individual basis, this might be termed altruism—behavior carried out to benefit another without anticipation of reward from an external source.[1] On a societal basis; it is usually referred to as humanitarianism —a concern for human social welfare.[2] When this concern becomes part of the ideology of an individual, group, state, or society, it is reflected in various social-welfare activities.

The roots of altruism are obscure. From a historical point of view, there appear to have been civilizations in which the idea of unselfishly helping another—particularly a stranger—would have seemed foolish, if not unnatural or even dangerous. Such a sentiment would probably have been alien to the Spartans, and wholehearted giving without corresponding personal gain would have puzzled an ancient Greek, who sought "attachment to another person chiefly as a means of strength for oneself."[3] In modern society, on the other hand, altruism has been termed the foundation of all social relations,[4] and in the early days of its investigation was considered of such overwhelming importance and ubiquity that a biological basis was imputed, if not proved.[5]

It seems more likely, however, that altruistic behavior arises from participation in mutual-aid activities, as a response to religious commandments, or even for egoistic reasons,[6] and later becomes an independent motivation, a value in itself.[7] In any case, there are discernible and measurable differences in the amount of altruism of individuals, and many variables that determine to what extent an individual will behave altruistically at any given time.[8] Like religious motivations, altruism may lead to direct involvement in social welfare, as by personally helping another, or to very indirect methods, such as voting for certain measures.[9]

When altruism is widely dispersed throughout a society, or even within a portion of society, it is generally thought of as an ideology, in which case it can be termed humanitarianism. There is little consensus concerning an exact definition of "ideology."[10] The word itself was first used in France—as *idéologie*—in 1797, and the school of thought that flowed from it was attacked by Napoleon. The word became popularized anew when Marx—for reasons not clearly understood—began to use it in a somewhat different context.[11] Although the concept is difficult to define, and thus used variously,[12] there is little disagreement as to the importance of ideology as a guide to thought and action. MacIver defines "ideology" as a system of political, economic, and social values and ideas from which objectives are derived.[13] Bluhm adds that ideologies not only tell us what is good and what we ought to do, but also explain the way things are and why they are that way.[14] Bell goes farther: "What gives ideology its force is its passion . . . the most important latent function of ideology is to tap emotion."[15] Ideology is also used to explain away inconvenient facts: "Facts are not indispensable to the central beliefs. They are rationalized with the beliefs if possible; otherwise they are ignored."[16]

In short, the way people view themselves and the world, the things they hold to be good and desirable, and the kind of world they prefer become a way of looking at things, a predisposition to assign values, and a guide to what is considered appropriate behavior. This is why a social-welfare plan that will reduce the cost of societal problems may be ignored or defeated, as noted in Chapter 6. "Quite often the ideological decision will have as much or more weight and meaning for an individual than his own immediate self-interest . . . and he will *behave* on the basis of ideology, rather than market considerations."[17]

In the political sphere, ideology is extremely important:[18]

The powerful political ideas of our time are almost all part of some ideology or other. To be sure, outposts of scholarship are to be found here and there in the intellectual landscape . . . but most of us see politics come to grips with the political world, and commit what paltry political acts we do commit under the influence of some ideology or other.[19]

Although it has been found that in new or developing states ideology becomes an even more central concept in making policy than it does in established or developed countries,[20] it is indeed a large and risky task to attempt to characterize a whole society's ideology.[21] Nevertheless, there is no lack of such attempts,[22] both general assertions that the social services cannot be understood apart from the particular culture in which they grew up[23] and specific delineations of national character: "The French character reveals two contradictory propensities: a very practical common sense with an immediate concern for material interests and, on the other hand, a great idealism, universalism, and humanism with intellectual brilliance."[24] Similarly: "There are cultural values that set us [the United States] apart from other nations—our economic individualism, our unusual emphasis on private property, the free market, and minimum government."[25]

Such delineations, whether they are correct or not, are not necessary as regards humanitarianism. Even cursory examination reveals that throughout the world purely humanitarian sentiments play a major part in the establishment and shaping of social-welfare programs. Particularly where irreversible conditions, such as aging and mental retardation, are concerned or where there is no prospect of equipping the person for, or returning him or her to, normal living (the severely disabled), one can only conclude that the helping activities undertaken spring from a desire to aid others. For example, two major motivations for OASDI in 1935 have been discussed previously—(1) the political fear of unrest and desire for political support by the aged and (2) the economic need to remove the aged from the labor force and to increase their consumptive capacity. The third root was a deep concern for the welfare of the aged. By and large, the aged were seen as among the "deserving poor": Their condition was not seen as resulting from their own behavior or deficiency (except, perhaps, by dyed-in-the-wool reactionaries who blamed them for not having saved for their old age), and they were therefore to be helped. It was the convergence of all three of these major motivations that resulted in the OASDI program. There were major objections to the entire Social Security Act, including opposition to the government's entering the insurance business and fears about the cost of the program, as well as concern for the "moral fiber" of recipients. Humanitarian considerations, however, combined with the other motivations to ensure passage. Conversely, it is most unlikely that such humanitarian goals would have resulted in passage of the bill had no political or economic considerations been involved, as witness the 27 million Americans currently living below the line declared by the American government to be the subsistence level. Humanitarian sentiments do not seem to be enough to overcome economic objections and the political powerlessness of the poor.

Similarly, humanitarian impulses and farm surpluses converged to result in the Food Stamp Program, discussed previously. It is doubtful whether such a program would have been instituted had there been a shortage of farm products in the United States. On the other hand, income maintenance is cheaper than "workfare,"[26] but the ideology of work proves stronger than the economic calculation.

Although humanitarianism as an ideology permeates most of human society, there are other ideologies that affect the scope and type of social welfare, and even its very existence. In some cultures there exists an ideology that the order of things has been foreordained, or decreed by God. Hence, not only are people powerless to effect change but attempts to do so are impious, if not heretical. Social welfare requires, therefore, an ideology of instrumental activism—a belief that people can change the world instead of having to accept a predestined order.[27] Or, in a somewhat different vein, a society may be characterized as tough-minded or tender-minded,[28] with consequent effects on social-welfare policies.

THE MYSTIQUE OF AGRICULTURE

Another ideology that structures social welfare sees agriculture as a mystique rather than as a job or a vocation. There are countries in which agriculture is invested with values over and above those resulting from the need for farm products. In such places, contact with the soil, with the seasons, with growing things is felt to have value for the individual. The farmer is idealized as the repository of the highest virtues of citizenship, and the farm family is visualized as self-sufficient, close-knit, and happy—sometimes either in spite of or because of poor soil, low income, and lack of amenities. In other settings, the value orientation is toward technology, scientism, large and rationally managed industries, and increasing industrialization. In such cases, the idealization might be that of happy workmen coming home from a factory where by their own efforts they have participated in a creative undertaking, and joining their families in constructive leisure activities. In either case, to the extent that these ideal types pervade the imagination of the people (or the planners), social-welfare services might be structured to strengthen the one or the other. Farm subsidies might flow from one orientation, together with little help for urban housing, and counseling services that literally urge people to go back to the farm. From the other orientation might flow very liberal fringe benefits, insurance plans linked to industrial work, plans for aiding labor mobility, and so forth.

In Israel, for example, there has been a heavy emphasis on agriculture since before independence. The Zionists and the founders of Israel reacted against the abnormal situation of European Jews—who were forbidden the ownership of land for many centuries—by emphasizing the necessity of forming a society with a broad base in agriculture. This led to measures to induce and help people to become farmers. New immigrants were allotted very cheap housing in farm villages and were given the necessary equipment, supplies, and instruction, while those who insisted on going to the cities received less help. Urban settlers were also given substantial help if they became farmers: "The main decisions concerning the development of agriculture were not taken on the basis of economic considerations. The high priority given to agricultural settlement over other types of development was motivated by political and ideological considerations."[29]

In Latin America too, there have been efforts to counteract the trend toward urbanization. Venezuela has used land reform, the establishment of rural services, and economic measures to this. end.[30] In African countries, on the contrary, there is no mystique of agriculture. Industrialization is the aim, and workers are recruited for industry from the farms and villages, with the approval and help of the government. In the United States, the mystique of agriculture converges with fear of unemployment, resulting in farm and acreage subsidies that keep millions of Americans on farms that otherwise would not support them. It has been estimated that almost twice as many Americans are farmers than are required for the same amount of production—or, put another way, that half the number of farmers could produce the same amount of farm products. The symbolic aspect of agriculture in American society is an important part of this situation.[31]

INDIVIDUALISM AND COLLECTIVISM

Ideologies concerning the comparative desirabilities of cooperative and individual endeavor also affect social-welfare policies and programs. Where individualism is seen as a virtue,[32] programs that are thought to create, encourage, or lay clients open to charges of dependence might be badly supported; where cooperation is a desideratum, programs that put a premium on mutual aid might receive much approbation:

If cultural tradition places a strong emphasis on individual responsibility, then collective solutions are likely to be resisted. On the other hand, a group can have values which stress the importance of collective action as a general rule, and, consequently, welfare problems, too, call forth a collective response.[33]

Israel places much stress on cooperatives and collectives: Almost the entire public health service is sponsored by labor unions, political parties, and other cooperative entities. In the United States, rugged individualism has always been considered an integral part of American ideology, to the extent that social-welfare programs, as noted previously, almost invariably start with the individual, and for some categories do not start at all. New immigrants, for example, are entirely dependent on voluntary agencies; there are no government units charged with the general absorption of new immigrants.[34] Africans, on the other hand, are said to lean toward cooperation rather than individualism: "I am because I participate" is the way this has been phrased.[35]

MISTRUST AS AN IDEOLOGY

Another ideological factor of major import for social welfare is the view, explicated by Tawney, that people are guided by an "acquisitive instinct"; that is, they are out to acquire all they can by any means.[36] Despite protestations of belief in democracy, and exaltations of mutual aid, a great deal of social welfare—policies, programs, and practices— is based on mistrust. Investigations into welfare programs almost invariably seek instances of ineligible clients receiving benefits. Very rare are efforts to determine if eligible clients are *not* receiving benefits.[37] The ideology of basic mistrust has its roots in history. Baron von Voght, writing of social welfare in Hamburg in 1796, says of the poor who declared their income to be only one shilling, sixpence a week, "We knew enough of our poor to suppose that one shilling sixpence avowed earning something more."[38] In modern times, the fear that someone, somewhere, will "rip off" the welfare system results in elaborate rules and stratagems to prevent this from happening. Safeguards against excessive costs become important parts of program planning, and arouse more interest and discussion than the benefits the programs are supposedly designed to impart.

It is understandable that aided citizens do not stand out or provide good copy, while "welfare cheats" do. So deeply has the ideology of mistrust entered into the welfare scene, however, that "welfare" and "cheating" have become almost synonymous in some minds. Hence, headlines about Medicare, Medicaid, or day-care frauds bring to mind cheating clients, rather than the doctors, politicians, and entrepreneurs involved. It is illustrative that when the commissioner of human resources of a large eastern city resigned in 1975, he did not discuss the number of people helped, rehabilitated, or made happy during his term of office, but rather the money saved by detection of fraudulent claimants. Similarly, campaign promises to "do something about welfare" are understood to mean to eliminate "rip-offs" rather than to eliminate poverty or other social problems.

In ancient days, the Talmud said, "Better that a thousand guilty go free than that one innocent should suffer." In a much later time (1655), a church historian said the same thing differently:

> Better it is, two drones should be fed, than one bee famished. We see the heavens themselves, in dispensing their rain, often water many stinking bogs and noisome lakes . . . only because much good ground lies insepara- bly intermingled with them; so that the bad with the good must be watered, or the bad with the good parched away.[39]

A hundred and forty years later there were still pleas, which would be valid today, against this type of imputation: "The mass of worthy, honest, and economical poor should not be treated as thieves and pau- pers, because large numbers of these last classes attempt to defraud us, or because a few of them may possibly succeed in doing so."[40]

Many unintended consequences flow from social welfare based on mistrust. For example, the fact that hospital care is subsidized at a higher level than home care arises from the remnants of an attitude that if people are not willing to be hospitalized, they can't be really sick, or that financial help to stay at home while sick (outdoor as opposed to indoor relief) can be more easily diverted to other purposes. As a result of this difference in subsidies, however, hospitals accept and keep peo- ple, rather than treating them as outpatients, because this increases hospital income.

The ideology of humanitarianism and that of basic mistrust of others are intrinsically incompatible, and one way of resolving the incompati- bility is to limit mistrust to a specific group. Thus, it is said that while most people are basically honest, hardworking, and trustworthy, the poor—or, more specifically, welfare recipients—cannot be trusted, and the larger society must guard itself against them. This view feeds into —nay, demands—a culture of poverty that is different from the major- ity culture. And among the 27 million poor people in the United States, one can identify an occasional cheat who owns two houses or rides up to collect his payment in a Cadillac.[41]

There are other ideologies, large and small, that impact on social welfare. In some cases—for instance, Sweden, as mentioned before— a classless society, or a society with less social stratification, is an ideolog- ical goal and social welfare is seen as one method through which in- comes can be redistributed more nearly equally.[42] In many African countries, national development is an overwhelmingly strong factor in ideology, at least on the part of the government, and social welfare is viewed as an important instrument toward this end. In Israel, the absorption of immigrants *(m'zug galiyot)* is seen as an almost sacred duty, and permeates social-welfare policies and programs. In other countries, as will be seen later, population control is the overwhelming goal, and social welfare is used as one instrumentality. Then there is the ideology of the elite[43] who believe that the poor can't plan, think, or be trusted,[44] and who may assign to the nonelite a different culture,[45] thereby rationalizing various measures they would not like to have applied to themselves. It has been said of Japanese ideology, for example, that the notion of rights is foreign: There is only the concept of duties.[46] Similarly, social welfare in the Yemen has traditionally been the personal responsibility of the privileged Muslim.[47]

RACISM

Perhaps the most salient ideology that has affected social welfare, as well as all other aspects of the society, in the United States has been racism, either among individuals or as institutional racism in societal structures. Although there have undoubtedly also been economic supports for this situation, the basis has been mainly attitudinal or ideological. In part, this is a belief that blacks are inferior in certain ways; in part, the ideology sees whites as destined to dominate. This is not simply an attitude in which some persist despite facts and logic, pleas and exhortations; it is an ideology that sees a predominantly white world or society as the desideratum, with nonwhites tolerated, or even, in individual instances, permitted to share equally.

Viewing the situation as an absorption problem, at least three views are possible. There is the ideology of assimilation, which holds that the existing culture or civilization, or that of the majority, is desirable, and that other groups must change themselves to become like the existing or majority group. A second view is that of mutual assimilation, or the "melting pot," which holds that each group must give up part of its heritage, while another part is absorbed by, and becomes integral to, the remainder of society—in short, that from an amalgam of all groups, a new entity arises. The third view is that of cultural pluralism, in which each group maintains the essential parts of its own culture, while sharing in an overall framework.[48] The "black revolt" of the 1960s, Supreme Court decisions, new laws and regulations, and changing public attitudes have led away from the assimilation model, but various groups see the melting pot and cultural pluralism as differing, and desirable, goals.

Institutional racism, dating back at least to slavery days, has been a major determinant in creating a predominantely black lower class in the United States. Unemployment among black teenagers and young adults is always two or three times higher than among whites, and the same is true of housing, educational, and health problems. The ideological factor was remarked in 1965: "Underlying much of the failure to provide equal service to Negro farmers in the South has been the preconception ... that Negro farmers have limited needs, capabilities, and aspirations."[49]

Similarly, the ideology that "it's a man's world"—and should remain so—is responsible for the sex discrimination presently being vigorously fought on many fronts, though no significant attempt to raise the retirement age for women to match that of men has been made so far.

Insofar as ethnic groups other than blacks are concerned, the firmly entrenched ideology of the United States, particularly with regard to immigrant groups, has been rhetorical support for the melting pot and practical support for assimilation. However, the assumption that ethnicity is a temporary phenomenon to be condoned as tactics in a strategy of long-term assimilation is no longer held as firmly as it once was. Hansen, a student of American assimilation, postulated that "what the grandparents want to forget, the grandchildren want to remember," but this refers only to the more exotic aspects—songs, dances, food, costumes—of the old culture. And he predicted that without encouragement and support, the fourth generation will no longer be interested in such things.[50] The fourth and succeeding generations of some immigrant groups are proving more tenacious in their attachment to ethnicity than Hansen foresaw, and there seems to be a growing move toward cultural pluralism. This expresses itself not only in education conducted in foreign languages in New York City schools, for example —including Russian, Spanish, Chinese, and various dialects of India— but in a resurgence of ethnic pride, the maintenance and rehabilitation of ethnic neighborhoods, and the recognition of ethnic groups as political forces to be reckoned with.[51] In Israel, for example, cultural pluralism expresses itself in schools where Arabic-speaking pupils are taught in their own language and the Koran is used instead of the Bible, as well as in religious courts for each religion and sect.

INDIRECT AND PARTICIPATORY DEMOCRACY

There is an ideology of indirect, as opposed to participatory, democracy. In the former, officials are elected at relatively infrequent intervals and appoint administrators who hire subadministrators and other employees. Although the elected officials are ultimately responsible to the electorate, the public has little influence between elections, and none at all on nonelected officials, except in the case of illegal acts. By and large, this is the ideology of government that prevails in the United

States. There is a view, however, especially as regards social welfare, that policy should be made, and programs effectuated, by participation of clients, staff, and public.[52] Such participatory democracy is said to result in more humane services, more responsiveness to local conditions, and more effective activities. Gartner and Reissman speak of social welfare as one of the "consumer intensive" services, in which the participation of the consumer is necessary for good service. They see this as an opening, a "crack in the system," which makes it a point of potential change.[53] Social welfare is more than simply consumer-intensive: The participation of clients and public in determining policy and programs distinguishes between business and public administration, on one hand, and the administration of social-welfare agencies, on the other. These differences are not merely methodological but in large measure ideological, reflecting belief systems as to how both social welfare and democracy should operate.

One of the most salient and controversial ideological components of the War on Poverty was the ruling that programs should include the "maximum feasible participation" of the poor.[54] Opinions as to what resulted from this provision tend to be quite divergent and passionately defended. They range from the feeling that maximum feasible participation was never fairly attempted to the view that it was solely responsible for the failure of the War on Poverty, the Office of Economic Opportunity (OEO), and the Model Cities Program. From the experience, however, has begun to emerge clearer understanding of what such participation can be and do.[55]

Katan categorizes the way in which indigenous personnel are used, and the reasons behind such utilization: Clients may be given a conforming role, where they are expected to accept the organization's goals and methods; a mediating role, which makes them the bridge between the agency and the community; or an innovative role, where they are expected to initiate program activities. Paraprofessionals are used to overcome manpower shortages, relocate work within the organization, solve problems of poverty and unemployment, change the image of the poor, provide therapeutic experiences, make services more meaningful to clientele, change the organization, or increase citizen participation.[56]

In an Israeli study, the reasons why more participants and other members of the public were not serving in policy-making positions over a two-year period were studied. The major reasons given by directors of multiservice centers as to underrepresentation of elected members on center boards were

1. Members were considered "not yet ready" to serve. They were considered not to know enough about the center or about centers in

general, or not to have achieved a "center outlook" transcending their own interests or needs or those of specific interest groups.

2. Directors did not know how to conduct such elections fairly, without opening up the center to politicalization, or how to prevent it from being "captured" by a specific interest group.

3. Members were felt to be disinclined to serve on boards, uninterested, or without sufficient time to devote.

4. Members identified not with the center but with only one segment —the health club, activities for the aged, the day camp, or the like.[57]

Another reason for the relative lack of success of participation by the poor is advanced by Warren. Although one tends to view autonomy, viability, and wide distribution of decision-making power as desiderata, it is possible that these are basically incompatible and that movement toward any one of them results in movement away from the other two. Failure to recognize this may lead to frustration because of unrealistic expectations.[58]

MORALITY

There is at least one more major ideological factor that operates in many social-welfare programs. This is a vision of what constitutes moral behavior and attitudes: While all who need help should receive it, they should behave in specified ways to be eligible for such help, or the amount of help should be conditioned upon the recipients' attitudes or behavior: For example, though lazy people should be kept alive (and even this is by no means universally agreed upon), they should certainly not be helped as much as industrious people who are unfortunate. During the Irish famine, with 8 million people starving, the ruling British were concerned that proposed relief measures would reward the Irish rather than punish them for their assumed improvidence— and hence did nothing.[59] This application of the distinction between the so-called deserving and undeserving poor can be matched by similar programs (or their lack) and regulations. For example, it has been proposed that mothers of illegitimate children be refused help if they bear another illegitimate child. The cost is not usually cited as the reason but, rather, their reprehensible desire to be dependent upon society despite their own immorality. Similarly, alcoholics, drug abusers, those who "waste" their grants, and even—at certain times—those who hold unpopular political views, such as alleged communists, are targets of attempts to deny them aid. This sometimes extends—in practice, if not in law—to applicants whose behavior on the premises of the welfare agency is considered objectionable.

Moral judgments concerning how recipients of help should behave, and moral indignation when they don't, is illustrated by the following case record presented to beginning social-work students, followed by their usual reaction:

Facts	*Reaction*
An able-bodied young man on relief, deprives himself of food and entertainment to buy books, which he spends his time study-ing.	Indignation
	Approbation
All the books, however, are pornographic, because he's writing a book to expose the deleterious effects of pornography on the young,	Indignation
	Approbation
while he is living with a girl who prostitutes herself to supply him with drugs.	Indignation

IDEOLOGIES REGARDING SOCIAL WELFARE

In addition to the ideological stances that influence social welfare, there is also ideology concerning social welfare itself to consider. Wilensky and Lebeaux argue that the major dichotomy is between a view of social welfare as residual—that is, "last resort" service when the family, mutual aid, the church, and the market place have failed—and a view of social welfare as structural, as part of the institutionalized ongoing activities of society.[60] The first view represents social welfare as a privilege to be earned, or as an undeserved charity, while the latter conceives of social welfare as the deserved right of everyone in society. The latter view has been carried farther by Smith, who points out that there is no constitutional or legal right to decent housing, sufficient food, or other necessities in American society. Although one can sue an agency for not fulfilling its obligations, one cannot sue the government or any of its organs simply because one does not have the necessities of life. He argues, therefore, for social welfare based upon the right to life: Benefits should not be based on what a person is or has done, how he behaves or what he believes, but should be offered him or her simply because he or she is alive.[61] This too is an ideology, though one held by very few people.

The view that gross inequality in the distribution of income is undesirable—whether seeing it as dysfunctional for the society, inimical to individuals, or simply immoral—is also an ideology, and the use of social-welfare programs to achieve a more nearly equal distribution is engaging the attention of more and more people. Whether the redistribution is achieved by direct means—children's allowances, a guaranteed minimum income, larger welfare payments—or indirectly, through improved education, affirmative action, or otherwise, the use of social welfare as an instrument for redistribution is a serious concern in some countries. There is a growing literature on this subject.[62]

Then, there is the view that social-welfare policies and programs are being used to maintain the capitalist system and that this should be resisted. This is the position of some of the "radical" social workers:

> We have to break with the professional doctrine that the institutions in which social workers are employed have benign motives; that the purpose of hospitals is to provide health care for the sick; that the purpose of welfare agencies is to provide assistance for the impoverished; that the purpose of child care agencies is to protect children.[63]

Contrariwise, there is a view that social welfare is immoral, at least in some of its particulars. That some welfare recipients are given more money in grants than others get in wages arouses great moral indignation in some people. Regardless of whether the wages of some individuals or families are woefully inadequate, or whether their needs are clear and pressing, it violates some ideologies for nonworking people of whatever category to get more than workers. This has been the expressed basis of a proposal to reduce welfare payments in New York State.[64]

It is clear from this partial listing of ideologies that impinge upon social welfare that different ideological positions, or even elements of single ideologies, may clash. The ideology that all people are equal conflicts with the belief that to deserve help, people must behave in ways seen as moral. Humanitarianism coexists with mistrust. It is not surprising, then, that "since social welfare goals touch a core of ideologies, they tend to polarize Americans. Priorities for funding programs for old people or children, for example, vie with programs meant to encourage work among employables."[65]

Even unopposed actions do not necessarily flow directly from ideologies. For one thing, there may be a gap between the rhetoric and the program. As Wilensky points out:

> Countries vary in the size of the universal gap between ideology and practice. Sweden and the USSR may represent extremes in the meshing of words and deeds: Sweden is most egalitarian in practice, and its political rhetoric comes close to its practice; the USSR is most egalitarian in ideology, and is one of the least egalitarian in practice. The United States is far from the Soviet Union in its ideology, but closer in its practice. The

failure to separate official rhetoric and popular sentiment from welfare practice creates great confusion in discussion of the welfare state.[66]

Further, ideologies do not remain static but vary with changes in tradition, setting, historical events, and political backgrounds, among other things.[67] To cite only two recent examples, ideologies regarding the "place" of blacks and the role of women have been radically altered since the 1960s. Such change in ideology is complicated, however, by what.has been called the "atavistic fallacy,"[68] which automatically attributes to what came first a more important meaning.

Finally, it should be noted that there are also anti-ideologies, which spring from antagonism toward existing ideologies. It has been a truism at certain times and in certain places in the United States that characterizing a social-welfare policy or program as communistic or socialistic was enough to ensure its defeat. An American congressman said, "The word 'social worker' is not a good word. People connect social worker with socialization, and socialized medicine, and socialism. I have suggested that we ought to get rid of that term."[69]

THE INSTITUTIONALIZATION OF IDEOLOGIES

Ideologies that lead to social welfare can become institutionalized, as do mutual-aid and religious motivations. From being informal and unstructured, as when one individual gives to another, giving may become structured but ad hoc. In the early days of the Charity Organization in England, for example, there were no regular clients, funds, or donors. On becoming aware of a needy person, the members (later, the secretary) of the society would gather the facts, determine the amount needed, and decide which well-to-do people would be amenable to helping the client. They would then, in effect, take up a collection for the client, after which the "system" of client, collector, and donor would dissolve. At a later period, philanthropy became formal, structured, and permanent. In this stage there are accepted roles, processes, and continuing structures.

Voluntary organizations are often organized around the interests of one person or a small group. Parents whose children are exceptional in one way or another, or people whose loved ones are suffering from a disease such as leukemia or Tay-Sachs disease, or those interested in certain groups such as American Indians, Vietnamese orphans, or patients in Israeli hospitals, or in causes such as prevention of child abuse, get together and undertake to do something about their interest.

The goal may be to comfort one another, spur research, or seek government intervention. Almost invariably, however, such voluntary organizations feel the need for funds, and fund-raising becomes one of the important activities of the organization. With fund-raising there often come licensing, legal controls, and accountability. Lack of accountability may lead to excessive administrative and fund-raising costs: Whereas 5 percent is considered the acceptable limit for fund-raising costs in some organizations, there are some that operate with a 2 percent limit; on the other hand, organizations accountable to no one have been known to use more than 50 percent of their proceeds in payments to the fund-raisers and others.

The proliferation of appeals for money that ensued from many competing fund-raising efforts, as well as recognition of the importance of many of the causes represented, led to cooperation and collaboration between some agencies, and finally to federation of fund-raising efforts in the form of a united drive, welfare-fund campaign, or other overall effort, in most cities. In almost every case, the combined drive produced more money than had all of the separate drives, taken together. Such success brings with it a series of problems. For example, how is the additional money to be distributed—equally among participating organizations, in proportion to their previous budgets, according to some index of fund-raising activities or results?

A second problem of federated fund-raising occurs in the diffusion of altruism that results.[70] Some of the people who were very active in raising funds for a specific cause might be equally active regarding the united fund, but others will feel the general good to be more remote than was the specific need, and will lose some momentum. Again, becoming a representative to, or even an officer of, the united organization often is more prestigious (or even more time-consuming) than working for the local or individual unit, thus draining leadership from the unit to the federation.

Further, as it becomes more difficult to raise all the money desired by each organization, an evaluative element begins to make itself felt, in which the federation makes judgments as to the efficiency and efficacy of the constituent organizations, and allocates funds to them accordingly. This sometimes extends to the goal of the organization, or its reason for existence. The federation, consequently, becomes an instrument for community control, and establishes planning, research, evaluative, and policy-making units. The make-up of the governing body of the federation thus becomes a matter of vital concern to the community. Part of the ideological struggle mentioned previously arises from the fact that at one time only the big givers were on the governing bodies, and their ideas of what the community, groups, or individuals needed did not always coincide with those of the professionals or of the clients. The move to co-opt representatives of client groups and staff onto boards is based, in part, on this aspect of organized philanthropy.

One outgrowth of the federation of individual units is more rational planning of services. The organization with the wealthiest or most active members is not able to offer more or better services in the face of less need. In addition, the combined resources of the units for publicity purposes make it possible to reach ever larger groups of givers and other participants. On the other hand, new organizations and causes are forced to compete with giant federations, which are not always receptive to allocating money for a new cause or to another organization. Thus, the process tends to be repeated: New organizations come into being, and the number of appeals in addition to the federated appeal becomes obtrusive. One solution, successfully undertaken in a number of cities, is to enlarge the federation into a superfederation, blanketing in the new organizations with the old. Interestingly, the result has usually been, again, larger collections than all of the individual donations, including those to the federation, taken collectively.

Organized philanthropy has become big business in a number of countries. Fund-raisers have their own professional association, code of ethics,[71] continuing education seminars, and employment services. Federation officials are also organized into a number of associations, and some universities offer extension courses for them. A good part of education for community organization in social work uses federation bodies and offices of various kinds as field-work settings.

The size of the voluntary sector has been estimated as 6 million organizations in America. One of every ten service workers in the United States is employed by a nonprofit organization, as is one of every six professional workers. One-ninth of all property is owned by voluntary organizations. Tax-exempt charitable, religious, literary, and educational organizations have annual revenues of more than $100 billion in money and other resources.[72]

In addition to membership groups, there are also foundations to take into consideration. Although one tends to think of philanthropic foundations as a feature of the modern world, these are ancient institutions. In the fourteenth and fifteenth centuries, bequests and large gifts by individual benefactors were not uncommon. At the time of the Reformation, there were at least 460 charitable foundations in England.[73] The giant foundations that exist today, however, were begun at the end of the nineteenth century and the beginning of the twentieth. This development was considerably influenced by an article entitled "Wealth" written by Andrew Carnegie, who called upon the rich to administer their wealth as a public trust because, "having proved themselves in the struggle for commercial success, they were particularly fitting agents of the public trust."[74] Carnegie channeled much of his money toward the building of libraries, parks, concert halls, museums, and educational institutions with a practical slant. John D. Rockefeller,

Sr., carried the idea farther, establishing trusts and engaging personnel whose lifework it would be to "manage benevolence properly and effectively."[75] Although Rockefeller may have been motivated by the desire to improve his image from that of the "most execrated name in American life,"[76] both he and Henry Ford took the lead in establishing immense nonprofit charitable foundations. The spread of foundations has been aided by tax laws that exempt contributions to philanthropy, in great part, from income taxes and make the property of such bodies tax-exempt. As a consequence, there were more than 25,000 grant-making foundations in 1975, with combined assets of around $25 billion.[77] The annual income of the Ford Foundation alone exceeds that of the world's largest bank; the income of the 596 largest tax-exempt foundations is more than twice the total net earnings of the nation's 50 largest commercial banks.[78]

The status of foundations has not gone unchallenged, however. Just as there are rising questions about tax-exemption for church properties other than the church buildings themselves, especially properties used for income-producing purposes, so questions are being raised about foundations with such enormous incomes—mostly from stock dividends, stock trading, and capital gains—being exempt from property taxes, as well as income taxes. In many American cities, estates on which owners can no longer afford the taxes, and whose tax burdens other individuals are reluctant to assume, are being purchased by tax-exempt bodies. A result is areas where large, well-kept estates pay no property taxes to the localities in which they exist, and consequent impoverishment of those localities.

The institutionalization of philanthropy has resulted, not only in professional careers for staff members as noted above, but also in what has been called the "philanthropic career" for lay people. Although record-keeping, public relations, fund dispensing, and even provision of services are carried out by the staff, it is an axiom of fund-raising that people do not give to causes: They give to people. The establishment of fund-raising machinery with which interested people involve their friends or associates and, by use of a repertoire of techniques—example, prestige, shame, friendship—induce them to contribute to the support of an organization, has become both an art and a science.[79] Testimonial dinners, award ceremonies, bazaars, door-to-door solicitations, and other fund-raising methods have become embedded in the social life of much of the United States, especially in large cities. Statuses are defined as "big giver," "effective fund-raiser," "hard worker," and the like. Social life comes to be focused around church or organizational affairs, and the network of activities and friendships thus created becomes an important part of a person's life style.

Nor is business immune to this syndrome. Fund-raising exploits the manufacturer's, wholesaler's, or retailer's suppliers to contribute to, or be active in, the chosen cause—the implied (but never spoken) threat being that failure to participate might give the edge to a competitor. Customers are also used, as when a firm posts a sign that it has given to a particular cause, presumably to court favor with that cause's adherents. Large firms are thus the favorite target of some fund-raisers, and firms that are concerned about public relations, or their "image," urge and expect employees to be active in civic and philanthropic endeavors.[80]

The institutionalization of philanthropy—whether in the historical mold of a Charity Organization Society, a social-services exchange to compare information about recipients, or the huge modern foundations and organizations—serves to rationalize services, to increase professionalization, to make possible long-range planning, and to increase accountability. On the other hand, such institutionalization often results in a type of paternalism, in which the umbrella organization gives or withholds according to deference to its wishes—for instance, on a small scale, it may require hymns to be sung or prayers to be said before offering food or funds may be available only for the higher education of deaf black orphans.

A second problem with institutionalized philanthropy is when the original founder, biggest giver, or most prestigious member exerts pervasive authority to the point that decisions are really made by him or her, thus reducing the philanthropy to an ad hominem proposition.

The problem of depersonalization—in which members begin to feel like units because of the size and impersonality of the organization—sometimes reduces, as mentioned previously, the amount of individual commitment and activity.

Then there is the phenomenon of goal displacement, when the activities required to keep the organization going become more important than the stated goal.[81] Such activities become necessary because of:

The percentage of purely nominal members.
The large turnover in membership.
The rising average age of the membership.
The necessity for a change-over from voluntary
    help to the introduction of salaried assistance.[82]

The result is that "interest groups are formed which are frequently concerned more with preserving and building up the organization itself than in helping it to serve its initial purpose."[83] It is not uncommon to see people becoming very active and engaging in membership solicitation, fund-raising, program presentations, and other aspects of the organization with little knowledge about or concern for the stated goals of the organization. Such activity can be carried out for very obscure, esoteric, and highly specialized organizations whose very reason for existence might be seriously challenged by others. What has happened in such cases is that the activity and its satisfactions have become free-standing motivations, detached from the original impulse toward mutual aid, altruism, religious acts, or the like. Fierce loyalties to, and strident competition between, such organizations may exist, with the ultimate goal playing a very minor role in determining actions.[84]

Goal displacement is not the same as goal substitution.[85] In the latter, the stated goal of the organization is reached, but either because the satisfactions of the members are too great to forgo or because it seems a waste to disband such a successful instrument, a new goal is chosen for the organization. Some of the rationalizations used to continue organizations in the event of goal attainment are

1. Agreed, the aims and objects have been achieved, but now watch must be kept to ensure that achievement is consolidated.
2. The aims are not in fact quite achieved; there are still all sorts of details to be dealt with.
3. The government has taken the work over, but it is vital that private initiative should continue to play a part.
4. The aims which we had in the past have been achieved, but in the meantime we have found new subsidiary ones.[86]

An example of an organization not wanting to disband because of its proved effectiveness is the Infantile Paralysis Foundation, with its very effective March of Dimes, spurred by President Franklin D. Roosevelt's personal interest. Rather than disband the organization, a new goal was sought in the fight against birth defects.

THE FUTURE OF INSTITUTIONALIZED IDEOLOGIES

Ideologies change, albeit very slowly, but there is little reason to believe that societies of the future will be less humanitarian, or that individuals will be less altruistic, than those of today. The thrusts of certain ideologies do seem to have reached a plateau, however, even if only temporarily, while others are receding. The mystique of agriculture seems less strong than it once was, and with the growth of the service economy, large farms as food factories will probably continue to grow, with consequently less idealization of farm life (though individuals who have never been farmers may continue to romanticize the vocation). Both technology and the need for immense resources to deal with social problems will militate against widespread collectives or cooperatives, with government intervention continuing to be the major thrust, as well as the most innovative and daring. There are few signs of any widespread return to openness, trust, and chance-taking, despite rhetoric that calls for those. Consequently, programs will probably continue to be guided in their regulations by fear of cheating rather than hope of success.

The move to overcome racism may also have reached a plateau, as affirmative action, class-action suits, integrated schools, and other devices appear to whites to have achieved "enough," or as much as can be expected to date. Similarly, the feminist movement, having achieved visibility and some gains, may suffer from overexposure in the near future. Ethnicity, on the other hand, is becoming more widely recognized as a permanent feature of American life, and emphasis may move from assimilation or the melting pot to cultural pluralism, with consequent concern about intergroup relations and ethnic pride. This does not necessarily mean that local participation in social-welfare programs will grow: The defeats and problems that accompanied the War on Poverty overshadow the gains in the public mind, and act to deter re-entry into that area. Finally, paucity of resources for social welfare will probably reinforce the ideology of morality, with "undeserving" or "immoral" clients being refused service under various subterfuges.

NOTES

1. J. Macaulay and L. Berkowitz (eds.), *Altruism and Helping Behavior: Social Psychological Studies of Some Antecedents and Consequences* (New York: Academic Press, 1970), p. 3.
2. *Webster's Third New International Dictionary* (Cleveland: World Book Co., 1961), p. 1100.
3. G. H. Palmer, *Altruism: Its Nature and Varieties* (Westport, Conn.: Greenwood Press, 1970), p. 2.
4. T. Brosse, "Altruism and Creativity as Biological Factors in Human Evolution," in P. A. Sorokin (ed.), *Explorations in Altruistic Love and Behavior* (Boston: Beacon Press, 1950), pp. 118–44.
5. Brosse says, "We need scientific research providing a biological basis for the fundamental problems of ethics, including the problem of altruization." *Ibid.*
6. Palmer, *op. cit.*, p. 5.
7. R. B. Perry, *Realms of Value* (Cambridge, Mass.: Harvard University Press, 1954), p. 69.
8. See Macaulay and Berkowitz, *op. cit.*
9. On altruism and social welfare, see R. M. Titmuss, *The Gift Relationship* (London: Allen & Unwin, 1971); E. S. Phelps (ed.), *Altruism, Morality, and Economic Theory* (New York: Sage, 1975); and A. L. Schorr, "Who Promised Us a Rose Garden?" *Social Work*, 20 (1975):200–205.

10. One definition is "A system of interdependent ideas . . . held by a social group or society, which reflects, rationalizes, and defends its particular social, moral, religious, political, and economic institutional interests and commitments. Ideologies serve as logical and philosophical justifications for a group's patterns of behavior, as well as its attitudes, goals, and general life situation." G. A. Theodorson and A. G. Theodorson, *A Modern Dictionary of Sociology* (New York: Crowell, 1969).

11. H. M. Drucker, *The Political Uses of Ideology* (New York: Barnes and Noble, 1974), p. 3.

12. Drucker (*ibid.*, p. xii) says, "We are largely ignorant about ideologies . . . we cannot agree how ideologies came to be—we do not agree about what an ideology is." On the difficulties of defining ideology, see "What Are Ideological Beliefs?" in D. Joravsky, *The Lysenko Affair* (Cambridge, Mass.: Harvard University Press, 1970).

13. R. M. MacIver, "Introduction," in F. Gross (ed.), *European Ideologies* (New York: Philosophical Library, 1948), p. 5.

14. W. T. Bluhm, *Ideologies and Attitudes: Modern Political Culture* (Englewood Cliffs, N.J.: Prentice-Hall, 1974), p. 4.

15. D. Bell, *The End of Ideology* (New York: Free Press, 1960), pp. 370–71.

16. A. L. Schorr, *Social Security and Social Services in France* (Washington, D.C.: Government Printing Office, 1965), p. 2.

17. Bell, *op. cit.*, p. 192. (Emphasis in original.)

18. Drucker, *op. cit.*, p. 142.

19. *Ibid.*, p. xi.

20. J. Neipris, "Some Origins of Social Work Policy in a New State," Ph.D. diss., University of California, Berkeley, 1966.

21. H. L. Wilensky and C. N. Lebeaux, *Industrial Society and Social Welfare* (New York: Free Press, 1958), p. 337.

22. M. Mead, "The Study of National Character," in D. Lerner and H. D. Lasswell (eds.), *The Policy Sciences* (Stanford, Calif.: Stanford University Press, 1951), p. 70.

23. R. M. Titmuss, *Essay on "the Welfare State"* (New Haven, Conn.: Yale University Press, 1959), p. 20.

24. W. A. Friedlander, *Individualism and Social Welfare* (New York: Free Press, 1962), p. 153.

25. Wilensky and Lebeaux, *op. cit.*, p. xvii.

26. R. D. Husby, "Child Day Care for Welfare Mothers," *Social Work*, 19 (July 1974): 420–26.

27. B. M. Gross, "Prefatory Comment," in B. Akzin and Y. Dror, *Israel: High Pressure Planning* (Syracuse, N.Y.: Syracuse University Press, 1966), p. xi.

28. H. J. Eysenck, *The Psychology of Politics* (New York: Praeger, 1954).

29. Y. Ben David, *Agricultural Planning and Village Community in Israel* (New York: UNESCO, 1964), pp. 9–10.

30. H. Hurtado, "Summary of Country Case Study," in H. D. Stein (ed.), *Planning for the Needs of Children in Developing Countries* (New York: UNICEF, 1964), p. 123.

31. D. Macarov, *Incentives to Work* (San Francisco: Jossey-Bass, 1970), pp. 83–84.

32. For example, G. Gurin and P. Gurin, "Personal Efficacy and the Ideology of Individual Responsibility," and G. Katona, "Persistence of Belief in Personal Financial Progress," both in B. Strumpel (ed.), *Economic Means for Human Needs: Social Indicators of Well-Being and Discontent* (Ann Arbor: University of Michigan Press, 1976).

33. M. N. Zald (ed.), *Social Welfare Institutions* (New York: Wiley, 1965), p. 141.

34. J. Moss, "Social Services," in *Britannica Book of the Year* (Chicago: Encyclopaedia Britannica, 1966), p. 686.

35. *Social Reconstruction in the Newly Independent Countries of East Africa* (New York: United Nations, 1965), p. 31.

36. R. H. Tawney, *The Acquisitive Society* (New York: Harcourt, Brace & World, 1948).

37. An exception is a study conducted by the City University of New York: See *Evaluation of the Welfare Declaration: Eligibility Simplification for Public Assistance* (New York: City University of New York, 1969), p. 3.

38. K. de Schweinitz, *England's Road to Social Security* (Philadelphia: University of Pennsylvania Press, 1943), p. 92.

39. Fuller, quoted in *ibid.*, p. 18.

40. J. Colcord, *Cash Relief* (New York: Sage, 1936), p. 10.

41. After investigating the empirical base of such stories, Liebling termed them "horsefeathers swathed in mink." A. J. Liebling, *The Press* (New York: Ballantine, 1964), p. 79.

42. "Social Welfare: Ends and Means," in *Current Sweden, No. 54* (Stockholm: Swedish Institute, 1974).

43. P. Thoenes, *The Elite in the Welfare State* (New York: Free Press, 1966).

44. For how this works out in the Food Stamp Program, see J. B. Williamson *et al.*, *Strategies against Poverty in America* (New York: Wiley, 1975).

45. Macarov, *op. cit.*, pp. 109–22.

46. *Local Government in Selected Countries* (New York: United Nations Technical Assistance Program, 1963), p. 75.

47. *The Arab World* (New York: Arab Information Center, 1965).

48. C. Price, "The Study of Assimilation," in J. A. Jackson (ed.), *Migration* (Cambridge, England: Cambridge University Press, 1969), pp. 181–237.

49. V. Fuller, "Rural Poverty and Rural Area Development," in M. S. Gordon (ed.), *Poverty in America* (San Francisco: Chandler, 1965), p. 395.

50. M. L. Hansen, *The Immigrant in American History* (New York: Harper & Row, 1964).

51. See, for example, J. L. Vigilante, "Back to the Old Neighborhood," *Social Service Review*, 50 (June 1976); A. Kogut, "The Settlement and Ethnicity," *Social Work*, 17 (1972):22; S. TeSelle (ed.), *The Rediscovery of Ethnicity: Its Implications for Culture and Politics in America* (New York: Harper & Row, 1973); and A. J. Naperstek and K. Kollias, "The Ethnic and Class Dimensions in Neighborhoods: A Means for the Reorganization of Human Service Delivery Systems," *Journal of Sociology and Social Welfare*, 2 (Spring 1975):406.

52. D. Macarov, "Management in the Social Work Curriculum," *Administration in Social Work*, 1 (October 1977).

53. A. Gartner and F. Riessman, *The Service Society and the Consumer Vanguard* (New York: Harper & Row, 1974), pp. 5–6.

54. D. P. Moynihan, *Maximum Feasible Misunderstanding* (New York: Free Press, 1969).

55. See, for example, L. E. Crown, "Meaningful Consumer Participation: A Challenge to the Social Agency Administrator," in H. A. Schatz, *Social Work Administration: A Resource Book* (New York: Council on Social Work Education, 1970), pp. 333–35.

56. Y. Katan, "The Utilization of Indigenous Workers in Human Service Organizations," in Y. Hasenfeld and R. A. English (eds.), *Human Service Organizations* (Ann Arbor: University of Michigan Press, 1974), pp. 448–67.

57. D. Macarov, *Boards and Directors: A Longitudinal Study* (Jerusalem: Paul Baerwald School of Social Work, Hebrew University, 1976) (in Hebrew).

58. R. L. Warren, "Toward a Non-Utopian Normative Model of the Community," *American Sociological Review*, 35 (1970):219.

59. S. Marcus, "Hunger and Ideology," in Zald, *op. cit.*, p. 164.

60. Wilensky and Lebeaux, *op. cit.*

61. A. D. Smith, *The Right to Life* (Chapel Hill: University of North Carolina Press, 1955).

62. A. L. Schorr (ed), *Jubilee for Our Times: A Practical Program for Income Equality* (New York: Columbia University Press, 1977).

63. R. A. Cloward, and F. F. Piven, "The Acquiesence of Social Work," *Social Science and Modern Society*, 14 (January-February 1975):55–63. See also R. Bailey and M. Brake (eds.), *Radical Social Work* (New York: Pantheon, 1976.)

64. W. T. Smith, II, *Public Welfare: The "Impossible" Dream.* Paper presented at the County Officers Association of the State of New York, Rochester, New York, 1975. (Mimeographed.)

65. J. Axinn and H. Levin, *Social Welfare: A History of the American Response to Need* (New York: Dodd, Mead, 1975), p. 1.

66. H. L. Wilensky, *The Welfare State and Equality: Structural and Ideological Roots of Public Expenditures* (Berkeley: University of California, 1975), p. 39.

67. E. Pusic, *Reappraisal of the United Nations Social Security Programme* (New York: United Nations, 1965).

68. R. B. Perry, *Realms of Value* (Cambridge, Mass: Harvard University Press, 1954).

69. J. P. Fogarty, *Hearings before a Sub-committee of the Committee on Appropriations, House of Representatives, Eighty-seventh Congress, Second Session* (Washington, D.C.: Department of Health, Education, and Welfare, 1962), p. 204.

70. The diffusion of individual altruism in the presence of other people has been repeatedly demonstrated and measured. See Macaulay and Berkowitz, *op. cit.*

71. Reputable fund-raisers will not, for example, undertake activities on a commission basis, as this has been found to lead to unscrupulous tactics that eventually injure the organizations by which they were employed.

72. *Giving in America: Toward a Stronger Voluntary Sector* (Washington, D.C.: Commission on Private Philanthropy and Public Needs, 1975), p. 11.

73. Schweinitz, *op. cit.*, pp. 63–64.

74. *Giving in America, op. cit.*, pp. 63–64.

75. *Ibid.*

76. D. Horowitz and D. Kolodny, "The Foundations: Charity Begins at Home," *Ramparts*, 7 (April 1969):39–48, reprinted in Roby, *op.cit.*, pp. 43–59.

77. *Giving in America, op. cit.*, p. 64.

78. Horowitz and Kolodny, *op. cit.*, p. 43.

79. "Thirty percent of higher-income contributors said they feel they are pressured into giving more time or money than they really want to." *Giving in America, op. cit.*, p. 62.

80. A. D. Ross, "Philanthropic Activity and the Business Career," in Zald, *op. cit.*, pp. 341–59.

81. A. Etzioni, *Modern Organizations* (Englewood Cliffs, N.J.: Prentice-Hall, 1964), p. 10.

82. Theoness, *op. cit.*, p. 150.

83. Etzioni, *op. cit.*, p. 10.

84. Such goal displacement is not confined to philanthropic organizations, of course, but may be observed in voluntary fire departments, Little League ball teams, and civic groups, for example.

85. Etzioni, *op. cit.*, p. 13; see also D. L. Sills, "The Succession of Goals," in D. L. Sills, *The Volunteers* (New York: Free Press, 1957), reprinted in A. Etzioni (ed.), *Complex Organizations: A Sociological Reader* (New York: Holt, Rinehart and Winston, 1961), pp. 146–59.

86. Thoeness, *op. cit.*, p. 150.

PART III

ATTITUDES THAT SHAPE SOCIAL WELFARE

8

People and Environment: Population Issues

Actions rarely proceed directly and in their intended form from motivations. Reality intrudes, in the shape of situations, structures, events, and processes. Further, the beliefs and convictions of the motivated person, as well as those of society, determine whether and in what manner motivations lead to action, and how motivations themselves change.

The major motivations for social welfare discussed in the previous part not only impact upon one another but are also acted upon by deeply held societal convictions. The ultimate shape of social-welfare policies and programs is determined, in large part, by the interplay of motivations and attitudes. The latter relate to population considerations, based on the thinking of Malthus; the question of who should survive, as raised originally by Darwin; the proper activities of people, about which Luther had firm ideas; laissez-faire economics, largely identified with Adam Smith; the structure of society, questioned by Marx; the methodology of social work, on which Freud had considerable influence; and desiderata for the social services, to which Beveridge addressed himself.

These do not, obviously, exhaust the attitudes that permeate society, nor even those most closely related to social welfare. Because they are, however, among those that impact most immediately and clearly on the thinking that shapes social welfare, they have been chosen for scrutiny in this and the four chapters following.

153

MALTHUSIAN THEORY

Predecessors and contemporaries of Thomas Malthus, who lived from 1766 to 1834, worried about the ability of the world to sustain its population,[1] but it was his book *An Essay on the Principle of Population as It Affects the Future Improvement of Society* (first published in 1798) that brought the problem to public attention and reverberated throughout the world of social planning.[2]

Although accurate world population figures were not available, Malthus deduced that the human population tended to double in each generation, thus attaining geometric progression—2, 4, 8, 16, 32, and so forth. He took as his modal family one with six children, two of whom die before maturity (which was normative in his day), leaving four grown children, or twice as many as their parents, to reproduce—a rather conservative estimate for that time.

However, the productivity of agriculture—man's basic source of sustenance—was seen by Malthus as increasing only by arithmetic progression—1, 2, 3, 4, 5, and so forth—and even this assumption was, in his time, wildly optimistic.[3] Then, on the basis of two seemingly irrefutable axioms—"First, that food is necessary to the existence of man. . . . Secondly, that the passion between the sexes is necessary and will remain nearly in its present state"[4]—Malthus contended that population *must* outstrip sustenance sooner or later.

The only reason that this had not already happened, according to Malthus, was that disease, war, natural calamities, and famine periodically decimated populations; but, he argued, geometric increase among humans invariably more than makes up the loss in a relatively short time, and the surge toward overpopulation—and consequent disease and starvation—continues. Malthus summarized his theory in three propositions, which the remainder of his book documents:

> That population cannot increase without the means of subsistence is a proposition so evident that it needs no illustration.
>
> That population does invariably increase where there are the means of subsistence, the history of every people that have ever existed will abundantly prove.
>
> And that the superior power of population cannot be checked without producing misery or vice, the ample portion of these two bitter ingredients in the cup of human life and the continuance of the physical causes that seem to have produced them bear too convincing a testimony.[5]

Malthus's proposition that population invariably outstrips agricultural production has been called a "dismal theorem."[6] He went further, though, pointing out that increases in the world's food supply reduce the discrepancy between population and sustenance only temporarily, and that increases in the food supply simply ensure more births, or more surviving children, and thus a larger population to live in hunger and eventually die of starvation. This is what happened in Ireland at the beginning of the eighteenth century. There, 2 million people were living miserably on small grains. The introduction of potatoes led to a better diet, and subsequently a decline in infant mortality, so that by 1845 there were 8 million people living at about the same level of misery on potatoes. As a result of blight, crop failure, and famine, 2 million starved to death, 2 million emigrated, and 4 million remained in modest comfort. Through continued emigration, and a relatively late age for marriage, the population of Ireland has remained at 4 million since then.[7] This proposition—that increased food supply simply increases the number of those who eventually die of starvation—has been called an "utterly dismal theorem."[8] The only hope that Malthus could hold out—or, rather, the only remedy that he could hope for—was that mankind would exercise "moral restraint" and not have so many children.[9]

The impact of Malthusian theory upon social welfare was as immediate as it was widespread. William Pitt the Younger, alarmed by what he thought was a declining British population, had introduced a bill in Parliament revising the Poor Laws to pay liberal allowances for children, for the specific purpose of boosting the population.[10] But, Malthus wrote:

> The poor-laws of England tend to depress the general condition of the poor in these two ways. Their first obvious tendency is to increase population without increasing the food for its support. . . . Secondly, the quantity of provisions consumed in workhouses . . . diminishes the shares that would otherwise belong to more industrious and more worthy members, and thus in the same manner forces more to become dependents.[11]

Pitt promptly withdrew his proposed bill.[12] Attitudes toward population questions have influenced social welfare ever since. Because much of Malthus's picture of the poor was seen as demeaning by early social workers, and because the early influence of Malthusian theory was seen as inimical to social workers' goals and values, Malthus was anathema to many of them. Grace Abbott, for example, wrote in 1941, "The doctrine of Malthus . . . has no more place in modern social organization than flogging as a cure for the delusions of the insane."[13] This view of Malthusianism as ignoring the problems of the poor and the unfit in order to reduce population persists in some quarters.

The Population/Agriculture Record

The extent to which Malthus's predictions concerning population on a worldwide basis have come true (even if not on a generational basis) is relatively clear: It took from the beginning of man until the beginning of the current era for the world's population to reach a quarter billion. By 1650, the population had doubled to half billion.[14] In 1850, the billion mark was reached. It took only another eighty years (1930) for the population to reach 2 billion; in another thirty years (1960) it had reached 3 billion; and fifteen years later (1975) the population was 4 billion.[15] Clearly, it has taken roughly half as long to add each successive billion people to the earth's population since 1850.

The accelerating increase in population is not solely the result of an increasing, or even a high, birth rate but is more closely linked to increasing longevity. In 1700, life expectancy at birth in Europe was 33 years; in 1950, it was 66;[16] and in 1976, it was 71.[17] This is partly due to the fact that though some of the calamities Malthus counted on to reduce the population continue, others have been mitigated, if not eliminated. Antibiotics and other new drugs have controlled many diseases. Pneumonia, for example, was once referred to as the "old person's friend" because death from pneumonia was common among the aged, and considered relatively painless. Pneumonia is now rather easily cured in most cases. Other diseases, such as smallpox, have been virtually eliminated through public health measures. Similarly, advances in sanitation; sounder construction of buildings, bridges, dams, and so forth; and more reliable forecasting of hurricanes, tornadoes, snowstorms, and—quite recently—earthquakes and volcanoes—all contribute to increased longevity.

The past record of agricultural productivity is more difficult to assess than that of population, because reliable worldwide data are available only for recent times. Overall food production, however, seems to have at least kept pace with population growth, until the most recent population increases. Tangential evidence includes the fact that in 1776, one farmer provided food for three people, and by 1976, one farmer provided food for fifty-seven people.[18] Since 1952–53, the average rate of increase in the production of food in the world at large has been 3 percent per year, while the population has increased on the average 1.7 percent per year.[19] It has, in fact, been estimated that since 1850, the increase in output has been more rapid than the increase in population,[20] and that this is not simply a result of population decreases caused by wars is evidenced by the fact that food production decreased more rapidly than population did, at least during World War II.[21]

One of the most dramatic increases in agriculture is the result of painstaking laboratory research to find new strains of corn and other grains, new pesticides, and new fertilizers. The success of these efforts has been such that they were termed the Green Revolution, and they have resulted in startling increases in productivity in some areas. It was, indeed, hoped that these new developments would enable production to at least keep pace with population growth until the latter is stabilized, and there was some evidence that it would.

Unfortunately, overall worldwide production figures do not indicate how the produce is distributed. When population and production increases are approximately the same, surpluses in one area almost inevitably leave untouched the famine in another. Thus, despite worldwide figures, population in the developing countries increased by 2.6 percent during the last five years, and agricultural production by only 2.5 percent.[22] As a result of such imbalances and distribution difficulties, one estimate holds that 10 million people died of hunger in the eighteenth century, 25 million in the nineteenth century, and 12 million in the twentieth century to date, with a total of at least 25 million projected for the full century ending in the year 2000.[23] An even more pessimistic view holds that of the 60 million deaths that occur each year, between 10 million and 20 million are the result of starvation or malnutrition.[24] In any case, even if the *proportion* of people suffering from malnutrition in the developing countries has declined in the last thirty years, the actual *number* of hungry people has certainly increased.[25] In 1970, for example, 462 million people suffered from malnutrition.[26]

The reasons why increasing agricultural production—including the Green Revolution—has had little impact on the number of hungry and starving people in the world reside in the difference between overall figures and actual distribution, as mentioned above. More than 2 billion people—roughly, half the world's population and, in some countries, as much as 90 percent of the population—live on small family farms in developing countries.[27] Their chance of sharing in a general advance in agriculture is small. Not only do new types of seeds, fertilizers, and pesticides require capital outlays beyond their means, but lack of storage facilities, roads, trucks, and even jute sacks makes transport and storage impossible.[28] Such lack of infrastructure in many areas means that the Green Revolution results in increased profits for large landowners, absentee landlords, and various middlemen but makes little difference in the life of the family farmer.[29] Further, not only do the hybrid seeds require much greater inputs of fertilizer, water, pesticides, and transportation,[30] they also—a fact rarely remarked—contain less protein than the open-pollinated varieties.[31]

Nor do the farmers themselves readily welcome innovations. Most farmers in developing countries lead a very precarious economic existence. By sticking to accepted practices, and living in accordance with conventional wisdom, they have managed to survive so far. "For most agricultural people, particularly the more peasant-like their systems and methods of production, the well-tried ways are known to work successfully (in their terms) at least most years."[32] Any innovation, no matter how large the possible rewards, involves the possibility of failure, and the margin for failure permitted such farmers may be very small.[33] In short, dependence on the Green Revolution results in undermining of traditional systems of social protection without substituting viable alternatives for huge segments of the rural sector of the developing world.[34]

Population/Agriculture Projections

Projecting future population and productivity trends is even more difficult than examining the past. Both estimates and opinions concerning future population growth vary widely, and are often based upon different assumptions and data.[35] If, however, the world's population were to continue to grow at the rate of 2 percent per year as it has recently, in 750 years the entire surface of the globe (land and water alike) would be covered by a solid mass of people.[36] Estimates as to what will actually happen—in contradistinction to what *could* happen—vary from a flat prediction that today's world population of 4 billion will double in thirty years[37] to a prediction that by the year 2000 the population will not have reached 6 billion.[38] However, there are virtually no serious predictions that the world population will *not* increase substantially over the present 4 billion by the year 2000.

Insofar as longer-term projections are concerned, the United Nations, in a carefully detailed and documented report, has extrapolated low, median, and high population trends. This report predicts that the increase in life expectancy will cease when it attains 74.8 years for both sexes combined (72.5 years for males and 77.5 years for females), and that zero population growth (2.08 births per couple) will be reached in various parts of the world between the years 2005 and 2070. Stabilization of the world population would then occur in the year 2075. Estimates of the population at that time range from 9.5 billion to 15.8 billion.[39] Although this may seem a long way off, we are closer to the beginning of the twenty-first century than we are to the beginning of World War II, and children born now who live sixty years or more will live most of their lives in the next century.[40] Consequently, whether one accepts the low or the high prediction, "it remains imperative to create the conditions permitting a healthy life for between 10,000 and 15,000 million human beings who will probably inhabit this earth in the coming century."[41]

Obviously, one of the essential aspects of a healthy life is the availability of food, but predictions of the future of agricultural productivity vary even more than those about population growth. There are, in fact, few predictions concerning ultimate levels of productivity, and most concern is understandably expressed in relation to what will happen in the short run—until zero population growth is achieved, if ever, or in the period until the year 2000, during which time the world's population will almost assuredly grow.

A typical view holds:

> Even the most enthusiastic boosters of the Green Revolution admit that it cannot possibly keep food production abreast of population growth for more than two decades or so. Since a birth control solution to the population explosion will inevitably take longer than that, the prospects for avoiding massive increases in the death rate from starvation are dim indeed."[42]

One reason for this pessimism is the opinion that farm production is living off past breakthroughs in agricultural technology: Agricultural research has been called "outmoded, pedestrian, and inefficient."[43] As a consequence of this, among other factors, it has been estimated that even using optimistic projections, by 1985 there will still be thirty-four countries with a combined population of 800 million whose food will fall short of their requirements.[44] Even views that rebut such predictions do so on the basis of worldwide overall production figures, and assume that the surpluses of one part of the world or one country will be distributed in another part of the world or another country, or that all the cultivable land in the world will be used, regardless of location or condition, or that lack of land area will be compensated by massive applications of fertilizers—none of which seems, remotely possible within the foreseeable future.[45]

Although the life-and-death problem of population-food ratios is the major thrust of Malthusian thinking, there are also other aspects of rapid population growth to consider: economic, social, political, educational, health, and environmental.[46] There is the question of the various kinds of pollution that will occur—smoke and fumes, junk, land exhaustion, pollution of waterways, crowded public places, traffic, and population density.[47] Housing is another area often neglected in such discussions. To maintain the present level of housing, ten new houses for every thousand of the population are needed annually—a rate attained only by Sweden, Switzerland, the Federal Republic of Germany, and Russia.[48] The correlation between crowdedness and number of school dropouts, mental illness, physical illness, delinquency, and unhappiness makes this aspect of direct importance to social welfare.

Each of these problems influences social-welfare policies and programs, and though questions of population and agricultural increases and the balance between them are dramatic and perhaps demanding, there are societies attempting to increase their populations or increase certain sectors, while others are more concerned with the health and happiness of the present population or with enlarging the area of freedom of choice to include family size and spacing of children.

SOCIAL WELFARE AND POPULATION CONSIDERATIONS

Before World War II, the desirability of population growth was hardly questioned.[49] Since that time, differing situations in various societies have led to different responses and, therefore, to different roles for social welfare. For example, while one of the highest population growth rates in the world is in Mexico (3.8 percent), the successful candidate for the Mexican presidency in 1969 called for population increases. Since then, Mexico has instituted one of the most comprehensive population policies in the Western Hemisphere, aimed at "responsible parenthood."[50] Other countries with high rates of annual population increase from 1966 to 1975 included Rhodesia (4.0 percent), South Africa (3.6 percent), and Thailand (3.3 percent).[51] Family-planning programs in these countries are relatively weak.[52] On the other hand, the Philippines, with a population increase in 1976 of 3.0 percent, Taiwan (1.9 percent), India (2.0 percent), and Japan (1.2 percent)[53] are engaged in massive campaigns, as are Iran, Kenya, Egypt, and Indonesia.[54] Mainland China is also thought to be engaged in a widespread population-control effort, reportedly with considerable success, though the available hard data are difficult to validate.[55]

Other countries engage in different social-welfare programs related to population. Although these can be separated for heuristic purposes, they actually merge, exist side by side, or conflict, even within the same society. A U.N. categorization of such programs is pronatalist, noninterventionist, human rights, social development, and population-growth limitation.[56]

Some of these programs have been further subdivided into family protection, protection of mothers, protection of children, responsible parenthood, family planning, and family-life education.[57] For purposes of discussion here, social-welfare activities related to population problems have been divided into seven categories, each of which will be examined under a separate heading.

1. Controlling Population Growth. In those countries where rapid population growth is seen as one of the major causes of physical, social, and economic problems, it is understandable that population control is an important goal of national policy. For reasons to be delineated, however, this is not a unanimous reaction. Indeed, of 130 developing countries with high fertility rates in 1976, only 33 have acknowledged government programs to lower fertility, 31 provide family planning for health and humanitarian reasons, 64 have no such programs; and information from 2 countries is lacking.[58] Of countries that have population-control programs (and these are not confined to developing countries), Japan, South Korea, Singapore, and Taiwan are among the most successful to date. In Taiwan, for example, the average annual growth rate before 1966 was more than 30 per thousand. During 1967-74, this was reduced to 21.2 per thousand, and in 1974 the rate had fallen to 18.67 per thousand.[59]

The world birth rate (which is not the same as the growth rate) declined from 34 per thousand people in 1965 to 30 per thousand in 1974. Birth rates dropped in 127 countries, including the most populous, but the drops in Latin America and Africa were very small.[60] The rate of natural increase (the birth-death ratio) throughout the world dropped slightly from 1965 to 1975, remaining steady in Latin America and the Near East, and actually rising in Africa.[61]

Although increasing life expectancy is as important a factor in population growth in many countries as is a high birth rate, the latter seems more susceptible to manipulation, and population control seems easier and cheaper than increasing resources or attempting to solve the problems caused by overpopulation: "Money spent to reduce births will be as much as 100 times more effective than money invested to raise output."[62]

The methods by which population control is attempted vary from the very indirect to the direct. Some countries, for example, depend on or encourage emigration. In the West Indies it is estimated that emigration reduces the net population increase in some years by 52 percent.[63] In fact, in four areas of the West Indies, emigration exceeded net population increase, and in four others it ranged from 70 to 90 percent of that increase.[64] Similarly, emigration has been a substantial factor in stabilizing the population of Eire. In some countries, emigration helps to reduce population though it is primarily favored for reasons that are unrelated to population: India derives a large part of its foreign-currency reserve from remittances sent home to family members by Indians abroad, while Lebanon considers such remittances an important part of its economy. Conversely, there are countries that prohibit or limit immigration for population-control reasons.

In other places reduction of the population is seen as a function of the general economic situation. There is a strong correlation between higher economic status and smaller families, and middle-class families are usually smaller than lower-class families. However, correlation is not causation, and it is also true that in many societies small families have a better chance of moving into the middle class.[65]

Another indirect method of encouraging smaller families is through legislation that favors small families through tax structures, housing policies, employment policies, and social-welfare programs. In some Indian states, for example, workers are threatened with dismissal if they continue having children after the first two. In other countries, income-tax exemptions grow progressively smaller with additional dependents, or children's allowances are reduced. Singapore makes it difficult for employed women with more than three children to get maternity benefits and for large families to find housing.[66] Some countries pay bonuses to men who undergo vasectomies.

These measures have been called "inducements," in contradistinction to voluntarism and compulsion.[67] More direct measures are used to encourage voluntarism in the area of population control. These include education, the availability of legal and inexpensive abortions, voluntary sterilization, and widespread distribution of contraceptives. In Pakistan, contraceptives are sold at more than 35,000 pharmacies, tea stalls, general provision stores, and others. No prescription is required, and as a sales incentive, the shopkeepers are permitted to keep 40 percent of the sales price.[68]

Even more direct measures are involved in compulsion, which, taken to its logical extreme, means enforced sterilization. Although no country admits to this practice, there are charges that so-called voluntary sterilization plans are enforced under various kinds of pressure.[69] Reports of such cases in the United States led to an investigation and strict measures against the practice[70]—measures that not everyone believes to be enforced. In 1976, the Indian Minister for Health and Family Planning stated that the government "might have to resort to making it a law."[71]

The extent and efficacy of the direct measures rest, in large part, on the religion, culture, and laws of the country concerned. Religious attitudes vary. The official attitude of the Roman Catholic Church as expressed by the Vatican opposes all methods of birth control except the rhythm method.[72] Protestants are generally in favor of contraception as a method of preventive birth control.[73] The Orthodox Jewish approach condones contraceptive methods on the part of the female, but proscribes them for the male, including coitus interruptus,[74] while Conservative and Reform Jews tend to condone contraceptive devices employed by either sex. Hindu belief systems provide little barrier to the use of family planning,[75] though Gandhi saw artificial birth control as reprehensible.[76] Buddhism has neither the injunction to multiply nor strict prohibitions on birth control: The well-being of the living is considered paramount.[77] In Islam, abortion is absolutely forbidden, but contraception is allowed for pressing reasons, providing both marriage partners agree, the agreement is voluntary, and the time period is limited.[78] Pragmatically, Saudi Arabia forbids the sale of contraceptives,[79] Pakistan encourages and subsidizes such sales,[80] and Bangladesh is reported to be moving toward legalized abortion.[81]

The culture of a country or a group may look down on large families as a manifestation of lower-class values. There are also individuals and groups who consider more than two children per couple as a form of environmental pollution, and aim for zero population growth. Conversely, there are cultures in which having many children (particularly boys) is considered proof of the masculinity ("machismo") of the father and the good fortune of the mother.[82] In Hinduism, a son is looked on as one of the greatest blessings because the father's fortune in the next world depends on the exact execution of the funeral rites by his son.[83] In Judaism too, a son to say the memorial prayers (Kaddish) for the departed is extremely important to some branches. There are also societies that value children as laborers—in the past, in factories or home sweatshops; and at present, on farms, picking flowers, making rugs, and in other specific occupations. In some cultures—for example, in African countries where the life expectancy is short—large families are based on the desire for enough grown children to provide for the parents' old age. (A Yiddish proverb, however, says that though two parents can support twelve children, twelve children can't seem to support two parents.)

Finally, the laws of a country may mandate birth-control measures; may legalize some, but not other, birth-control activities; or may outlaw any such activities. There are many combinations and variations in this area. In some places, governmental involvement is illegal or otherwise impossible, but voluntary organizations may be permitted, or even encouraged, to engage in such programs, or the law may permit dissemination of information but not devices. Again, information and devices may be permitted while abortions are outlawed. Finally, abortions may be permitted but not through use of public funds. In addition, states or other local authorities may be permitted what the national government is forbidden, or vice versa.

The rationales for laws affecting contraceptives may be viewed as based on the following:

1. *Human survival:* the high rate of child mortality.
2. *Nationalism:* fear of being outnumbered by a rival religious, cultural, or racial group (the Singhalese and Tamils in Sri Lanka) or a national rivalry requiring large armies (Honduras and El Salvador).
3. *Doctrinaire issues:* Malthusianism and neo-Malthusianism.
4. *Religious opposition:* in many predominantly Catholic countries.

5. *Protection of public morals:* birth-control information seen as ob-
scenity, indecency, or promoting promiscuity.[84]

There are also factors that, though extraneous to government or
policy considerations, might influence individual sets of parents regarding having or not having additional children. One of these is education,
because there is a rough inverse correlation between education and
number of children. The number of previous children who have survived also influences the decision to have more children, as does the
amount of family income. The mother's employment opportunities or
actual employment outside the house also has an effect.[85] Finally, the
rise of the feminist movement, which has cast doubt on woman's rele-
gation to *Kinder, Kirche, und Küche* and led many women to demand
a voice in family decisions, is not without effect.

Although individuals and couples have probably practiced some sort
of birth control since the earliest times, it was in 1807 that the Code
Napoleon was introduced in France, giving daughters the same inheritance rights as sons. French workers and peasants immediately em-
braced the advantages of family limitation, using folk methods handed
down for generations.[86] The first birth-control clinics in the world were
established in Holland in 1878,[87] and it was after that date that acceptance of contraceptive techniques in England is said to have been
responsible for the sudden drop in the English birthrate.[88] The term
"birth control," however, dates back to 1914. It won out over "family
limitation," "conscious generation," "neo-Malthusianism," "voluntary
parenthood," "voluntary motherhood," "race control," and "birthrate
control,"[89] though "family planning" has become the preferred term of
late, and does denote a somewhat different approach.

The growth of birth control or family planning throughout the world
is forever linked with the name of Margaret Sanger, who virtually
single-handedly brought the importance of population questions to the
attention of governments and people.[90] She was jailed eight times (all
in the United States)[91] but persisted in her contentions that birth-
control information is not obscene, that it is an integral part of public
health and education, and that both societies as a whole and individuals
have a right to decide population questions on the basis of knowledge,
rather than ignorance.

It is possible to trace the development of the birth-control movement
through a series of important events, but these hardly do credit to the
rich history of what is, essentially, the evolution of a social movement,
and they have been documented elsewhere.[92] The first issue of Margaret Sanger's *Woman Rebel* appeared in 1914, and the first birth-control
clinic in America opened in Brooklyn in 1916, only to be closed by the
police. In 1921, the National Birth Control Association was founded,

and in 1925, the International Association. In 1931, as a result of such activities and growing interest, the Federal Council of Churches of Christ in America called for the repeal of both federal and state laws that prohibited communication about birth control by physicians and other qualified people, and the Vatican sanctioned the rhythm method of birth control in the early 1930s. In 1936, court rulings made possible for the first time the mailing of contraceptive materials and information to and from doctors and other qualified people. In 1942, the Birth Control Association changed its name to the Planned Parenthood Federation of America.[93] After continuing interest and agitation, the American Public Health Association, in 1959, passed a "stunning" resolution stressing the importance of birth control.[94] In 1960, the birth-control pill was released to the general public,[95] and family planning became a generally accepted activity.

In 1965, the Supreme Court found in *Griswald* v. *Connecticut* that the "right to privacy" guaranteed by the Constitution governs the right to decide "whether and when to bear or beget a child." Consequently, distribution of contraceptives and contraceptive information is now legal in all states.[96]

Two caveats regarding this history of birth control and family planning are in order. The first is that it has been concerned solely with the activities of voluntary organizations, rather than with those of governments, and the second is that the history concerns birth-control information and materials but not abortions, which have their own record.

Although the Surgeon General had ruled in 1942 that states could use federal funds for family-planning services, few states used these funds at first. However, government concern for widespread knowledge concerning family planning—in contradistinction to that available through private medicine—began to grow with the realization that poverty and large families are correlated, presumably owing to poor families' inability to acquire the necessary information and devices.[97] With the Supreme Court ruling in 1965 that married couples have a constitutional right to practice contraception, the Office of Economic Opportunity began to make grants to finance family-planning projects, and in 1967 this became an object of "special emphasis."[98] In the same year, the Social Security Act was amended to offer educational and practical services to families with dependent children.[99]

Family-planning activities can be divided into giving information, giving or implanting devices, and performing abortions. As heated as was the controversy over the first two activities, and as halting as was their growth, they were minor issues as compared to the passions, controversies, and campaigns around abortion. The abortion issue not only arouses deep moral fervor on both sides but has medical, legal, sociological, philosophic, demographic, and psychological aspects.[100]

Nevertheless, abortion is now probably the most widespread method of limiting birth.[101] The number of pregnancies terminated each year by induced abortion throughout the world is not known. Recent estimates have ranged from 30 million to 55 million.[102] It is probable that some form of abortion has been in use since the earliest days of mankind, and it had evidently become widespread enough in relatively modern times for Pope Pius XI to feel constrained in 1679 to condemn the notion that the unborn fetus may be killed to escape personal or social complications.[103]

It was, indeed, the widespread use of illegal abortions, which often resulted in injury or death to the mother, that motivated many people to support contraceptive measures. Margaret Sanger, for one, was originally opposed to abortion and urged contraception as a measure that would make abortion unnecessary.

In the United States, a number of forces combined to change attitudes and the law regarding abortions. The rediscovery of poverty led to recognition that the poor, dependent on societal resources and agencies, were denied the relevant goods and services available to others through the private market, including information, devices, and abortions. Simultaneously, the student revolt and the black revolt led to more concern for individual freedom and rights, and they were soon joined by the women's movement. The revealed correlation between large families and societal problems had an impact on attitudes toward abortion no less than on other methods of birth control. Finally, the dangers of illegal abortions were brought to public notice in a number of dramatic ways.[104]

The battle for legalized abortion involved, and continues to involve, deeply held ideological and moral positions, the poles of which have evolved into the right-to-life position and the right-to-choose position and produced rhetoric that, on one side, speaks of the fetus as a "bit of vegetating unborn matter," and, on the other, speaks of "socially convenient murder."[105]

The middle 1960s appear to have been a watershed in the liberalization of laws regarding abortion throughout the world. Until then, abortion laws had generally been very strict—in some states, even stricter than those of the Catholic Church. In Japan and certain parts of Europe, however, abortions—safely performed—were associated with spectacular drops in birthrates. In the 1960s, it was estimated that there were about a million abortions a year in the United States. The great majority of these were illegal because abortion was permitted only to save the life of the mother. Beginning in 1967, about a dozen states enacted somewhat more liberal laws,[106] and a Supreme Court decision in 1973 invalidated the antiabortion laws of most states.[107] Although by late 1975 this decision had not yet been fully implemented in every state, it was noted that in 1973 somewhere between 600,000 and 750,000 legal abortions were reported in the United States.[108] In Canada, the life of the mother remains the only legal basis for abortion, but the law is not strictly enforced; medically dictated abortions are common, and women wishing to terminate a pregnancy for a nonmedical reason often cross the border and undergo the operation in the United States.[109]

In 1976, it was estimated that 8 percent of countries rule abortions to be illegal; 13 percent allow abortions under very restricted conditions; 16 percent allow abortions if based upon medical, eugenic, or humanitarian conditions; 24 percent allow abortions for societal reasons; 36 percent allow abortions on request; and in 3 percent of the countries the situation is unknown.[110] In fact, common acceptance of abortion has grown throughout the world to the point that Pope Paul VI thought it necessary to reaffirm the church's traditional position in 1974,[111] which surprised and disappointed many who were hoping for a liberalization of the church's stand.

The move toward more liberal attitudes regarding abortion in the United States has not been without opposition. Those who oppose abortion on moral grounds hope to override the decision of the Supreme Court with a constitutional amendment. The attitudes of the candidates toward such an amendment became an issue during the presidential campaign of 1976.

Aside from morality as such, one of the controversial and major issues is whether abortions should be made available through welfare programs, thus using tax payments of a portion of the population to perform what they consider illegal and immoral acts. Owing to the passionate intensity with which views on both sides are held, it is probable that laws and activities will continue to fluctuate from side to side with political, judicial, and administrative changes.

The activities of social-welfare agencies and social workers involved in population-control measures in the United States have been almost nonexistent because there is no policy of controlling population growth as such: Efforts have been directed toward family planning, family welfare, and family-life education. In other parts of the world, however, social-welfare agencies and workers have taken the lead in population-control activities, carrying almost the entire burden in some countries.

The United Nations has been active in the area of population problems. There is U.N. Fund for Population Activities, the World Health Organization has incorporated family planning into its worldwide activities, and conferences are periodically sponsored on subjects as various as social-welfare aspects of family planning,[112] law and population,[113] and world population as a challenge to development.[114]

Perhaps the most salient evidence of social work's involvement in population problems is the active role taken by schools of social work throughout the world, under the leadership of the International Association of Schools of Social Work. Beginning in 1970 with a conference in Hawaii,[115] the Association undertook a five-year project to stimulate the development of qualified social-work personnel in various regions of the world for effective participation in family-planning and population policies, programs, and services. The goal of the project was to establish pilot projects in up to thirty schools of social work throughout the world, in which the development of indigenous curricula, teaching materials, demonstration projects, and field instruction placements would be stimulated. Among other things, a 57-item "reference bookshelf" has been distributed and a "Reader's Guide" to the bookshelf circulated.[116] As might be expected, success has been greater in some areas than in others. Initial success was achieved in Asia, later success in Africa, and the least to date in Latin America.

Many professionals, in addition to social workers, participate in family-planning activities. These include nurses, public health workers, specially trained population workers, and even agricultural extension personnel. In some countries, it has been found efficacious to combine family-life education with literacy and nutrition campaigns.[117] In this manner, the material used to increase literacy relates to family-life and nutritional education. In other countries, family planning is an integral part of the community movement.[118] In such settings two of the important subjects for group discussion in community meetings are the need for and methods of family planning.

Worldwide involvement in population planning passed a landmark in 1974 with a U.N. World Population Conference held in Bucharest, Rumania.[119] One hundred and thirty-six member states discussed population problems openly and freely, and though various positions were espoused, a plan of action was adopted, albeit with what many observers saw as weaknesses. The major positions and their principal proponents were

1. Population growth is desirable to fill empty lands (Brazil), for development and defense purposes in the developing world (China), or to stimulate the economy (France).
2. Population growth is not an important variable, but development is (many African and Latin American states).
3. Rapid population growth intensifies problems in socio-economic development (most of Asia, Western Europe, the United States, Oceania, Japan, and some Latin American states).
4. Population is a key variable in socio-economic development (Bangladesh).

5. There is no need for population policy: in a well-organized society the demographic trends are adjusted automatically by social and economic factors (Eastern Europe, excluding Rumania and Yugoslavia).[120]

Whether or not as a result of this conference, developments fostering more widespread distribution of birth-control information and devices, and liberalization of laws concerning abortion, have been increasingly rapid throughout the world during the last few years. Although the policies that flow from these developments are not always (or even often) thought of as or called social-welfare services, the use of social workers to implement them is widespread. Most of the social workers would deny that they are carrying out activities based on Malthusian theory and would, instead, define their work as improving the quality of life in their respective countries.

2. Increasing Resources. One method of attempting to overcome the population/agriculture imbalance is, as outlined above, to try to limit population. The other possibility is to try to increase available resources. The latter was the major counterthrust to population control at the Bucharest Conference. Many countries, including mainland China, argued that economic development is the major need, that with proper development population growth would be no problem, and that attempts to concentrate on population control divert attention from the need for economic development.

One does not ordinarily think of social-welfare policies as designed primarily to increase resources, though, as pointed out previously, the goal of returning welfare clients to productive activities runs through many programs. Throughout the developing world, however, massive programs to increase agricultural production are seen as encompassing the goals of social welfare and the activities of social workers. It is in this sense that many developing countries posit social welfare as an integral tool in national development. Because this is often seen as different from, and even in opposition to, the tradition of social work as a one-to-one relationship dealing with intrapsychic problems as it has evolved in many Western countries, efforts to promote indigenous social welfare often mean transforming the Western tradition to serve national interests.

The massive programs that attempt to increase agricultural productivity, especially on small family farms, use many workers with a variety of titles—social worker, village worker, rural worker, cadre member, and so forth—who have different kinds of training, to carry out social-welfare policies as part of national development programs. Whether or not they are called social workers, they use the values and methods of social work—consciously or unwittingly[121]—including beginning where people are, individualizing, motivating, respecting local tradition and cultures, and using what has been termed "cultural empathy."[122] Similarly, the goal of improving the quality of life makes it possible to view the policies as social-welfare policies, regardless of their official titles.

In addition, a method of choice for increasing agricultural productivity has been the formation of cooperatives. Through the cooperative endeavors of a number of farmers, facilities denied individuals can be obtained. Consequently, there are purchasing and marketing cooperatives; transportation and credit cooperatives; cooperative tilling of fields, fertilizing, spraying, and harvesting. In 1975, Taiwan, for example, had 3,616 cooperatives of various kinds, including cooperative farms.[123] The agricultural extension worker operates, in many cases, as a community organizer; conversely, the community organizer is often used to help solve agricultural problems.

It is interesting that within the rather limited experience of developed countries in utilizing so-called industrial social workers, the social workers have seen their roles as helping workers to solve personal problems, rather than as aiding production by reducing absenteeism and turnover; whereas in the developing countries the "personal problem" is most likely to be the need for increased production.

This need for social workers who can help small farmers increase production—and the specialized training it entails—is one strand in the tapestry of the increasing effort to make social-welfare programs and social work throughout the world indigenous. There are real and pressing needs in the countries concerned, and they are far from the content of social work imported from elsewhere, via consultants, teaching materials, or training abroad.[124] In any case, for social-welfare personnel to whom population-control methods as such are counterindicated, for whatever reason, the use of social-work methods and social-welfare programs to increase resources offers a logical alternative.

3. Distributing Resources. A third field of service for social welfare is the attempt to bridge the gap between available resources and needy people. Whether or not the resources now available are and will be sufficient,[125] the problem of distribution will remain. The avowed goal of social welfare in some countries, such as Sweden, is a more equitable distribution of welfare,[126] but in other countries it is more fundamentally a matter of helping poor people acquire more resources. Consequently, it is probably safe to say that most social workers throughout the world spend some, if not most, of their time helping their clients with additional resources or indicating to them how or where they can acquire additional resources. Not only does poverty remain one of the most widespread and pressing of social problems;[127] it has also been increasingly recognized as both the cause and effect of many other ills. The client who says, "Let's not talk about my kid anymore. Let's talk dollars and cents," is exemplifying the interrelatedness of these problems.[128]

Of the six basic social-welfare program fields listed by Kamerman and Kahn, distribution of material resources is paramount in the areas of income maintenance and housing, and indirectly in employment. Even within health, education, and the "personal" or "general" services, there are elements of resource distribution.[129] Such resource distribution takes the shape of monetary programs—both of the insurance type and grants—vouchers such as rent orders and food stamps, and the direct distribution of food, clothing, prosthetic devices, and so forth. Resource distribution is also the focus of long-term planning in social welfare, deriving from such formulations as "The whole experience of the last century is that if parents are given work, responsibility, enough food and safe water, they have the sense to see they do not need endless children as insurance against calamity."[130]

4. Family and Child Welfare. Much social-welfare policy and many social-work activities are concerned not with the size of populations or the amount of resources but, rather, with the mental and physical health of children, and thus, perforce, with families. Such services include surrogate care and adoption for children whose homes or parents are no longer suitable or available; protection against abuse and neglect; institutionalization, including group-care homes; day-care programs; and school lunches—as well as counseling, guidance, and referral for all family members. In Israel, there are even arrangements to add rooms to the houses of large families.[131]

Population considerations enter when it is recognized that all over the world it is a commonplace that large families and poverty very often go hand in hand,[132] and when social-welfare efforts are then directed toward achieving smaller families for the sake of health and well-being, rather than as an instrument of national policy. Indeed, aggregate family planning does not add up to population control: "Millions of individual private reproductive decisions do not automatically control population for society's benefit."[133] From a transnational viewpoint, it appears that there is a preference in social-welfare programs for in-kind benefits where the end in view is the healthy nurture of children, while cash benefits are more often linked to demographic policy.[134]

As remarked in Chapter 3, the United States has no official policy regarding family size or family welfare. Indeed, in December 1971, President Nixon vetoed large-scale child-care legislation on the basis that it would commit the government to communal, rather than family-centered, child rearing.[135] Nevertheless, the fact that in the United States 41 percent of mothers of children less than eighteen years old work—including 29 percent of mothers of children under three, 45 percent of mothers of children under six, and 57 percent of mothers with children from six to seventeen—indicates both the need for and the scope of child-welfare activities in America.[136] Further, increasing entry of women into the labor force—either voluntarily or as required by the WIN program—has created a need for day-care facilities, which represent one of the faster-growing services in the United States. And, as with most emergency situations, bureaucratic foul-ups, problems of the establishment of standards, and corruption among suppliers remain to be remedied.

5. *Family Planning.* Family planning is related to family welfare inso-far as the size of families can be a determinant of their economic position or of the incidence of various problems connected with family size. The basic reason for family planning, however, is a desire to offer choice to parents as a right. Demand for this right, like many others, seems to be linked to larger-scale reactions to government control, as well as to improved technology that makes choice concerning family size and spacing realistic and effective.

Although the "right to choose" is often used as a proabortion slogan, it is applicable on a wider scale related to birth-control information and devices. Proliferation of this concept can be traced in the literature of social welfare. In 1966, for example, the Adelphi University School of Social Work cosponsored with the United Cerebral Palsy Association a conference entitled "Mothers-at-Risk";[137] a 1968 conference was co-sponsored by the American Public Health Association, the Child Wel-fare League of America, and the Family Service Association of America and was entitled "Family Planning";[138] and in 1971 the Council on Social Work Education made available readings and case materials on family planning.[139] Education on family planning may range from questions of personal hygiene, through sexuality, to birth-control informa-tion, and is often subsumed under the heading "family-life education."[140] As such, it is firmly seated in many social-welfare agen-cies, as well as government programs. In 1965, for example, family-planning services were permitted states using federal Title XIX funds; in 1972, family-planning services were made a mandatory element of state Medicaid plans; and in 1975, Title XX gave states the right to develop their own social-service provisions, but retained family plan-ning as the only specifically mandated service.[141]

6. *Selective Policies.* Social-welfare policies regarding population con-trol or family planning are not always applicable to the entire popula-

tion affected. There may be programs to control growth of only segments of the population or to offer family-planning help to selected groups. In Israel, for example, there is a recognition of the correlation between large families and various problems, and hence activity designed to offer information concerning family planning to families with such problems, while at the same time there is a unit within the Prime Minister's office charged with encouraging population growth for the country as a whole. Little wonder that this has been termed a "schizophrenic policy toward large families."[142]

Selectivity regarding population growth (or control) can be and has become a serious bone of contention, with the more disadvantaged segments of the population sometimes convinced that such measures are designed solely to decimate or weaken them. For this reason, zero population growth has been denounced as a fascist movement by the American Progressive Labor Party,[143] and some developing countries are known to view family planning as a type of colonialism, designed to keep them small and weak. History offers some support for such accusations and feelings: In Victorian England, it was permissible to say things about the poor that would later come to be regarded as outrageous,[144] and it is not surprising that such beliefs can lead to support for eugenic selection.[145]

The eugenics movement—or, at least, its philosophy—was spurred by a book published in 1877. Richard Dugdale, a prison inspector, became interested in the large number of prisoners who bore the family name Juke, and on tracing 1,200 people of Juke blood, he found 280 on relief, 200 criminals, 50 prostitutes, and numerous others with similar records. Blaming heredity, *The Jukes* created a sensation.[146] Two books published in 1912, one in London and one in New York,[147] demonstrated how much certain families of "hereditary criminals" and mental defectives had cost society,[148] and contributed to the foundation of a eugenics movement that called for the repression of "defective stock."[149] It was implicit that those who should be allowed—perhaps encouraged—to reproduce were mature, well-to-do, college-trained citizens.[150] By 1915, twelve U.S. states had adopted sterilization laws.[151]

On a more genteel level, President Theodore Roosevelt had remarked, around the turn of the century, that the "worst evil" in population-growth rates in America was the relative infertility of the "old native American stock, especially in the North East, as compared with the immigrant population."[152] Further, during lectures on population problems at the University of Chicago in 1929, one participant called for action that would prevent the overwhelming of the white race by colored people.[153] The fact that this person was one of Mussolini's chief spokesmen is obviously not without significance.[154]

Such suspicion of the true intent of population-control measures, and even of family-planning programs, continues to apply to current activities: "Whispers of 'planned starvation' emerged from the economic crisis of 1967, after huge cotton production cutbacks and highly automated farm machinery left the Deep South with thousands of no-longer-needed, unemployed blacks."[155] And:

> The prevailing view as to the best means is remarkably unanimous and abundantly documented. It is set forth in . . . seventeen volumes of Congressional hearings so far published on the "population crisis." . . . The essential recommendation . . . is that the government should give highest priority to ghetto-oriented family-planning programs.[156]

So deep are these suspicions that when the 1967 amendments to the Social Security Act ruled that public welfare programs for families with dependent children should include educational and practical services in family planning, rather than being seen as an attempt to give poor families equal access to such facilities with other families, they were interpreted in some circles as singling out the poor as promiscuous,[157] and many social workers balked or inwardly resisted them on the grounds that by designing the program for the poor alone, the government might arouse feelings of undue pressure in the minds of some of the families involved.[158]

These charges indicate the strength of emotions aroused around the entire question of population control or family planning. When the government withholds family-planning information in its programs, it is accused of depriving the poor of what is available to others. When it offers such information to the poor, it is accused of discrimination. When it offers information on a universal basis, it is still accused of discrimination because only the poor participate in government social-welfare programs.

7. Encouraging Population Growth. At the opposite end of the spectrum from population control are what are termed pro-natalist policies. From the earliest times population laws, at least, have been pro-natalist. "The early codes dating back to Hammurabi and the Emperor Augustus contained such provisions. The United States of America's Declaration of Independence accused King George III of Britain: 'He has endeavored to prevent the population of these states.' "[159]

One of the most widespread reasons for pro-natalist policies is quasi-xenophobic fears that other groups, countries, philosophies, or races are threatening by virtue of their very size. Unable to affect their growth, the effort is turned inward, toward increasing population. Appleman cites a number of such examples:

> A distinguished Egyptian demographer told me in 1963 that the military leaders there were against population limitation because "Egypt must

become great"; an Indian demographer told me that since the Chinese invasion, Indian militarists have increasingly criticized the government's family planning program; a leader of the Family Planning Association in Thailand told me the army had been a powerful and effective foe of the organization there from the beginning; and an important Chinese government official on Formosa . . . told me: "Our population increase means we *must* go back to the mainland. That's what we're working for."[160]

There are other countries such as Israel, however, which are short of labor, and some that see some minimum population figure as necessary for viability and independence: The 4 million people in Ireland and Denmark are sometimes cited as a model. Argentina and Brazil have been called "frankly pro-natalist," with their large tracts of empty land given as the reason.[161] In India, despite a change in the inheritance law dating to 1956, custom still limits succession to males, exerting a pro-natalist effect because "a family which already has several daughters will want more children in the hope of producing a son, in order to keep property within the family."[162]

Then there is simply the tradition, which the women's liberation movement is seeking to uproot, that it is the proper role of women to have babies and raise families—or, more precisely, that a woman is or should be happy only when there is a baby on the way or in the family.[163] Finally, there are pro-natalist practices that do not derive from stated policy: In Egypt, Indonesia, Iran, and Sri Lanka, a woman can be divorced on one of many grounds and find herself without alimony, a job opportunity, or custody of her children; this forces her to bear as many children as her husband demands.[164]

Regardless of motivations for enlarging populations, certain activities are generally directed to that end. Tax exemptions that take into consideration the cost of raising children are perhaps the most universal of all such devices. Generally speaking, however, these are of limited utility, because exploitation of tax exemptions requires an income sufficiently large to take advantage of them. And because poor people pay lower income taxes, such exemptions act to subsidize the more affluent, who generally do not refrain from having children for financial reasons, rather than the poor, who might.

Another method of encouraging higher birthrates, as well as healthy parents and children, is the establishment of maternity benefits. In many countries, such benefits are limited to working mothers and take the form of financial benefits during time off from work, guarantee of a job on return, and reduction in work hours for a specified period. Some maternity benefits may be available to all mothers, not just those who work.[165] In Israel, these include a grant for a layette and the cost of transportation (usually by ambulance) to the hospital. (Medical expenses are covered by insurance.) The repayment of transportation costs and hospital bills has induced many mothers, particularly those from outlying areas, to give birth in hospitals rather than at home, with a consequent decrease in infant mortality.[166] Israel also has a network of maternal- and child-health clinics that give prenatal and postnatal care to all mothers and are patronized by all strata of the society.[167]

Of all measures avowedly designed to increase the birthrate, however, children's or family allowances are the most ubiquitous. In some cases, the motivation was mixed: "A combination of low birth rates . . . and difficult economic conditions for large families."[168] In other cases, it was straightforward: "With its present rate of reproduction, the British race cannot continue and childrens' allowances can at least help to restore the birth rate."[169] Some countries resisted: "Governments . . . feared that they might weaken parental responsibility for the family if they subsidised persons who produced more children than they could support."[170]

The terms "children's allowances," "family allowances," and "demogrants" are often used synonymously (and will be here), though they are technically different. Family allowances are paid to all family units, children's allowances are linked to the number of children, and demogrants are paid to each individual. There is no known instance of demogrants, and the term is often used in a generic manner, encompassing both of the other two. As noted previously, such allowances began in Europe, when employers paid differential wages based on family size —a method that was later taken over by governments. Such programs have grown from 7 in 1940 to about 65 in 1975.[171] Of the 128 countries reporting to the United Nations, 58 have no family or children's allowances; 49 have programs related to present or past employment status; 13 have universal programs, with no such linkage; 4 have dual programs, partly related to employment and partly universal; 2 (including the United States, with its AFDC) make payments based on a means test; 1 makes funds available only to those in military service; and 1 has a program of a mixed nature.[172] Every industrialized country in the West, with the exception of the United States, has a children's- or family-allowance program, as do such developing countries as Chad, Nauru, and Togo. In some cases, there are residency requirements for eligibility for family allowances, and in others, stipulation as to where the births must have occurred.[173]

There is no consistency in arrangements for family or children's allowances. Although most countries pay increasing sums as the number of children increases, some have limits, while others pay progressively less with each additional child.[174] In Norway, one-parent families get paid as for an additional child.[175] In the Canadian province of Alberta, the allowance rises with the age of the child, in recognition of increasing needs.[176] Prince Edward Island adds $10 to the allowance for the fifth and each following child.[177] Although twins do not result in disproportionate payments, Ireland pays double the normal allowance in the case of triplets or more, and in addition makes a grant of 100 pounds on the birth of triplets, and 150 pounds on the birth of quadruplets or more.[178] New Zealand pays a straight $3 per week per child, but payments can be received in a lump sum if necessary to help acquire suitable housing.[179] In Poland, payments are made for the first child, and the rate goes up with succeeding children—but only for workers' families—and there is also a means test by which poorer families are given more help.[180] The Soviet Union begins payments only with the fourth child.[181] Great Britain specifies that family allowances belong to the mother, rather than to the father or the children.[182] Israel at one time gave a cash bonus to every family having ten children. Switzerland pays more for children living in the mountains.[183] Finally, some countries tax family allowances as part of income[184] while others declare them nontaxable.[185]

There is little question but that children's and family allowances were originally instituted to increase the birthrates and thus enlarge populations. France was one of the first countries to institute such a program, and it is in that country that aid to families is largest.[186] It is also clear that in France, "the policy of encouraging a higher birth rate is reflected in the raising of family allowances for the third and fourth children."[187] This goal of children's allowances has been termed "stimulation of procreation."[188]

The evaluation of the success of children's allowances can proceed from a number of different assumptions. The variety of variables that must be taken into account in seeking to evaluate family planning as a whole has been emphasized by a World Health Organization report,[189] and some of the side effects that can occur have been mentioned in a Swedish report that finds that children's allowances tend to reduce other types of child- and family-oriented programs such as summer camps for children and vacations for housewives.[190] But France's program was the prototype of children's allowances to raise birthrates, and the French experience is instructive.

In 1939, France extended coverage of its previous children's-allowance program to the entire population, and immediately after World War II the average number of births per year rose from 630,000 to 856,000. However, Schorr notes that during the same period, the United States experienced a comparable increase without a children's allowance, and the birthrate in Sweden declined, despite that country's family-allowance system.[191] Canada, in 1945, also instituted a family-allowance program, but its birthrate continues to parallel that of the United States, which has no such program.[192] It seems, therefore, that children's or family allowances do not create higher birthrates.[193] Even if taken together, family allowances, tax measures, and maternity benefits for working mothers have not increased birthrates, while, on the contrary, compulsory education, child-labor laws, and social security do seem to have nudged fertility downward.[194]

There remains the argument about family allowances, not as an incentive for population increase but as a method—or even the preferred method—of fighting poverty and its related ills. The argument for this program,[195] as opposed to existing antipoverty programs, embodies the dilemma of universal versus categorical programs that was mentioned briefly in Chapter 2.

Proponents of a children's allowance in the United States point out that universal programs, by making benefits available to every stratum of the population, ensure that there will be an influential, sophisticated body of users who will demand, and receive, good service. They point out that services for poor people almost invariably become poor services.[196] Further, they argue that because payments are based on the number of children, large families will receive the bulk of the payments, and—because they constitute the portion of the population most at risk—their problems will thereby be solved or alleviated in disproportionate numbers. They also argue that payments going to everyone and being paid automatically will eliminate the need for a means test and all other stigmatizing features. Finally, it is argued that because everyone in the country, regardless of class or position, will benefit from such cash payments, there will be little political opposition to such a program, as there is likely to be toward new programs in aid of the poor alone. Indeed, the dismantling of some current programs that might be made possible by a universal allowance would, it is argued, be seen as sufficient reason to support such an allowance.

Proponents of categorical, or selective, programs contend that the limited money available to fight social problems should be concentrated on those with the problems rather than dispersed to others. They view children's allowances as a bonus to middle- and upper-class families at the expense of the poor. They hold that the amounts to be paid would be insignificant to the affluent, while often the difference between hunger and satisfaction, or dignity and humility, for the poor. They point out that services for the poor need not become poor services, provided they are adequately funded[197] and clients are allowed to participate in policy determination and organized into self-interest groups. They contend that means tests need not be degrading, as witness the experiment with simple statements mentioned in Chapter 2, as well as applications for loans, credit cards, charge accounts, and scholarships. Finally, they hold that "something for everybody" as the price for political support is polite bribery, and that there is little evidence that the affluent would object to further efforts to eradicate or alleviate poverty, or even that they would be unwilling to sacrifice to do so, if they were convinced that the effort would bear fruit.

Objectively, there is no question but that a universal children's or family allowance in the United States, set at a level that would raise the bulk—or even a sizable number—of poor people out of poverty, would be an extremely expensive program, even when offset by current costs of programs to be abandoned. Were the principle termed claw-back in Britain applied—that is, taxing the payments so that those in the higher income-tax brackets would pay most of it back in taxes—costs would be reduced somewhat, but because people in the 50 percent bracket would still retain half the payments, and so forth proportionately, with everyone who pays taxes, including the affluent, retaining at least part of the payments, the cost would still be enormous. The alternative would then be to reduce the payments, thereby raising fewer people out of poverty, and helping the remaining poor less. Thus, from a purely bookkeeping point of view, any program that uses resources for those not in need reduces the amount of help given the needy. Specifically, the cost of the three major proposed programs, in 1969 dollars, would be:

Vadakin's proposal: $7 billion cost, of which $1 billion would go to 16 million poor people among 144 million recipients.

Schorr's proposal: $13 billion cost, less a "substantial" fragment recovered in taxes, of which $2 billion would go to 13 million poor people among 111 million recipients.

McGovern's proposal: $42 billion cost, less taxes recovered, of which $6 billion would go to 14 million poor people among 144 million recipients.[198]

On the question of the willingness of the affluent to aid the poor, it should be pointed out that many taxpayers subsidize services for others: Childless couples pay school taxes, and people who own no car pay highway taxes. Further, in a survey conducted in nine states, 54 percent of the sample opted for a tax-supported program "for all those who have a clear need for assistance,"[199] which fits the definition of a categorical program. In a similar survey in Israel, 54 percent indicated willingness to pay more taxes to fight poverty, but 10 percent demurred on the ground that the money collected would not be, in fact, used for that purpose.[200] Public-opinion polls do not, of course, determine policies, and the major argument for a universal children's allowance, family allowance, or demogrant remains its supposed political feasibility.

SOCIAL WELFARE AS NATIONAL DEVELOPMENT

The role of social welfare in countries that use it in an attempt to increase or decrease their population, or to bring about internal changes in population composition, is an example of its use for national-development purposes. Although many countries, including the United States, have no clearly enunciated goals for the future, and therefore no medium- or long-range plans,[201] other countries have clear targets in terms of literacy, various levels of education, manpower resources, or even housing units, and these targets result in plans in which various sectors of the economy and the society are given intermediate and ultimate goals. Increasingly, social-welfare activities are being seen as an integral and important component in achieving national-development goals.

In countries where social welfare has traditionally been seen as primarily preventive and remedial, a developmental role may seem strange, and even antithetical to concern for the needs of individuals. However, a United Nations definition points out that

> ... in addition to, and extending beyond the range of its responsibilities for specific services, social welfare has a further function within the broad area of a country's social development. In this larger sense, social welfare should play a major part in ensuring that the human and material resources of the country are effectively mobilized and deployed to deal successfully with the social requirements of change and thus contribute to nation-building.[202]

Assessing the relative needs of individuals, families, groups, and the country or society as a whole, when they do not seem identical, involves difficult questions of ends and means, short-term and long-term change, and conflicting needs of individuals and groups. Increasingly, and particularly in the developing world, social welfare is being seen as an instrument of national development, with participation in population-related activities as an important—sometimes the most important—element.

SOCIAL WELFARE AND POPULATION-RELATED ACTIVITIES IN THE FUTURE

In countries with excess-population problems, social welfare will probably play an increasingly important role through future activities designed to control population growth. At the same time, it may be forced to play a more active role than heretofore in terms of both planning for increases in resources and actively engaging in some sort of agricultural extension work. This will be more important in countries with resource deficiencies, while more equitable distribution of resources will be its role in countries where poverty is perceived in relative, rather than absolute, terms.

Continually increasing life expectancy, on the other hand, can be expected to require social welfare's greater involvement in other activities. One problem will arise as the number of the aged who must be supported or helped in one way or another increases in proportion to the number of people working or able to help: Plans to lighten or equalize the burden on the young will be required. There also will be an increase in the amount of leisure time available to those who have retired (or been retired) while still able-bodied. Satisfying use of such leisure time will require planning and establishing appropriate frameworks.[203]

Finally, the increase in population that will almost surely take place through and beyond the year 2000 will bring with it new and increasing problems of environmental pollution—a subject with which social welfare will be forced to grapple if it is to remain effective in contributing to the welfare of the society.

NOTES

1. Plato, Aristotle, Tertullian, and Botero among them. See J. Mayer, "Toward a Non-Malthusian Population Policy," in D. Callahan (ed.), *The American Population Debate* (Garden City, N.Y.: Doubleday, 1971), pp. 135–53.

2. T. R. Malthus, *An Essay on the Principle of Population; or, A View of Its Past and Present Effect on Human Happiness with an Inquiry into Our Prospects Respecting the Future Removal or Mitigation of the Evils Which It Occasions* (7th ed.); see also T. R. Malthus, *Population: The First Essay* (Ann Arbor: University of Michigan Press, 1959).

3. K. E. Boulding, "Foreword," in Malthus, 1959, *op. cit.*, p. vi.

4. Malthus, 1959, *op. cit.*, p. 4.

5. *Ibid.*, p. 13.

6. Boulding, *op. cit.*, p. vii.

7. *Ibid.*, p. ix.

8. *Ibid.*, p. vii.

9. Two hundred years later this was still the major hope of a person as prominent as a 1976 presidential aspirant: "Every family with two or more children would make a personal, voluntary decision to have no more children. Every couple with no children or one child would voluntarily agree to stop with the second." M. K. Udall, "Spaceship Earth: Standing Room Only," in Callahan, *op. cit.*, pp. 84–95.

182   DESIGN OF SOCIAL WELFARE

10. R. L. Heilbroner, *The Worldly Philosophers* (New York: Simon & Schuster, 1953), p. 69.
11. Malthus, 1959, *op. cit.*, p. 29.
12. Heilbroner, *op. cit.*, p. 86.
13. G. Abbott, *From Relief to Social Security* (Chicago: University of Chicago Press, 1941), p. 8.
14. Mayer, *op. cit.*, p. 139.
15. *Population and Vital Statistics Report: Data Available as of 1 July 1976* (New York: United Nations, 1976), ST/ESA/STAT/SER.A/117, p. 1.
16. Mayer, *op. cit.*, p. 140.
17. P. Myers, *1976 World Population Data Sheet* (Washington, D.C.: Population Reference Bureau, 1976).
18. *The Secret of Affluence* (Washington, D.C.: Department of Agriculture, 1976).
19. Mayer, *op. cit.*, p. 144.
20. *Ibid.*
21. *Ibid.*, p. 143.
22. *New York Times*, August 8, 1976, p. E3, based on reports of the 1974 World Conference on Food and from the International Food Policy Research Institute.
23. "Starvation," *Parade*, December 14, 1975, p. 5.
24. P. R. Ehrlich and A. H. Ehrlich, *Population, Resources, Environment: Issues in Human Ecology* (San Francisco: Freeman, 1970).
25. *Population, Food Supply and Agricultural Development* (Rome: Food and Agriculture Organization of the United Nations, 1975) (originally published as Chapter 3 of *The State of Food and Agriculture: 1974* [Rome: Food and Agriculture Organization, 1975]), p. 11.)
26. *Ibid.*, p. 32.
27. D. Macarov and G. Fradkin, *The Short Course in Development Activities* (Ramat Gan, Israel: Massada Press, 1973), p. 17.
28. S. Samant, S. Sawant, and B. Talati, *Distribution of Fertilizers in Ralnagiri (India) District* (Tel Aviv: Foreign Training Department, Ministry of Agriculture, 1970) (mimeographed), p. 6.
29. S. L. Parmar, "What Good Is Economic Betterment ...," *CERES*, 3 (1970): 21; W. Ladejinsky, *Foreign Affairs*, quoted in *CERES*, 3 (1970):13; D. Tweddle, "What People Who Care Really Think," *CERES*, 3 (1970): 27; A. Krassowski (ed.), *British Development Policies: Needs and Prospects 1970* (London: Overseas Development Institute, 1970), p. 62; and Macarov and Fradkin, *op. cit.*, p. 26.
30. V. K. Oppenheimer, *Population* (New York: Foreign Policy Association, 1971).
31. M. Perelman, "The Generation of Technology and Agricultural Efficiency," *Review of Social Economy*, 29 (October 1976):217–24.
32. G. E. Jones, "Rural Development and Agricultural Extension: A Sociological View," *Community Development Journal*, 6 (1967):26.
33. Macarov and Fradkin, *op. cit.*, p. 97.
34. N. Gilbert, "Alternative Forms of Social Protection for Developing Countries," *Social Security Review*, 50 (September 1976):363–87.

35. For passionate views on various sides, see Callahan, *op. cit.*

36. Boulding, *op. cit.*, p. vi.

37. *New York Times*, May 31, 1976, p. 3.

38. L. R. Brown, "The Growth of Population Is Slowing Down," *New York Times*, November 21, 1976, p. E8.

39. *Concise Report on the World Population in 1970-75 and Its Long-Range Implications* (New York: United Nations, Department of Economic and Social Affairs, 1974), ST/ESA/SER.A/56.

40. "Man's Population Predicament," *Population Bulletin*, Vol. 27, No. 2, Population Reference Bureau, 1971; quoted in K. B. Oettinger and J. D. Stansbury, *Population and Family Planning: Analytical Abstracts for Social Work Educators and Related Disciplines* (New York: International Association of Schools of Social Work, 1972).

41. *Concise Report . . ., op. cit.*, p. 68.

42. Ehrlich and Ehrlich, *op. cit.*

43. V. R. McElheny, "Scientific Impasse Faces U.S. in Its Agricultural Technology," *New York Times*, May 31, 1976, pp. 1, 22.

44. *Population, Food Supply and Agricultural Development, op. cit.*, p. 27.

45. Mayer, *op. cit.*

46. *Rapid Population Growth: Consequences and Policy Implications* (Baltimore: Johns Hopkins Press, 1971).

47. W. H. Davis, "Overpopulated America," in Callahan, *op. cit.*, pp. 161–67.

48. *World Population: Challenge to Development* (New York: United Nations, 1966), E/CONF.41/1, pp. 26–27.

49. *Law and Population* (New York: United Nations Fund for Population Activities, n.d.), p. 9.

50. *World Population Growth and Response: 1965–1975—A Decade of Global Action* (Washington, D.C.: Population Reference Bureau, 1976), pp. 147–48.

51. *Social Welfare Indicators: Republic of China, 1976* (Taipei: Executive Yuan, 1976), p. 98.

52. *World Population Growth . . ., op. cit.*

53. Myers, *op. cit.*

54. *Social Welfare and Family Planning* (New York: United Nations, 1976), ST/ESA/27, p. 52.

55. Although there are a number of studies of population activities in China —such as Chen Pi-chao, *Population and Health Policy in the People's Republic of China* (Washington, D. C.: Smithsonian Institution, 1976); *Population and Family Planning in the People's Republic of China* (Washington, D.C.: Population Crisis Committee, 1971); J. S. Aird, *Population Policy and Demographic Prospects in the People's Republic of China* (Washington, D.C.: Department of Health, Education, and Welfare, 1972)—the Chinese delegation to the World Population Conference refused to publish reports or statistics, demanded that all such information be deleted from the official conference proceedings, and "came out in extreme terms with an attack on the population explosion 'myth.' " A. McCormack, "Driving a Stake into the Heart of Old Malthus," *People*, 1 (1974):5–14, 39.

56. *Report of the Interregional Meeting of Experts on the Social Welfare Aspects of Family Planning* (New York: United Nations, 1971), ST/SOA/111, pp. 12–13; *Social Welfare and Family Planning, op. cit.*, pp. 42–43.
57. A. Gindy, "Social Welfare and Family Planning: A New Priority for the United Nations," *New Themes in Social Work Education* (New York: International Association of Schools of Social Work, 1972), pp. 180–81.
58. D. Nortman and E. Hofstatter, "Population and Family Planning Programs: A Factbook," *Reports on Population and Family Planning*, 2 (October 1976).
59. *A Review of Public Administration: The Republic of China* (Taipei: Executive Yuan, 1975), p. 3.
60. *World Population Growth . . ., op. cit.*, p. 3.
61. *Ibid.*, p. 265.
62. S. Enkes, "The Economic Case for Birth Control in Underdeveloped Nations," *Challenge Magazine*, May-June 1967; quoted in H. L. Sheppard, *Effects of Family Planning on Poverty in the United States* (Kalamazoo, Mich.: Upjohn, 1967), p. 10.
63. "Social Realities and the Social Work Response: Report from the English-Speaking Caribbean." Paper presented at the Eighteenth International Conference of Schools of Social Work, San Juan, Puerto Rico, July 13–17, 1976.
64. *Ibid.*
65. Sheppard, *op. cit.*
66. *World Population Growth . . ., op. cit.*, p. 98; see also *India: An Introduction* (New Delhi: Ministry of External Affairs, 1975).
67. H. D. Stein, "Values, Family Planning, and Development: Implications for Social Work," in *A Developmental Outlook for Social Work Education* (New York: International Association of Schools of Social Work, 1974), p. 50.
68. *World Population Growth . . ., op. cit.*, p. 93.
69. K. Gulhati, "Compulsory Sterilization: A New Dimension in India's Population Policy," *Draper World Population Fund Report*, 3 (Autumn-Winter 1976): 26–29.
70. S. B. Kamerman and A. J. Kahn, *Social Services in the United States: Policies and Programs* (Philadelphia: Temple University Press, 1976), p. 395; see also S. M. Rothman, "Sterilizing the Poor," *Social Science and Modern Society*, 14 (January-February 1977): 36–40.
71. Gulhati, *op. cit.*
72. F. J. Ayd, Jr., "The Catholic Church," in E. T. Tyler (ed.), *Birth Control: A Continuing Controversy* (Springfield, Ill.: Thomas, 1967), p. 88.
73. J. Fletcher, "The Protestant Churches," in Tyler, *op. cit.*, pp. 99–106. This, despite Luther's attitude: "If a woman grows weary and at last dies from childbearing, it matters not. Let her only die from bearing; she is there to do it." Quoted in M. Sanger, *Margaret Sanger: An Autobiography* (New York: Norton, 1938), p. 210.
74. A. F. Guttmacher, "Judaism," in Tyler, *op. cit.*, pp. 107–17.
75. Stein, *op. cit.*, p. 52.

76. D. Callahan, *Abortion: Law, Choice and Morality* (New York: Macmillan, 1970), p. 153.
77. Stein, *op. cit.*, p. 52.
78. A. A. Maududi, *Birth Control: Its Social, Political, Economic, Moral, and Religious Aspects* (Lahore: Islamic Publications, 1974); see also S. Soemardjan, "Social Attitudes toward Population Policies in Less Developed Societies," in K. A. Kendall (ed.), *Population Dynamics and Family Planning: A New Responsibility for Social Work Education* (New York: Council on Social Work Education, 1971), p. 113. Nevertheless, "some Moslem authorities do not consider the termination of pregnancy before foetal viability as forbidden by Islam." *Law and Population, op. cit.*, p. 32.
79. *World Population Growth . . ., op. cit.*, p. 173.
80. *Ibid.*, p. 98.
81. *Ibid.*, p. 71.
82. In Arabic, the father without sons is derisively called *abu banot*—"father of daughters."
83. Callahan, *Abortion, op. cit.*, p. 154.
84. J. Stepan and E. H. Kellogg, *Comparative Study of World Law on Contraceptives: Revised and Updated* (Washington, D.C.: Smithsonian Institution, 1974), pp. 5–6.
85. Stein, *op. cit.*, p. 58; specifically, see D. W. Bowers and D. W. Hastings, "Childspacing and Wife's Employment Status Among 1940–41 University of Utah Graduates," *Rocky Mountain Social Science Journal, 7* (1970):125–36.
86. L. Lader, *The Margaret Sanger Story and the Fight for Birth Control* (Garden City, N.Y.: Doubleday, 1955), pp. 50–51.
87. *Ibid.*, p. 76.
88. *Ibid.*, p. 68.
89. *Ibid.*, p. 53.
90. M. Sanger, *Margaret Sanger: An Autobiography* (New York: Norton, 1938).
91. E. T. Douglas, *Margaret Sanger: Pioneer of the Future* (New York: Holt, Rinehart & Winston, 1970), p. 1.
92. *Ibid.*; Lader, *op. cit.*; Sanger, *op. cit.*; D. M. Kennedy, *Birth Control in America: The Career of Margaret Sanger* (New Haven, Conn.: Yale University Press, 1970).
93. Lader, *op. cit.*
94. A. F. Guttmacher, "Family Planning: Humanism and Science," in F. Haselkorn (ed.), *Family Planning: The Role of Social Work* (Garden City, N.Y.: Adelphi University School of Social Work, 1968), pp. 18–29.
95. Douglas, *op. cit.*, p. 259.
96. Stepan and Kellogg, *op. cit.*, p. 17.
97. "The United States Government quietly supported a few family planning programs as early as the 1930s, but it neither publicly acknowledged nor vigorously pursued those activities. . . . By 1967, the Agency for International Development was spending almost 9 million dollars annually on birth control abroad, and the Office [sic] of Health, Education, and Wel-

fare, with the Office for [sic] Economic Opportunity, spent over 20 million dollars for contraceptive programs in this country." Kennedy, *op. cit.,* p. viii.

98. Kamerman and Kahn, *op. cit.,* pp. 390–91.
99. Oettinger and Stansbury, *op. cit.,* p. 21.
100. Callahan, *Abortion, op. cit.,* p. 1.
101. Oettinger and Stansbury, *op. cit.,* p. 56.
102. C. Tietze and M. J. Murstein, "Induced Abortion: 1975 Factbook," *Reports on Population/Family Planning,* 14 (December 1975):1–76.
103. Pope Pius XI, *Casti Connubi,* March 4, 1679.
104. For example, through such movies as *Love with a Proper Stranger.*
105. H. B. Munson, "Abortion in Modern Times: Thoughts and Comments," *Renewal,* February 1967, p.9; M. Hentoff, "Abortion: Murder as a Liberal Art," *Jubilee,* April 1967, pp. 4–5; both quoted in Callahan, *Abortion, op. cit.,* p. 4.
106. See *Workbook on the First National Affiliate Workshop on Planning and Providing Abortion Services* (New York: Planned Parenthood–World Population, 1973).
107. Tietze and Murstein, *op. cit.,* p. 7.
108. *Ibid.,* p. 14.
109. M. Zimmerman, "Abortion Law and Practice: A Status Report," *Population Reports,* E (March 1976):25–40.
110. *Ibid.*
111. *Declaration on Abortion,* Sacred Congregation for Doctrine, June 28, 1974; released November 18, 1974, by Pope Paul VI per Franciscus Cardinal Sper, Prefect.
112. *Report of the Interregional Meeting . . ., op. cit.*
113. *The Symposium on Law and Population* (New York: United Nations Fund for Population Activities, 1975).
114. *World Population Growth . . ., op. cit.*
115. Kendall, *op. cit.*
116. Oettinger and Stansbury, *op. cit;* see also K. B. Oettinger, *Social Work in Action: An International Perspective on Population and Family Planning* (New York: International Association of Schools of Social Work, 1975).
117. *Social Welfare and Family Planning, op. cit.,* p. 49.
118. *Korea: Past and Present* (Seoul: Kwangnyong, 1972), pp. 348–50.
119. "A Report on Bucharest," *Studies in Family Planning,* 5 (December 1974):357–95.
120. *Ibid.,* p. 359.
121. D. Macarov and G. Fradkin, "Principles of Manpower Training for Agricultural Development: The Israeli Experience," *Community Development Journal,* 10 (October 1975):171–78; W. F. Whyte, *Organizing for Agricultural Development: Human Aspects in the Utilization of Science and Technology* (New Brunswick, N.J.: Transaction, 1975).
122. W. H. Goodenough, *Cooperation in Change* (New York: Sage, 1963).
123. *China Yearbook 1976* (Taipei: Republic of China, 1976), p. 319.
124. See, for example, D. Macarov, "Some Aspects of Teaching from Foreign Records," *Indian Journal of Social Work,* 24 (January 1964):315–20.

125. For varying views, see Mayer, *op. cit.*, and W. G. Marston, "The Population Crisis: Myth or Menace?" in W. M. Gerson (ed.), *Social Problems in a Changing World* (New York: Crowell, 1969), pp. 527–46.

126. "Social Welfare: Ends and Means," in *Current Sweden*, No. 54 (Stockholm: Swedish Institute, 1974).

127. R. Bendiner, "Poverty Is a Tougher Problem than Ever," in H. L. Sheppard (ed.), *Poverty and Wealth in America* (Chicago: Quadrangle, 1970), pp. 76–88. For some insight into poverty and related problems in a Communist state, see G. Konrad, *The Case Worker* (New York: Harcourt Brace Jovanovich, 1974).

128. E. M. Elman, *The Poorhouse State* (New York: Pantheon, 1966), p. 292.

129. Kamerman and Kahn, *op. cit.*, pp. 6–7.

130. B. Ward, "Not Triage, but Investment in People, Food, and Water," *New York Times*, November 15, 1976, p. L31.

131. D. Macarov, "Israel's Social Services: Historical Roots and Current Situation," in D. Thursz and J. L. Vigilante (eds.), *Meeting Human Needs*, Vol. 1: *An Overview of Nine Countries* (Beverly Hills, Calif.: Sage, 1975), p. 145.

132. *Ibid.*, and *Introduction to Social Security: A Workers' Education Manual* (Geneva: International Labour Organization, 1970), p. 46.

133. K. Davis, "Population Policy: Will Current Programs Succeed?" *Science*, November 10, 1967, pp. 730–39; quoted in L. Rapoport, "The Social Work Role in Family Planning: A Summation," in F. Haselkorn (ed.), *Family Planning: The Role of Social Work* (Garden City, N. Y.: Adelphi University School of Social Work, 1968), pp. 144–59.

134. *Introduction to Social Security, op. cit.*, p. 47.

135. A. J. Kahn and S. B. Kamerman, *Not for the Poor Alone: European Social Services* (Philadelphia: Temple University Press, 1975), p. 172.

136. *Ibid.*, p. 174.

137. F. Haselkorn (ed.), *Mothers-at-Risk* (Garden City, N.Y.: Adelphi University School of Social Work, 1966).

138. Haselkorn, *Family Planning, op. cit.*

139. F. Haselkorn (ed.), *Family Planning: Readings and Case Material* (New York: Council on Social Work Education, 1971).

140. In El Salvador, for example, though family-planning clinics are active throughout the country, "the philosophy of these activities respects the individual right of self-determination." *El Salvador* (New York: El Salvador Consulate, n.d.), p. 15.

141. Kamerman and Kahn, *op. cit.*, pp. 393–94.

142. E. D. Jaffe, "Poverty in the Third Jewish Commonwealth: Sephardi-Ashkenazi Divisions," *Journal of Jewish Communal Service*, 52 (Fall 1975):91–99.

143. "ZPG: A Fascist Movement!" in Callahan, *The American Population Debate, op. cit.*, pp. 68–76.

144. V. Shlakman, "Social Work's Role in Family Planning: Social Policy Issues," in Haselkorn, *Family Planning: The Role of Social Work, op. cit.*, p. 71.

145. *Ibid.*, p. 70.

146. R. L. Dugdale, *The Jukes: A Study in Crime, Pauperism, Disease and*

Heredity, 4th ed. (New York: Arno Press, 1970), quoted in Goldman, *op. cit.,* p. 92.

147. K. Pearson, *Darwinism, Medical Progress and Eugenics* (London: University College, 1912); H. H. Goddard, *The Kallikak Family: A Study in the Heredity of Feeble-Mindedness* (New York: Arno Press, 1973).

148. P. Thoenes, *The Elite in the Welfare State* (New York: Free Press, 1966), p. 61. It should be noted that the data of both the Juke and the Kallikak studies have been re-examined, leading to considerable question as to their correctness; the importance of environment as opposed to inheritance is recognized to a much greater extent today than when those books were published.

149. R. Lubove, *The Professional Altruist: The Emergence of Social Work as a Career: 1880–1930* (New York: Atheneum, 1973), p. 69.

150. R. Hofstadter, *Social Darwinism in American Thought* (Boston: Beacon Press, 1944), p. 163.

151. Thoenes, *op. cit.,* p. 61.

152. Kennedy, *op. cit.,* p. 43.

153. C. Gini, "The Cyclical Rise and Fall of Population," in C. Gini *et al., Population* (Chicago: University of Chicago Press, 1930), pp. 1–91.

154. Lader, *op. cit.,* p. 242.

155. N. Kotz, *Let Them Eat Promises* (Garden City, N.Y.: Doubleday, 1971), p. 31.

156. J. Blake, "Population Policy for Americans: Is the Government Being Misled?" in Callahan, *The American Population Debate, op. cit.,* p. 298.

157. Kamerman and Kahn, *op. cit.,* p. 409.

158. Oettinger and Stansbury, *op. cit.,* p. 21.

159. *Law and Population, op. cit.,* p. 9.

160. P. Appleman, *The Silent Explosion* (Boston: Beacon Press, 1965), p. 47. (Emphasis in original.)

161. McCormack, *op. cit.,* p. 6.

162. *Law and Population, op. cit.,* p. 8.

163. E. Peck and J. Senderowitz, *Pronatalism: The Myth of Mom and Apple Pie* (New York: Crowell, 1974).

164. *Law and Population, op. cit.,* p. 26.

165. Israel includes women who adopt children, while Sweden pays benefits to fathers who stay home to take care of newborn children. *Social Security Programs Throughout the World, 1975* (Washington, D.C.: Department of Health, Education, and Welfare, 1975), p. xi.

166. D. Macarov, *Social Welfare* (No. 15 in *Israel Today* Series) (Jerusalem: Ministry of Foreign Affairs, 1975).

167. For other arrangements for young children, see A. Doron, *Cross-National Studies of Social Service Systems: Israeli Reports* (New York: Columbia University Press, 1976).

168. L. Holgersson and S. Lundstrom, *The Evolution of Swedish Social Welfare* (Stockholm: The Swedish Institute, 1975), p. 9.

169. W. H. Beveridge, *Social Insurance and Allied Services* (New York: Macmillan, 1942), p. 154.

170. *Introduction to Social Security, op. cit.,* p. 46.

171. *Social Security Programs Throughout the World, 1975, op. cit.*, p. xi.

172. *Ibid.*

173. *Ibid.*, p. 49.

174. Although Williamson *et al.* say, "There is no country that pays less for each subsequent child," both Hungary and Rumania do. See J. B. Williamson *et al.*, *Strategies Against Poverty in America* (New York: Wiley, 1975), p. 78; and *Social Security Programs Throughout the World, 1975, op. cit.*, pp. 99, 133.

175. *Facts About Norway* (Oslo: Royal Ministry of Foreign Affairs, 1975).

176. *Health and Welfare in Canada*, Reference Paper No. 94 (Ottawa: Department of External Affairs, 1975).

177. *Ibid.*

178. *Guide to the Social Services* (Dublin: Stationery Office, 1974), p. 56.

179. *New Zealand Official Yearbook, 1974* (Wellington: Government of New Zealand, 1975).

180. *Poland: A Handbook* (Warsaw: Interpress, 1974).

181. *Social Security Programs Throughout the World, 1975, op. cit.*, p. xxvi.

182. *Social Services in Britain* (New York: British Information Services, 1975).

183. *Social Security Programs Throughout the World, 1975, op. cit.*, p. 215.

184. *Health and Welfare in Canada, op. cit.*

185. *Social Benefits in Sweden: 1974–1975* (Stockholm: Tryg Hansa, 1974), p. 2.

186. *Social Security and National Health Insurance in France* (New York: Ambassade de France, N.D.), p. 15.

187. *Ibid.*

188. E. M. Burns, "Childhood Poverty and the Children's Allowance," in E. M. Burns (ed.), *Children's Allowances and the Economic Welfare of Children* (New York: Citizens Committee for Children of New York, 1968), p. 12; quoted in N. Gilbert and H. Specht, *Dimensions of Social Welfare Policy* (Englewood Cliffs, N.J.: Prentice-Hall, 1974), p. 63.

189. *Evaluation of Family Planning in Health Services* (Geneva: World Health Organization, 1975).

190. Holgersson and Lundstrom, *op. cit.*

191. A. L. Schorr, "Income Maintenance and the Birth Rate," *Social Security Bulletin*, 28 (December 1965):2.

192. Gilbert and Specht, *op. cit.*, p. 64.

193. Kahn and Kamerman, *op. cit.*, p. 153. In this connection, a former official (female) of the U.S. Department of Health, Education, and Welfare commented to a congressional committee that the assumption that women have children in order to collect money always seems to emanate from men: No women seem to make this charge!

194. Oettinger and Stansbury, *op. cit.*, p. 67.

195. For example, Schorr, "Income Maintenance . . .," *op. cit.*, and D. P. Moynihan, "The Case for a Family Allowance," *New York Times Magazine*, February 5, 1967, pp. 13, 68–73.

196. As Yarmolinsky points out, "Legal Aid clients can get separations, but divorces are for the paying clients. Legal Aid clients can get arrangements to pay off their accumulated debts, but bankruptcy . . . proceed-

ings are for the paying clients. Legal Aid clients brought up on criminal charges are encouraged to accept the plea bargain offered by the prosecutor." A. Yarmolinksy, "The Service Society," *Daedalus,* 97 (Fall 1968): 1263.

197. That services confined to one group of people, and even including some means-tested programs, can be quality service is evidenced by the Veterans' Administration: "Veterans benefits pay better and come easier; the recipients are not badgered or made to feel they are a drag on society. These programs are, in fact, the very model of a modern humanistic socialism: they are characterized by federal standards and financing; a presumption of eligibility and of earned right; easy application and easy appeals; and a warmhearted collaboration of intercessor groups." H. L. Wilensky, *The Welfare State and Equality: Structural and Ideological Roots of Public Expenditures* (Berkeley: University of California, 1975), pp. 41–42.

198. Williamson, *op. cit.,* pp. 78–79.

199. G. W. Carter, L. H. Fifield, and H. Shields, *Public Opinions toward Welfare: An Opinion Poll* (Los Angeles: Regional Research Institute in Social Welfare, School of Social Work, University of Southern California, 1973), p. 8.

200. D. Macarov and U. Yannai, *Images of Poverty and the Poor in Jerusalem* (Jerusalem: Paul Baerwald School of Social Work, Hebrew University, 1975) (in Hebrew).

201. On national medium- and long-range plans, see *Approaches and Methods Used in Long-Term Social Planning and Policy-Making* (New York: United Nations, 1973), ECE/EC.AD/3.

202. *Training for Social Welfare: Fifth International Survey—New Approaches in Meeting Manpower Needs* (New York: United Nations, 1971), ST/SOA/105, p. 2.

203. For current thinking in this direction, see Kaplan, *op. cit.;* and for transnational perspectives, A. Szalai (ed.), *The Use of Time: Daily Activities of Urban and Suburban Populations in Twelve Countries* (The Hague: Mouton, 1972).

9

Who Deserves to Survive?: The Influence of Social Darwinism

BIOLOGICAL DARWINISM

For fifty years before Charles Darwin published *The Origins of Species* in 1859,[1] the problems of variation, adaptation, heredity, and environment had been receiving considerable attention from scientists[2] but no one had developed a comprehensive theory as widely accepted as evolution. It was while Darwin was engaging in the systematic inquiry that led to his book that he happened to read Malthus's famous essay on population. He was at once struck by the fact that under circumstances of insufficient sustenance for all, "favorable variations would tend to be preserved and unfavorable ones to be destroyed."[3] From this grew the concept that later came to be generally termed "survival of the fittest."[4]

Although Darwin knew nothing of the principles of Mendelian genetics, he based his theory of natural selection on the universal somatic variations among organisms.[5] Consequently, his theory dealt with species rather than individuals, and with somatic (that is, genetically determined) differences rather than those that are attributable to nurture, environment, or socialization. In short, Darwin dealt with the biological world, in which genetic mutations favorable to survival eventually resulted in a changed species—provided the mutation was transmitted to sufficient progeny.

Indeed, the major challenge to Darwin's theory, and to the genetic principles on which it was based, came from the Soviet biologist Trofim Denisovich Lysenko, who claimed to have caused environmentally induced changes to continue genetically, through breeding. Lysenko held, for example, that by subjecting wheat to heat at certain periods, it could be made to produce rye, and that cuckoos could be hatched from warblers' eggs.[6] The Chevalier de Lamarck, in France, had argued many years previously that acquired characteristics could be inherited, but his ideas had been discredited.[7] Lysenko's contention that environmental conditions could be manipulated in such a manner that plants would change while growing, and thus produce a new species, was highly compatible with Communist ideology under Stalin because it indicated that the Soviet socio-economic system could produce a new type of citizen who would transmit his or her characteristics biologically, obviating the necessity of continuing educational or socialization efforts. As a consequence, Lysenko and his theory were elevated to high positions in the Soviet Union and all question—let alone dissent—was suppressed until after Stalin's death, at which time Lysenko and his theories were repudiated by Khrushchev, once a farmer. It is believed that forced acceptance of Lysenko's theory set Soviet agriculture back, perhaps by generations, and may be at least partly responsible for the famines in Stalin's day and the Russian food shortages that still exist at this writing.

Darwin's theory of genetically carried mutations and subsequent development of new species had little direct impact on social welfare. For one thing, evolutionary change was felt to occur over time periods difficult for the ordinary mind to grasp, and secondly, conscious intervention in the evolutionary process was seen as impossible.

SOCIAL DARWINISM

The major impact of Darwinian theory on social welfare came about not as the result of a massive perversion like Lysenko's but, rather, through a vulgarization of Darwin's thesis, which came to be called Social Darwinism. Social Darwinism is distinct from biological Darwinism in that it attempts to apply Darwin's theory of the evolution of the species to human individuals and—more recently—social institutions. Social Darwinism concerned itself less with the process through which individuals and institutions were presumed to have evolved than with the end result—that the fittest had survived:

> Biological Darwinism asserted that all species of organic life had evolved and were evolving by a process of the survival of the fittest. According to . . . "Social Darwinism," society, too, was an organism that evolved by the survival of the fittest. Existing institutions were therefore the "fittest" way of doing things, and businessmen who bested their competitors had thereby proved themselves "the fittest to enjoy wealth and power."[8]

Herbert Spencer, philosopher, writer, and teacher, was one of the earliest proponents of Social Darwinism, and though he was English he was enormously influential in America from about 1870 to 1890. From the very beginning, Spencer carried Social Darwinism to its logical conclusion:

> He who loses his life because of his stupidity, vice, or idleness is in the same class as the victims of weak viscera or malformed limbs. Under nature's laws all alike are put on trial. "If they are sufficiently complete to live, they *do* live, and it is well they should live. If they are not sufficiently complete to live, they die, and it is best they should die"[9]

No philosophy or theory could have suited the upper classes of America in the days of the robber barons so well. It mattered not how a man became rich or powerful; his having done so proved that he was entitled to his wealth and power, for he was one of the fit. And the cries of those whom he hurt, and the outrage of those who observed his methods, were merely fulminations of the jealous unfit, not worthy of consideration. Thus, John D. Rockefeller could say to a Sunday school:

> The growth of a large business is merely a survival of the fittest. . . . The American Beauty rose can be produced in the splendor and fragrance which bring cheer to its beholder only by sacrificing the early buds which grow up around it. This is not an evil tendency in business. It is merely the working-out of a law of nature and a law of God.[10]

America did not lack for its own prophets of Social Darwinism. William Graham Sumner,[11] one of the most articulate and influential, had no patience with those who would lavish compensations upon the virtueless:

> . . . "the strong" and "the weak" are terms which admit of no definition unless they are made equivalent to the industrious and the idle, the frugal and the extravagant . . . if we do not like the survival of the fittest, we have only one possible alternative, and that is the survival of the unfittest. The former is the law of civilization; the latter is the law of anti-civilization . . . a plan for nourishing the unfittest and yet advancing in civilization, no man will ever find.[12]

Social Darwinism, as it has evolved, differs from classical Darwinism, and even from early Social Darwinism, in a number of ways. In some versions, it does not admit the existence of mutations—that is, breaks with the past or with tradition—but holds that individuals and groups, and even entire social classes, must move upward step by step: specifically, that the "virtues" of the elite class can only be attained by first achieving the virtues of the lower classes and continuing to develop.[13] In the developmental view, immigrant groups too were presumed to be moving along a continuum from peasant village to modern urban culture.[14] If a group did not emerge as successful in comparison with other groups, the defect was obviously inherent in the group: Its members were too "primitive" or "uncultured." The success of immigrant groups was sometimes put in terms of the group's assimilability—the more difficult to assimilate, to become like Americans (that is, white Anglo-Saxon Protestants), the more negative the group image. A similar pattern emerged during the period of mass immigration into Israel: A status-ladder emerged in which immigrants from Yemen were on the upper rungs, as clean, healthy, and hardworking, albeit exotic, thus exemplifying the aspiration values of Israel, while immigants from Kurdistan were viewed as stolid, unambitious, and unintelligent. Efforts to increase the assimilation of the latter group were often countered with appeals to developmentalism: Only time could effect the desired change. The major thrust of the developmental viewpoint is that efforts to reform society, or even social welfare, are doomed to failure because only slow evolutionary change in people can bring about changes in society.

Another result of Social Darwinism is the displacement of "equality" as the basic social goal in America by "equality of opportunity."[15] Equality, obviously not having been achieved, can be dismissed as antievolutionary and, therefore, unnatural. It is rationalized, instead, that America offers everyone equality of opportunity. If there are those who cannot take advantage of such opportunity, it can only be because of their own lacks—or, more bluntly—their inferiority.[16]

Sometimes the superiority-inferiority dichotomy is expressed in terms of class, as when F. Scott Fitzgerald wistfully remarks that the very rich "are different from you and me,"[17] but class consciousness has been relatively ephemeral in America as compared to consciousness of race, color, or creed,[18] and it was to the latter kinds of minorities that the inferiority postulated by Social Darwinism was imputed. Social Darwinism thus offered special opportunities to those who sought "scientific bolstering of their prejudices, and the opportunities were fully exploited to reduce the Negro and 'non-Anglo-Saxon' immigrants to a position of permanent inferiority."[19]

As the early Social Darwinist view that the defects that caused personal and group failure were inherent and inherited came to be identified with such prejudice and racism, a later, more genteel variation came into prominence:

The new ideology is very different from the open prejudice and reactionary tactics of the old days. Its adherents include sympathetic social scientists with social consciences in good working order, and liberal politicians with a genuine commitment to reform. They are very careful to dissociate themselves from vulgar Calvinism or crude racism; they indignantly condemn any notions of innate wickedness or genetic defect. "The Negro is *not born* inferior," they shout apoplectically. "Force of circumstance . . . has *made* him inferior" . . . he is "caught in the cycle of poverty." He is trained to be poor by his culture and his family life, endowed by his environment . . . with those unfortunately unpleasant characteristics that make him ineligible for a passport into the affluent society. . . . But the stigma, the defect, the fatal difference . . . is still located within the victim.[20]

This new version of Social Darwinism has been termed "blaming the victim," and it is illustrated by Ryan:

The miserable health care of the poor is explained away on the grounds that the victim has poor motivation and lacks health information. The problems of slum housing are traced to the characteristics of tenants who are labeled as "Southern rural migrants" not yet "acculturated" to life in the big city. The "multiproblem" poor, it is claimed, suffer the psychological effects of impoverishment, the "culture of poverty," and the deviant value system of the lower classes; consequently, though unwittingly, they cause their own troubles.[21]

In its several variants—developmentalism, equality of opportunity, and blaming the victim—the net effect of Social Darwinism is to rationalize away the inequalities of society on the grounds that some people are smarter, stronger, more moral, or even more finely tuned in their ego defenses than others[22] and, conversely, that the cognitive capacity, moral development, and psychodynamic organization of the needy, the lower class, or the unsuccessful are inferior.[23] In this way, hunger can be explained away on the grounds that parents are ignorant as to what constitutes a balanced diet, or child neglect on the basis of mentally retarded parents.[24]

Through defining need as individual deficiency, rather than as institutional or resource deficiency,[25] poverty comes to be viewed as a normal state for large segments of the population,[26] and almost all of society's members come to agree that the prevailing system of inequality is "acceptable and just."[27] In short, Social Darwinism offers a theoretical basis for elevating selfishness to a science.[28] As such, it is obviously diametrically opposed to the basis of mutual aid, a fact that caused Kropotkin to remark that evolutionists might admit the importance of mutual aid among animals, but like Spencer, they refused to admit it for man.[29]

As a method of analyzing society, Social Darwinism was less useful than it was as a rationalization for the status quo, and it soon lost the interest and support of intellectuals. Thorstein Veblen, however, turned from individual behavior to that of institutions and saw the social institution, rather than the individual, as the subject of selection, or survival of the fittest.[30] Because it is more difficult to achieve consensus on the success of institutions than on that of individuals, and thus it is harder to impute inherent defects to unsuccessful institutions, the very continuation of institutions, rather than their success, becomes the criterion for "fitness." Social Darwinism thereby becomes an ultraconservative tautology: Whatever is has proved its fitness by continuing to exist; whatever exists is fittest to exist. Everything, therefore, is as it should be, and nothing should be changed. In this manner, Social Darwinism leads to the practice of defending the status quo.[31]

EFFECTS ON SOCIAL WELFARE

Because Social Darwinism was seen as the working out of natural law, as immutable as the laws of evolution, any attempt to alter or disturb its workings by aiding the unfit (that is, the needy) was not only futile; it was also immoral—an attempt to thwart the will of God or nature. In addition, helping the unfit must be at the expense of the fit—a further immorality. Spencer's categorical repudiation of state interference with the "natural," unimpeded growth of society led him to oppose all state aid to the poor. They are unfit and should be eliminated: "The whole effort of nature is to get rid of such, to clear the world of them, and make room for better."[32] Sumner spoke more directly to social welfare:

> The next time that you are tempted to subscribe a dollar to a charity, I do not tell you not to do it, because after you have fairly considered the matter, you may think it right to do it, but I do ask you to stop and remember . . . that if you put your dollar in the savings bank it will go to swell the capital of the country which is available for division amongst those who, while they earn it, will reproduce it with increase.[33]

Mostly as a result of the influence of Spencer and Sumner, the Charity Organization Society movement accepted Social Darwinism as a theoretical base for its activities. The theory strengthened the belief that the cause of social problems lay in the individuals afflicted with them, rather than in the rest of society,[34] and these individuals were thus seen as existing outside the mainstream of the country's activities and development. Unfit to survive, they were nevertheless kept alive by humanitarian charity. Far from contributing to the development of mankind and society, they were deadweight—a drag on the movement to ultimate perfection.

Consequently, pity for those afflicted with problems was replaced with blame, leading to the creation of an outcast class viewed and treated not with indifference but with contempt.[35] Those who have "made it" are sure they have done so through their inherent fitness, motivation, and efforts, and any lingering doubts are exorcised by comparison with the purported unfit, unmotivated, and inactive.[36]

This underlying feeling of superiority of the successful to the unsuccessful, of the fit in relation to the unfit, is a major influence in the formulation of social-welfare policies and programs. Regulations that once denied the vote to paupers, nonowners of property, or nontaxpayers have been revoked,[37] but the question of whether the mentally ill should be allowed to have children, or even get married, is still subject to passionate debate in some places. Similarly, help to the poor must be gingerly legislated and extended, lest the agency or the government be accused of pampering the poor. The help given the ill, the aged, and the disabled is usually less than sufficient to make a decent life possible, because they are no longer in a position to contribute to societal development.

The working out of Social Darwinism in social-welfare programs is exemplified in urban renewal. Many American cities, concerned about the decay of their inner cities, the low quality of life thus engendered, and the conditions under which people were living, requisitioned the land on which slum dwellings stood—using various legal devices—and evicted the tenants. In many cases, equivalent (that is, equally bad) housing was found for the tenants, on the supposition that once the new housing was ready, they could move back. But the cost of replacing slums with more suitable housing resulted in rentals too high for the former tenants, with the result that more affluent people moved into the new housing. This move was not decried by the private or government developers, not only because the new tenants paid more rent but also because, as a common expression put it, "those people" (the former tenants) would not have known how to maintain the new housing in a desirable manner. In short, urban renewal became a stratagem for keeping the unfit out of sight, and leaving them with only such housing as they "deserved." This pattern repeated itself so often in American cities that it gave rise to the dictum, among the knowledgeable, that "urban renewal means Negro removal."

Further hints as to the strength of Social Darwinism in American thought are contained in the results of various surveys concerning the plight of the needy, and particularly of the poor. In one such survey, for example, though only 32 percent of the responses felt that people were poor because of their own faults or shortcomings, 54 percent felt that they could pull themselves up if they wanted to badly enough.[38] In other words, 22 percent of the respondents believed that people are poor because of circumstances beyond their control, and yet that they could control those circumstances if they wanted to.

The force of Social Darwinism is emphasized by the fact that though the major thesis of biological Darwinism—that of evolution—has come to be generally accepted throughout the world, the survival of the fittest as applied to individuals and institutions has long since lost any factual basis it might have had. With the discovery of new medicines such as antibiotics, and with the invention of life-sustaining devices such as kidney-dialysis machines, toughness and durability in the individual have been replaced by "medicated survival," practically independent of any inherent quality of the individual. Similarly, protective tariffs, monopolies and cartels acquiesced in by governments, international consortia and conglomerates, and government subsidies and cost over-runs, not to mention the "packaging" of "images" engaged in by the public-relations industry, divest organizational survival of any basis in fitness, except in the most self-interested sense. As Tawney puts it:

> Few tricks of the unsophisticated intellect are more curious than the naive psychology of the businessman, who ascribes his achievements to his own unaided efforts, in bland unconsciousness of a social order without whose continuous support and vigilant protection he would be as a lamb bleating in the desert.[39]

Social Darwinism is, therefore, an example of a theory no longer supported by facts that has become a free-standing belief system, with little relationship to reality or logic. Speaking of the blaming-the-victim brand of Social Darwinism, Ryan says:

> It is central in the mainstream of contemporary American social thought, and its ideas pervade our most crucial assumptions so thoroughly that they are hardly noticed. Moreover, the fruits of this ideology appear to be fraught with altruism and humanitarianism, so it is hard to believe that it has principally functioned to block social change.[40]

Not only does Social Darwinism block social change; it is also at the root of some opposition to social welfare, sees it vaguely as somehow maintaining the unfit at the expense of the fit, defending the "rights" of those who should have no rights, and thus undermining the rights of those who strengthen society and support the development of a new and better way of life. Hence, the derogatory term "do-gooders."

Social welfare has been singularly ineffective in breaking down the self-fulfilling prophecy that is Social Darwinism's contribution to society, namely: The needy are unfit to survive; we therefore make it difficult for them to survive; their difficulty in surviving proves that they are unfit.

NOTES

1. C. Darwin, *The Origin of Species* (London: Murray, 1859).
2. S. Persons, "Darwinism and American Culture," in *The Impact of Darwinian Thought on American Life and Culture* (Austin: University of Texas Press, 1959), p. 2.
3. F. Darwin, *The Life and Letters of Charles Darwin* (New York: Appleton, 1888), Vol. 1, p. 68; quoted in R. Hofstadter, *Social Darwinism in American Thought* (Boston: Beacon Press, 1944), p. 39.
4. A phrase actually coined in H. Spencer, "A Theory of Population, Deduced from the General Law of Animal Fertility," *Westminster Review*, 57 (1852):468–501; quoted in Hofstadter, *loc. cit.*
5. Persons, *op. cit.*, p. 4.
6. D. Joravsky, *The Lysenko Affair* (Cambridge, Mass.: Harvard University Press, 1970), pp. 157–58, 212.
7. Hofstadter, *loc. cit.*, H. G. Cannon, *Lamarck and Modern Genetics* (Westport, Conn.: Greenwood Press, 1959).
8. E. F. Goldman, *Rendezvous with Destiny: A History of Modern American Reform* (New York: Vintage, n.d.), pp. 70–71.
9. Hofstadter, *op. cit.*, p. 41.
10. *Ibid.*, p. 45.
11. W. G. Sumner, *Social Darwinism* (Englewood Cliffs; N.J.: Prentice-Hall, 1963).
12. Hofstadter, *op. cit.*, p. 57.
13. M. Lerner, "Respectable Bigotry," in M. Friedman (ed.), *Overcoming Middle Class Rage* (Philadelphia: Westminster Press, 1971), p. 253.
14. R. J. Vecoli, "Ethnicity: A Neglected Dimension of American History," in Friedman, *op. cit.*, p. 172.
15. R. Parker, *The Myth of the Middle Class* (New York: Harper & Row, 1972), p. xviii.
16. The black revolt of the 1960s, with its demands for recompense for past deprivations rather than mere compensation for present lacks, added a further dimension to the equality issue and led to demands for equity, rather than equality, and demands that needs be the criteria for help, rather than equality of opportunity or of services.
17. To which Ernest Hemingway, no Social Darwinist, is said to have responded, "Yes, Scott. They have more money."
18. D. Danzig, "The Social Framework of Ethnic Conflict in America," in Friedman, *op. cit.*, p. 253.
19. Goldman, *op. cit.*, p. 96.
20. W. Ryan, "Blaming the Victim: Ideology Serves the Establishment," in P. Roby (ed.), *The Poverty Establishment* (Englewood Cliffs, N. J.: Prentice-Hall, 1974), p. 173. (Emphasis in original.)
21. *Ibid.*
22. Lerner, *op. cit.*, p. 151.
23. *Ibid.*, p. 148.
24. N. Kotz, *Let Them Eat Promises* (Garden City, N. Y.: Doubleday, 1971), p. 107.

25. N. Gilbert and H. Specht, *Dimensions of Social Welfare Policy* (Englewood Cliffs, N. J.: Prentice-Hall, 1974), p. 97.

26. J. W. Eaton, "Community Development Ideologies," *International Review of Community Development,* 2 (1963):40–41.

27. J. V. Til, "Social Inequality: How Did We Get Here Anyway?" in A. B. Shostak, J. V. Til, and S. B. V. Til, *Privilege in America: An End to Inequality?* (Englewood Cliffs, N.J.: Prentice-Hall, 1973), p. 4.

28. Goldman, *op. cit.,* p. 71.

29. P. Kropotkin, *Mutual Aid: A Factor of Evolution* (New York: Knopf, 1925), quoted in R. Nisbet, *The Social Philosophers: Community and Conflict in Western Thought* (New York: Crowell, 1973), p. 376.

30. Persons, *op. cit.,* p. 6.

31. P. Thoenes, *The Elite in the Welfare State* (New York: Free Press, 1966), p. 37.

32. Hofstadter, *op. cit.,* p. 41.

33. Sumner, *op. cit.,* p. 120.

34. J. Axinn and H. Levin, *Social Welfare: A History of the American Response to Need* (New York: Dodd, Mead, 1975), pp. 89–90.

35. F. F. Piven and R. A. Cloward, *Regulating the Poor: The Functions of Public Welfare* (New York: Random House, 1971), pp. 165–66.

36. As Tawney points out: "The demonstration that distress is a proof of demerit . . . has always been popular with the prosperous." R. H. Tawney, "Economic Virtues and Prescriptions for Poverty," in H. D. Stein and R. A. Cloward (eds.), *Social Perspectives on Behavior* (New York: Free Press, 1958), p. 284.

37. As late as 1934, the constitutions of fourteen states deprived relief recipients of the rights to vote and to hold office. K. Woodroofe, *From Charity to Social Work in England and the United States* (Toronto: University of Toronto Press, 1962), p. 154.

38. *Public Opinion Poll of Social Services* (Los Angeles: University of Southern California, 1971), pp. 23–24 (mimeographed).

39. Tawney, *op. cit.,* p. 284.

40. Ryan, *op. cit.,* p. 179.

10

Work and Welfare: The Influence of the Protestant Ethic

When Martin Luther nailed his ninety-five theses to the church door in Wittenberg in 1517, he set in motion two influences on social welfare that have continued to the present. The first (mentioned in Chapter 4) was emphasis on faith rather than on good works. Among the causes for Luther's break with Catholicism were the methods by which one could obtain absolution for sins by undertaking good works. These had degenerated to the point where indulgences could be purchased in advance for sins not yet committed, and indeed, one could "shop around" for the priest who gave the greatest bargains. Further, the money thus collected did not necessarily go to the poor and needy: It might be used to pay the priest's personal debts.[1] This led Luther to deny the efficacy of good works in one's lifetime to earn grace or to guarantee salvation. Luther insisted that faith alone had merit, and he repeatedly attacked as pagan and corrupt the church's emphasis on good works as a road to heaven.[2] This had its effect on later attitudes toward charity, which have been described as "anti-social welfare stands."[3] However, Protestantism served as a powerful factor in the establishment of voluntary social-welfare organizations, and in the emergence of labor unions.[4]

But a second influence of the Reformation is more widespread, and it has left a deeper and more pervasive mark on all social-welfare policies and programs. This is the attitude toward work that is often referred to as the Protestant Ethic.

Luther viewed work—of any kind—as service to God, and he endowed work with religious dignity by defining it as a vocation, or a calling. In his view, each person serves God best by doing most perfectly the work of his own vocation. Conversely, one who does not work, or will not work to the full extent of his ability, is a sinner. John Calvin went a step farther: Not only is work a religious duty, but people are called upon to work without desire for the fruits of their labor, simply because to work is to carry out the will of God. Such work will establish God's kingdom on earth, and this is its value and its end. Thus, it does not matter whether people receive less than their subsistence needs for their work or become rich; whether the work is satisfying or stultifying, socially useful or harmful, degrading or elevating: God-fearing people work.

Further, the concomitant doctrine of predestination indicated that it was already decided (though unknown) who would be saved, and nothing that people did would affect that decision. Because the command was to work without regard for issue, success was seen as coming from God, as a mark of favor, and if a person was poor, that was also the working out of God's will. Consequently, the Protestant Ethic added to Social Darwinism's doctrine, that the unsuccessful are unfit, the tenet that it is God's will that they be so. In this light, it is possible to understand the complacency with which a proper Bostonian was heard to remark, "God made me a rich man!"[5]

By giving work a religious cast, the Protestant Ethic deepened the roots of work in society and intensified society's fervor for work. More important, Luther's stance and influence added impetus to the creation of a work-centered society. The religious motivation for work combined with the manpower needs of the Industrial Revolution,[6] the economic philosophy called mercantilism, new inventions, and changing forms of government to make work the central factor of people's lives and of socio-economic structures. The Protestant Ethic placed a religiotheoretic base under the demands of industrialization.

In this type of society, few need-satisfying methods other than work are provided. The society—and certainly the state—is under no legal obligation to do more than provide a system wherein work is linked with satisfaction. The state may create legal bodies that are obligated *to the state* to assist needy individuals, but they are not so obligated to the needy themselves.[7] The person whose needs are not satisfied by a public agency has a case only if the agency is not carrying out its legal charge or is discriminatory. If neither is true, then the fact that his needs remain unsatisfied cannot be the legitimate basis of action. In fact, the individual has no legal claim on the community for subsistence.

Work takes on a number of functions in such a society. It not only provides income, but it also gives structure to the day, week, and year, as well as to the lifetime; it provides a means of identification ("What do you do?"); it determines with whom one associates for large segments of time; it provides a sense of belonging; and it provides almost indefinable psychic rewards.[8] Succinctly:

In our work-oriented society all adult males are expected to be productive wage earners. In most cases, gainful employment is a necessary though not a sufficient condition for a man to consider himself and be considered a responsible and respected member of the community. In addition, the kind of job he holds helps to determine both his self-image and his status in society. In short, work is a major life task and unless a man performs it adequately, he is a failure by his own standards and those of society.[9]

This overwhelming emphasis on work, which developed in Western civilization, was not inevitable. Human societies display great variations in their priority lists—some emphasizing commerce; others, military expansion, religion, or some other thing.[10] The ancient Greeks, for example, saw many kinds of work as inherently degrading, fit to be done only by slaves. Their eschewing of such work, far from proving sterile or destructive, resulted in the beginnings of literature, mathematics, theater, art, and democratic government.

In the Yoga tradition of Hinduism, on the other hand, the devotee is advised to work for Krishna, not for any benefit inherent in work, but simply to avoid idleness. The work must not be done for the fruits of profit, which gratify one's senses, because gratification of the senses leads away from oneness with Krishna: "A real Yoga does not desire such fruits. He has no desire other than Krishna, and Krishna is already there."[11] Japan is said to be moving from a period in which life took its major meaning from a person's work to an age where concern is similarly given to the larger aspects of life.[12]

There are also many cultures in which work has always been seen as demeaning and to be avoided if possible. This does not seem to arise from constitutional laziness on the part of individuals but is rather a question of social connotation. Successful people rise above such work, or have other people do the physical work for them; the symbol of success is a pair of hands that have not been dirtied by work. This attitude is particularly true in very status-conscious countries with clear class or caste distinctions.[13]

Elsewhere, particularly in preindustrial societies, there is a tendency to work only for satisfaction of current needs. Farmers in such cultures grow only what they and their families need for immediate consumption.[14] Without transport facilities, means of storage, or credit, it is of very little use to a farmer to produce a surplus, which will only take up space and eventually rot. Consequently, if work has no religious connotation, it makes little sense for the farmer to engage in useless or unproductive labor. Instead, he may take up the slack in his time schedule with other activities—cockfighting, for example. For this reason, some preindustrial societies guarantee a hundred or more holidays a year,[15] and this tends to be reinforced in countries where Catholicism is predominant, with its "whole assortment of work-dismissing, leisure-providing feast days."[16] In fact, without a religious motivation, "people who are clear-sighted, undeluded, and sober-minded will not go on working once their reasonable needs are satisfied ... the readiness to work springs from trivial, questionable motives."[17]

In industrializing and industrialized countries, however, if Protestantism is strong,[18] there is a mutual reinforcing of these two factors. In those places, it is agreed that people should want to "get ahead," should want to make money, and should work.[19] Work becomes more than an income-producing activity: It takes on aspects of an article of faith.

EFFECTS ON SOCIAL WELFARE

There are few areas of social welfare in the industrialized world that have not been influenced by the rise of the Protestant Ethic. By adding an imputation of sinfulness or immorality to those who do not work, it sharpened the distinction between the deserving and the undeserving poor. It reinforced the need for a work test to determine an applicant's willingness to work, even in cases where no work is offered or available. It helped transform almshouses, for those who could not take care of themselves in their own homes, into workhouses, thereby weakening outdoor relief and strengthening indoor relief. It added consideration of "potential" assets, in the form of possible employability, to the actual assets examined by means tests. Finally, the Protestant Ethic led to relief work, in contradistinction to direct relief.

The Deserving and the Undeserving

The distinction between those who deserve help and those who do not has many connotations. One criterion is the ability of the recipient to use the help—or, more accurately, to use the help properly or well. Those who are adjudged to be unable to use the help may be refused it. In social-work terms, they are sometimes labeled "resistant," "unsuitable for service," or "unable to arrive at (or maintain) the contract." In community-organization and even in international-aid parlance, the community or country must not only need the aid but be able to use it wisely (that is, "deserve" it). The dilemma arises when need is created by inability to use aid wisely. Helping only those who can use help wisely results in "creaming"—dealing with the easiest situations and ignoring or neglecting the more difficult.

This distinction has been made in many social-welfare programs. Great care is taken to distinguish the able, deserving client temporarily in crisis from the chronically disabled or disadvantaged client for whom continuous support but no solution to his or her problems is feasible. Help given the former usually exceeds that given the latter. Investments are more acceptable than expenses. The deserving client thus becomes defined as one who can be helped to leave the rolls, while the others are considered less deserving. This is why work relief is usually more liberal in payments and less restrictive concerning eligibility than poor relief:[20] There is hope that one who can work will move from relief rolls to employment rolls, and it is important to maintain his morale and abilities.

Whereas Social Darwinism says, in effect, that the needy were unfit, and therefore—at least to a certain extent—blameless, the Protestant Ethic says that those who do not work are immoral—in fact, sinners. These differences have implications for policies and programs. If "laziness is . . . a sickness rather than a moral defect,"[21] the lazy are the victims of pathology and, as noted previously, must be treated rather than punished. At least since the 1800s it has been considered respectable to treat paupers as pathological.[22] In this respect at least, the economic sector has been held blameless, and the fault has been imputed to just those institutions that strike a moral stance: "churches, trade unions, and the bar."[23]

If the pathological are not responsible for their own situations, obviously they cannot be expected to treat themselves. Pathology, therefore, carries in its wake paternalism on the part of society. Decisions and actions must be taken on their behalf and in their places. It is not only possible but necessary to interfere in their lives, because patients are not supposed to know what is good for them, and society has not only the right but the responsibility to cure the pathological, even against their will, and even if the cure is both painful and uncertain.

If not working is deviance, however, rather than pathology, it is both purposeful and reprehensible. The image of the deviant is of one who is responsible for his own situation and therefore deserves punishment for willfully violating the norms of society. Hence the poor are exhorted to conform to middle-class standards of dress, conduct, speech, thrift, and other such virtues. At the same time, like any deviants, they are considered unsuitable for normal company and are kept at arm's length, which makes it difficult to have effective and significant participation of the poor in social-welfare programs. The manner in which poverty is viewed as deviance, and refusal to work is considered the cause, dates back to the Puritans' dictum that those who will not work should not be permitted to eat—an attitude not conspicuously absent from the public mind today.

Although presumed willingness to work has always been an important element in determination of the deserving poor, other elements inevitably enter in. The habits, personalities, and cultural backgrounds of applicants have always played a role in determining if they were "worthy" to receive relief.[24] To this can be added race and, in some cases, the humility or politeness with which the application is made, or the insistence or persistence.

Work Tests

When work is available, the willingness of the deserving poor to work can easily be tested, but when no jobs are to be had, some other method has to be devised. It should be noted that even when the agency can neither provide work nor refer the client, motivation remains important.

In the early days of social welfare, a wood yard was usually maintained for test purposes. The applicant who would not lift the axe was ipso facto unworthy. Or "applicants moved a pile of rock from one side of a yard to the other and back again."[25] The work test was originally designed to determine suitability for relief,[26] but it began to change into make-work or relief work when specific standards were established, such as three hours of work in the wood yard entitling the applicant to three meals and lodging.[27] Work tests for women included sewing garments, some of which were later ripped up, but some of which went to relief clients. Work tests were employed in shelters for the homeless with a deterrent motive—to keep the undeserving out.[28]

As work tests required applicants to demonstrate their willingness to work, even if the work itself was unnecessary, unimportant, or inefficient, the distinction between the deserving and the undeserving poor began to move from the realm of ability to that of motivation. This aspect of the work test remains today, as when a recipient of unemployment compensation must "prove that he is, in truth, seeking work—[by] the practice of urging [and in some cases, of requiring] applicants to maintain . . . registration on a current basis by re-registering at specific intervals,"[29] and in person. As noted, the shift from ability to motivation also applied to morals. Sometimes a work test is made so difficult—that is, the conditions under which assistance is offered are so unattractive —so as to deter the unworthy from seeking relief.[30]

Workhouses

One of the earliest institutionalized methods of dealing with social problems was the almshouse, which was intended to take care of the helpless—the aged, the disabled, the chronically ill, and those who for any other reason could not take care of themselves at home. In fact, the almshouse became "a dumping ground for dependents of any age, of either sex and with every kind of disability."[31]

The theory underlying sending the able-bodied poor to workhouses[32] was that they could learn to support themselves, the wealth of the nation would increase, and—even if the program should fall short of all that was promised for it—the poor (particularly, poor children) would acquire skills and habits of industry so that the country would profit through the increase in the number of efficient workers.[33]

Workhouses, as a rule, were less successful than almshouses in achieving their aims,[34] but such was the prevailing belief in the justice and efficacy of work that almshouses were gradually transformed into workhouses "in which work is provided for every degree of ability in the pauper; and thus the able poor [are] made to provide, partially at least for their own support, and also to the support, or at least the comfort of the impotent poor."[35] As the work element in almshouses and workhouses took on more importance, it became more and more like relief work or, synonymously, work relief. For example, it often occurred that the cost of supervising almshouse workers who did farm work was greater than that of hiring farmhands to do the work.[36] As work relief became more prominent, workhouses began to diminish in number and importance. Workhouses are a thing of the past today, on both sides of the Atlantic, but as Graham points out, we continue to keep recipients on desert islands in the midst of our cities[37]—islands called ghettos, low-cost housing projects, and the like.

Work Relief

Work relief is a method of making relief payments through the mechanism of work. It differs from public works as a method of relieving need in that work relief is predominantly a relief, rather than an employment, measure. It selects workers according to their need, engages in projects for maximum employment, and pays on the basis of amount needed. It often involves a means test and sometimes limits the number of hours that can be worked or the amount earned.[38] Public-works programs, on the other hand, select workers according to competence, choose projects by intrinsic value, and pay on the basis of the amounts paid by private employers. With the growth of the service sector of the economy, another distinction is coming into being: the difference between public-service jobs and public-works projects.[39]

Work relief was originally undertaken as a test of the willingness of the unemployed to work, and as the test of motivation became a schedule of amounts of work for amounts of help, the requirement of work for help became the norm. Whereas public works were used as means of relief for the unemployed in the 1850s,[40] the depression of the 1890s resulted in extensive use of work relief, which at that time was quite honestly called "made work."[41] The rationale for work relief was very positive: to help able-bodied workers who were unemployed before they became completely destitute, and to allow them to avoid the humiliation that accompanied application for relief.[42] As noted, work relief usually pays more than does outright relief not connected to work.

It was during the Great Depression that work relief came into its own, so to speak, in America. The number of able-bodied people out of work far outstripped the work available, including public-works projects. Indeed, the number of public-works projects that would ordinarily have been available was drastically curtailed as states and communities found themselves unable to finance them. The choice was between direct relief, which meant payments in cash and in kind, and work relief, with payments made as salaries. For those unable to work there was no choice but to give direct relief, but for the employable, work relief was instituted.

Franklin Roosevelt was quite clear that Americans would rather work than "go on the dole," and most Americans agreed with him, including those who needed work or the dole. The WPA (Works Progress Administration)[43] was accordingly established. With mounting demand, and continuing experience, the WPA paid salaries that, though not technically "adequate," kept people from starving. More, it abandoned salaries based on individual need and paid standard salaries to all workers, with some differences between the states. Workers were picked for ability to work, and many—especially artists, musicians, writers, and other skilled people—were allowed to work in their chosen fields. A good deal of the work provided by the WPA met the standard established by the American Association of Social Workers, which had called for work that was productive in itself, and not just a technique for avoiding idleness.[44]

The actual amount of work accomplished under the WPA, simply in terms of projects, is staggering: construction or improvement of 600,000 miles of highways, roads, and streets; building or rebuilding 116,000 bridges and viaducts; more than 110,000 public buildings constructed or reconstructed; nearly 80 million books renovated; and more than half a billion school lunches served.[45] Plays written on WPA commission are still being performed, to say nothing of the playwrights thus encouraged, and there still are murals in post offices and other public buildings that owe their existence to the WPA.

After the Depression, work relief returned to a low standard:

> Wages . . . dropped to a starvation level, and are paid on the . . . "budget deficiency basis." There is no test of "employability" and little attempt to fit the skill or experience of the worker to the demands of the job. The system has taken on many characteristics of the poor relief work-test in which the needy person is required to prove his "worthiness" to receive relief.[46]

Moreover, despite the successes of the WPA, many of the experiences were perceived as negative, while from others important lessons were learned. Take, for example, the question of costs. It seems patently true that if people capable of work are being given relief, any work they do in return is an asset, even if their efficiency is low. As a matter of fact, however, work relief involves many nonlabor costs—for tools, transportation, supervision, recording, bookkeeping, insurance, and so forth. Just as it was found in the almshouse that the farm labor would be cheaper if done by farmhands, so work relief during the Depression was more expensive than direct relief would have been.[47] Whether the work accomplished was worth the extra costs is debatable, but that it would have been cheaper to give out checks is hardly questionable.

A second problem is competition with the private sector. Every job given out through work relief represents work that could have been done through the regular market.[48] The manufacture of goods is even more problematic, as it competes directly with manufacturers, wholesalers, and retailers. "The problem facing work relief sponsors was to select for production goods for which there was no normal commercial demand, but which at the same time were not useless"[49]—a formidable challenge. In fact, it was found difficult, if not impossible, to find work-relief jobs that did not compete in one way or another with private business.[50]

On the other side stood the unions, which demanded for their members jobs they saw as being subsumed under work relief. Worse, they saw the low salaries being paid to those on work relief as undermining the salaries they had fought hard to achieve. Giving work to nonunion people, even relief work, while union members were also idle was another source of contention.

It also proved very difficult to provide work for everyone who wanted it. There were estimated to be half a million to a million people certified for WPA employment without assignment most of the time, and another two million eligible but not certified.[51] Of those employed, 77 percent were employed in public construction and maintenance work. It proved exceedingly difficult to devise other types of work that would absorb large numbers of unskilled workers and at the same time not compete with private industry. Housing projects, for example, were intended to employ 25 percent of the people who were on work relief, but actually they averaged less than 1 percent.[52]

These aspects of work relief were relatively minor, however, compared to the expectation that working for relief would enable the unemployed to maintain their work habits and skills, and—more important—their morale. In the event, however, very little skilled work was or can be provided, and most participants are assigned unskilled work.

Most relief work is make-work, and is perceived as such by those who engage in it and—more important—by others. The image of the WPA worker that has entered American folklore is that of the leaf raker leaning on his rake while gossiping with his fellows. The classic story is of the worker who complained about lack of a rake. Informed that without the rake he would not be expected to do anything, he continued to complain—because everyone else had a rake on which to lean! It might well be that relief work gave the unemployed some of the benefits of working—structure to the day, companionship, and relief from boredom—but whether morale is maintained under such circumstances is at least open to question. Charnow, commenting on the belief that work relief is superior to direct relief as a means of maintaining morale and work habits, says:

> As a matter of fact, the extent to which work relief has preserved these values has depended upon conditions which varied with the type of program and with individual workers [and with] needs tests, makeshift projects, poor planning and supervision, assignment of skilled workers to unskilled work, low efficiency, irregular hours, lax discipline, [and] unstable financing . . . injurious rather than desirable work habits and attitudes were likely to develop. . . . Community attitudes became . . . derisive as the program assumed a semi-permanent character.[53]

Not only did the workers become disillusioned: The view of work relief as a method of exacting a moral duty from recipients of public support faded as costs mounted, taxes increased, and the workers seemed to be developing an attitude that the government was obligated to provide work.[54]

The lessons of history must be learned again and again, and as the Depression with its massive work-relief programs ceases to be a living memory, the demand is again heard that people receiving welfare should be required to give some work in return, even if only symbolically.

> Paying a person the monetary equivalent of wages to do nothing shocks Anglo-American sensibilities. The act of handing . . . dollars to healthy men and women generates a collective insanity among the nonwelfare population that precludes serious debate. Perhaps an ugly worm in all of us wants to control the behavior of other humans.[55]

Even during relative prosperity, the demand that people work continues:

> It is a notorious fact that a picture of men at ease and in the middle of plenty most often makes people contemplating it both nervous and abusive . . . the antiutopians appear to be saying that the world must have

pain—deprivation and impairment in it.... It may be good for themselves and surely could not be too bad for others.[56]

WORK AND WELFARE

The close relationship between work and welfare that spread with
the Protestant Ethic is further illustrated by the extent to which social-
welfare programs are administered through, or linked to, the mechanism of employment. It will be recalled, for example, that the
Speenhamland experiment in overcoming poverty was a wage-
supplementation program. Those who were not workers received no
benefits at all from it. This remains the pattern for many, if not the
majority of, social-welfare programs throughout the world. Of 118
countries reporting old-age, survivors, and disability insurance programs, only 13 have programs not linked with work; 7 have work-linked
programs that nonworkers may volunteer to join; while 98 limit benefits
to workers or ex-workers.[57] As noted previously, in 53 countries family
allowances are linked in whole or in part to employment status, and in
only 13 are they wholly unrelated to jobs. Unemployment compensation almost invariably requires a record of prior employment, and even
sickness and maternity benefits are usually available only to "employed
persons."[58]

The linkage of social-welfare programs and work records is not solely
due to the necessity or desirability of worker and employer contributions to the funds, for in some programs (for example, Unemployment
Insurance in the United States and old-age pensions in Australia) there
are no contributions by the insured. The underlying feeling, stemming
from views of work as moral and idleness as immoral, seems to be that
only those who contribute to society by working are entitled to auto-
matic, stigma-free benefits, while others must justify their claims as best
they can.

In view of the overwhelming importance attached to work in modern
society, it is understandable that the ultimate goal of many social-
welfare policies and programs is to prepare people for, or return them
to, the labor force. Vocational-guidance, counseling, training, retraining, and rehabilitation programs are all established to help people find
their way into productive employment, and hence the mainstream of
normal life. Ordinarily, such programs are deemed successful when
they enable the participant to take a job. Some programs, however,
follow up farther, in an attempt to help the participant remain on the
job, by dealing with problems that arise either on the job or in other
areas. Increasingly, it is being recognized in some countries that a
rapidly changing employment situation may require mobility from job
to job, or from occupation to occupation, and that such changes may be

necessary more than once in a lifetime career. In recognition of this fact, Great Britain, for example, passed the Employment and Training Act in 1973, which gives each person over nineteen the right to one year's training every five years at a tax-free stipend equal to 60 percent to 90 percent of his or her income.[59]

The normative nature of work in society also adds a psychiatric or, at least, a psychosomatic aspect to lack of work, and casts work in a therapeutic role. The fact that aged retirees become ill at a higher rate than nonretirees[60] has been attributed to their reputed need to work. Another point of view holds that much illness among those who are not working is psychosomatic, because illness is a more socially acceptable reason for not working than is retirement or any similar reason.[61] Some observers even speak of a "toxic condition" that is caused by long periods of unemployment.[62] In short, anything that prohibits people from working or entices or induces them not to work renders them unhappy, immoral, or ill,[63] and social-welfare programs, to be geared to achieving a happy, healthy population, must be geared toward providing work opportunities.

In this same vein, work is assumed to have therapeutic qualities. Because working is normative in most societies, those who cannot work, for any reason, tend to feel diminished, damaged, stigmatized, and outside the mainstream. In regard to many individuals, and even whole groups, the aim of social welfare may be to help them to enter or return to employment. Aside from, or in addition to, the economic benefits this may bestow on the individual or on society, becoming like everyone else, acquiring self-esteem, avoiding stigma, and strengthening positive self-image are important therapeutic goals. For this reason, many programs dealing with the retarded, the mentally ill, the disabled, the unemployed, the acting out, and—to some extent—deviants undertake work activities. The supposed therapeutic qualities of work lead to work programs within institutions—prisons, reform schools, hospitals for the mentally ill, and so forth—as well as in noninstitutional settings such as sheltered workshops for the aged, the disabled, and others, which are free-standing social services. The goals of sheltered workshops, both in and outside of institutions, include acquisition and retention of skills, restoration of a normal atmosphere, recreation, and income. Workshops are also used purely as an evaluative device by staff.

Certain dilemmas are inherent in the use of sheltered workshops. One of these is that in attempting to rehabilitate clients for the larger society, the workshop becomes a subculture of deviant people, bringing with it ridicule and subnormal role expectations.[64] For some participants, being able to work only in a sheltered setting symbolizes their failure and hopelessness. Another problem arises from the fact that though the workshop may not be intended for "real" work, the need for production—seen either by the sponsors or the participants—often begins to dominate the scene. This may lead to screening out from the workshop the least productive—who may need it most. The emphasis on production may also move the workshop into the area of marketing its products, and here it comes up against the same problems as does work relief–competition with private business on one side and the unions on the other. Contrariwise, the operating workshop must be able to keep the participants busy, and therefore may accept contract work at prices that substantially reduce the income of the project or result in véry low wages to the workers, if it is a profit-sharing institution. Consequently, workshops have the notorious reputation of paying substandard wages.[65]

Because sheltered workshops may have several different aims, it is difficult to assess relative goal attainment. However, there seems to be a discrepancy between the goals of the staff, which are often therapeutic, recreational, or rehabilitative, and those of participants, which often include acquiring some additional income. In one study, the suggestion for change that was offered with greatest frequency was that of increasing wages,[66] but sponsors often refuse to recognize this motivation, perhaps because they deem it unworthy.

In any case, it would seem that in sheltered workshops, the principle of individualization would lead those who run them to distinguish among those participants who enjoy working, those who are conditioned to work, those who feel they are expected to work, those who are willing to or must work for additional income, those who feel they have worked enough, and those who never wanted to work. Generally, however, the Protestant Ethic operates to create the assumption that people want to work, must work, and find health in working.

From this view of work as moral in its own right, there flows the natural extension that work is a means of instilling moral discipline. Consequently, work is seen not only as helpful to those who participate in sheltered workshops but also as required in institutions for criminals or juvenile delinquents. Not only is work generally considered a highly efficacious means of reforming the individual wrongdoer, but it is also regarded as the best thing in the world for the morality of the poor and the disadvantaged.[67]

The Protestant Ethic has played a part in the development of programs and proposals that term grants or subsidies "wages" or "salaries" and mask welfare by calling it "work" or "training." The mothers in training under the WIN program receive payments, but these are "educational subsidies," and hence these women are not included in unemployment or welfare statistics. There have also been proposals to use attitudes toward work to enable mothers to stay home: Gil, among others, has proposed that mothers be paid salaries for the duty they perform in raising children.[68] Others have proposed that housewives be paid for the work they do. It is hoped by the proponents of such plans that in this way society's desire to see people working, rather than on welfare, will be satisfied.

THE WAGE STOP

There is an asymmetric relationship between work and welfare. When employment policies are prepared and debated, the effects they will have on the welfare population are a minor consideration. If this were not so, the minimum wage would be pegged at a point where no working person's income would be below the poverty line. When welfare policies are prepared and debated, however, the effects on recipients' employment patterns are a major consideration. An important underlying concern of all income-maintenance programs, and many service programs, is the presumed effect of the program on the recipients' incentive to work.

This concern has roots that go back to the beginnings of organized welfare, under the title "less eligibility." In the earliest attempts at organized welfare in Europe, it was emphasized that measures must be taken to prevent "any man from securing a shilling which he was able to earn himself."[69] In 1834, this became one of the foundations of social welfare in Britain: "His situation on the whole shall not be made really or apparently so eligible as the situation of the independent laborer of the lowest class."[70]

The inclusion of the word "apparently" is indicative of the force, or the fear, of public opinion, which might misjudge the situation of the pauper as being the equivalent of that of nonpaupers, and react accordingly. This fear that the situation of the poor might approximate that of others now marks most social-welfare programs, and its apparent violation is sometimes the object of the deepest and most emotional antiwelfare expressions.

In modern terms, less eligibility is often referred to as the "wage stop." The wage stop operates to guarantee that recipients of welfare will not receive through welfare as much as they could make by working. Almost all social-welfare programs throughout the world, whether in the guise of insurance or grants, are implicitly pegged at rates that presumably will not induce people now working to abandon their jobs, and will not discourage people who are not working from seeking employment.

The manner in which the earning capacity of the individual is determined varies with program and place. One method is to base payments on the last salary, paying a proportion. Another, used by American

Social Security, is to average out the individual's lifetime earnings, based on representative periods. Again, it is possible to determine the average wage for a country or a region, for an occupation or a group of occupations (for example, white-collar work). The extent to which these averages take into consideration different salaries for different age groups, fringe benefits, and so forth is part of the problem of reaching an equitable determination.[71] Perhaps the nadir in cynicism concerning such matters was reached by Huey Long when he was governor of Louisiana. Informed that federal law required the payment of prevailing wages to participants in federally financed employment programs, Long defined prevailing wages as the "lowest wages you can prevail upon a man to take."

The wage stop operates to limit payments to a percentage of the prevailing wage in a clearly discernible and almost universal manner. In Israel, for example, social-welfare grants are limited to 40 percent of the average wage.[72] In France, old-age pensions are limited to 25 percent of the annual wage on retirement at age sixty, and 50 percent at age sixty-five,[73] and unemployment benefits can only be 70 percent of the average wage, which is an increase from the 40 percent formerly prevalent.[74] In the United States, Unemployment Insurance payments compensate for only 25 percent of the wages lost,[75] and payments as high as average weekly salaries are virtually nonexistent. Retirement pay covers about 30 percent of recent earnings of single retired people, or 45 percent of the earnings of couples, while only 20 percent of the people over sixty-five have any type of supplementary benefits, such as private insurance or a pension plan.[76] Local relief payments are almost invariably limited to a small proportion of the average or the lowest salary, and the proportion is growing smaller.[77]

That such payments are based on the principle of less eligibility, rather than on need, is obvious. There is no reason to believe that someone who becomes unemployed thereby reduces his or her living expenses to one quarter of what they formerly were, or that the needs of a single person fall by 70 percent on the day that he becomes sixty-five, or she reaches sixty-two.[78]

So deep and pervasive is the fear of a work disincentive due to welfare payments that not only employables but also those who cannot work, such as the aged, the handicapped, and children; those who public policy says should not work, such as mothers of young children; and those who are willing to work but cannot find jobs, the unemployed, are all limited as to the amount they can receive from welfare payments—regardless of their need—to a proportion of what they presumably could (but actually cannot) earn from work. In this way the principle of less eligibility virtually guarantees the continuation of poverty, because a fraction of the average or lowest wage, or of payments made in the preinflation days of twenty or thirty years ago, is in many cases below the poverty line.

The poverty line itself is set according to criteria discussed in Chapter 2. There is the concept of relative poverty, which measures a condition against that of others, in other countries or at other times or in the here and now, or uses a statistical group such as the lowest 10 percent in the income distribution. This concept also includes self-images and reference groups as indices of poverty.[79] Poverty may also be viewed as normative for some people or some groups. Monks and nuns are usually thought of as poor, at least in material terms. The mentally retarded, the physically disabled, and the very old are often equated in the public mind with poor people.[80] Viewing poverty as normative has certain societal advantages, for in this way poverty can be made invisible, or seen as inevitable, or even as desirable.[81] There does seem to be a need for poor people to do the "dirty, dead-end jobs of society,"[82] to serve as horrid examples, or to be scapegoats for others.[83] Poverty may even be seen as character-building and a desirable discipline.

Another definition of poverty, in absolute terms, is the one most commonly used to determine who is poor, where the poor are, how they manage, and how best to plan and evaluate antipoverty programs. The absolute measure used in the United States since the early 1960s is based on the number of calories necessary to sustain life during a short emergency period, translated into the types of food normally available on the American market, and their costs.[84] These food costs are taken to be one-third of the required budget,[85] which can then be determined for single individuals and families of various sizes. The most careful work in this area has been done by Orshansky, who arrived at differential budgets for farm and nonfarm families, people of various ages, and inhabitants of different parts of the United States.[86] Her figures were vulgarized by others, who used a round figure for an "average" family of four as the poverty line. Orshansky's poverty line stood at $3,000 in 1964 and rose to $5,500 in 1977. This represents a rise in per-meal costs from 22 cents to 42 cents.[87] In other words, anyone who received as much as 42 cents per meal in 1977 was not considered poor, nor was he or she included in official statistics on poverty in the United States.[88]

There is some question as to whether the benefits from food stamps, Medicaid, day care, and so forth should be included in the computation of poverty statistics, with proponents arguing that such income reduces the incidence of poverty considerably. Opponents point out, however, that of 27.1 million people below the poverty line in 1975,[89] only 19.0 million used food stamps;[90] and because the Food Stamp Program is so devised that the closer a family approaches the poverty line from below, the smaller will be the available benefit from food stamps, the number of people actually raised above the poverty line by the use of food stamps is probably very small.[91] Similarly, Medicaid programs become income only if they are used, which means only if there is illness in the family. Attempts to impute such income to all poor families creates a misleading statistical artifact.

Regardless of how poverty is defined and measured, it is created and perpetuated in part by social-welfare policies that limit payments to all recipients, in order to convince them that they would be better off working. Yet most of them cannot work: Of the poor in the United States, 40 percent are less than sixteen years old; 20 percent are sixty-five or more; 5 percent are disabled; 25 percent are female heads of families; 1 percent are unemployed and actively looking for work; and 9 percent are poor despite the fact that they are already employed (and half of them are working full time and the year round).[92] In Israel too, the proportion of the poor who cannot work is overwhelming. In 1973, 49 percent were under seventeen; 11 percent were over sixty-five; 14 percent were disabled or in institutions; 9 percent were employed; 3 percent were self-employed; and 2 percent were officially registered as unemployed—leaving only 12 percent as legitimate targets of the wage stop.[93] Nevertheless, the income of *all* the poor is limited by the fear of work disincentives.

There are few beliefs as widely held and deeply felt as the tenet that people will not work if they can achieve the same income, or even nearly the same income, in some other way, and it is on this belief that social-welfare payments are based. Yet closer examination of the belief indicates that it entails many contradictions and paradoxes, and is supported by little empirical evidence.

Generally speaking, work motivations are thought to arise from instincts and physiological drives, from desire for material goods, from social pressures, and from a combination of these.[94] For each belief, however, there is a counterbelief, and these can be summarized as follows:

Belief: People work in order to satisfy instinctual and biological needs and drives, and are unhappy to the point of illness if they are not allowed to work.
Counterbelief: People are basically lazy; no one really wants to work or does so unless he has to; efforts to avoid work are the basis of all social and mechanical progress.
Belief: People work only to achieve material ends, and would not work if they could achieve the same ends by other means.
Counterbelief: People work even when their material needs are satisfied, because of personal needs and social pressures.

Belief: Only people whose sustenance needs are unmet are motivated by the need to work; others must be artificially stimulated by advertising, social pressure, and other devices, or else they would be satisfied.
Counterbelief: People are insatiable, and they will therefore always work to achieve more and more satisfactions.
Belief: People work because of the satisfactions inherent in working— the sense of creativity, fulfillment, productivity, and performing an expected and useful social role.
Counterbelief: Most people find their work boring, unsatisfying, and uncreative, and constantly seek to reduce the hours they must spend at it.
Belief: People work because in their work groups they find primary group relationships, companionship, enjoyment, status, and recognition.
Counterbelief: The major focus of people's lives is outside their work places, major interests center on nonwork activities, and most satisfying personal relationships are not found with fellow workers.
Belief: People work because of the social identity that work offers them, the regulation of daily life activity it entails, and the way it defines them to the rest of society.
Counterbelief: People define themselves and are defined according to their leisure-time activities, their interests and expertise, and their familial and ethnic backgrounds.

McGregor summarizes these conflicting views of work motivations as Theory X and Theory Y.[95] Theory X assumes that people are lazy, dislike and shun work, have to be driven, and need both carrot and stick. It assumes that most people are incapable of taking responsibility for themselves and have to be looked after.[96] Theory Y, contrariwise, assumes that people have a psychological need to work and want achievement and responsibility. Given the proper opportunity, they want to work.

The paradox of the simultaneous existence of both of these views on work motivation can be understood as involving ambivalence, goal displacement, cognitive dissonance, cultural lag, the gap between norms and behaviors, the postulation of two cultures, and scapegoating.[97] For purposes of social-welfare policies and practices, the last two are of major importance.

As a method of avoiding the discomfort of holding contradictory views on work motivation, the postulation of two cultures has great appeal. There is the majority culture, known as "we," which is based on Theory Y. We like to work, enjoy our work, and understand that people should work for their living. All we ask is the opportunity to work, and we are willing to do unpleasant or badly paid work if that is all that is available. And then there is "they." They are lazy, avoid work as much as possible, waste what little money they do acquire, and have no qualms about living at the expense of others: In short, they are Theory X people.

The belief that the poor do not want to work is so widespread and so deeply held that it warrants examination. One useful area of investigation is that of work incentives themselves; the other concerns specific attitudes of the poor toward work.

The literature on work motivation and incentives is enormous. Since Adam Smith published *The Wealth of Nations* more than two hundred years ago, devoting part of it to "The Causes of the Improvement in the Productive Powers of Labour," inquiry into methods of increasing productivity has never ceased. One of the pioneers in this area was Frederick W. Taylor, with whose name the concept of "scientific management" is associated.[98] At later dates, Fritz A. Roethlisberger and Elton Mayo,[99] in the empirical area, and George C. Homans,[100] as a theorist, called attention to the "human relations" factors in industry. Following this school, F. Herzberg distinguished between "hygiene factors" and "motivators," holding that satisfaction-dissatisfaction does not constitute a continuum.[101] This work caused attention to focus on methods of creating worker satisfactions. However, though the satisfaction of workers may be seen as a desirable goal in itself, the question has been raised as to whether more satisfied workers work harder or produce more. Little hard evidence has been found that they do either,[102] and even the "self-actualization" aspects that A. H. Maslow holds to be the highest, or final, potent need [103] and that have been found in some studies of work,[104] have been questioned as, in fact, being the product of hard work, rather than its cause.[105]

There seems to be increasing evidence that individual work patterns are more or less stable lifetime patterns affected only slightly, or for short periods, by the conditions or the content of work. The range of possible patterns is from "workaholics"[106] through what Sigmund Freud calls a "natural human aversion to work,"[107] to the patterns of those who believe with Sumner that work kills.[108] Little work has been done as yet on the reasons for these different approaches to work. Dalton studied the 9 rate-busters among the 300 workmen he investigated, and hinted that their growing up on farms or in urban lower-class families, and being Protestants, might have some connection with their behavior.[109] McClelland attributes varying achievement needs to child-rearing practices;[110] Whyte discusses role models;[111] Kohn and Schooler look to previous job histories;[112] and Goodwin examines work motivations of mothers, fathers, and sons.[113] Definitive studies on the development of attitudes to work remain to be done, however.[114]

By the same token, few empirical studies have been done specifically

on attitudes of poor people toward work.[115] One exception was Goodwin's study of four thousand people that compared attitudes of welfare
families and participants in federal work-training programs with those
of middle-class families having steady employment. His findings:

> Evidence from this study unambiguously supports the following conclu-
> sion: poor people—males and females, blacks and whites, youths and
> adults—identify their self-esteem with work as strongly as do the non-
> poor. They express as much willingness to take job training if unable to
> earn a living and to work even if they were to have an adequate income.
> They have, moreover, as high life aspirations as do the nonpoor and want
> the same things, among them a good education and a nice place to live.
> This study reveals no differences between poor and nonpoor when it
> comes to life goals and wanting to work.[116]

Another study, conducted on a wide scale and continuing for three
years, actually made payments to the members of an experimental
group, bringing them to 50 percent, 75 percent, 100 percent, and 125
percent of the poverty line, and comparing their consequent labor
patterns with those of a similar control group. The study reached 1,357
families in four cities. The major finding is that there was only a small
(5–6 percent) reduction in average hours worked by the male heads of
families who received payments, and this occurred entirely among
white men.[117]

Despite these findings that most people, including poor people,
would not stop working for welfare if welfare income were the same,
or even a bit more, than their work income, the fear of work disincentives continues to guide the hand of those who design social-welfare
policies and programs. This fear is the biggest obstacle to sweeping
welfare reform in the shape of a reverse income tax or some other kind
of guaranteed minimum income.[118]

In 1962, Milton Friedman proposed a reverse income tax (alterna-
tively termed a negative income tax) to replace all existing welfare
programs.[119] In 1964, Schwartz proposed a "family security benefit."[120]
Various forms of guaranteed income have been advanced since then,
including President Nixon's Family Assistance Plan.[121] All of these plans
are intended to place an income floor beneath the population, guaranteeing that no one will have less than a predetermined minimum.
Supporters from the conservative side favor wiping out the crazy quilt
of programs that exists today, with different conditions of eligibility,
different payments, and overlaps and gaps. They also favor less government control, through giving cash rather than goods or services, and a
reduction in the number of social-welfare service employees. Supporters from the liberal wing want to do away with means tests and categories of recipients, and to make sure that everyone is above the poverty

line, regardless of location, occupation, work linkage, race, and other distinctions.

How much such programs would cost depends, obviously, on the level of payments to be made. Comparisons are difficult because variables include not only levels of payment but also the rates at which earned income would reduce such payments, as well as whether offsets of reduced or discarded alternative programs are included, and at what point in the inflationary economy the proposal was made. The least expensive proposal was that of Friedman, which would have cost $4 billion in 1969, of which $3 billion would have gone to those under the poverty line, increasing the minimum income of a family of four to $1,775, about one-third of the way up to the officially designated poverty line. Although Friedman envisioned his plan as eliminating public assistance, Social Security, and public housing, among other things, the gap that would remain between payments and subsistence would require retention of many of these programs.[122]

The most ambitious of the guaranteed-income proposals is that of the National Welfare Rights Organization. This proposal would pay up to $5,500 for a family of four; in other words, it would guarantee that no family in the United States had less income than it needed to purchase items at the poverty-line level of 42 cents per meal. Estimates of the cost of this program ranged in 1969 from $50 billion per year to $71 billion above the then current welfare expenditures,[123] with one-half of the costs going to the nonpoor.[124]

The guaranteed minimum income or the reverse income tax is the major alternative program to family allowances, children's allowances, or demogrants as a sweeping welfare-reform measure, and the major difference between them is the fear of a work disincentive in the former. Demogrants, of whatever form, would be paid on the basis of family size and, hence, presumed differential need. They would, as pointed out previously, make payments to those not in need, in addition to the poor, and they would not—according to any proposal currently under consideration—pay enough to raise any families out of poverty except those that are already very close to the poverty line.[125] For the latter reason, demogrants are not usually opposed as weakening work incentives, though there are such accusations in France, where family allowances may be as large as salaries.

Guaranteed-income measures, on the other hand, would be paid on the basis of individual incomes, and it is the fear of work disincentives that keeps proposed rates low, guarantees payments to the nonpoor (as discussed below), and in the final analysis, would alleviate but not eliminate poverty. On the face of it, guaranteeing everyone at least 42 cents per meal, taking part of the cost from the elimination of other income-maintenance programs (such as AFDC and General Assistance) and savings in other social costs associated with poverty (such as the costs of crime and mental illness), and paying the rest out of general revenues would eliminate poverty, insofar as that is defined in absolute financial terms. The operative questions are whether, in such a case, everyone making a salary below the poverty line would stop working (increase his or her leisure-to-work ratio, in economists' terms) and many other people, slightly or even far above that line, would prefer less income with no work.

Because there is general agreement that this would, indeed, eventuate, income-guarantee proposals have work-incentive programs built into them. Under such provisions, people would be given only a portion of the guarantee, and of any additional money that they would make, only a certain percentage (say, 30 percent or 50 percent) would be taken into account in computing their income (and thereby the amount to which they are entitled). The percentage would increase as income from work increased, but there would still be an absolute amount added to the income until the predetermined minimum, or "break-even" point, was reached. In this way, there would be advantage in continuing to earn while receiving the guaranteed income until one reached the guaranteed minimum.

In order for these work incentives to be effective, obviously, there has to be a gap between the amount given when there is no other income and what can be achieved by a combination of guarantee and work. It is in the amount of the basic guarantee, the rates and progression of diminishing payments, and the maximum attainment, or break-even, point that the various plans differ.

Further, on the supposition that people immediately above the poverty line would reduce their work to receive some of the subsidy and have more leisure, most plans include the near poor, fixing the break-even point above the poverty line. In this way, portions—sometimes substantial portions—of the costs of guaranteed-income proposals go to the nonpoor, as noted above.

Because of feared work disincentives in the face of unearned income, work incentives are built into guaranteed-income proposals. These incentives require beginning payments lower than the poverty line, and therefore people who cannot work—the aged, children, the disabled, and mothers of small children—would not be raised out of poverty by such programs, though it is possible that some of them would receive more than they do now, and with less hassle.

In these ways, the belief that people should work, and the fear that they will not, operates to emasculate programs designed originally to eliminate poverty. Because the consequences of this belief are so enormous, and the evidence on which it is based is so flimsy, it is interesting to speculate on the possible origins and intensity of these feelings.

Despite the fact that work has always been a pervasive norm in American society, the need for human labor in the American economy has almost imperceptibly but steadily diminished. Increases in efficiency and advances in automation have reduced the hours, days, weeks, and years required of human laborers. There are, to be sure, factors that mask the extent of this change: Farm subsidies operate to keep millions more people on farms than are needed in terms of output; automation is resisted as strongly, if not as violently, as in the days of the Luddites (for example, on the waterfront); union printers set up and take apart type for copy set on linotype machines; and other forms of featherbedding abound. Nevertheless, the amount of work required of Americans steadily decreases. The average American has four hours a day more leisure than his grandfather had,[126] and if the rate of reduction in work hours continues as it has since 1880, before today's children retire their work week will be halved.[127] The four-day week has been introduced into some major industries.[128] The long-term trend of work hours has been generally downward,[129] and as the work week has contracted and life expectancy has been extended, the average American has added about twenty-two more years of leisure to his life.[130] This trend not only continues but is accelerating, with reduction in the length of the work year through longer vacations and added holidays more prevalent than increases in overtime work.[131]

Not only are people working less; they are also less happy with their work. The fears and resistance concerning automation exhibited by organized labor indicate that there are many workers who know that their jobs could be done by machines—perhaps faster, better, and for twenty-four hours a day. Not only do they view with fear the threat of being replaced by machines; they feel degraded that they are forced to work to acquire material necessities when such work is basically unnecessary. In light of ecological questions that have recently come to the fore, and questions as to whether more is necessarily better, many people have begun to question the social desirability of their work. Further, the accelerating shift from the production of goods to the production of services (discussed previously) carries with it, for some people, the stigma of not producing tangible, and therefore more acceptable, products.

Such dependence on unnecessary, socially questionable, and little-understood work, like any enforced dependence, has ramifications in people's feelings about themselves. Empirically, work and the work place have been found no longer to be the central life interests of a vast majority of workers,[132] with only a small minority of workers' ideas centering around their jobs.[133] Half of all workers "say they could accomplish more work if they tried,"[134] and "most employees accept (or become resigned to) their lot."[135] It is small wonder, then, that a study of industrial workers raises "serious questions concerning the general conditions of psychological and social health of our industrial workers,"[136] and that a government task force found that many "workers accept the necessity of work but get little satisfaction from their specific jobs."[137]

The American norm is that work is good in itself, people should want to work, work is ennobling, people should work as hard as they can and with enjoyment, and the well-being of the country depends on the efficiency and the amount of human labor. But in reality, Americans are constantly working shorter hours and fewer days per week, taking more and longer vacations, and retiring earlier. They do not enjoy working, do not work as hard or as long as they can and feel they should, enjoy their leisure more than their work, define themselves in terms of their leisure-time occupations,[138] know that they do not work as hard as their fathers and grandfathers are said to have worked, and secretly wish that they did not have to work. They have doubts about the social necessity or even usefulness of their work, and they are often troubled by the image it bestows on them.

One way of dealing with the discomforting gap between the norms a person accepts and the behavior he or she exhibits is the age-old practice of scapegoating. The origin and meaning of the term "scapegoat" are found in the Bible, where the High Priest placed upon the head of a goat the sins of the people and sent it off to die in the wilderness.[139] By transferring to the goat the sins of the people and punishing it, he relieved the people of their feelings of guilt. Scapegoating, in its classical sense, occurs when an individual or group feels guilty of holding unacceptable views. The guilt and the feelings are denied, that is, repressed, and the individual or group often becomes vehement in advocating the existing norms. Indeed, the more guilt, the more vehemence. ("Methinks the lady doth protest too much.") Such repression does not allay the tension created by the conflict between real and expressed feelings, however, and the next steps are to accuse others of having the proscribed views or feelings—that is, projection—and then punish them for so doing. The more one shares or admires the projected traits, the more reprehensible they become in the scapegoat. There is nothing scapegoats can do to change their roles, because the reason for the punishment lies in the feelings of others, rather than in the victim's own feelings or behavior.[140]

Many people who have questions about the necessity, desirability, or usefulness of their work—questions that may be unspoken, diffuse, even close to unconscious—but ostensibly share the prevailing societal norms concerning working, being productive, and being useful[141] need a scapegoat, and find one in the poor. The poor are fantasized as happy connivers who live without work, enjoying guiltless leisure, sexual freedom, immunity from laws and morals, exemption from obligations, and total lack of concern about the future. Thus a culture of poverty is not only established but made the scapegoat for the more affluent. The fact that this picture of the culture of poverty resembles the situation of no poor people who have been found in studies—and, indeed, is a travesty of the tense, bitter, anxious, humiliated people who cannot afford 42 cents a meal who make up the poor—does not, of course, affect the process of scapegoating. Once assigned these reprehensible characteristics, the poor can—nay, *must*—be punished, changed, and isolated because of them.

In this respect, at least, social welfare has changed but little since its earliest days:

> The Elizabethan lawmaker proposes work as training for youth, as prevention of roguery, as a test of good intent, and as a means of providing employment for the needy. In the background is the House of Correction with its threat of punishment. How ancient is the confusion about work, and how deep-rooted is our conflict of feeling concerning it![142]

And: "The most vigorous opponents of FAP [the Family Assistance Plan] ... were ... preoccupied with the morality of giving support to non-working males/females at all."[143]

THE FUTURE OF THE WORK-WELFARE LINK

It is very likely that drastic reforms of the welfare system in the United States will be made in the relatively near future. The unwieldiness of the present system, the built-in growth factors, its inefficiency, and lack of effectiveness—all seem to be building up disenchantment with what is often termed the "welfare mess." In addition to purely structural changes, it seems very probable that either some sort of family allowance, children's allowance, or demogrant, or a variant of the Family Assistance Plan, or some other guaranteed-income proposal will be adopted. In no case, however, are public attitudes ready to accept payments as high as wages. Working people will not stand for nonworkers matching or exceeding their income, regardless of need. Others, not threatened by such equity, will see such payments as immoral, demoralizing, and injurious to the economy and the society. The voice of Luther will be heard in the land for many a year yet.

In the long run, however, the need for human labor will continue to decrease. As people enjoy their leisure more, the work week and day will shrink even further. Methods of sharing the labor will become more crisis-ridden. Although experts by no means agree on the ultimate results of automation,[144] or on whether the shift to service jobs will be limitless, part of the affluent society enjoys greater and greater amounts of leisure. Eventually, social-welfare planners may have to face the question of how society's resources should be distributed when 10 percent of the population will be able to produce all the goods and services needed by the nation.[145] In an almost workless society, who will do what work there is, and what will be the inducement or recompense? And what will be the role of the others? It is possible to construct a series of rather fantastic scenarios depicting societies in which something other than work is the central value. In a music-centered society, for example, stellar performers might be the elite; musicians, the upper class; and there would be distinct societal roles for the manufacturers of instruments, the music printers, record and tape manufacturers, and so forth. The tone-deaf would be relegated to the role of the poor and the needy in our current society. In any case, with the possibility of most necessary work being done by machines, work need not be the touchstone of merit, morality, and social usefulness forever.

NOTES

1. E. H. Erikson, *Young Man Luther: A Study in Psychoanalysis and History* (New York: Norton, 1958), pp. 226–27.
2. R. Nisbet, *The Contribution of Religion to Social Work* (New York: Columbia University Press, 1932), pp. 207–8.
3. H. G. Gutman, *Work, Culture and Society in Industrializing America* (New York: Knopf, 1976).
4. *Ibid.*
5. C. Amory, *The Proper Bostonians* (New York: Dutton, 1947), p. 91.
6. J. W. Osborne, *The Silent Revolution: The Industrial Revolution in England Source of Cultural Change* (New York: Scribner's, 1970).
7. G. Simmel, "The Poor," *Social Problems,* 13 (1965):123.
8. See E. A. Friedmann and R. J. Havighurst, *The Meaning of Work and Retirement* (Chicago: University of Chicago Press, 1954); V. H. Vroom, *Work and Motivation* (New York: Wiley, 1964); R. Barlow, H. E. Brazer, and J. N. Morgan, *Economic Behavior of the Affluent* (Washington, D.C.: The Brookings Institution, 1966); and R. Dubin, "Industrial Workers' Worlds: A Study of the Central Life Interests of Industrial Workers," in A. M. Rose (ed.), *Human Behavior and Social Processes* (Boston: Houghton Mifflin, 1962).
9. J. H. Pfouts, *Vocational History of 309 Arm, Leg, and Bilateral Amputees of World War II* (Baltimore: Veterans' Administration Outpatient Clinic, n.d.).
10. H. L. Wilensky and C. N. Lebeaux, *Industrial Society and Social Welfare* (New York: Free Press, 1958).

11. A. C. B. Prabhupada, *The Perfection of Yoga* (Los Angeles: International Center for Krishna Consciousness, 1972), pp. 9–10.

12. K. Yakabe, *Labor Relations in Japan: Fundamental Characteristics* (Tokyo: International Society for Educational Information, 1974), p. 76.

13. D. Macarov and G. Fradkin, *The Short Course in Development Activities* (Ramat Gan, Israel: Massada Press, 1973), p. 93.

14. M. Weber, *The Protestant Ethic and the Spirit of Capitalism* (New York: Scribner's, 1952).

15. W. Buckingham, *Automation* (New York: Mentor, 1961).

16. Nisbet, *op. cit.*, p. 213.

17. E. Hoffer, *Working and Thinking on the Waterfront* (New York: Harper & Row, 1969).

18. Bell equates Protestant culture with wages based on tasks, and Catholic culture with wages based on need. D. Bell, *The End of Ideology* (New York: Free Press, 1960), p. 227.

19. W. F. Whyte, *Money and Motivation* (New York: Harper Bros., 1955), p. 12.

20. J. Charnow, *Work Relief Experience in the United States* (Washington, D.C.: Social Science Research Council, 1943), p. 6.

21. D. Gilbert, "The Changing Work Ethic and Rehabilitation," *Journal of Rehabilitation,* 39 (1973):14–17.

22. J. J. Graham, *The Enemies of the Poor* (New York: Random House, 1970), p. 7.

23. *Ibid.*

24. Charnow, *op. cit.*, p. 7.

25. L. H. Feder, *Unemployment Relief in Periods of Depression* (New York: Sage, 1936).

26. *Ibid.*, p. 73.

27. *Ibid.*, p. 352.

28. *Ibid.*, p. 169.

29. D. S. Howard, *The WPA and Federal Relief Policy* (New York: Sage, 1943), p. 481.

30. Charnow, *op. cit.*, p. 7.

31. K. Woodroofe, *From Charity to Social Work in England and the United States* (Toronto: University of Toronto Press, 1962), p. 155.

32. R. C. Federico, *The Social Welfare Institution: An Introduction* (Lexington, Mass.: Heath, 1973), p. 14.

33. K. de Schweinitz, *England's Road to Social Security* (Philadelphia: University of Pennsylvania Press, 1943), p. 49.

34. D. J. Rothman, *The Discovery of the Asylum: Social Order and Disorder in the New Republic* (Boston: Little, Brown, 1971), p. 318n.

35. J. Quincy, *Report of the Committee to Whom Was Referred the Consideration of the Pauper Laws of This Commonwealth;* reprinted in *Poverty, U.S.A.: The Almshouse Experience* (New York: Arno Press, 1971); quoted in J. Axinn and H. Levin, *Social Welfare: A History of the American Response to Need* (New York: Dodd, Mead, 1975), p. 43.

36. Charnow, *op. cit.*, p. 80.

37. Graham, *op. cit.*, p. 18.

38. J. Colcord, *Cash Relief* (New York: Sage, 1936), p. 13; Charnow, *op. cit.*, pp. iv–v.
39. W. H. Leahy, "An Economic Perspective of Public Employment Programs," *Review of Social Economy,* 34 (October 1976):198.
40. Feder, *op. cit.,* p. 31.
41. *Ibid.,* p. 169.
42. Charnow, *op. cit.,* p. 5.
43. There were bewildering numbers of agencies and name changes, including the Public Works Administration (PWA), the Federal Emergency Relief Administration (FERA), the National Youth Administration (NYA), the Civilian Conservation Corps (CCC), the Civil Works Administration (CWA), and both Works Progress Administration and Works Projects Administration (WPA). For the sake of simplicity, they are all referred to herein as the WPA.
44. Axinn and Levin, *op. cit.,* p. 189.
45. D. S. Howard, *The WPA and Federal Relief Policy* (New York: Sage, 1943), p. 128.
46. J. C. Brown, *Public Relief 1929–1939* (New York: Holt, 1940), pp. 379–80.
47. Charnow, *op. cit.,* p. 112.
48. *Ibid.,* p. 99.
49. *Ibid.*
50. Feder, *op. cit.,* p. 279.
51. Charnow, *op. cit.,* p. 3.
52. *Ibid.,* p. 84.
53. *Ibid.,* pp. 114–15.
54. *Ibid.,* pp. 115–16.
55. Graham, *op. cit.,* p. 22.
56. G. Kateb, *Utopia and Its Enemies* (New York: Schocken, 1963), p. 126.
57. *Social Security Programs Throughout the World 1975* (Washington, D.C.: Department of Health, Education, and Welfare, 1975).
58. *Ibid.*
59. H. E. Striner, "Recurrent Educational and Manpower Training in Great Britain," *Monthly Labor Review,* 98 (September 1975):30–34.
60. E. W. Busse, "Psychoneurotic Reactions and Defense Mechanisms in the Aged," in P. H. Hock and J. Zabin (eds.), *Psychopathology of Aging* (New York: Grune & Stratton, 1961).
61. M. G. Field, "Structured Strain in the Role of the Soviet Physician," *American Journal of Sociology,* 63 (1953):493.
62. Friedmann and Havighurst, *op. cit.*
63. D. Macarov, *Incentives to Work* (San Francisco: Jossey-Bass, 1970), pp. 64–65.
64. P. W. Power and R. P. Marinelli, "Normalization and the Sheltered Workshop: A Review and Proposals for Change," *Rehabilitation Literature,* 35 (1974):66–72, 78.
65. P. R. Friedman, "The Mentally Handicapped Citizen and Institutional Labor," *Harvard Law Review,* 87 (1974):567–87.
66. J. Reingold, R. L. Wolk, and S. Schwartz, "Attitudes of Adult Children

Whose Aging Parents Are Members of a Sheltered Workshop," *Aging and Human Development,* 3 (1972):331–37.

67. J. M. Martin, *Lower-Class Delinquency and Work Programs* (New York: New York University Press, 1966).

68. D. G. Gil, *Unravelling Social Policy* (Cambridge, Mass.: Schenkman, 1973).

69. Schweinitz, *op. cit.,* p. 92.

70. *Ibid.,* p. 123.

71. For some of the complexities involved in determining prevailing rates, see Charnow, *op. cit.,* p. 62.

72. D. Macarov, "Work Without Pay: Work Incentives and Patterns in a Salaryless Environment," *International Journal of Social Economics,* 2 (Summer 1975):106.

73. "Current Information: France—Recent Developments in Social Security Legislation," *International Labour Review,* 106 (October 1972):367–72.

74. J. J. Oechslin, "The Role of Employers' Organisations in France," *International Labour Review,* 106 (November 1972):391–413.

75. Although Unemployment Insurance is intended to pay "adequate" benefits, no examination of the adequacy of payments has been conducted for the past twenty years. J. M. Becker, "Income Maintenance Through Unemployment Insurance," *Review of Social Economy,* 34 (October 1976): 163–71.

76. I. C. Merriam, "Financing Social Welfare," in *Encyclopedia of Social Work* (New York: National Association of Social Workers, 1971). Only about half of the labor force was covered by private pension plans in 1973. J. Galper, "Private Pensions and Public Policy," *Social Work,* 18 (May 1973):5–12.

77. "The weekly sickness benefit ... in 1911 represented a much higher proportion of the average wage; it was worth more in purchasing power and ... was altogether more generous than the amount paid today." R. N. Titmuss, *Essays on "The Welfare State"* (New Haven, Conn.: Yale University Press, 1959), p. 24.

78. Different amounts are available at different ages to principal wage earners, survivors, the disabled, and so forth. *Your Social Security Earnings Record* (Washington, D.C.: Department of Health, Education, and Welfare, 1975).

79. Macarov, *Incentives to Work, op. cit.,* pp. 18–25.

80. Axinn and Levin, *op. cit.,* pp. 4–5.

81. Macarov, *Incentives to Work, op. cit.,* pp. 25–32.

82. H. Gans, "Income Grants and 'Dirty Work,'" *The Public Interest,* 6 (1967):110; H. Gans, *More Equality* (New York: Vintage, 1968); A. Walinsky, "Keeping the Poor in Their Place: Notes on the Importance of Being One-Up," in A. B. Shostak and W. Gomberg (eds.), *New Perspectives on Poverty* (Englewood Cliffs, N.J.: Prentice-Hall, 1965); Macarov, *Incentives to Work, op. cit.,* pp. 32–35.

83. Macarov, *Incentives to Work, op. cit.,* pp. 35–36.

84. Both the Bureau of Labor Statistics and the Social Security Administra-

tion publish budgets on which the poverty line is based. The Social Security Administration's figures are the more frequently used.

85. The average American family actually spends 16 percent of its income on food (J. B. Williamson *et al., Strategies Against Poverty in America* [New York: Wiley, 1975], p. 20), but because the smaller incomes of the poor allow little reduction in this "fixed" cost, the percentage of income spent for food among the poor is estimated to be twice that among the more affluent.

86. M. Orshansky, "Counting the Poor: Another Look at the Poverty Profile," in L. A. Ferman, J. L. Kornbluh, and A. Haber (eds.), *Poverty in America* (Ann Arbor: University of Michigan Press, 1972); "Who's Who Among the Poor," *Social Security Bulletin,* 28 (1965):3; "More About the Poor in 1964," *Social Security Bulletin,* 29 (1966):3.

87. The formula is $mc = pl/(p)(m)(d)(f)$

where mc = meal cost

pl = poverty line

p = people in family

m = meals per day

f = proportion of budget spent on food

d = days per year

or $\$0.42 = \$5,500/(4)(3)(365)(3)$

88. For comparative purposes, it should be noted that in 1977, a loaf of white bread cost 58 cents.

89. R. D. Plotnick and F. Skidmore, *Programs Against Poverty* (New York: Academic Press, 1975).

90. S. B. Kamerman and A. J. Kahn, *Social Services in the United States: Policies and Programs* (Philadelphia: Temple University Press, 1976), p. 542.

91. For tables of food-stamp eligibility and payments, see N. Kotz, *Let Them Eat Promises* (Garden City, N.Y.: Doubleday, 1971), pp. 246–51.

92. S. R. Wright and J. D. Wright, "Income Maintenance and Work Behavior," *Social Policy,* 6 (September–October 1975):24–32.

93. F. Ginor, *Analysis of Low Income Groups* (Tel Aviv: University of Tel Aviv, 1974) (in Hebrew); A. Nizan and H. Avidor, *An Empirical Study of Handicapped Persons in Israel in Need of Vocational Rehabilitation* (Jerusalem: National Insurance Institute, 1974) (in Hebrew); *Statistical Abstract of Israel* (Jerusalem: Central Bureau of Statistics, 1975).

94. Macarov, *Incentives to Work, op. cit.,* pp. 61–108.

95. D. McGregor, *The Human Side of Management* (New York: McGraw-Hill, 1960).

96. For views regarding Theory X, see H. Levinson, *The Great Jackass Fallacy* (Cambridge, Mass.: Harvard University Press, 1973).

97. Macarov, *Incentives to Work, op. cit.,* pp. 100–108.

98. F. W. Taylor, *The Principles of Scientific Management* (New York: Harper Bros., 1911).

99. F. A. Roethlisberger and W. J. Dickson, *Management and the Worker* (Cambridge, Mass.: Harvard University Press, 1939); E. Mayo, *The Human Problems of an Industrial Civilization* (New York: Macmillan, 1933).

100. G. C. Homans, *The Human Group* (London: Routledge & Kegan Paul, 1951).

101. F. Herzberg, B. Mausner, and B. B. Snyderman, *The Motivation to Work* (New York: Wiley, 1959); F. Herzberg, *Work and the Nature of Man* (Cleveland: World Publishing, 1966); D. Macarov, "Work Patterns and Satisfactions in an Israeli Kibbutz: A Test of the Herzberg Hypothesis," *Personnel Psychology*, 25 (1972):483–93.

102. L. P. Brayfield and W. H. Crockett, "Employee Attitudes and Performance," *Psychological Bulletin*, 52 (November 1975):396–424; P. C. Smith, L. M. Kendall, and C. C. Hulin, *The Measurement of Satisfactions in Work and Retirement: A Strategy for the Study of Attitudes* (Chicago: Rand McNally, 1969); G. Strauss, "Job Satisfaction, Motivation and Job Redesign," *Organizational Behavior: Research and Issues* (Madison, Wis.: Industrial Relations Research Association, 1974).

103. A. H. Maslow, *Motivation and Personality* (New York: Harper Bros., 1954).

104. G. Huizinga, *Maslow's Need Hierarchy in the Work Situation* (Groningen, Netherlands: Walters-Noordhoff, 1970).

105. D. Macarov, "Reciprocity Between Self-Actualization and Hard Work," *International Journal of Social Economics*, 3 (1976):39–44.

106. M. M. Machlowitz, *The Workaholic.* New Haven, Conn.: Yale University 1976. (Mimeographed.)

107. S. Freud, *Civilization and Its Discontents* (New York: Paperback, 1958), pp. 20–21.

108. W. G. Sumner, *Social Darwinism* (Englewood Cliffs, N.J.: Prentice-Hall, 1963), p. 1.

109. W. G. Whyte, *op. cit.*

110. D. C. McClelland, *The Achieving Society* (Princeton, N.J.: Van Nostrand, 1961).

111. W. F. Whyte, *Organisational Behaviour: Theory and Application* (Homewood, Ill.: Irwin, 1969).

112. M. L. Kohn and C. Schooler, "Occupational Experience and Psychological Functioning: An Assessment of Reciprocal Effects," *American Sociological Review*, 38 (February 1973):97–118.

113. L. Goodwin, *Do the Poor Want to Work?: A Social-Psychological Study of Work Orientations* (Washington, D.C.: The Brookings Institution, 1972).

114. As has been pointed out, "the inclination as well as the ability to make successful efforts is not independent of inborn physical and psychological gifts and environmental advantages and disadvantages." E. Van den Haag, "Economics Is Not Enough: On the Anti-Capitalist Spirit," *Public Interest*, 45 (Fall 1976):109–22.

115. For an overview of incentive studies, see G. G. Cain and H. W. Watts (eds.), *Income Maintenance and Labor Supply: Econometric Studies* (Chicago: Markham, 1973).

116. Goodwin, *op. cit.*, p. 112.

117. J. A. Pechman and P. M. Timpane (eds.), *Work Incentives and Income Guarantees: The New Jersey Negative Income Tax Experiment* (Washington, D.C.: The Brookings Institution, 1975); for a critique of this experi-

ment, see P. H. Rossi and K. C. Lyall, *Reforming Public Welfare: A Critique of the Negative Income Tax Experiment* (New York: Sage, 1976).

118. Echoes of Malthus thus continue to reverberate: "If our benevolence be indiscriminate . . . we shall raise the worthless above the worthy; we shall encourage indolence and check industry; and in the most marked manner subtract from the sum of human happiness." Quoted in D. Bell, *op. cit.*, p. 245.

119. M. Friedman, *Capitalism and Freedom* (Chicago: University of Chicago Press, 1962).

120. E. E. Schwartz, "A Way to End the Means Test," *Social Work*, 4 (1963):3.

121. D. P. Moynihan, *The Politics of a Guaranteed Income: The Nixon Administration and the Family Assistance Plan* (New York: Vintage, 1973).

122. Williamson, *op. cit.*, p. 88.

123. *Ibid.*, p. 90.

124. For comparative purposes, the budget of the U.S. Department of Defense at this writing is $120 billion.

125. The most generous of these proposals—George McGovern's—would raise 64 percent of poor families out of poverty. Williamson, *op. cit.*, p. 79.

126. M. Kaplan, *Leisure in America: A Social Inquiry* (New York: Wiley, 1960), p. 43.

127. Buckingham, *op. cit.*

128. A. H. Raskin, "Shorter Workweek: A New Breakthrough," *New York Times*, October 8, 1976, p. 14.

129. This is true even when "moonlighting" is considered. M. Kaplan, *Leisure: Theory and Policy* (New York: Wiley, 1975), pp. 284, 368.

130. R. L. Cunningham, *The Philosophy of Work* (New York: National Association of Manufacturers, 1964), p. 14.

131. *Methods of Adjusting to Automation and Technological Change* (Washington, D.C.: Department of Labor, n.d.), p. 15; see also J. Barbash, "Final Report on the Conference," *Work in a Changing Industrial Society* (Paris: Organization for Economic Cooperation and Development, 1974), p. 24; and A. A. Evans, *Flexibility in Working Life* (Paris: Organization for Economic Cooperation and Development, 1973), p. 36.

132. A. Kornhauser, *Mental Health of the Industrial Worker* (New York: Wiley, 1965), p. 8.

133. Dubin, *op. cit.*, pp. 262–63.

134. G. Strauss, "Workers' Attitudes and Adjustments," in J. M. Rosow (ed.), *The Worker and the Job: Coping with Change* (Englewood Cliffs, N.J.: Prentice-Hall, 1974), pp. 73–98.

135. *Ibid.*

136. Kornhauser, *op. cit.*, p. 9.

137. *Work in America* (Cambridge, Mass.: MIT Press, 1973), p. 14.

138. Kaplan, *Leisure in America, op. cit.*

139. Lev. 16:10, 22.

140. For an excellent description of scapegoating, see K. Heap, "The Scapegoat Role in Youth Groups," *Case Conference* (London), 12 (January 1966):215.

141. R. Coles, "Work and Self-Respect," *Daedalus,* 104 (Fall 1976):29–38.
142. Schweinitz, *op. cit.,* p. 27.
143. Rossi and Lyall, *op. cit.,* p. 176.
144. See, for example, F. Best (ed.), *The Future of Work* (Englewood Cliffs, N.J.: Prentice-Hall, 1973).
145. Cunningham, *op. cit.*

11

Laissez-Faire Economics, Psychoanalysis, and Economic Determinism

THE INFLUENCE OF ADAM SMITH

As is true of most major societal changes, it is difficult to say when the Industrial Revolution began: with the flying shuttle in 1733, with the steam engine in 1765, with the spinning jenny in 1770, or at some other point.[1] In any case, the advent of the Industrial Revolution both utilized and strengthened the Protestant Ethic. Previously, the Protestant emphasis on work had been mainly observable in agriculture and small handicrafts, but the time had come when many people had no work. In some places there was too little arable land for too many family members, and primogeniture, the custom of the Middle Ages whereby the eldest son inherited and the younger joined the army or the clergy, was dying out. Hence, the Elizabethan Poor Laws emphasized keeping people in their home locations, putting vagrants to work, and making work for those who had none.

With the establishment of factories, a wage economy began to take the place of the agricultural barter economy. And because wages were easily convertible into goods, the limiting boundary of work hours and effort was no longer the acquisition of sustenance. It was possible to convert more work into more possessions. A religious belief that added to these utilitarian considerations the concept that work was also a duty owed God was admirably suited to the new economy. Factories needed workers, and workers needed jobs, not just to make money but also to be moral, religious, law-abiding people. Factory owners thus did people a favor by allowing them to work, and workers were expected to be grateful to the point of not biting the hand that fed them by asking for higher wages or better working conditions. This was not only ingratitude but almost blasphemy.

The new economic system resulted in a shift away from the limited production of high-priced objects for the few to large-scale production of low-priced goods for the many. The economic circle went from salaries to purchases to production to jobs to salaries. With this change in the economic situation, a new economic theory was required to explain and predict the behavior of the market. That theory was supplied by Adam Smith.

Smith was a man of enormous knowledge and wide-ranging interests. Although he was basically an economist, his *Wealth of Nations* is encyclopedic in its subject matter. Among other things, Smith commented on the tremendous increase in production that division of labor and specialization bring in their wake, using a pin factory as his model. These comments became the basis of Max Weber's attribution of these aspects to bureaucracy,[2] and of the scientific-management principle of Taylor, mentioned previously. Smith's economic theory has been termed that of "laissez-faire." Basically, Smith held that if everyone would seek to maximize his own economic condition, everyone would benefit. If each were to compete with all others, the most efficient enterprise would survive, and society would profit by a supply of the best merchandise at the cheapest prices. The inefficient would, of course, go into some other enterprise, where they would be the most efficient. Smith's classic example has to do with manufacturing gloves and shoes:

> Suppose we have one hundred manufacturers of gloves. The self-interest of each one will cause him to wish to raise his price above his cost of production and thereby to realize an extra profit. But he cannot. If he raises his price, his competitors will step in and take his market away from him by underselling him. . . . Let us suppose that consumers decide they want more gloves than are being turned out, and fewer shoes. . . . Glove prices will tend to rise as consumers try to buy more of them than there are ready at hand, and shoe prices will tend to fall . . . but as glove prices rise, profits in the glove industry will rise, too; and . . . profits in shoe manufacturing will slump. . . . Workers will be released from the shoe business . . . they will move to the glove business . . . glove production will rise and shoe production fall.
>
> And this is exactly what society wanted in the first place. As more gloves come on the market to meet demand, glove prices will fall back into line. As fewer shoes are produced, shoe prices will again rise up to normal. . . . Society will have changed . . . production to fit its new desires. Yet no one has issued a dictum, and no planning authority has established schedules of output. Self-interest and competition . . . have accomplished the transition.[3]

According to Smith, not only will prices and goods be regulated by supply and demand, but so will the income of those who produce the goods.[4] The important thing is that no one should interfere in any way with the free operation of supply and demand, self-interest and competition. This is the source of the term "laissez-faire." The competitive network, when not interfered with, becomes an "invisible hand," ensuring everyone's benefit.

Smith has become one of *the* classical economists in the modern pantheon. Classical economics is based on supposedly perfect knowledge and rational behavior: The economic theorist knows all the pertinent facts and assumes that people will behave in what is, to him, a rational manner.[5] Consequently, there naturally flowed from laissez-faire economics the concept of the economic man. This is the person who responds to rational stimuli that are, in the nature of things, economic. Hence, it is perfectly certain, in Smith's view, that a worker— pursuing his or her own interest—will take the job offering the highest salary. Considerations of enjoyment, working conditions, work companions, distance from home, or career opportunities were not assumed to affect economic considerations, nor were apathy and lethargy taken into account. This image of the "economic man," though specifically disavowed in modern theory, continues to exist in the minds of many who determine or discuss social-welfare policies, and it finds expression in the wage stop discussed in the preceding chapter, and in the belief that women have children in order to collect benefits.

Because the invisible hand that regulates the market is the economic man's competition with everyone else, people who do not choose to compete, or do not maximize their economic conditions, upset the market; and so do agencies or institutions that enable them to drop out of competition. Such people should be penalized, and such institutions should be minimized. The social-welfare system is a prime offender in this regard. It enables recipients of social welfare to exist outside of the market system, and it gives people choices other than those offered by the market. It interferes with the supply of labor, and allows people to purchase items (and thus keep prices up) with resources other than their own labor. In short, whereas the Protestant Ethic said it is good for men to work, laissez-faire adds, "Don't let social welfare interfere with the supply of labor or the operations of the free market."

In social-welfare terms, the influence of Adam Smith reinforces Social Darwinism, which casts the needy into the role of the unfit, and the Protestant Ethic, which makes them seem immoral, by making them deviant in that because they are presumed to be unconcerned about competing with others in the open market, they disrupt the economic picture. It is in this sense that Danzig speaks of "the conservatism which has captured America, based on Adam Smith's economics and John Calvin's ethics."[6]

The fact that social welfare operates outside the market economy not only causes problems for its clients but also results in difficulties for social-welfare programs and for the entire social-welfare institution. In a culture that measures most things in economic terms, social welfare is hard to understand and even harder to evaluate. Drucker, for example, holds that social welfare cannot succeed, basically because it does not have a "bottom line" of profit or loss against which it can evaluate its success.[7] Without such an evaluative device, success can only be judged in terms of continuation of activities, which means, in turn, continuation of, or increase in, social-welfare budgets. Hence, social-welfare agencies undertake the activities that will ensure their budgets, rather than those that are in the best interests of their clients.

The acknowledged difficulty of evaluating social-welfare programs and activities is made doubly difficult by the need to couch the evaluation in terms meaningful to businessmen.[8] This is even more of a problem for services that do not result in reduced costs to society. For example, as noted previously, whereas preventive medical services for the aged can be said to reduce hospitalization and institutionalization costs, recreation services for the aged cannot be evaluated on the same basis. The necessity to quantify what are essentially qualitative services results in distortions in services, as well as in bookkeeping. As Etzioni points out, emphasis on measurement leads to undertaking the most easily measurable activities.[9]

Further, whereas competition in business is believed to result in increased efficiency, the lack of a profit motive or measurement in social-welfare activities militates against competition between agencies, and there is a drive to achieve coordination of services. The attempt to achieve coordination of services often uses time, energy, and funds that could have gone into the services as such. In addition, coordination often acts to deny clients choice. Finally, coordination often results in more standardized services, less innovation, and a generally more conservative stance.

Emphasis upon the economic system as the norm to which social welfare should aspire has another influence. This is the insistence upon fees. The question of whether to charge fees for services has many factors, including eligibility, means tests, and revenues.

One assumption is that it is morally good and even therapeutic for clients to pay for services. In private psychotherapeutic settings, not only is discussion of the cost of treatment considered part of the contract between practitioner and client, but the manner in which the client relates to money, the necessity to discuss it, and the arrangements for payment are all used for both evaluative and treatment purposes. Indeed, even when private practitioners deal with people of very limited means—perhaps as a public service—a symbolic fee is often insisted upon. This attitude is also evident in many community centers and settlement houses, in which everyone pays something, even if only symbolically. The stated rationale for this attitude is that it is good for people to have to pay. Examined deeper, the assumption is that people who pay behave differently, appreciate the service more, and therefore use the service better. It is interesting that this belief, like many others, rests upon little, if any, evidence.[10] There is no proof that symbolic payment for services affects behavior or even attitudes. Contrariwise, it is possible that payments, no matter how small, act as a selective device, barring certain participants, and that any differences in behavior that are felt to exist arise from differences in clientele.

Smith's laissez-faire philosophy not only resulted in questions about welfare's being outside the market system, it also caused welfare to be seen as an economic activity in its own right, subject to the rules of the marketplace. In this way, the insurance-type programs are expected to operate with actuarial soundness, and fears that the Social Security system will "go bankrupt" are widely heard, despite the fact that there is no necessity, outside of marketing practice, that income match payments. Similarly, administrators of insurance-type programs view participants as "investors" who must receive a reasonable return. Thus, while the wage stop limits the amount of payments, it is necessary that there be a limit to premiums as well. The rationale for a limitation on the income taxed for Social Security in the United States—$16,500[11] at this writing—is that the 16 million people making more than that would not recover their premiums in benefits, which would amount to a poor investment from their point of view and seem to be "unfair." However, not only do citizens pay for many benefits they do not personally use, as pointed out previously, but the "put in–take out" principle does not operate at the lower end of the scale: Those paying into Social Security too few premiums, or for too few quarters, receive no benefits, nor are their premiums returned to them.

In a general way, Smith's influence upon social welfare can be summed up as being opposed to government influence in the market, particularly for social-welfare purposes.[12] One of Franklin Roosevelt's problems regarding the proposed Social Security Act was the fear that it would be seen—and opposed—as the government entering the life-insurance business. Each extension of social welfare on the part of the government is greeted by some people as unwarranted government encroachment into the area of individual responsibility. Even during the period of massive need known as the Great Depression, the voluntary agencies, despite their own lack of resources, opposed government measures.

In the 1960s, one of the first proposals for a guaranteed minimum income came, as noted previously, from Milton Friedman, an avowedly conservative economist who became Senator Barry Goldwater's economic adviser during the latter's campaign for the presidency. So reactionary were Senator Goldwater's views believed to be that letters in *Social Work*, the American journal for professional social workers, called on social workers to oppose the new proposal because of its source. Indeed, the motivation for Friedman's proposal was to get the government out of the welfare business, and to free clients from dependence on the bureaucracy. In short, back to Smith's free market.

THE INFLUENCE OF SIGMUND FREUD

Although Sigmund Freud's impact on social work is greater than on social welfare, the effect on the latter includes four elements: impact on the reform movement, the medical model, the assumption of "real" underlying problems, and reaffirmation of the importance of work.

American society entered the so-called progressive era slightly before the turn of the present century, and for about twenty years social reform was a goal of voluntary agencies, settlement houses,[13] and individuals. The movement for women's rights began, muckrakers exposed the evils perpetrated on the immigrants in the city slums, and the evils of corporate rapacity were denounced. After World War I, however, the prevailing mood was one of wanting to return to the "old familiar," rather than to continue the fight for changes. The arrival of Freudian theory, with its emphasis on the inner self rather than the outer reality, gave social workers, at least, a rationalization to move from social reform to individual adjustment as their goal.[14] Social work became deeply engaged with the one-to-one relationship, and casework assumed a predominance in social-work activities and in training for social work, which has continued until today.[15] Even within settlement houses and community centers, emphasis shifted from community changes to recreational and therapeutic group work. The psychoanalytic aspects of both casework and group work became prestigious, and doubts about the efficacy of psychiatry and psychoanalysis, let alone their efficiency,[16] had little effect on this retreat from social reform.

A second effect of Freudian theory on social welfare was the establishment and continuation of a medical model as the pattern for social-work activities. According to the medical model, a patient is brought involuntarily or brings himself voluntarily to a mental-health therapist or institution, and it is assumed that he is ill.[17] Because the disease is assumed to be the result of some motivation the patient does not recognize, the therapist plays a rather passive role, helping him or her to become aware of the problem, after which he or she is assumed to be able to deal with it. This is in contrast to the human-service model, which adds to the above the possibility of externally caused problems, and casts the practitioner in the role of expediter, facilitator, ombudsman, advocate, broker, and adviser, as well as therapist. Although the concept of social welfare as a human service, in the terms just outlined, is proliferating, the great bulk of social work continues to be taught and practiced according to the medical model.

The dysfunctional aspects of the medical model are underlined in formulations that emphasize that heart disease cannot be eradicated by appropriate legislation but that poverty can. Polio can be eliminated by vaccines; marital discord cannot. Sick people can be prescribed for; unhappy people cannot buy prescriptions for their condition. The nurse may be handmaiden to the doctor, but the social worker must be self-determining.

Freudian thinking led to another aspect of social welfare. Because one of the assumptions of the Freudian process is that the presenting problem is rarely the real problem, dealing with the former will not solve the latter. In other words, because the problem is assumed to be in the unconscious, not known to the patient, whatever the patient describes as the problem cannot be the underlying difficulty. Although this theory is being challenged by the emerging school of behavioral modification in social work, the Freudian assumption can lead to conflicts and ambivalences concerning the possibility of separating making payments from giving other kinds of service.

On the one hand, massive amounts of social workers' time have been used in financial investigations of clients and in preparing payment orders—time taken from dealing with emotional and environmental problems. On the other hand, it was felt that the request for money either masked other felt problems or was indicative of a situation that was responsible for the money shortage. Therefore, the request for money was seen as the presenting problem, which made possible and necessary a search for deeper difficulties.[18] In many cases, this assumption was seen by both clients and outsiders as postulating problems that did not exist, and for which no help had been sought. In some cases, clients appeared to be accepting services as a necessary adjunct of receiving funds. The payment became the bait for other services.

As a result of these feelings, there have been some experiments in which payments and services have been disconnected. For people requesting funds, there are eligibility clerks who are not trained as social workers,[19] while the assumption is that people needing services other than financial will apply to the service agencies.[20] While no large-scale investigation as to the results of this division between payments and services has yet been made, there is some evidence that the services have been made less accessible, even for those who want and need them, as the payments have been controlled more strictly and been made available from more convenient places.

There is one more influence of Freudian thinking to consider. As Freudian theory became more important and more familiar to social workers, Freud's dictum concerning happiness became more controlling. His prescription for happiness is "to love and to work." Although love is more or less out of the control of social workers, Freud's imprimateur on the need to work reinforces the Protestant Ethic, and work is seen not only as an economic and social necessity but as therapy for troubled souls. The facts that Freud remarked, as noted previously, that people seem to have a natural aversion to work and that Freud's patients were mostly from the leisure class of Viennese society do not seem to be given as much weight in deducing social-welfare policies from Freudian imperatives.[21]

THE INFLUENCE OF KARL MARX

As noted in Chapter 7, one of the strongest influences of the thinking of Karl Marx on American social welfare has been negative: To label a program "communist" or even "socialist" is often to ensure its defeat. However, throughout the non-Soviet world, Marxian philosophy may have influenced social welfare more than is realized. Perhaps its largest contribution has been in directing attention away from individual deficiencies while creating a focus on institutional or societal deficiencies that afflict people with problems. As Marx stated it, "what constitutes the proletariat is not naturally existing poverty, but poverty artificially produced."[22] The need to change the system, rather than the people, did not originate with Marx, of course, nor is it exclusive to his thinking, but as a social philosophy it has impacted on social welfare to the point that there are those who call for exclusive concern with this area.[23]

The early pronouncements concerning the goals of the communist state included "comprehensive social insurance for all hired workers and for all urban and rural poor." Specifically: "(1) inclusion of all wage and salary earners and all urban and rural indigents, (2) coverage of all income hazards, (3) financing entirely by employers, (4) compensation to equal at least full wages in case of loss of work capacity and unemployment, and (5) complete self-administration by the insured."

When the communist state actually came into being, however, "concrete programs . . . were pragmatically trimmed to the dimensions of reality."[24]

Today, studies that compare social-security coverage in communist and non-communist countries find little difference in coverage attributable to a difference in political philosophy or structure.[25] There are, however, differences in methods of delivering services, the services offered, and the outcomes. Marxian theory places heavy emphasis on economic determinism, and in the early days of communism, it was assumed that a "utopian" economic situation would obviate all personal problems, and even in noncommunist utopian societies, such as the Israeli kibbutz, social work was seen as irrelevant for a long time—until social problems that arose in spite of absence of economic difficulties reached the number and intensity that required professional help. Traces of this attitude continue in Soviet social work. Marital counseling, for example, is available only at the point of divorce, under court auspices, but not sooner,[26] and social services in general are much less publicized and much less available and accessible than income-maintenance payments. Many social services are not assigned a clearly designated place in bureaucratic hierarchies, and they are often offered inconsistently.[27] When services are offered, work is often the prescription, the process, and the solution.[28] This is both reinforced and made necessary by the fact that psychoanalysis is generally rejected in the Soviet Union as an invalid technique.[29]

Despite this emphasis on work, the retirement age in the Soviet Union is sixty for men and fifty-five for women (with earlier ages for those engaged in difficult or dangerous work),[30] as compared to sixty-five and sixty in the United States, respectively. Further, no contributions are required of recipients covered by the Soviet social-security program.[31]

In a more general way, states based on egalitarian, labor, or socialist principles seem to provide more protection against the exigencies of life (with other variables held constant) than do more individualistically oriented states. A U.N. report, for example, holds that it is the inelasticity of wages with respect to family size that is the "prime cause of undernourishment and other hardship among the families of the able-bodied workers."[32]

In Israel, which is usually considered within the labor, if not the socialist, camp,[33] salaries are geared not only to the size of workers' families but also to a cost-of-living index, increasing automatically with inflation. Most jobs carry tenure (guaranteed permanence) after six months of employment, and relatively generous severance pay, which is required by law. Pension plans are insured and cannot be withdrawn; maternity leave and pay are legally required; and there is almost universal health insurance.

Taking into account such differences between societies of the left and those of the right, what is their ultimate result? Who has better living conditions? This question entails so many definitions and value judgments that it cannot be answered. There have, however, been a few comparative studies of problems and situations. Cantril studied human concerns in a number of countries, and the differences cannot be categorized as between communist and noncommunist countries.[34] Apel and Strumpel, however, studied Greece, a non-communist country, and

Bulgaria, a communist country, matching them on a number of important variables. Their findings include: "There is a more [nearly] equal income distribution in Bulgaria than in Greece ... social status and participation, material well-being, and security are higher in Bulgaria."[35]

It would be wrong to leave a discussion of the influence of Marx without mentioning welfare in China, a massive country, and Cuba, a relatively small one. Unfortunately, unbiased evaluations of their policies and programs are not yet available.

NOTES

1. J. W. Osborne, *The Silent Revolution: The Industrial Revolution in England as a Source of Cultural Change* (New York: Scribner's, 1970).
2. M. Weber, "Bureaucracy," in H. H. Gerth and C. W. Mills (eds.), *From Max Weber: Essays in Sociology* (London: Routledge & Kegan Paul, 1948).
3. Quoted in R. L. Heilbroner, *The Worldly Philosophers* (New York: Simon & Shuster, 1953).
4. *Ibid.*
5. An example of this thinking applied to welfare is found in F. E. Durbin, *Welfare Income and Employment: An Economic Analysis of Family Choice* (New York: Praeger, 1969).
6. D. Danzig, "The Social Framework of Ethnic Conflict in America," in M. Friedman (ed.), *Overcoming Middle Class Rage* (Philadelphia: Westminster, 1971), pp. 247.
7. P. F. Drucker, "Why Service Institutions Do Not Perform," in *Management: Tasks, Responsibilities, Practices* (New York: Harper & Row, 1973), pp. 137-47.
8. On social-work evaluation, see E. J. Mullen *et al., Evaluation of Social Intervention* (San Francisco: Jossey-Bass, 1972). On the evaluation of social-welfare programs, see C. H. Weiss, *Evaluation Research: Methods of Assessing Program Effectiveness* (Englewood Cliffs, N.J.: Prentice-Hall, 1972); C. H. Weiss, *Evaluating Action Programs: Readings in Social Action and Education* (Boston: Allyn & Bacon, 1972); and M. B. Meld, "The Politics of Evaluation of Social Programs," *Social Work*, 19 (July 1974): 448–55.
9. A. Etzioni, *Modern Organizations* (Englewood Cliffs, N.J.: Prentice-Hall, 1964), p. 9.
10. J. Shireman, "Client and Worker Opinions About Fee-Charging in a Child Welfare Agency," *Child Welfare*, 44 (1975): 331–40.
11. *Your Social Security Earnings Record* (Washington, D.C.: Department of Health, Education, and Welfare, 1975).
12. Smith's opposition to social welfare was related to the ideal world of his economic theories. In the real world, he was much more sympathetic to

the poor. G. V. Rimlinger, "Smith and the Merits of the Poor," *Review of Social Economy,* 34 (December 1976): 333–44.

13. The establishment of the U.S. Children's Bureau was due to the thirty-year fight begun in 1900 by a small group of women affiliated with settlement houses. A. Hanlan, "From Social Reform to Social Security: The Separation of ADC and Child Welfare," in P. E. Weinberger (ed.), *Perspectives on Social Welfare: An Introductory Anthology* (New York: Macmillan, 1974), pp. 109-20.

14. H. Borenzweig, "Social Work and Psychoanalytic Theory: A Historical Analysis," in Weinberger, *op. cit.,* pp. 97-109.

15. Students in direct-practice concentrations (multi-method, casework, direct service, group work), in contradistinction to those in indirect practice (community organization, administration, macro-track, social problems, research, and "other" concentrations) made up 74 percent of all students in master's programs in the United States in 1974. L. Ripple, *Statistics on Social Work Education in the United States: 1974* (New York: Council on Social Work Education, 1975).

16. H. J. Eysenck, "The Effects of Psychotherapy," in H. J. Eysenck (ed.), *Handbook of Abnormal Psychology* (London: Pitman, 1969).

17. W. Fisher, J. Mehr, and P. Truckenbrod, *Human Services: The Third Revolution in Mental Health* (New York: Alfred, 1974), p. 32.

18. Relief in kind was resisted by the social workers from the earliest days of the profession; they saw it as an indirect substitute for clients' education in home economics and workers' knowledge about clients. J. Colcord, *Cash Relief* (New York: Sage, 1936), p. 17.

19. When, on the other hand, trained social workers are used in highly simplified jobs, for instance, as eligibility clerks, they tend to expand their functions to make use of their knowledge and experience. *Evaluation of the Welfare Declaration: Eligibility Simplification for Public Assistance* (New York: City University of New York, 1969), p. 6; see also D. Macarov and N. Golan, "Goals in Social Work Practice: A Longitudinal Study," *International Social Work,* 16 (2/3, 1973): 2.

20. *The Separation of Services from the Determination of Eligibility for Assistance Payments* (Washington, D.C.: Government Printing Office, 1970); G. Hoshino, "Separating Maintenance from Social Service," *Public Welfare,* 30 (Spring 1972): 54–61; H. Chaiklin and C. F. Landau, "Separation, Service Delivery and Family Functioning," *Public Welfare,* 31 (Winter 1973): 2–7; E. D. Jaffe, "Separation in Jerusalem," *Public Welfare,* 31 (Winter, 1973): 33–38.

21. D. Macarov, *Incentives to Work* (San Francisco: Jossey-Bass, 1970), pp. 64, 89-90; G. Friedmann, *The Anatomy of Work* (New York: Free Press, 1964); E. Z. Friedenberg, "Neo-Freudianism and Erich Fromm," *Commentary,* 34 (1962):389.

22. K. Marx, *Early Writings* (New York: McGraw-Hill, 1964).

23. For example: "Social services, as they presently function, do not and cannot be of great service to clients or to social welfare in general . . . social services will not be of full service to clients and to us all unless their task is seen as a struggle for the creation of a fundamentally changed

society." J. H. Galper, *The Politics of Social Services* (Englewood Cliffs, N.J.: Prentice-Hall, 1975), p. x.

24. G. V. Rimlinger, "Social Security, Incentives and Controls in the U.S. and U.S.S.R.," in M. N. Zald (ed.), *Social Welfare Institutions* (New York: Wiley, 1965), pp. 102–22.

25. See H. L. Pryor, *Public Expenditures in Communist and Capitalist Nations* (Homewood, Ill.: Irwin, 1968); P. Cutright, "Political Structure, Economic Development, and National Social Security Programs," *American Journal of Sociology,* 70 (March 1965):537; H. L. Wilensky, *The Welfare State and Equality: Structural and Ideological Roots of Public Expenditures* (Berkeley: University of California Press, 1975); and H. J. Aaron, "Social Security: International Comparisons," in O. Eckstein, *Studies in the Economics of Income Maintenance* (Washington, D.C.: The Brookings Institution, 1967).

26. B. Madison, "Social Service Administration in the U.S.S.R.," in D. Thursz and J. L. Vigilante (eds.), *Meeting Human Needs,* Vol. 1: *An Overview of Nine Countries* (Beverly Hills, Calif.: Sage, 1975), p. 255.

27. *Ibid.,* p. 242.

28. *Ibid.,* p. 245.

29. C. I. Schottland, "Social Welfare in the Soviet Union," in *Social Welfare Forum, 1959* (New York: Columbia University Press 1959), p. 230.

30. *Ibid.,* p. 225.

31. *Ibid.*

32. *Introduction to Social Security: A Workers' Education Manual* (Geneva: International Labour Organization, 1970), p. 46.

33. The mixture of "pure" communistic forms, in the shape of the kibbutz, large cooperatives, government ownership of railroads, telephone and postal services, and so forth, and a large—perhaps a majority—private business sector, makes Israel hard to classify. See D. Macarov, "Political Ideologies and Social Welfare: The Case of Israel," *International Social Work* (forthcoming).

34. H. Cantril, *The Patterns of Human Concerns* (New Brunswick, N.J.: Rutgers University Press, 1965).

35. H. Apel and B. Strumpel, "Economic Well-Being as a Criterion for System Performance: A Survey in Bulgaria and Greece," in B. Strumpel (ed.), *Economic Means for Human Needs: Social Indicators of Well-Being and Discontent* (Ann Arbor: University of Michigan Press, 1976), p. 174.

12
The Welfare State

ITS HISTORY

Although the term "welfare state" does not seem to have been used before 1941,[1] the concept of a state taking full responsibility for the needs of its citizens has its roots in antiquity. The Athenian state distributed grain to citizens during times of famine and inflated corn prices; it provided pensions for disabled soldiers and the orphans of those killed in battle; other orphans were supported until their eighteenth birthday. With the additional benefits that were available, "in the fourth century all full citizens were in receipt of a sufficient amount of food and money to secure them their livelihood."[2] With the distribution of income from captured territories, Greece was indeed an ancient approximation of the welfare state.[3]

As religion and state fused throughout the West, however, the welfare responsibilities of governments were dispersed throughout other institutions—the church, the family, the market, the locality—and it was not until the reemergence of governments as distinct from religions that state responsibility for social welfare again began to make itself felt. Bismarck's motives in instituting social insurance may have had political undertones, as remarked previously, but the result was a system of payments in the event of contingencies—payments that were made as of right, regulated by law, and which could be anticipated by recipients. These payments covered only certain exigencies, however, and did not provide a complete system of government supplied and guaranteed social services.

There were similar and additional measures in other countries between that time and World War I, but this was a period when it was overwhelmingly agreed that voluntary organizations (or, in more common terms, "private charities") were the proper agencies for social-welfare activities. During World War I there was a movement in Great Britain to broaden government social-welfare activities, particularly in terms of wide reforms in housing, employment, and other basic areas. This was a reaction to the suffering undergone by the soldiers at the front, and was popularly expressed in terms of building "homes fit for heroes." The postwar depression damped these plans considerably, and it was not until the Great Depression that further basic steps were taken to insure people against more of the vicissitudes of life. European countries were already ahead of the United States in several respects, insofar as this goal was concerned, but the Social Security Act enacted in 1935 in the United States brought the country more or less in line with all the Western countries.

It was not until World War II that the next large step toward a deliberately conceived plan to guarantee citizens against most of the unforeseen exigencies of life was proposed. Again, the impetus was provided by war. In England particularly, the magnitude of the war effort, the sacrifice required of everyone, the shared losses, and the joint endeavors engaged in by all classes set the stage for Britons' concern for one another's welfare. The Atlantic Charter, with its call for freedom from want and fear,[4] epitomized this determination to—in the words used by William Faulkner years later in accepting the Nobel Prize for Literature—not just to have endured the rigors of war, but to have prevailed in the search for a better way of life. In England, it was felt that the war could not be won unless millions of ordinary people, in Great Britain and overseas, were convinced that they had something better to offer than their enemies had—not only during but also after the war.[5]

THE BEVERIDGE REPORT

The general effect of war on social welfare has been traced by Titmuss,[6] but the drive for a welfare state was dramatically emphasized when *The Times* of London called for social justice, abolition of privilege, more equitable distribution of income and wealth, and other drastic changes in English life immediately after the terrible retreat from Dunkirk.[7] As a result, Sir William Beveridge reviewed a series of surveys made between 1928 and 1937, and came to the conclusion that poverty and want in England in 1942 were "needless."[8] Beveridge had proposed in 1924, in a pamphlet, "insurance for all and everything," and in 1942 he published *Social Insurance and Allied Services,*[9] since generally known as the Beveridge Report. More than any other single document, the Beveridge Report brought about a decision and a series of actions designed to turn Great Britain into a "welfare state."

Marshall holds that there were three possibilities before Great Britain. One was represented by the socialist school, which believed that the capitalist system of private enterprise and a free market economy was inefficient and unjust and should be replaced by a rational order of things planned and directed by the political power. In such an order, normal needs would be met automatically and some needs would cease to exist, because there would be no more poverty or squalor. The second school held that though problems existed, the socio-economic system could be remedied by the state's intervention to modify some of its operations. The third school had the conservative view that nothing was wrong that the then current system would not correct in the normal course of events, without changes.[10] The welfare state, when it arrived, fell somewhere between the first and second schools:

> The total ultimate responsibility of the State for the welfare of its people was recognized more explicitly than ever before. . . . The social services were not to be regarded as regrettable necessities to be retained only until the capitalist system had been reformed or socialized; they were a permanent and even a glorious part of the social system itself. They were something to be proud of, not to apologize for.[11]

It is easier to define the nucleus of the welfare state than its boundaries.[12] Beveridge phrased the former as simply a unified and comprehensive structure of social services designed to combat the "Five Giants of Want, Disease, Ignorance, Squalor and Idleness," but in what manner and to what extent is not clear.[13] A more formal definition is:

> The assumption by the community, acting through the State, of the responsibility for providing the means whereby all its members can reach minimum standards of health, economic security, and civilized living, and can share according to their capacity in its social and cultural heritage.[14]

Thoenes would add to this description the proviso that the government-sponsored programs be maintained "concurrently with the maintenance of a capitalist system of productions."[15] This specifically denies the possibility of communist states, regardless of their social-welfare systems, being defined as welfare states.

Galper also equates the welfare state with capitalism, but he views this as malevolence, rather than, as does Thoenes, benevolence. According to Galper:

> The welfare state emerges as a series of programs and policies organized to meet a limited and distorted notion of human needs, within a frame-

work of support for capitalist institutions and values . . . the welfare state represents a historically specific form of social organization that has emerged as a result of the continuing ability of capitalist institutions to mold and transform human needs and social struggles within the logic of capitalist requirements.[16]

Thoenes's view of the welfare state requires not only a capitalist system but a democratic political process as well:

Whenever society has come to certain elements of the Welfare State, these elements have been introduced by democratic means; and it is by democratic methods that they are controlled and kept in being. . . . Democracy is at the present time a reasonable guarantee for the survival of a Welfare State, but the Welfare State is no guarantee for the survival of democracy.[17]

If, however, services are examined rather than definitions, the social services of the communist and socialist countries—as noted in the preceding chapter—are not markedly different from those in capitalist and democratic countries, including the countries that are referred to as welfare states. The Soviet Union, for example, not only has a universal children's allowance; it also requires no contributions by employees for other kinds of social insurance: They are all financed by employer and government contributions. On the other hand, there is no unemployment insurance,because there is,by definition,no unemployment.However, legal restrictions on travel and change of residence, denial of social welfare to those leaving farms without permission, and other such limitations conceal, rather than eliminate, unemployment. Russian citizens applying for visas to Israel, for example, are almost invariably deprived of their jobs and are not eligible for any social welfare, but not being defined as unemployed, they do not appear in unemployment statistics.

As noted above, the nucleus of the welfare state is more easily defined than its boundaries. For the latter, a look at the factors leading to the establishment of welfare-state policies is necessary. In addition to welfare, there are at least five other developmental aspects:

The basic transformation in the attitude towards poverty . . . ; the detailed investigation of the "social contingencies" . . . ; the close association between unemployment and welfare policy; . . . the development . . . of welfare philosophies and practices; and . . . the influence of working-class pressures on the content and tone of welfare legislation.[18]

Given these conditions, the welfare state uses its power deliberately to guarantee individuals and families a minimum income irrespective of the market value of their work or property, and to reduce insecurity by enabling all citizens to meet "social contingencies," such as illness or unemployment, and by offering them the best possible social services.[19]

The welfare state, then, is the abandonment of a residual conception of social welfare, which sees the market and the family—and perhaps the church and voluntary groups—as the natural, desirable first-line sources of help, with the government acting only to help the few who fall through that network.[20] In its place there is a structural conception which sees social welfare built into the ongoing activities of government, in the same way as the educational system is in the United States, or as the police system, the courts, defense, and so forth are built into government activities more universally. The structural aspect stops not with social welfare as generally defined but with what Titmuss calls the "trichotomy" of social welfare systems—the social, fiscal, and occupational.[21]

Not only is the structural, rather than the residual, concept of social welfare inherent in the definition of a welfare state, there are also those who see universal programs, in contradistinction to categorical or selective ones, as epitomizing the welfare state. This view, however, is not as generally accepted as the structural or the residual concept.

The inclusion of the word "state" in "welfare state" indicates that only government activities are included, and, indeed, it would be difficult to include a business firm, no matter how widespread or lavish its social services, under the definition.[22] However, there are welfare states that not only take cognizance of voluntary organizations but also include them in the planning for universal coverage. Great Britain, for example, relies on many voluntary organizations to deliver the services guaranteed by the state.[23]

Again, it would be an error to think of the welfare state as an all-or-nothing proposition. There are many views as to what constitutes the good or the desirable life, and as many opinions as to how to achieve it, and what appears incomplete to some will appear exaggerated to others. The lack of health insurance and children's or family allowances may make the United States seem far from being a welfare state to some, while lack of a clearly defined poverty line and guarantees that no one will sink below it may make states with health insurance and family allowances seem retrograde to others. Even countries with structured social-welfare services may find the results insufficient. In Great Britain, for example, the universal coverage must be supplemented by "superannuation" related to work, which double-decker system still results in providing only 50 percent to 66 percent of wages. Free medical care and prescriptions have been superseded by partial payment, and means tests are sometimes added to what were originally universal payments, for example, in allocating additional old-age pensions.

Further, the welfare state's goal of protection from the cradle to the grave is not seen as a proper societal goal by everyone. In 1949, former President Herbert Hoover described the welfare state as a "disguise for the totalitarian state,"[24] and declared that it put America on the "last mile to collectivism."[25] Others have pointed out that if the money invested by individuals in contributory social-welfare programs were used to buy private insurance, the costs would be less and the benefits greater.[26] In addition, welfare-state programs are seen to be infinitely expansible, and their continual expansion is seen by some as disastrous.[27] More widespread than these caveats, however, is the fear that under the welfare state individuals will lose their taste for responsibility, freedom, and decision-making.[28] It is feared that if people no longer have the spur of fear of possible future disaster to cause them to work, to save, and to plan ahead, the human race will become "amiable idiots," and the progress of civilization will cease.

In no case is the welfare state seen as completely successful:

> Even the strongest advocates of welfare will attest to its failure to eliminate poverty. . . . The welfare state has been accompanied by disruptive political struggles over the appropriate level of expenditure for welfare and by unresolved debate about the fraction of the gross national product required for capital investments to sustain economic growth.[29]

Nor have the principles of the welfare state been incorporated into America's basic laws: "The courts have not found in the Constitution a right to social welfare."[30]

THE FUTURE OF THE WELFARE STATE

Insofar as the welfare state is characterized by programs built into the architecture of a society, there is every likelihood that these programs will not only continue but grow, as demonstrated by Wilensky.[31] It is almost impossible to envision the dismantling of the Social Security system of the United States, for example,[32] or discontinuation of children's allowances in other countries.

On the other hand, the very existence of such structured programs often creates the feeling that nothing more need be done, and it becomes increasingly difficult to mount categorical programs or ensure that there are sufficient benefits in them, despite the fact that there may be pockets, or even widespread strata, of needy people. In fact, it is even hard to couch the necessity or desirability of a welfare state in terms that move the spirit of the average citizen: "To the socialist it is nothing but semi-socialism, to the liberals only semi-liberalism. To each and all it is an inevitable half-way house; to nobody is it a noble and inspiring ideal [rather than] a half-hearted, Christianity-flavoured, middle-class respectability."[33]

Another problem of the welfare state is that it usually attempts to react to situations with planning and prevention, but rarely with societal changes, radical new solutions, or bold experimentation. The welfare state can act to prevent things that people do not want (for instance, danger, hunger, thirst, cold, unemployment, squandering of food or talents) but rarely to bring about things that people do want (such as more leisure, less pollution, interpersonal kindness and consideration).

Then there is the question of the social costs of the welfare state. Does lack of fear in fact lead to lack of ambition or effort? Do the social benefits received tend to be outweighed by the social problems created?

Insofar as the first question is concerned, there is little feeling or evidence that in Sweden, one of the most advanced states in terms of welfare, work incentives have been affected. The reputation of Swedes as hard, steady, and productive laborers is maintained by that country's record of economic health. However, the rates of drunkenness, divorce, and suicide are often cited as correlated with, if not caused by, the presumed boredom of a country without the fear of social problems. More careful analysis, however, reemphasizes the research dictum that correlation is not causation, because the Swedish rates of each of these are exceeded in countries that offer substantially less coverage than the Swedish system.

It is almost impossible to compare national rates of alcoholism, because definitions of "alcoholism," laws, and reporting vary too widely. Insofar as suicides are concerned, however, the highest rate in Europe for males is in Hungary, which reports 48.3 suicides in every 100,000 deaths. Finland follows with 37.4, then Austria with 31.3, and Sweden's rate is only 31.2.[34] As for divorce: Sweden's rate of 3.3 per 1,000 population is topped by that of the United States, which is 4.6, and the U.S. Virgin Islands have the world's highest rate, 7.0.[35]

Probably the universal programs that welfare states offer will continue to grow and expand, while the categorical and selective programs will wax and wane with changes in economies and ideologies. In the final analysis, as Thoenes points out, the welfare state cannot be considered complete, or even viable, unless its citizens consider its achievements their achievements: Where there is pride in the welfare state, its programs will probably continue to grow, but where pride is invested in individual competition and success, the welfare state will develop slowly, if at all.[36]

NOTES

1. W. Temple, "The State," in C. I. Schottland (ed.), *The Welfare State* (New York: Harper & Row, 1967), pp. 20–24.
2. J. Hasebroek, *Trade and Politics in Ancient Greece* (London: Bell, 1933), p. 35; quoted in A. W. Gouldner, *The Hellenic World: A Sociological Analysis* (New York: Harper & Row, 1969), p. 137.
3. Gouldner, *op. cit.*, p. 137.
4. In his domestic aims, Franklin D. Roosevelt added freedom of speech and religion.
5. R. M. Titmuss, *Essays on "the Welfare State"* (New Haven, Conn.: Yale University Press, 1959), p. 82.
6. "War and Social Policy," in *ibid.*, pp. 75–87.
7. *Ibid.*
8. K. Woodroofe, *From Charity to Social Work in England and the United States* (Toronto: University of Toronto Press, 1962), p. 12.
9. W. H. Beveridge, *Social Insurance and Allied Services* (New York: Macmillan, 1942).
10. T. H. Marshall, *Social Policy* (London: Hutchinson, 1965), pp. 28–29.
11. *Ibid.*, p. 77.
12. Woodroofe, *op. cit.*, p. 144.
13. M. P. Hall, *The Social Services of Modern England* (London: Routledge & Kegan Paul, 1955), p. 305.
14. P. Thoenes, *The Elite in the Welfare State* (New York: Free Press, 1966), p. 125.
15. J. H. Galper, *The Politics of Social Services* (Englewood Cliffs, N.J.: Prentice-Hall, 1975), pp. 22–23.
16. Thoenes, *op. cit.*, pp. 136–37.
17. R. C. Birch, *The Shaping of the Welfare State* (London: Longmans, 1974).
18. A. Briggs, "The Welfare State in Historical Perspective," in M. N. Zald (ed.), *Social Welfare Institutions* (New York: Wiley, 1965), pp. 38–39.
19. *Ibid.*, p. 29.
20. H. L. Wilensky and C. N. Lebeaux, *Industrial Society and Social Welfare* (New York: Free Press, 1958); Thoenes, *op. cit.*, p. 130.
21. D. G. Neill, "Unfinished Business of the Welfare State," in Schottland, *op. cit.*, p. 74.
22. *Ibid.*, p. 70.
23. Beveridge, for example, felt obliged to write a sequel in 1948 on voluntary organizations. W. H. Beveridge, *Voluntary Action: A Report on Methods of Social Advance* (New York: Macmillan, 1948).
24. R. M. Titmuss, "The Welfare State: Images and Realities," in Schottland, *op. cit.*, p. 117.
25. A. Schlesinger, Jr., "The Welfare State," in Schottland, *op. cit.*, p. 117.
26. C. Clark, "Welfare and Taxation," quoted in W. Ropke, "Reflections on the Welfare State," in Schottland, *op. cit.*, p. 173.
27. Ropke, *op. cit.*, p. 176.
28. *Ibid.*, p. 177.

29. M. Janowitz, *Social Control of the Welfare State* (New York: Elsevier Scientific Publishing, 1976), p. 1.
30. P. B. Kurland, "The Judicial Road to Social Welfare," *Social Service Review*, 48 (1974): 481–93.
31. H. L. Wilensky, *The Welfare State and Equality: Structural and Ideological Roots of Public Expenditures* (Berkeley: University of California Press, 1975).
32. Although New York City threatened to withdraw from Social Security (which a municipality may do), it could only do so if it provided similar benefits for participants.
33. Thoenes, *op. cit.*, p. 133.
34. E. M. Brooke (ed.), *Suicide and Attempted Suicide* (Geneva: World Health Organization, 1974), p. 110.
35. *Statistical Yearbook 1975* (New York: United Nations, 1976), pp. 79–83.
36. Thoenes, *op. cit.*, p. 133.

13
Conclusion

Typical of postindustrial societies is the extent to which they become service-oriented, rather than oriented towards material goods. As this happens, the need to develop research and build knowledge on the reciprocal impacts of technologies and services becomes acute. It is important that the mutuality of these relationships be explored and understood as more and more people move into service experiences, both as offerers and as recipients. One way of understanding these relationships is by identifying the basic concepts—motivations and influences—that determine their present shapes.

Social welfare has become one of the largest areas of government activity, in terms of absolute amounts of resources used, their proportion of the total available, and the number of people affected. Understanding of some of the major concepts that bring social welfare into being and shape it into its present structure offers possibilities of moving from description to prediction to prescription. The intention of the previous chapters was to illuminate some of the major motivations that result in social-welfare policies, programs, and practices, together with some of the important attitudes, beliefs, and processes that act upon the resultant structures.

To summarize briefly, the desire or the need to engage in mutual aid characterizes or leads to such structures as families, neighborhoods, small groups, and cooperatives, communes, and collectives. The desire to strengthen these forms, on the one hand, and to make use of them, on the other, results in social-welfare policies designed to strengthen families, such as AFDC in the United States or generous family allowances in France, and in restrictive policies such as relatives' responsibility laws and residency requirements. The interaction of these two elements sometimes weakens, rather than strengthens, mutual aid.

Religious motivations for social welfare differ among religions, and even among sects of the same belief, but one of the strong motivations for individuals to engage in charity has always been the desire to fulfill a commandment. Two of the problems created are (1) whether this extends to nonmembers of the group and (2) the relationship of these activities to government-sponsored programs. Nevertheless, the religious motivation has deep roots in history and is responsible for the bulk of voluntary social-welfare activities.

One political reason for social-welfare policies is the desire of a person or group to acquire or retain power. Bismarck's early social insurances arose from his fear of the Social Democrats, and Franklin Roosevelt's espousal of Social Security was strengthened by competition from the Townsend Plan. There is also the desire to avoid social unrest, to which veterans' bonuses and ghetto-oriented programs can both be traced. And, finally, there are policies that arise from the political process itself —logrolling, compromises, and appendages to other policies, such as the day-care provisions occasioned by the WIN program.

The economic basis for social welfare rests on the desire to reduce the costs of social problems, as when rehabilitation costs are balanced against the taxpaying potential of the rehabilitated. There are also policies designed to increase productivity, ranging from sheltered workshops to public work requirements. Economic motivations also include the desire to increase consumption, the best example being the motivation for the Food Stamp Program of the Department of Agriculture. Finally, there are policies that arise from the structure and the process of the economic system, such as cost cutting in times of depression, despite increased need.

The ideology of social welfare is rooted mainly in a humanitarian outlook, though there are more circumscribed ideologies that affect policies variously. The institutionalization of social welfare into organized philanthropy results in personal and societal motivations for social welfare that take on a life of their own.

Acting on this congeries of motivations is a series of attitudes and beliefs that can be traced back to, or identified with, certain seminal philosophers.

Thomas Malthus called attention to population questions, and though his view of the poor and needy remains anathema to many people engaged in social-welfare endeavors, the problems he posed are now the very basis of social-welfare policies in many countries. These policies range from pro-natalism to population control, but there is increasing acceptance of the fact that the quality of life on this planet as a whole is related, in large part, to the number of its inhabitants. There is also the growing view that couples should have the right to choose how large a family they want, as well as spacing of their children. Attitudes toward these questions, and toward the rights of women, minorities, and personal freedom, affect social-welfare policies.

Charles Darwin's "survival of the fittest" has been transmuted to apply to social institutions and to individuals, rather than to species, in the form of Social Darwinism. The extent to which this philosophy causes the poor, needy, and minorities to be seen as "unfit," and therefore not entitled to survive (at least on the same level as others), molds some social-welfare policies, as is evidenced in those policies based upon "blaming the victim."

The morality attached to working, as well as work seen as rehabilitative and problem-solving, can be traced in large part to the influence of Martin Luther. The impact of this thinking on social-welfare policies is clearly illustrated by the almost universal existence of a wage stop in welfare programs, guaranteeing that no one, including those who cannot work, will receive more through welfare than through working. The major obstacle to the adoption of a guaranteed minimum income is the fear of a work disincentive.

Adam Smith's influence on social welfare was to cause it to be viewed as unwarranted interference by the government in the economic system through maintaining unproductive people. Sigmund Freud had enormous influence on social work, in contradistinction to social welfare, through imposing a medical model on practice. There were, however, impacts on policy, as evidenced in the controversy concerning separation of payments from services. Marx had little influence on American social work, except in a "backlash" manner: Programs deemed "socialist" were resisted.

The welfare state, in which the necessary provisions would be part of the structure of society (rather than merely residual), universal, stigma-free, and of good quality, was advocated by the English author of the Beveridge Report, which saw social welfare as an important function of government.

These motivations and influences offer a matrix, or a paradigm, through which many social-welfare policies can be better understood, both in their historical development and their present situation and trends. There are, to be sure, other motivations and other important influences that deserve the same scrutiny and analysis, and these will lead to even better understanding of social welfare. Nor are motivations and influences the whole story: Social welfare is also molded by relatively immutable situations, such as lack or presence of resources, or geographical considerations; by structures, such as age groups, classes, and castes; by events, such as wars, natural catastrophes, and historic changes; and by the very processes through which policies are made in various arenas.

The almost limitless variety of the combinations of motivations and influences that shape social welfare—only a few of which have been examined here—can be likened to a kaleidoscope, in which even a little movement of one part results in changes in the entire design. There is a danger, however, that as people engaged in social-welfare activities become aware of the scope and the complexity of these formative influences, they may feel incapable of making significant changes in social welfare. This could lead to a retreat into exclusive concern with specific types of problems, or to further refinement of existing methodology. This would be unfortunate for society, social-welfare recipients, and the social-work profession alike. It is not enough for social welfare to take into account, and acknowledge the impact of, ideology, for instance. Social-welfare personnel must attempt to change those ideologies that are inimical to human beings and the quality of their lives.

Political considerations will certainly continue to impact on social welfare, but it is important that social workers, their clients, and the public make effective inputs into the political process. Others may judge social welfare by its economic results, but people committed to social-welfare goals must be able to point out the social-welfare implications of economic moves. Similarly, unemployment may continue to be a problem that must be dealt with in its own right, but social workers, of all people, should understand and point out that full employment will not eliminate poverty, let alone emotional and relationship problems.

The ways in which these activities can be undertaken, and the possibilities of success, are beyond the scope of this book, having been dealt with in a number of other places.[1] However, it is important that students of social work, and all others who intend to become engaged in the social-welfare endeavor, should understand that the design of social welfare consists not only of its structure but also of its goals, and that attaining the latter necessitates dealing with the former.

That this will be no easy job goes without saying. However, as *The Ethics of the Fathers* puts it, "The task is difficult, the time is short, and the goals are urgent. . . . It may not be given you to complete the job, but neither are you free to desist."[2]

NOTES

1. R. Morris and R. H. Binstock, *Feasible Planning for Social Change* (New York: Columbia University Press, 1966); R. Mayer, R. Moroney, and R. Morris (eds.), *Centrally Planned Change: A Reexamination of Theory and Experience* (Urbana: University of Illinois Press, 1974); L. Goodwin, *Can Social Science Help Resolve National Problems?: Welfare, a Case in Point* (New York: Free Press, 1975).
2. S. Raskin, *Ethics of the Fathers* (New York: Bloch, 1969).

Sources Cited

Aaron, H. J. "Social Security: International Comparisons," in O. Eckstein, *Studies in the Economics of Income Maintenance*. Washington, D.C.: The Brookings Institution, 1967.

Abbott, G. *From Relief to Social Security*. Chicago: University of Chicago Press, 1941.

Abt Associates, Inc. *A Study of the Neighborhood Center Pilot Program*, Vol. 3: *The Neighborhood Services Program Model*. Washington, D.C.: Executive Office of the President, Bureau of the Budget, 1969.

Agate, J. *The Practice of Geriatrics*. London: Heinemann, 1970.

Agouba, I. M. "Social Realities and the Response of Social Work Education in Africa." Paper presented at the Eighteenth International Conference of Schools of Social Work, San Juan, Puerto Rico, July 13–17, 1976.

Aird, J. S. *Population Policy and Demographic Prospects in the People's Republic of China*. Washington, D.C.: Department of Health, Education, and Welfare, 1972.

Akzin, B., and Y. Dror. *Israel: High Pressure Planning*. Syracuse, N.Y.: Syracuse University Press, 1966.

Almanzor, A. C., and E. C. Viloria. "Social Realities and the Response of Social Work Education in Asia." Paper presented at the Eighteenth International Conference of Schools of Social Work, San Juan, Puerto Rico, July 13–17, 1976.

Altmeyer, A. J. *The Formative Years of Social Security*. Madison: University of Wisconsin Press, 1966.

Amendment to Family Law (Support), 1959. Jerusalem: Government of Israel, 1959. (In Hebrew.)

Amory, C. *The Proper Bostonians*. New York: Dutton, 1947.

Anderson, J., and E. Lourey. *Issues in the Development, Implementation and Evaluation of Simplified Eligibility Methods for Public Assistance.* Minneapolis: American Rehabilitation Foundation, 1969.

Andrews, F. M., and S. B. Withey. *Social Indicators of Well-Being: Americans' Perceptions of Life Quality.* New York: Plenum, 1976.

Annual Report: Ministry of Social Affairs and Labour. Amman: Hashemite Kingdom of Jordan, 1974.

Apel, H., and B. Strumpel. "Economic Well-Being as a Criterion for System Performance: A Survey in Bulgaria and Greece," in B. Strumpel (ed.), *Economic Means for Human Needs: Social Indicators of Well-Being and Discontent.* Ann Arbor: University of Michigan Press, 1976.

Appleman, P. *The Silent Explosion.* Boston: Beacon Press, 1965.

Approaches and Methods Used in Long-Term Social Planning and Policy-Making. New York: United Nations, 1973.

Aptekar, H. H. "The Values, Functions, and Methods of Social Work," in *An Intercultural Exploration: Universals and Differences in Social Work Values, Functions, and Practice.* New York: Council on Social Work Education, 1967.

Arab World, The. New York: Arab Information Center, 1965.

Ardrey, R. *The Territorial Imperative.* New York: Delta, 1966.

———. *The Hunting Hypothesis.* New York: Atheneum, 1976.

Attlee, D. R. *The Social Worker.* London: Bell, 1920.

Axinn, J., and H. Levin. *Social Welfare: A History of the American Response to Need.* New York: Dodd, Mead, 1975.

Ayd, F. J., Jr. "The Catholic Church," in E. T. Tyler (ed.), *Birth Control: A Continuing Controversy.* Springfield, Ill.: Charles C. Thomas, 1967.

Babylonian Talmud. "Ktuvim," samech zion, p. 2.

Bachrach, P., and M. S. Baratz. *Power and Poverty: Theory and Practice.* New York: Oxford University Press, 1970.

Badran, H. "Egypt's Social Service System: New Ideology, New Approaches," in D. Thursz and J. L. Vigilante (eds.), *Meeting Human Needs,* Vol. 1: *An Overview of Nine Countries.* Beverly Hills, Calif.: Sage, 1975.

Bailey, R., and M. Brake (eds.). *Radical Social Work.* New York: Pantheon, 1976.

Bandler, J. T. D. "Family Issues in Social Policy: An Analysis of Social Security." Ph.D. diss., Columbia University, New York, 1975.

Barbash, J. "Final Report on the Conference," *Work in a Changing Industrial Society.* Paris: Organization for Economic Cooperation and Development, 1974.

Barlow, R., H. E. Brazer, and J. N. Morgan. *Economic Behavior of the Affluent.* Washington, D.C.: The Brookings Institution, 1966.

Barnett, S. A. *Canon Barnett: His Life, Work, and Friends.* London: Murray, 1921.

Barth, M. C., G. J. Carcagno, and J. L. Palmer. *Toward an Effective Income Support System: Problems, Prospects, and Choices.* Madison: University of Wisconsin Press, 1974.

Bauer, R. A. (ed.). *Social Indicators.* Cambridge, Mass.: MIT Press, 1966.

Becker, H. S. *Outsiders: Studies in the Sociology of Deviance.* New York: Free Press, 1963.

Becker, J. M. "Income Maintenance Through Unemployment Insurance," *Review of Social Economy*, 34 (October 1976): 163–71.

Bedger, J. E. "Cost Analysis in Day Care and Head Start," *Child Welfare*, 53 (1974): 514–23.

Bell, D. *The End of Ideology*. New York: Free Press, 1960.

Bell, W. "Relatives' Responsibility: A Problem in Social Policy," *Social Work*, 12 (January 1967): 32–39.

Ben David, Y. *Agricultural Planning and Village Community in Israel*. New York: UNESCO, 1964.

Bendiner, R. "Poverty Is a Tougher Problem than Ever," in H. L. Sheppard (ed.), *Poverty and Wealth in America*. Chicago: Quadrangle, 1970.

Benson, R. S., and H. Wolman (eds.). *Counterbudget: A Blueprint for Changing National Priorities 1971–76*. New York: Praeger, 1971.

Berger, G. *Innovation by Tradition: Articles on Jewish Communal Life*. New York: Federation of Jewish Philanthropies of New York, 1976.

Best, F. (ed.). *The Future of Work*. Englewood Cliffs, N.J.: Prentice-Hall, 1973.

Beveridge, W. H. *Social Insurance and Allied Services*. New York: Macmillan, 1942.

———. *Voluntary Action: A Report on Methods of Social Advance*. New York: Macmillan, 1948.

Billingsley, A. *Black Families in White America*. Englewood Cliffs, N.J.: Prentice-Hall, 1968.

Birch, R. C. *The Shaping of the Welfare State*. London: Longmans, 1974.

Bird, C. *The Invisible Scar*. New York: Pocket Books, 1966.

Birdwhistell, R. L. "The Idealized Model of the American Family," *Social Casework*, 51 (1970): 195–98.

Birenbaum, A., and E. Sagarin. *Social Problems: Private Troubles and Public Issues*. New York: Scribner's, 1972.

Black, B. J. "Vocational Rehabilitation," in *Encyclopedia of Social Work*. New York: National Association of Social Workers, 1965.

Blake, J. "Population Policy for Americans: Is the Government Being Misled?" in D. Callahan (ed.), *The American Population Debate*. Garden City, N.Y.: Doubleday, 1971.

Blaug, M. "The Myth of the Old Poor Law and the Making of the New," *Journal of Economic History*, 23 (June 1963): 151.

Blechman, B. M., E. M. Gramlich, and R. W. Hartman. *Setting National Priorities: The 1975 Budget*. Washington, D.C.: The Brookings Institution, 1974.

Bluhm, W. T. *Ideologies and Attitudes: Modern Political Culture*. Englewood Cliffs, N.J.: Prentice-Hall, 1974.

Borenzweig, H. "Social Work and Psychoanalytic Theory: A Historical Analysis," in P. E. Weinberger (ed.), *Perspectives on Social Welfare: An Introductory Anthology*. New York: Macmillan, 1974.

Boulding, K. E. "Foreword," in T. R. Malthus, *Population: The First Essay*. Ann Arbor: University of Michigan Press, 1959.

Bowers, D. W., and D. W. Hastings. "Childspacing and Wife's Employment Status Among 1940–41 University of Utah Graduates," *Rocky Mountain Social Science Journal*, 7 (1970): 125–36.

Braybrooke, D., and C. E. Lindblom. *A Strategy of Decision: Policy Evaluation as a Social Process.* New York: Free Press, 1963.

Brayfield, L. P., and W. H. Crockett. "Employee Attitudes and Performance," *Psychological Bulletin,* 52 (November 1955): 396–424.

Bremner, R. H. *From the Depths: The Discovery of Poverty in the United States.* New York: New York University Press, 1956.

Brieland, D., *et al. Contemporary Social Work.* New York: McGraw-Hill, 1975.

Briggs, A. "The Welfare State in Historical Perspective," in M. N. Zald (ed.), *Social Welfare Institutions.* New York: Wiley, 1965.

Brooke, E. M. (ed.). *Suicide and Attempted Suicide.* Geneva: World Health Organization, 1974.

Brosse, T. "Altruism and Creativity as Biological Factors in Human Evolution," in P. A. Sorokin (ed.), *Explorations in Altruistic Love and Behavior.* Boston: Beacon Press, 1950.

Brown, J. C. *Public Relief 1929–1939.* New York: Holt, 1940.

Brown, L. R. "The Growth of Population Is Slowing Down," *New York Times,* November 21, 1976, p. E8.

Browne, Sir Thomas, *Religio Medici* (1643); quoted in K. de Schweinitz, *England's Road to Social Security.* Philadelphia: University of Pennsylvania Press, 1943.

Brzozowski, R., *et al. Social Welfare and the Lines of Its Development in the Polish People's Republic.* Warsaw: Polish Medical Publishers, n.d.

Bubis, G. B. "Professional Education for the Jewish Component in Casework Practice," *Journal of Jewish Communal Service,* 52 (Spring 1976): 270–77.

Buckingham, W. *Automation.* New York: Mentor, 1961.

Bulletin: 1975–1976. Philadelphia: University of Pennsylvania School of Social Work, 1974.

Burns, E. M. (ed.). *Childrens' Allowances and the Economic Welfare of Children.* New York: Citizens Committee for Children of New York, 1968.

Burton, A. (ed.). *Encounter.* San Francisco: Jossey-Bass, 1969.

Busse, E. W. "Psychoneurotic Reactions and Defense Mechanisms in the Aged," in P. H. Hock and J. Zabin (eds.), *Psychopathology of Aging.* New York: Grune & Stratton, 1961.

Cahn, E. S., and J. C. Cahn. "Maximum Feasible Participation: A General Overview," in E. S. Cahn and B. A. Passett (eds.), *Citizen Participation: Effecting Community Change.* New York: Praeger, 1971.

Cahn, E. S., and B. A. Passett (eds.). *Citizen Participation: Effecting Community Change.* New York: Praeger, 1971.

Cain, G. G., and H. W. Watts (eds.). *Income Maintenance and Labor Supply: Econometric Studies.* Chicago: Markham, 1973.

Callahan, D. *Abortion: Law, Choice and Morality.* New York: Macmillan, 1970.

Callahan, D. (ed.). *The American Population Debate.* Garden City, N.Y.: Doubleday, 1971.

Campbell, J. (ed.). *The Portable Jung.* New York: Viking, 1971.

Cannon, H. G. *Lamarck and Modern Genetics.* Westport, Conn.: Greenwood Press, 1959.

Cantril, H. *The Patterns of Human Concerns.* New Brunswick, N.J.: Rutgers University Press, 1965.

Carp, J. M. "The Social Work Function of the Jewish Community Center," *Journal of Jewish Communal Service,* 52 (Fall 1975): 43–58.

Carter, G. W., L. H. Fifield, and H. Shields. *Public Opinions Toward Welfare: An Opinion Poll.* Los Angeles: Regional Research Institute in Social Welfare, School of Social Work, University of Southern California, 1973.

Chaiklin, H., and C. F. Landau. "Separation, Service Delivery and Family Functioning," *Public Welfare,* 31 (Winter 1973): 2–7.

Chakerian, G. C. "Religious Sponsorship," in *Encyclopedia of Social Work.* New York: National Association of Social Workers, 1965.

The Challenge of Crime in a Free Society. Washington, D.C.: President's Commission on Law Enforcement and Administration of Justice, 1967. (Excerpted in "Crime in America," in A. Birenbaum and E. Sagarin, *Social Problems: Private Troubles and Public Issues* [New York: Scribner's, 1972]).

Chambers, C. A. (ed.). *A Century of Concern: 1873–1973.* Columbus, Ohio: National Conference on Social Welfare, 1974.

Charnow, J. *Work Relief Experience in the United States.* Washington, D.C.: Social Science Research Council, 1943.

Chen Pi-chao. *Population and Health Policy in the People's Republic of China.* Washington, D.C.: Smithsonian Institution, 1976.

"Child's View of Old Age, A," *New York Times,* October 10, 1976, p. 6E.

China Yearbook 1976. Taipei: Republic of China, 1976.

Chipkin, I. S. "Judaism and Social Welfare," in L. Finkelstein (ed.), *The Jews.* Philadelphia: Jewish Publication Society of America, 1949.

Claflin, B., and P. Thaler. "Banding Together: The Best Way to Cope," *New York Magazine,* 5 (February 28, 1977): 41–48.

Clark, C. "Welfare and Taxation"; quoted in W. Ropke, "Reflections on the Welfare State," in C. I. Schottland (ed.), *The Welfare State.* New York: Harper & Row, 1967.

Cloward, R. A., and R. M. Elman. "Social Justice for the Poor," in L. A. Ferman, J. L. Kornbluh, and A. Haber (eds.), *Poverty in America.* Ann Arbor: University of Michigan Press, 1972.

Cloward, R. A., and F. F. Piven. "The Acquiescence of Social Work," *Social Science and Modern Society,* 14 (January-February 1975): 55–63.

Code of Federal Regulations: Public Welfare, Parts 200 to 499. Washington, D.C.: Office of the Federal Register, General Services Administration, 1974.

Cohen, N. E. "Changing Perspectives on United States Social Services," in D. Thursz and J. L. Vigilante (eds.), *Meeting Human Needs,* Vol. 1: *An Overview of Nine Countries.* Beverly Hills, Calif.: Sage, 1975.

Cohen, N. E. (ed.). *Social Work and Social Problems.* New York: National Association of Social Workers, 1964.

Cohen, W. J. "Social Indicators," in F. M. Loewenberg and R. Dolgoff (eds.), *The Practice of Social Intervention: Goals, Roles and Strategies.* Itasca, Ill.: Peacock, 1972.

Colcord, J. *Cash Relief.* New York: Sage, 1936.

Coleman, J. S. *Community Conflict.* New York: Free Press, 1957.

Coles, R. "Work and Self-Respect," *Daedalus,* 104 (Fall 1976):29–38.

Coll, B. D. *Perspectives in Public Welfare.* Washington, D.C.: Department of Health, Education, and Welfare, 1969.

Concise Report on the World Population in 1970–75 and Its Long-Range Implications. New York: United Nations, Department of Economic and Social Affairs, 1974.

Constantelos, D. *Byzantine Philanthropy and Social Welfare.* New Brunswick, N.J.: Rutgers University Press, 1968.

Conze, E. *Buddhism: Its Essence and Development.* New York: Harper & Row, 1959.

Coser, L. A. *The Functions of Social Conflict.* New York: Free Press, 1954.

———. *Continuities in the Study of Social Conflict.* New York: Free Press, 1967.

Coughlin, B. J. *Church and State in Social Welfare.* New York: Columbia University Press, 1965.

Crampton, H. M., and K. K. Keiser. *Social Welfare: Institution and Process.* New York: Random House, 1970.

Croner, H. B. *National Directory of Private Social Agencies 1975–1976.* Queens Village, N.Y.: Croner, 1969. (Updated monthly.)

Crown, L. E. "Meaningful Consumer Participation: A Challenge to the Social Agency Administrator," in H. A. Schatz, *Social Work Administration: A Resource Book.* New York: Council on Social Work Education, 1970.

Cunningham, M. "Eligibility Procedures for AFDC," *Social Work,* 22 (January 1977): 21–26.

Cunningham, R. L. *The Philosophy of Work.* New York: National Association of Manufacturers, 1964.

"Current Information: France—Recent Developments in Social Security Legislation," *International Labour Review,* 106 (October 1972): 367–72.

"Current Operating Statistics," *Social Security Bulletin,* 39 (March 1976): 35.

"Current Operating Statistics," *Social Security Bulletin,* 40 (April 1977): 58, 87.

Cutright, P. "Political Structure, Economic Development, and National Social Security Programs," *American Journal of Sociology,* 70 (March 1965): 537.

Danzig, D. "The Social Framework of Ethnic Conflict in America," in M. Friedman (ed.), *Overcoming Middle Class Rage.* Philadelphia: Westminster, 1971.

Darwin, C. *The Origin of Species.* London: Murray, 1859.

Darwin, F. *The Life and Letters of Charles Darwin.* New York: Appleton, 1888. 2 vols.

Davis, K. "Population Policy: Will Current Programs Succeed?" *Science,* November 10, 1967, pp. 730–39.

Davis, W. H. "Overpopulated America," in D. Callahan (ed.), *The American Population Debate.* Garden City, N.Y.: Doubleday, 1971.

Declaration on Abortion, Sacred Congregation for Doctrine, June 28, 1974; released November 18, 1974, by Pope Paul VI per Franciscus Cardinal Sper, Prefect.

Demographic Yearbook 1974. New York: United Nations, 1975.

Derthick, M. *Uncontrollable Spending for Social Service Grants.* Washington, D.C.: The Brookings Institution, 1975.

Deuteronomy, 14:29; 24:19–21.

Development of National Social Service Programmes, The. New York: United Nations Social Commission, 1959.

Development Outlook for Social Work Education, A. New York: International Association of Schools of Social Work, 1973.

Doron, A. *Cross-national Studies of Social Service Systems: Israeli Reports.* New York: Columbia University Press, 1976.

Douglas, E. T. *Margaret Sanger: Pioneer of the Future.* New York: Holt, Rinehart & Winston, 1970.

Drucker, H. M. *The Political Uses of Ideology.* New York: Barnes & Noble, 1974.

Drucker, P. F. *Management: Tasks, Responsibilities, Practices.* New York: Harper & Row, 1973.

Dubin, R. "Industrial Workers' Worlds: A Study of the Central Life Interests of Industrial Workers," in A. M. Rose (ed.), *Human Behavior and Social Processes.* Boston: Houghton Mifflin, 1962.

Dugdale, R. L. *The Jukes: A Study in Crime, Pauperism, Disease and Heredity.* New York: Arno Press, 1970.

Dumont, R. G., and D. C. Foss. *The American View of Death: Acceptance or Denial.* Cambridge, Mass.: Schenkman, 1972.

Durbin, E. F. *Welfare Income and Employment: An Economic Analysis of Family Choice.* New York: Praeger, 1969.

Eagle, E. "Charges for Care and Maintenance in State Institutions for the Mentally Retarded," *American Journal of Mental Deficiency,* 65 (September 1960): 199.

Eaton, J. W. "Community Development Ideologies," *International Review of Community Development,* 2 (1963): 40–41.

Eckardt, R. W., Jr. "Evangelical Christianity and Professional Social Work: A Study of the Beliefs and Practices of the Social Work Majors of Philadelphia College of the Bible and Temple University." Ph.D. diss. University of Pennsylvania, Philadelphia, 1974.

Eckstein, O. *Studies in the Economics of Income Maintenance.* Washington, D.C.: The Brookings Institution, 1967.

Ehrlich, P. R., and A. H. Ehrlich. *Population, Resources, Environment: Issues in Human Ecology.* San Francisco: Freeman, 1970.

El Salvador. New York: El Salvador Consulate, n.d.

Elman, E. M. *The Poorhouse State.* New York: Pantheon, 1966.

Enkes, S. "The Economic Case for Birth Control in Underdeveloped Nations," *Challenge Magazine,* May-June 1967.

Erikson, E. H. *Young Man Luther: A Study in Psychoanalysis and History.* New York: Norton, 1958.

Etzioni, A. *Modern Organizations.* Englewood Cliffs, N.J.: Prentice-Hall, 1964.

Etzioni, A. (ed.). *Complex Organizations: A Sociological Reader.* New York: Holt, Rinehart & Winston, 1961.

Evaluation of Family Planning in Health Services. Geneva: World Health Organization, 1975.

Evaluation of the Welfare Declaration: Eligibility Simplification for Public Assistance. New York: City University of New York, 1969.

Evans, A. A. *Flexibility in Working Life.* Paris: OECD, 1973.

Exodus, 16:3, 8.

Eysenck, H. J. *The Psychology of Politics.* New York: Praeger, 1954.

————. "The Effects of Psychotherapy," in H. J. Eysenck (ed.), *Handbook of Abnormal Psychology.* London: Pitman, 1969.

Facts about Norway. Oslo: Royal Ministry of Foreign Affairs, 1975.

Family, Child and Youth Welfare Services in Africa. New York: United Nations, 1966.

Faris, E., *et al. Intelligent Philanthropy.* Chicago: University of Chicago Press, 1930.

Feder, L. H. *Unemployment Relief in Periods of Depression.* New York: Sage, 1936.

Federal Republic of Germany at a Glance, The. Wiesbaden, West Germany: Franz Steiner, 1974.

Federico, R. C. *The Social Welfare Institution: An Introduction.* Lexington, Mass.: Heath, 1973.

Feine, Z., *et al. Interagency Collaboration in Drug Rehabilitation.* Richmond, Va.: Department of Mental Health and Mental Retardation, 1974.

Feldman, R. A. "Family Theory, Family Development and the Future of American Social Work," *International Social Work,* 16 (1973): 61.

Feldman, S. *The Administration of Mental Health Services.* Springfield, Ill.: Thomas, 1973.

Ferman, L. A., J. L. Kornbluh, and A. Haber (eds.). *Poverty in America.* Ann Arbor: University of Michigan Press, 1972.

Field, M. G. "Structured Strain in the Role of the Soviet Physician," *American Journal of Sociology,* 63 (1953): 493.

Findings of the 1973 AFDC Study—Part I: Demographic and Program Characteristics. Washington, D.C.: Department of Health, Education, and Welfare, 1973.

Findings of the 1973 AFDC Study—Part II-B. Washington, D.C.: Department of Health, Education, and Welfare, 1973.

Fink, A. E. *The Field of Social Work.* New York: Holt, Rinehart & Winston, 1974.

Finkelstein, L. (ed.). *The Jews.* Philadelphia: Jewish Publication Society of America, 1949.

Fishbein, B. K. *Social Welfare Abroad: Comparative Data on the Social Insurance and Public Assistance Programs of Selected Industrialized Democracies.* White Plains, N.Y.: Institute for Socioeconomic Studies, 1975.

Fisher, W., J. Mehr, and P. Truckenbrod. *Human Services: The Third Revolution in Mental Health.* New York: Alfred, 1974.

Fletcher, J. "The Protestant Churches," in E. T. Tyler (ed.), *Birth Control: A Continuing Controversy.* Springfield, Ill.: Thomas, 1967.

Fogarty, J. P. *Hearings Before a Sub-Committee of the Committee on Appropriations, House of Representatives, Eighty-seventh Congress, Second Session.* Washington, D.C.: Department of Health, Education, and Welfare, 1962.

Folsom, M. B. "Measures to Reduce Poverty," in M. S. Gordon (ed.), *Poverty in America.* San Francisco: Chandler, 1965.

Freud, S. *Civilization and Its Discontents.* New York: Paperback, 1958.

Friedenberg, E. Z. "Neo-Freudianism and Erich Fromm," *Commentary*, 34 (1962): 389.

Friedlander, W. A. *Individualism and Social Welfare.* New York: Free Press, 1962.

Friedman, M. *Capitalism and Freedom.* Chicago: University of Chicago Press, 1962.

Friedman, M. (ed.). *Overcoming Middle Class Rage.* Philadelphia: Westminster, 1971.

Friedman, P. R. "The Mentally Handicapped Citizen and Institutional Labor," *Harvard Law Review*, 87 (1974): 567–87.

Friedmann, E. A., and R. J. Havighurst, *The Meaning of Work and Retirement.* Chicago: University of Chicago Press, 1954.

Friedmann, G. *The Anatomy of Work.* New York: Free Press, 1964.

Fuller, T. *The Church History of Britain from the Birth of Jesus Christ Until the Year MDCXLVIII*, Book 2 (London, 1655): quoted in de Schweinitz, *England's Road to Social Security.* Philadelphia: University of Pennsylvania Press, 1943.

Fuller, V. "Rural Poverty and Rural Area Development," in M. S. Gordon (ed.), *Poverty in America.* San Francisco: Chandler, 1965.

Galper, J. "Private Pensions and Public Policy," *Social Work*, 18 (May 1973): 5–12.

Galper, J. H. *The Politics of Social Services.* Englewood Cliffs, N.J.: Prentice-Hall, 1975.

Gans, H. "Income Grants and 'Dirty Work,' " *The Public Interest*, 6 (1967): 110.

———. *More Equality.* New York: Vintage, 1968.

Garrett, J. F., and B. W. Griffis. "The Economic Benefits of Rehabilitation of the Mentally Retarded," *Welfare in Review*, 9 (March-April 1971): 1–7.

Gartner, A., and F. Riessman. *The Service Society and the Consumer Vanguard.* New York: Harper & Row, 1974.

Gerson, W. M. (ed.). *Social Problems in a Changing World.* New York: Crowell, 1969.

Gersuny, C., and W. R. Rosengren. *The Service Society.* Cambridge, Mass.: Schenkman, 1973.

Gerth, H. H., and C. W. Mills (eds.). *From Max Weber: Essays in Sociology.* London: Routledge & Kegan Paul, 1948.

Gil, D. G. *Unravelling Social Policy.* Cambridge, Mass.: Schenkman, 1973.

Gilbert, C. E. "Policy Making in Public Welfare," *Political Science Quarterly*, 81 (June 1966): 197–98.

Gilbert, L. D. "The Changing Work Ethic and Rehabilitation," *Journal of Rehabilitation*, 39 (1973): 14–17.

Gilbert, N. "Alternative Forms of Social Protection for Developing Countries," *Social Security Review*, 50 (September 1976): 363–87.

Gilbert, N., and H. Specht. *Dimensions of Social Welfare Policy.* Englewood Cliffs, N.J.: Prentice-Hall, 1974.

Gindy, A. "Social Welfare and Family Planning: A New Priority for the United Nations," *New Themes in Social Work Education.* New York: International Association of Schools of Social Work, 1972.

Gini, C. "The Cyclical Rise and Fall of Population," in C. Gini *et al.*, *Population.* Chicago: University of Chicago Press, 1930.

Gini, C., *et al. Population.* Chicago: University of Chicago Press, 1930.

Ginor, F. *Analysis of Low Income Groups.* Tel Aviv: University of Tel Aviv, 1974. (In Hebrew.)

Giving in America: Toward a Stronger Voluntary Sector. Washington, D.C.: Commission on Private Philanthropy and Public Needs, 1975.

Glazer, N. "A Sociologist's View of Poverty," in M. S. Gordon (ed.), *Poverty in America.* San Francisco: Chandler, 1965.

Glennerster, H. *Social Service Budgets and Social Policy: British and American Experience.* New York: Barnes & Noble, 1975.

Goddard, H. H. *The Kallikak Family: A Study in the Heredity of Feeble-mindedness.* New York: Arno Press, 1973.

Goldman, E. F. *Rendezvous with Destiny: A History of Modern American Reform.* New York: Vintage, n.d.

Goldston, R. *The Great Depression: The United States in the Thirties.* Greenwich, Conn.: Fawcett, 1968.

Gollub, S. L. "A Critical Look at Religious Requirements in Adoption," *Public Welfare*, 32 (1974): 23–28.

Goodenough, W. H. *Cooperation in Change.* New York: Sage, 1963.

Goodwin, L. *Do the Poor Want to Work?: A Social-Psychological Study of Work Orientations.* Washington, D.C.: The Brookings Institution, 1972.

————. *Can Social Science Help Resolve National Problems?: Welfare, a Case in Point.* New York: Free Press, 1975.

Gordon, M. S. (ed.). *Poverty in America.* San Francisco: Chandler, 1965.

Gouldner, A. W. *The Hellenic World: A Sociological Analysis.* New York: Harper & Row, 1969.

Graham, J. J. *The Enemies of the Poor.* New York: Random House, 1970.

Graycar, A. *Social Policy: An Australian Introduction.* Melbourne: Macmillan, 1976.

Green, A. W. *Social Problems: Arena of Conflict.* New York: McGraw-Hill, 1975.

Gross, A. M. *Is Cost Benefit Analysis Beneficial? Is Cost Effectiveness Analysis Effective?* Waltham, Mass.: Heller School, Brandeis University, 1976. (Mimeographed.)

Gross, B. M. "Prefatory Comment," in B. Akzin and Y. Dror, *Israel: High Pressure Planning.* Syracuse, N.Y.: Syracuse University Press, 1966.

Gross, F. (ed.). *European Ideologies.* New York: Philosophical Library, 1948.

Guide to the Social Services. Dublin: Stationery Office, 1974.

Guidelines on Reporting Child Abuse and Maltreatment. Hauppage, N.Y.: Suffolk County Department of Social Services, 1974.

Gulhati, K. "Compulsory Sterilization: A New Dimension in India's Population Policy," *Draper World Population Fund Report*, 3 (Autumn-Winter 1976): 26–29.

Gurin, G., and P. Gurin. "Personal Efficacy and the Ideology of Individual Responsibility," in B. Strumpel (ed.), *Economic Means for Human Needs: Social Indicators of Well-Being and Discontent.* Ann Arbor: University of Michigan Press, 1976.

Gutman, H. G. *Work, Culture and Society in Industrializing America.* New York: Knopf, 1976.

Guttmacher, A. F. "Judaism," in E. T. Tyler (ed.), *Birth Control: A Continuing Controversy.* Springfield, Ill.: Thomas, 1967.

———. "Family Planning: Humanism and Science," in F. Haselkorn (ed.), *Family Planning: The Role of Social Work.* Garden City, N.Y.: Adelphi University School of Social Work, 1968.

Halberstam, D. *The Best and the Brightest.* New York: Random House, 1972.

Hall, M. P. *The Social Services of Modern England.* London: Routledge & Kegan Paul, 1955.

Hallman, H. W. *Neighborhood Control of Public Programs: Case Studies of Community Centers and Neighborhood Boards.* New York: Praeger, 1970.

Hamlin, R. H. *Voluntary Health and Welfare Agencies in the United States.* New York: Schoolmaster Press, 1961.

Hampden-Turner, C. *From Poverty to Dignity.* Garden City, N.Y.: Anchor, 1975.

Handler, J. F., and E. J. Hollingsworth. *The "Deserving Poor": A Study of Welfare Administration.* New York: Academic Press, 1971.

Hanlan, A. "From Social Reform to Social Security: The Separation of ADC and Child Welfare," in P. E. Weinberger (ed.), *Perspectives on Social Welfare: An Introductory Anthology.* New York: Macmillan, 1974.

Hansen, M. L. *The Immigrant in American History.* New York: Harper & Row, 1964.

Hardwick, K. D. "As Long as Charity Shall Be a Virtue," in P. Smith (ed.), *Boston Private Charities from 1657 to 1800* (privately printed pamphlet); quoted in H. D. Stein, "Observations on Determinants of Social Work Education in the United States," in *An Intercultural Exploration: Universals and Differences in Social Work Values, Functions, and Practice.* New York: Council on Social Work Education, 1967.

Hareven, T. K. "Societal Problems," in C. A. Chambers (ed.), *A Century of Concern: 1873–1973.* Columbus, Ohio: National Conference on Social Welfare, 1974.

Harrington, M. *The Other America.* New York: Macmillan, 1963.

Hasebroek, J. *Trade and Politics in Ancient Greece.* London: Bell, 1933.

Haselkorn, F. *Family Planning: Readings and Case Material.* New York: Council on Social Work Education, 1971.

Haselkorn, F. (ed.). *Mothers-at-Risk.* Garden City, N.Y.: Adelphi University School of Social Work, 1966.

———. *Family Planning: The Role of Social Work.* Garden City, N.Y.: Adelphi University School of Social Work, 1968.

Hasenfeld, Y., and R. A. English (eds.). *Human Service Organizations.* Ann Arbor: University of Michigan Press, 1974.

Hayes, Patrick Cardinal. Letter in *1934–1935 Catalogue* (New York: Fordham University School of Social Service, 1934); quoted in S. C. Kohs, *The Roots of Social Work.* New York: Association Press, 1966.

Health and Welfare in Canada. Reference Paper No. 94. Ottawa: Department of External Affairs, 1975.

Heap, K. "The Scapegoat Role in Youth Groups," *Case Conference* (London), 12 (January 1966): 215.

Heilbroner, R. L. *The Worldly Philosophers.* New York: Simon & Schuster, 1953.

Helfer, R. E., and C. H. Kemps. *The Battered Child.* Chicago: University of Chicago Press, 1974.

Hentoff, M. "Abortion: Murder as a Liberal Art," *Jubilee,* April 1967, pp. 4–5.

Herberg, W. *Protestant, Catholic and Jew: An Essay in American Religious Sociology.* Garden City, N.Y.: Doubleday, 1955.

Herzberg, F. *Work and the Nature of Man.* Cleveland: World Publishing, 1966.

Herzberg, F., B. Mausner, and B. B. Snyderman. *The Motivation to Work.* New York: Wiley, 1959.

Hess, B. B. "America's Aged: Who, What, When, and Where?" in B. B. Hess (ed.), *Growing Old in America.* New Brunswick, N.J.: Transaction, 1976.

Hess, B. B. (ed.), *Growing Old in America.* New Brunswick, N.J.: Transaction, 1976.

Hines, F. K. *Factors Related to Participation in the Food Stamp Program.* Washington, D.C.: Department of Agriculture, 1975.

Hock, P. H., and J. Zabin (eds.). *Psychopathology of Aging.* New York: Grune & Stratton, 1961.

Hoffer, E. *Working and Thinking on the Waterfront.* New York: Harper & Row, 1969.

Hofstadter, R. *Social Darwinism in American Thought.* Boston: Beacon Press, 1944.

Holgersson, L., and S. Lundstrom. *The Evolution of Swedish Social Welfare.* Stockholm: The Swedish Institute, 1975.

Holtzman, A. *The Townsend Movement.* New York: Bookman, 1963.

Homans, G. C. *The Human Group.* London: Routledge & Kegan Paul, 1951.

Hoos, T. R. *Retraining the Work Force: An Analysis of Current Experience.* Berkeley: University of California Press, 1969.

Hopkins, H. L. *Hearings before the Subcommittee of the House Committee on Appropriations on H.R. 7527, Federal Emergency and Civil Works Programs.* Washington, D.C.: Seventy-third Congress, Second Session, House of Representatives, January 20, 1934.

Horowitz, D., and R. Erlich. "Proving Poverty Pays: Big Brother as a Holding Company," in P. Roby (ed.), *The Poverty Establishment.* Englewood Cliffs, N.J.: Prentice-Hall, 1974.

Horowitz, D., and B. Kimmerling. "Some Social Implications of Military Service and the Reserve System in Israel," *Archives of European Sociology,* 15 (1974): 77–91.

Horowitz, D., and D. Kolodny. "The Foundations: Charity Begins at Home," *Ramparts,* 7 (April 1969): 39–48; reprinted in P. Roby (ed.), *The Poverty Establishment.* Englewood Cliffs, N.J.: Prentice-Hall, 1974.

Horton, G. T. *Readings on Human Services Planning.* Arlington, Va.: Human Services Institute for Children and Families, 1975.

Hoshino, G. "Separating Maintenance from Social Service," *Public Welfare,* 30 (Spring 1972): 54–61.

"Hospital Affiliation Stirs Religious Issue," *New York Times,* October 20, 1976, p. 1.

How I Found a Way to Eat Better for Less Money. Albany: New York State Department of Social Services, 1976.

Howard, D. S. *The WPA and Federal Relief Policy.* New York: Sage, 1943.

Huizinga, G. *Maslow's Need Hierarchy in the Work Situation.* Groningen, Netherlands: Walters-Noordhoff, 1970.

Hurtado, H. "Summary of Country Case Study," in H. D. Stein (ed.), *Planning for the Needs of Children in Developing Countries.* New York: UNICEF, 1964.

Husby, R. D. "Child Day Care for Welfare Mothers," *Social Work,* 19 (July 1974): 420–26.

Impact of Darwinian Thought on American Life and Culture, The. Austin: University of Texas Press, 1959.

Inciardi, J. A., and H. A. Siegel (eds.). *Emerging Social Issues: A Sociological Perspective.* New York: Praeger, 1975.

India: An Introduction. New Delhi: Ministry of External Affairs, 1975.

Intercultural Exploration: Universals and Differences in Social Work Values, Functions, and Practice. New York: Council on Social Work Education, 1967.

Introduction to Social Security: A Workers' Education Manual. Geneva: International Labour Organization, 1970.

Jackson, J. A. *Migration.* Cambridge, England: Cambridge University Press, 1969.

Jackson, J. J. "Aged Blacks: A Potpourri in the Direction of the Reduction of Inequality," in B. B. Hess (ed.), *Growing Old in America.* New Brunswick, N.J.: Transaction, 1976.

Jaffe, E. D. "Separation in Jerusalem," *Public Welfare,* 31 (Winter 1973): 33–38.
————. "Poverty in the Third Jewish Commonwealth: Sephardi-Ashkenazi Divisions," *Journal of Jewish Communal Service,* 52 (Fall 1975): 91–99.

Janowitz, M. *Social Control of the Welfare State.* New York: Elsevier Scientific Publishing, 1976.

Jones, G. E. "Rural Development and Agricultural Extension: A Sociological View," *Community Development Journal,* 6 (1967): 26.

Joravsky, D. *The Lysenko Affair.* Cambridge, Mass.: Harvard University Press, 1970.

Judiciary—Court Acts—29A Part 1: New York State Family Court Act; Family Court Rules and Forms, Sections 413–416. Albany: State of New York.

Kadushin, A. *Child Welfare Services.* New York: Macmillan, 1974.

Kahn, A. J. *Social Policy and Social Services.* New York: Random House, 1973.
————. "Service Delivery at the Neighborhood Level: Experience, Theory, and Facts," *Social Service Review,* 50 (March 1976): 23–56.

Kahn, A. J., and S. B. Kamerman. *Not for the Poor Alone: European Social Services.* Philadelphia: Temple University Press, 1975.

Kamerman, S. B., and A. J. Kahn. *Social Services in the United States: Policies and Programs.* Philadelphia: Temple University Press, 1976.

Kaplan, M. *Leisure in America: A Social Inquiry.* New York: Wiley, 1960.

————. *Leisure: Theory and Policy.* New York: Wiley, 1975.

Kaslow, F. W. *Issues in Human Services.* San Francisco: Jossey-Bass, 1972.

Katan, Y. "The Utilization of Indigenous Workers in Human Service Organizations," in Y. Hasenfeld and R. A. English (eds.), *Human Service Organizations.* Ann Arbor: University of Michigan Press, 1974.

Kateb, G. *Utopia and Its Enemies.* New York: Schocken, 1963.

Katona, G. "Persistence of Belief in Personal Financial Progress," in B. Strumpel (ed.), *Economic Means for Human Needs: Social Indicators of Well-Being and Discontent.* Ann Arbor: University of Michigan Press, 1976.

Katz, A. H., and E. I. Bender. *The Strength in Us: Self-Help Groups in the Modern World.* New York: New Viewpoints, 1976.

Keefe, T. "Empathy and Social Work Education: A Study," *Journal of Education for Social Work,* 11 (Fall 1975): 69–75.

Kendall, K. A. *Population Dynamics and Family Planning: A New Responsibility for Social Work Education.* New York: Council on Social Work Education, 1971.

Kennedy, D. M. *Birth Control in America: The Career of Margaret Sanger.* New Haven, Conn.: Yale University Press, 1970.

Kershaw, J. A. "The Attack on Poverty," in M. S. Gordon (ed.), *Poverty in America.* San Francisco: Chandler, 1965.

Kingdom of the Netherlands: The Facts and Figures The Hague: Government Printing Office, 1971.

Kogut, A. "The Settlement and Ethnicity," *Social Work,* 17 (1972): 22.

Kohler, K. "Charity," in I. B. Singer (ed.), *The Jewish Encyclopedia,* Vol. 3. New York: Funk & Wagnalls, 1903.

Kohn, M. L., and C. Schooler. "Occupational Experience and Psychological Functioning: An Assessment of Reciprocal Effects," *American Sociological Review,* 38 (February 1973): 97–118.

Kohs, S. C. *The Roots of Social Work.* New York: Association Press, 1966.

Konrad, G. *The Case Worker.* New York: Harcourt Brace Jovanovich, 1974.

Korea: Past and Present. Seoul: Kwangnyong, 1972.

Kornhauser, A. *Mental Health of the Industrial Worker.* New York: Wiley, 1965.

Kotz, N. *Let Them Eat Promises.* Garden City, N.Y.: Doubleday, 1971.

Kraft, L., and C. J. Bernheimer. *Aspects of the Jewish Community Center.* New York: National Association of Jewish Center Workers, 1954.

Krassowski, A. (ed.). *British Development Policies: Needs and Prospects 1970.* London: Overseas Development Institute, 1970.

Kropotkin, P. *Mutual Aid: A Factor of Evolution.* New York: Knopf, 1925.

Kubler-Ross, E. *On Death and Dying.* New York: Macmillan, 1969.

Kurland, P. B. "The Judicial Road to Social Welfare," *Social Service Review,* 48 (1974): 481–93.

Labor and Social Legislation in Uruguay. New York: Consulate of Uruguay, n.d.

Ladejinsky, W. *Foreign Affairs,* quoted in *CERES,* 3 (1970): 13.

Lader, L. *The Margaret Sanger Story and the Fight for Birth Control.* Garden City, N.Y.: Doubleday, 1955.

Law and Population. New York: United Fund for Population Activities, n.d.

Leahy, W. H. "An Economic Perspective of Public Employment Programs," *Review of Social Economy,* 34 (October 1976): 189–200.

Leiby, J. "Provision and Management of Social Services," in C. A. Chambers (ed.), *A Century of Concern: 1873–1973.* Columbus, Ohio: National Conference on Social Welfare, 1974.

Leichter, H., and W. Mitchell. *Kinship and Casework.* New York: Sage, 1967.

Lerner, D., and H. D. Lasswell (eds.). *The Policy Sciences.* Stanford, Calif.: Stanford University Press, 1951.

Lerner, M. "Respectable Bigotry," in M. Friedman (ed.), *Overcoming Middle Class Rage.* Philadelphia: Westminster Press, 1971.

Leuchtenberg, W. E. *Franklin D. Roosevelt and the New Deal.* New York: Harper & Row, 1963.

Levinson, H. *The Great Jackass Fallacy.* Cambridge, Mass.: Harvard University Press, 1973.

Levinson, R. W. "Access to Health Care: An Information and Referral Approach," *Proceedings of the Information and Referral Roundtable 1975.* Phoenix, Ariz.: Alliance of Information and Referral Services, 1976.

Levitan, S. A. "Manpower Programs Under New Management: Some Lessons Learned and Their Applications," in G. F. Rohrlich (ed.), *Social Economics for the 1970's: Programs for Social Security, Health, and Manpower.* New York: Dunellen, 1970.

———. *Programs in Aid of the Poor in the 1970s.* Baltimore: Johns Hopkins Press, 1973.

Leviticus, 16: 10, 22.

Lewis, O. "The Culture of Poverty," *Scientific American,* 215 (October 1966): 19–25.

Leyendecker, H. M. *Problems and Policy in Public Assistance.* New York: Harper Bros., 1955.

Lieberman, E. J. (ed.). *Mental Health: The Public Health Challenge.* Washington, D.C.: American Public Health Association, 1975.

Liebling, A. J. *The Press.* New York: Ballantine, 1964.

Lindblom, C. E. "The Science of 'Muddling Through,'" *Public Administration Review,* 19 (1959): 79–88.

Local Government in Selected Countries. New York: United Nations Technical Assistance Program, 1963.

Loewenberg, F. M. "Social Work, Social Welfare, and Social Intervention," in F. M. Loewenberg, and R. Dolgoff (eds.), *The Practice of Social Intervention: Goals, Roles and Strategies.* Itasca, Ill.: Peacock, 1972.

Loewenberg, F. M., and R. Dolgoff (eds.). *The Practice of Social Intervention: Goals, Roles and Strategies.* Itasca, Ill.: Peacock, 1972.

Lorenz, K. *On Aggression.* New York: Bantam, 1971.

Lowenstein, E. R. "Social Work in Postindustrial Society," *Social Work,* 18 (November 1973): 40–47.

Lubove, R. *The Professional Altruist: The Emergence of Social Work as a Career: 1880–1930.* New York: Atheneum, 1973.

Macarov, D. "Some Aspects of Teaching from Foreign Records," *Indian Journal of Social Work,* 24 (January 1964): 315–20.

————. "The Concept of Empathy and the Educational Process," *Applied Social Studies,* 2 (1970): 107.

————. *Incentives to Work.* San Francisco: Jossey-Bass, 1970.

————. "Work Patterns and Satisfactions in an Israeli Kibbutz: A Test of the Herzberg Hypothesis," *Personnel Psychology,* 25 (1972): 483–93.

————. "The Israeli Community Center During the Yom Kippur War," *Journal of Jewish Communal Service,* 51 (Summer 1975): 340.

————. "Israel's Social Services: Historical Roots and Current Situation," in D. Thursz and J. L. Vigilante (eds.), *Meeting Human Needs,* Vol. 1: *An Overview of Nine Countries.* Beverly Hills, Calif.: Sage, 1975.

————. *Social Welfare.* No. 15 in Israel Today Series. Jerusalem: Ministry of Foreign Affairs, 1975.

————. "Work Without Pay: Work Incentives and Patterns in a Salaryless Environment," *International Journal of Social Economics,* 2 (Summer 1975): 106.

————. *Boards and Directors: A Longitudinal Study.* Jerusalem: Paul Baerwald School of Social Work, Hebrew University, 1976. (In Hebrew.)

————. "How Function Follows Form: The Relationship of Social Welfare Services to Societal Structure." Paper presented at the Annual Spring Meeting, School of Social Work, Adelphi University, Garden City, N.Y., May 20, 1976.

————. "Reciprocity Between Self-Actualization and Hard Work," *International Journal of Social Economics,* 3 (1976): 39–44.

————. "Management in the Social Work Curriculum," *Administration in Social Work,* 1 (October 1977) (forthcoming).

————. "Political Ideologies and Social Welfare: The Case of Israel," *International Social Work* (forthcoming).

————. "Social Welfare as a By-Product: The Effect of Neo-Mercantilism," *Journal of Sociology and Social Welfare* (forthcoming).

Macarov, D., and G. Fradkin. *The Short Course in Development Activities.* Ramat Gan, Israel: Massada Press, 1973.

————. "Principles of Manpower Training for Agricultural Development: The Israeli Experience," *Community Development Journal,* 10 (October 1975): 171–78.

Macarov, D., and N. Golan. "Goals in Social Work Practice: A Longitudinal Study," *International Social Work,* 16 (2/3, 1973): 2.

Macarov, D., and U. Yannai. *A Study of Centers for Discharged Reservists.* Jerusalem: Ministry of Labour, 1974. (In Hebrew.)

————. *Images of Poverty and the Poor in Jerusalem.* Jerusalem: Paul Baerwald School of Social Work, Hebrew University, 1975. (In Hebrew.)

Macarov, D., *et al.* "Consultants and Consultees: The View from Within," *Social Service Review,* 43 (September 1967): 283.

Macaulay, J., and L. Berkowitz (eds.). *Altruism and Helping Behavior: Social Psychological Studies of Some Antecedents and Consequences.* New York: Academic Press, 1970.

McCaghy, C. H. *Deviant Behavior: Crime, Conflict, and Interest Groups.* New York: Macmillan, 1976.

McClelland, D. C. *The Achieving Society.* Princeton, N.J.: Van Nostrand, 1961.

McCormack, A. "Driving a Stake into the Heart of Old Malthus," *People,* 1 (1974): 5–14, 39.

McCormick, M. J. *Diagnostic Casework in the Thomistic Pattern.* New York: Columbia University Press, 1954.

MacDonald, D. "Our Invisible Poor," *New Yorker,* January 19, 1963.

McElheny, V. R. "Scientific Impasse Faces U.S. in Its Agricultural Technology," *New York Times,* May 31, 1976, pp. 1, 22.

McFarland, K. "Why Men and Women Get Fired," *Personnel Journal,* 25 (1957): 307.

McGregor, D. *The Human Side of Management.* New York: McGraw-Hill, 1960.

Machlowitz, M. M. *The Workaholic.* New Haven, Conn.: Yale University, 1976. (Mimeographed.)

MacIver, R. M. "Introduction," in F. Gross (ed.), *European Ideologies.* New York: Philosophical Library, 1948.

McKinney's Consolidated Laws of New York: Social Welfare Laws. Brooklyn, N.Y.: Thompson, 1966.

Madison, B. "Social Services Administration in the U.S.S.R.," in D. Thursz and J. L. Vigilante (eds.), *Meeting Human Needs,* Vol. 1: *An Overview of Nine Countries.* Beverly Hills, Calif.: Sage, 1975.

Maimonides, M. Mishna Torah, viii (Seeds), "Giving to the Poor," Chapter 7, Part 3.

Malthus, T. R. *An Essay on the Principle of Population; or, A View of Its Past and Present Effect on Human Happiness with an Inquiry into Our Prospects Respecting the Future Removal or Mitigation of the Evils Which It Occasions.* 7th ed. Homewood, Ill.: Irwin, 1963.

————. *Population: The First Essay.* Ann Arbor: University of Michigan Press, 1959.

Manchester, W. *The Glory and the Dream: A Narrative History of America 1932–1972.* Boston: Little, Brown, 1973.

Mangum, G. L., and J. Walsh. *A Decade of Manpower Development and Training.* Salt Lake City: Olympus, 1973.

"Man's Population Predicament," *Population Bulletin,* Vol. 27, No. 2, Population Reference Bureau, 1971; quoted in K. B. Oettinger and J. D. Stansbury, *Population and Family Planning: Analytical Abstracts for Social Work Educators and Related Disciplines.* New York: International Association of Schools of Social Work, 1972.

March, M. S., and E. Newman. "Financing Social Welfare: Governmental Allocation Procedures," in *Encyclopedia of Social Work.* New York: National Association of Social Workers, 1971.

Marcus, S. "Hunger and Ideology," in M. N. Zald (ed.), *Social Welfare Institutions.* New York: Wiley, 1965.

Marland, S. P., Jr., *Career Education: A Proposal for Reform.* New York: McGraw-Hill, 1974.

Marshall, H. E. *Dorothea Dix: Forgotten Samaritan.* Chapel Hill: University of North Carolina Press, 1937.

Marshall, T. H. *Social Policy*. London: Hutchinson, 1965.

Marston, W. G. "The Population Crisis: Myth or Menace?" in W. M. Gerson (ed.), *Social Problems in a Changing World*. New York: Crowell, 1969.

Martin, J. M. *Lower-Class Delinquency and Work Programs*. New York: New York University Press, 1966.

Marx, K. *Early Writings*. New York: McGraw-Hill, 1964.

Maslow, A. H. *Motivation and Personality*. New York: Harper Bros., 1954.

Maududi, A. A. *Birth Control: Its Social, Political, Economic, Religious, and Moral Aspects*. Lahore: Islamic Publications, 1974.

Mayer, J. "Toward a Non-Malthusian Population Policy," in D. Callahan (ed.), *The American Population Debate*. Garden City, N.Y.: Doubleday, 1971.

Mayer, R., R. Moroney, and R. Morris (eds.). *Centrally Planned Change: A Reexamination of Theory and Experience*. Urbana: University of Illinois Press, 1974.

Mayo, E. *The Human Problems of an Industrial Civilization*. New York: Macmillan, 1933.

Mead, M. "The Study of National Character," in D. Lerner and H. D. Lasswell (eds.), *The Policy Sciences*. Stanford, Calif.: Stanford University Press, 1951.

Meld, M. B. "The Politics of Evaluation of Social Programs," *Social Work*, 19 (July 1974): 448–55.

Melville, K. *Communes in the Counter Culture: Origins, Theories, Styles of Life*. New York: Morrow, 1972.

Menefee, S. C. *Vocational Training and Employment of Youth*. New York: Da Capo Press, 1971.

Merriam, I. C. "Financing Social Welfare," in *Encyclopedia of Social Work*. New York: National Association of Social Workers, 1971.

Methods of Adjusting to Automation and Technological Change. Washington, D.C.: Department of Labor, n.d.

Middleman, R. R., and G. Goldberg. *Social Service Delivery: A Structural Approach to Social Work Practice*. New York: Columbia University Press, 1974.

Miller, H. "Government's Role in Social Welfare" (address delivered at the Second National Conference on the Churches and Social Welfare, National Council of the Churches of Christ in the U.S.A., Cleveland, 1961); quoted in B. J. Coughlin, *Church and State in Social Welfare*. New York: Columbia University Press, 1965.

Miller, L. S. "The Structural Determinants of the Social Welfare Effort: A Critique and a Contribution," *Social Service Review*, 50 (March 1976): 57–79.

Morris, D., and K. Hess. *Neighborhood Power: The New Localism*. Boston: Beacon Press, 1975.

Morris, R., and R. H. Binstock. *Feasible Planning for Social Change*. New York: Columbia University Press, 1966.

Morris, R., and M. Freund (eds.). *Trends and Issues in Jewish Social Welfare in the United States, 1899–1952*. Philadelphia: Jewish Publication Society of America, 1966.

Moss, J. "Social Services," in *Britannica Book of the Year*. Chicago: Encyclopaedia Britannica, 1966.

Moynihan, D. P. "The Case for a Family Allowance," *New York Times Magazine*, February 5, 1967, pp. 13, 68–73.

———. *Maximum Feasible Misunderstanding*. New York: Free Press, 1969.

———. *The Politics of a Guaranteed Income: The Nixon Administration and the Family Assistance Plan*. New York: Free Press, 1969.

Mullen, E. J., *et al. Evaluation of Social Intervention*. San Francisco: Jossey-Bass, 1972.

Munson, H. B. "Abortion in Modern Times: Thoughts and Comments, *Renewal*, February 1967, p. 9; quoted in D. Callahan (ed.), *The American Population Debate*. Garden City, N.Y.: Doubleday, 1971.

Munts, R., and I. Garfinkel. *The Work Disincentive Effects of Unemployment Insurance*. Kalamazoo, Mich.: Upjohn, 1974.

Myers, P. *1976 World Population Data Sheet*. Washington, D.C.: Population Reference Bureau, 1976.

Naparstek, A. J. *Neighborhood Decentralization: An Option for Urban Policy*. Washington, D.C.: National Center for Urban Ethnic Affairs, 1976.

Naparstek, A. J., and K. Kollias. "The Ethnic and Class Dimensions in Neighborhoods: A Means for the Reorganization of Human Service Delivery Systems," *Journal of Sociology and Social Welfare*, 2 (Spring 1975): 406.

Neill, D. G. "Unfinished Business of the Welfare State," in C. I. Schottland (ed.), *The Welfare State*. New York: Harper & Row, 1967.

Neipris, J. "Some Origins of Social Work Policy in a New State," Ph.D. diss., University of California, Berkeley, 1966.

New Themes in Social Work Education. New York: International Association of Schools of Social Work, 1972.

New Zealand Official Yearbook 1974. Wellington: Government of New Zealand, 1975.

Niebuhr, R. *The Contribution of Religion to Social Work*. New York: Columbia University Press, 1932.

Nisbet, R. *The Social Philosophers: Community and Conflict in Western Thought*. New York: Crowell, 1973.

Nizan, A., and H. Avidor. *An Empirical Study of Handicapped Persons in Israel in Need of Vocational Rehabilitation*. Jerusalem: National Insurance Institute, 1974. (In Hebrew.)

Nortman, D., and E. Hofstatter. "Population and Family Planning Programs: A Factbook," *Reports on Population and Family Planning*, 2 (October 1976).

O'Collins, M. "Introducing Social Work Education at the University of Papua New Guinea," *International Social Work*, 16 (1973): 20.

O'Donnell, E. J., and O. M. Reid. "The Multiservice Neighborhood Center: Preliminary Findings from a National Survey," *Welfare in Review*, 9 (May/June 1971): 1.

Oechslin, J. J. "The Role of Employers' Organizations in France," *International Labour Review*, 106 (November 1972): 391–413.

Oettinger, K. B. *Social Work in Action: An International Perspective on Popula-tion and Family Planning.* New York: International Association of Schools of Social Work, 1975.

Oettinger, K. B., and J. D. Stansbury. *Population and Family Planning: Analytical Abstracts for Social Work Educators and Related Disciplines.* New York: International Association of Schools of Social Work, 1972.

Oppenheimer, V. K. *Population.* New York: Foreign Policy Association, 1971.

Organization and Administration of Social Welfare Programmes: Romania. New York: United Nations, 1967.

Orshansky, M. "Who's Who Among the Poor," *Social Security Bulletin,* 28 (1965): 3.

———. "More About the Poor in 1964," *Social Security Bulletin,* 29 (1966): 3.

———. "Counting the Poor: Another Look at the Poverty Profile," in L. A. Ferman, J. L. Kornbluh, and A. Haber (eds.). *Poverty in America.* Ann Arbor: University of Michigan Press, 1972.

Osborne, J. W. *The Silent Revolution: The Industrial Revolution in England as a Source of Cultural Change.* New York: Scribner's, 1970.

Palmer, G. H. *Altruism: Its Nature and Varieties.* Westport, Conn.: Greenwood Press, 1970.

Papell, C. P. "Sensitivity Training: Relevance for Social Work Education," *Jour-nal of Education for Social Work,* 8 (Winter 1972): 42.

Parker, R. *The Myth of the Middle Class.* New York: Harper & Row, 1972.

Parmar, S. L. "What Good Is Economic Betterment . . ." *CERES,* 3 (1970): 21.

Pearson, K. *Darwinism, Medical Progress and Eugenics.* London: University College, 1912.

Pechman, J. A., and P. M. Timpane (eds.). *Work Incentives and Income Guaran-tees: The New Jersey Negative Income Tax Experiment.* Washington, D.C.: The Brookings Institution, 1975.

Peck, E., and J. Senderowitz. *Pronatalism: The Myth of Mom and Apple Pie.* New York: Crowell, 1974.

Perelman, M. "The Generation of Technology and Agricultural Efficiency," *Review of Social Economy,* 29 (October 1976): 217–24.

Perrett, G. *Days of Sadness, Years of Triumph: The American People 1939–1945.* Baltimore: Penguin, 1973.

Perry, R. B. *Realms of Value.* Cambridge, Mass.: Harvard University Press, 1954.

Persons, S. "Darwinism and American Culture," in *The Impact of Darwinian Thought on American Life and Culture.* Austin: University of Texas Press, 1959.

Peters, V. *All Things Common: The Hutterian Way of Life.* New York: Harper & Row, 1965.

Peterson, W. *The Welfare State in France.* Omaha: University of Nebraska Press, 1960.

Pfouts, J. H. *Vocational History of 309 Arm, Leg, and Bilateral Amputees of World War II.* Baltimore: Veterans' Administration Outpatient Clinic, n.d.

Phelps, E. S. (ed.). *Altruism, Morality, and Economic Theory.* New York: Sage, 1975.

Pimlott, J. A. R. *Toynbee Hall.* London: Dent, 1935.

Pincus, A., and V. Wood. "Retirement," in *Encyclopedia of Social Work.* New York: National Association of Social Workers, 1971.

Pius XI. *Casti Connubi.* March 4, 1679.

Piven, F. F. "Federal Interventions in the Cities: The New Urban Programs as a Political Strategy," in E. O. Smigel (ed.), *Handbook on the Study of Social Problems.* Chicago: Rand McNally, 1971.

Piven, F. F., and R. A. Cloward. *Regulating the Poor: The Functions of Public Welfare.* New York: Random House, 1971.

Plotnick, R. D., and F. Skidmore. *Programs Against Poverty.* New York: Academic Press, 1975.

Poland: A Handbook. Warsaw: Interpress, 1974.

Population, Food Supply and Agricultural Development. Rome: Food and Agriculture Organization, 1975. Originally published as Chapter 3 of *The State of Food and Agriculture: 1974.* Rome: Food and Agriculture Organization, 1975.

Population and Family Planning in the People's Republic of China. Washington, D.C.: Population Crisis Committee, 1971.

Population and Vital Statistics Report: Data Available as of July 1, 1976. New York: United Nations, 1976.

Poverty, U.S.A.: The Almshouse Experience. New York: Arno Press, 1971.

Power, P. W., and R. P. Marinelli. "Normalization and the Sheltered Workshop: A Review and Proposals for Change," *Rehabilitation Literature,* 35 (1974): 66–72, 78.

Prabhupada, A. C. B. *The Perfection of Yoga.* Los Angeles: International Center for Krishna Consciousness, 1972.

President's Commission on Income Maintenance Programs: Background Papers. Washington, D.C.: Government Printing Office, 1970.

Price, C. "The Study of Assimilation," in J. A. Jackson (ed.), *Migration.* Cambridge, England: Cambridge University Press, 1969.

Prigmore, C. J. *Social Work in Iran Since the White Revolution.* University: University of Alabama Press, 1976.

"Program Operations," *Social Security Bulletin,* Vol. 40 (April 1977).

Pryor, H. L. *Public Expenditures in Communist and Capitalist Nations.* Homewood, Ill.: Irwin, 1968.

Public Opinion Poll of Social Services. Los Angeles: University of Southern California, 1971. (Mimeographed.)

Pusic, E. *Reappraisal of the United Nations Social Security Programme.* New York: United Nations, 1965.

Quincy, J. *Report of the Committee to Whom Was Referred the Consideration of the Pauper Laws of This Commonwealth;* reprinted in *Poverty, U.S.A.: The Almshouse Experience.* New York: Arno Press, 1971.

Quinney, R. "The Future of Crime," in J. A. Inciardi and H. A. Siegel (eds.), *Emerging Social Issues: A Sociological Perspective.* New York: Praeger, 1975.

Ramos, J. "Migrant Farmworkers," in *Encyclopedia of Social Work.* New York: National Association of Social Workers, 1971.

Rapid Population Growth: Consequences and Policy Implications. Baltimore: Johns Hopkins Press, 1971.

Rapoport, L. "The Social Work Role in Family Planning: A Summation," in F. Haselkorn (ed.), *Family Planning: The Role of Social Work*. Garden City, N.Y.: Adelphi University School of Social Work, 1968.

Rashid, R. "Social Work Practice in West Pakistan," in *An Intercultural Exploration: Universals and Differences in Social Work Values, Functions, and Practice*. New York: Council on Social Work Education, 1967.

Raskin, A. H. "Shorter Workweek: A New Breakthrough," *New York Times*, October 8, 1976, p. 14.

Rein, M. *Social Policy: Issues of Choice and Change*. New York: Random House, 1970.

Reingold, J., R. L. Wolk, and S. Schwartz. "Attitudes of Adult Children Whose Aged Parents Are Members of a Sheltered Workshop," *Aging and Human Development*, 3 (1972): 331–37.

Report of the Interregional Meeting of Experts on the Social Welfare Aspects of Family Planning. New York: United Nations, 1971.

"Report on Bucharest, A," *Studies in Family Planning*, 5 (December 1974): 357–95.

Rescher, N. *Welfare: The Social Issues in Philosophical Perspective*. Pittsburgh: University of Pittsburgh Press, 1972.

Review of Public Administration, A: The Republic of China. Taipeh: Executive Yuan, 1975.

Richardson, J. *Food Stamp Program Reform: 94th Congress*. Washington, D.C.: Library of Congress, 1976.

Rimlinger, G. V. "Social Security, Incentives and Controls in the U.S. and U.S.S.R.," in M. N. Zald (ed.), *Social Welfare Institutions*. New York: Wiley, 1965.

———. "Smith and the Merits of the Poor," *Review of Social Economy*, 34 (December 1976): 333–44.

Ripple, L. *Statistics on Social Work Education in the United States: 1974*. New York: Council on Social Work Education, 1975.

Robb, J. H. "Family Structure and Agency Coordination: Decentralization and the Citizen," in M. N. Zald (ed.), *Social Welfare Institutions*. New York: Wiley, 1965.

Roby, P. (ed.). *The Poverty Establishment*. Englewood Cliffs, N.J.: Prentice-Hall, 1974.

Rodman, H. "On Understanding Lower Class Behavior," *Social and Economic Studies*, 8 (1959): 441.

Roethlisberger, F. A., and W. J. Dickson. *Management and the Worker*. Cambridge, Mass.: Harvard University Press, 1939.

Rohrlich, G. F. (ed.). *Social Economics for the 1970's: Programs for Social Security, Health, and Manpower*. New York: Dunellen, 1970.

Ropke, W. "Reflections on the Welfare State," in C. I. Schottland (ed.), *The Welfare State*. New York: Harper & Row, 1967.

Rose, A. M. (ed.). *Human Behavior and Social Processes*. Boston: Houghton Mifflin, 1962.

Rosenheim, M. K. "*Shapiro* v. *Thompson:* 'The Beggars Are Coming to Town,'" *1969 Supreme Court Review 303*.

Rosow, J. M. (ed.). *The Worker and the Job: Coping with Change.* Englewood Cliffs, N.J.: Prentice-Hall, 1974.

Ross, A. D. "Philanthropic Activity and the Business Career," in M. N. Zald (ed.), *Social Welfare Institutions.* New York: Wiley, 1965.

Rossbach, G. "Caseworkers' Use of the 'Third Ear,' " *Smith College Studies in Social Work,* 36 (October 1965): 127.

Rossi, P. H., and K. C. Lyall. *Reforming Public Welfare: A Critique of the Negative Income Tax Experiment.* New York: Sage, 1976.

Rothman, D. J. *The Discovery of the Asylum: Social Order and Disorder in the New Republic.* Boston: Little, Brown, 1971.

Rothman, S. M. "Sterilizing the Poor," *Social Science and Modern Society,* 14 (January-February 1977): 36–40.

Roueche, B. *Eleven Blue Men.* New York: Berkley, 1965.

Roundtree, Folsom, and Pelligrino v. *New York State Department of Social Services.* New York: U.S. District Court, Eastern District of New York, 1976, Memorandum and Order, and Dissenting Opinion, 75-C-1052.

Rubinow, I. M. "What Do We Owe to Peter Stuyvesant?" in R. Morris and M. Freund (eds.), *Trends and Issues in Jewish Social Welfare in the United States, 1899–1952.* Philadelphia: Jewish Publication Society of America, 1966.

Rue, V. M. "A U.S. Department of Marriage and the Family," *Journal of Marriage and the Family,* 35 (1973): 689–99.

Ryan, W. "Blaming the Victim: Ideology Serves the Establishment," in P. Roby (ed.), *The Poverty Establishment.* Englewood Cliffs, N.J.: Prentice-Hall, 1974.

Samant, S., S. Sawant, and B. Talati. *Distribution of Fertilizers in Ralnagiri (India) District.* Tel Aviv: Foreign Training Department, Ministry of Agriculture, 1970. (Mimeographed.)

Sanger, M. *Margaret Sanger: An Autobiography.* New York: Norton, 1938.

Sansom, A. B. *The Western World and Japan.* New York: Knopf, 1958.

Saxer, A. *Social Security in Switzerland.* Berne: Paul Haupt, 1965.

Schatz, H. A. *Social Work Administration: A Resource Book.* New York: Council on Social Work Education, 1970.

Scheler, M. F. *The Nature of Sympathy.* London: Routledge & Kegan Paul, 1954.

Schlesinger, A., Jr. "The Welfare State," in C. I. Schottland (ed.), *The Welfare State.* New York: Harper & Row, 1967.

Schofield, J. A. "The Economic Return to Preventive Social Work," *International Journal of Social Economics,* 3 (1976): 167–78.

Schorr, A. L. *Filial Responsibility in the Modern American Family.* Washington, D.C.: Government Printing Office, 1960.

———. "Income Maintenance and the Birth Rate," *Social Security Bulletin,* 28 (December 1965): 2.

———. *Social Security and Social Services in France.* Washington, D.C.: Government Printing Office, 1965.

———. "On Selfish Children and Lonely Parents," *The Public Interest,* 4 (Summer 1966): 8.

——. *Poor Kids.* New York: Basic Books, 1966.

——. "Who Promised Us a Rose Garden?" *Social Work,* 20 (May 1975): 200–205.

——. "Enforcing Child-Support," *New York Times,* October 8, 1976, p. 29.

——. *Jubilee for Our Times: A Practical Program for Income Equality.* New York: Columbia University Press, 1977.

Schottland, C. I. "Social Welfare in the Soviet Union," in *Social Welfare Forum, 1959.* New York: Columbia University Press, 1959, pp. 217–36.

——. *The Social Security Program in the United States.* New York: Appleton-Century-Crofts, 1963.

——. "The Changing Roles of Government and Family," in P. E. Weinberger (ed.), *Perspectives on Social Welfare: An Introductory Anthology.* New York: Macmillan, 1974.

Schottland, C. I. (ed.). *The Welfare State.* New York: Harper & Row, 1967.

Schumacher, E. F. *Small Is Beautiful: Economics as if People Mattered.* New York: Harper & Row, 1973.

Schwartz, E. E. "A Way to End the Means Test," *Social Work,* 4 (1963): 3.

Schweinitz, K. de. *England's Road to Social Security.* Philadelphia: University of Pennsylvania Press, 1943.

Secret of Affluence, The. Washington, D.C.: Department of Agriculture, 1976.

Select Committee on Nutrition and Human Needs, U.S. Senate. *Who Gets Food Stamps?* Washington, D.C.: Government Printing Office, 1975.

Separation of Services from the Determination of Eligibility for Assistance Payments, The. Washington, D.C.: Government Printing Office, 1970.

Service Directory of National Voluntary Health and Social Welfare Organizations. New York: National Assembly of National Voluntary Health and Social Welfare Organizations, 1974.

Shapira, M. "Reflections on the Preparation of Social Workers for Executive Positions," *Journal of Education for Social Work,* 7 (Winter 1971): 55–68.

Shapiro v. *Thompson,* 394 U.S. 618 (1969).

Sheidman, E. S. (ed.). *Death: Current Perspectives.* Palo Alto, Calif.: Mayfield, 1971.

Sheldon, E. B., and W. Moore (eds.). *Indicators of Social Change: Concepts and Measurements.* New York: Sage, 1968.

Sheppard, H. L. *Effects of Family Planning on Poverty in the United States.* Kalamazoo, Mich.: Upjohn, 1967.

Sheppard, H. L. (ed.). *Poverty and Wealth in America.* Chicago: Quadrangle, 1970.

Shireman, J. "Client and Worker Opinions About Fee-Charging in a Child Welfare Agency," *Child Welfare,* 44 (1975): 331–40.

Shlakman, V. "Social Work's Role in Family Planning: Social Policy Issues," in F. Haselkorn (ed.), *Family Planning: The Role of Social Work.* Garden City, N.Y.: Adelphi University School of Social Work, 1968.

Shonfield, A., and S. Shaw. *Social Indicators and Social Policy.* London: Heinemann, 1972.

Shostak, A. B., and W. Gomberg (eds.). *New Perspectives on Poverty.* Englewood Cliffs, N.J.: Prentice-Hall, 1965.

Shostak, A. B., J. V. Til, and S. B. V. Til. *Privilege in America: An End to Inequality?* Englewood Cliffs, N.J.: Prentice-Hall, 1973.

Siegel, S. "Judaism and Liberalism: A Conservative View," in P. E. Weinberger (ed.), *Perspectives on Social Welfare: An Introductory Anthology.* New York: Macmillan, 1974.

————. *Social Service Manpower Needs: An Overview to 1980.* New York: Council on Social Work Education, 1975.

Sills, D. L. *The Volunteers.* New York: Free Press, 1957.

Simmel, G. "The Poor," *Social Problems,* 13 (1965): 123.

Simon, K. A., and M. M. Frankel. *Projections of Educational Statistics to 1983–84.* Washington, D.C.: Department of Health, Education, and Welfare, 1974.

Singer, I. B. (ed.). *The Jewish Encyclopedia.* New York: Funk & Wagnalls, 1903.

Skolnick, J. H. *The Politics of Protest: A Task Force Report Submitted to the National Commission on the Causes and Prevention of Violence.* New York: Simon & Schuster, 1969.

Skolnik, L. R. *Public Assistance and Your Client: A Handbook.* Garden City, N.Y.: Adelphi University School of Social Work, 1977.

Smigel, E. O. (ed.). *Handbook on the Study of Social Problems.* Chicago: Rand McNally, 1971.

Smith, A. D. *The Right to Life.* Chapel Hill: University of North Carolina Press, 1955.

Smith, P. C., L. M. Kendall, and C. L. Hulin. *The Measurement of Satisfactions in Work and Retirement: A Strategy for the Study of Attitudes.* Chicago: Rand McNally, 1969.

Smith, W. T., II. "Public Welfare: The 'Impossible' Dream." Paper presented at the County Officers Association of the State of New York, Rochester, N.Y., 1975. (Mimeographed.)

Social Benefits in Sweden: 1974–1975. Stockholm: Tryg Hansa, 1974.

Social Conditions and Social Security: Germany Reports. Bonn: Press and Information Office, Federal Government of Germany, 1964.

Social Insurance in Norway. Oslo: National Insurance Institute, 1973.

Social Realities and the Social Work Response: Report from the English-speaking Caribbean. Paper presented at the Eighteenth International Conference of schools of Social Work, San Juan, Puerto Rico, July 13–17, 1976.

Social Reconstruction in the Newly Independent Countries of East Africa. New York: United Nations, 1965.

Social Security: 1974. Canberra: Australian Government Printing Service, 1974.

Social Security and National Health Insurance in France. New York: Ambassade de France, n.d.

Social Security Programs Throughout the World, 1975. Washington, D.C.: Department of Health, Education, and Welfare, 1975.

Social Services in Britain. New York: British Information Services, 1975.

"Social Welfare: Ends and Means," in *Current Sweden* No. 54. Stockholm: Swedish Institute, 1974.

Social Welfare and Family Planning. New York: United Nations, 1976.

Social Welfare in Thailand. Bangkok: Department of Public Welfare, Ministry of the Interior, 1962.

Social Welfare Indicators: Republic of China 1976. Taipeh: Executive Yuan, 1976.

Social Welfare Law, 1958: Regulations Concerning Helping the Needy. Jerusalem: Government of Israel, 1958. (In Hebrew.)

Soemardjan, S. "Social Attitudes Toward Population Policies in Less Developed Societies," in K. A. Kendall (ed.), *Population Dynamics and Family Planning: A New Responsibility for Social Work Education.* New York: Council on Social Work Education, 1971.

Sorokin, P. A. (ed.). *Explorations of Altruistic Love and Behavior.* Boston: Beacon Press, 1950.

Spencer, H. "A Theory of Population, Deduced from the General Law of Animal Fertility," *Westminster Review,* 57 (1852): 468–501.

Stack, C. B. *All Our Kin: Strategies for Survival in a Black Community.* New York: Harper & Row, 1974.

Stallings, R. A. "The Community Context of Crisis Management," *American Behavioral Scientist,* 16 (January-February 1973): 312.

"Starvation," *Parade,* December 14, 1975, p. 5.

Statistical Abstract of Israel. Jerusalem: Central Bureau of Statistics, 1975.

Statistical Yearbook 1975. New York: United Nations, 1976.

Stein, H. D. "Observations on Determinants of Social Work Education in the United States," in *An Intercultural Exploration: Universals and Differences in Social Work Values, Functions, and Practice.* New York: Council on Social Work Education, 1967.

———. "Values, Family Planning, and Development: Implications for Social Work," in *A Developmental Outlook for Social Work Education.* New York: International Association of Schools of Social Work, 1974.

Stein, H. D. (ed.). *Planning for the Needs of Children in Developing Countries.* New York: UNICEF, 1964.

Stein, H. D., and R. H. Cloward (eds.). *Social Perspectives on Behavior.* New York: Free Press, 1958.

Steiner, G. Y. *Social Insecurity: The Politics of Welfare.* Chicago: Rand McNally, 1966.

Stepan, J., and E. H. Kellogg. *Comparative Study of World Law on Contraceptives: Revised and Updated.* Washington, D.C.: Smithsonian Institution, 1974.

Stevens, R., and R. Stevens. *Welfare Medicine in America: A Case Study of Medicaid.* New York: Free Press, 1974.

Stock, M. *Freud: A Thomistic Approach.* Washington, D.C.: Thomist Press, 1963.

Strauss, A. *George Herbert Mead on Social Psychology.* Chicago: University of Chicago Press, 1956.

———. "Transformations of Identity," in A. M. Rose (ed.), *Human Behavior and Social Processes.* Boston: Houghton Mifflin, 1962.

Strauss, G. "Job Satisfaction, Motivation and Job Redesign," *Organizational Behavior: Research and Issues.* Madison, Wis.: Industrial Relations Research Association, 1974.

————. "Workers' Attitudes and Adjustments," in J. M. Rosow (ed.), *The Worker and the Job: Coping with Change.* Englewood Cliffs, N.J.: Prentice-Hall, 1974.

Striner, H. E. *1984 and Beyond: The World of Work.* Kalamazoo, Mich.: Upjohn, 1967.

————. "Recurrent Educational Manpower Training in Great Britain," *Monthly Labor Review,* 98 (September 1975): 30–34.

Strumpel, B. (ed.). *Economic Means for Human Needs: Social Indicators of Well-Being and Discontent.* Ann Arbor: University of Michigan Press, 1976.

Studt, E. "Crime and Delinquency: Institutions," in *Encyclopedia of Social Work.* New York: National Association of Social Workers, 1971.

Sumner, W. G. *Social Darwinism.* Englewood Cliffs, N.J.: Prentice-Hall, 1963.

Supplemental Security Income for the Aged, Blind, and Disabled. Washington, D.C.: Department of Health, Education, and Welfare, 1973.

Sussman, M. B. "Family," in *Encyclopedia of Social Work.* New York: National Association of Social Workers, 1971.

Swai, A. Z. N. "Developmental Planning Related to Needs of Children in Tanganyika," in H. D. Stein (ed.), *Planning for the Needs of Children in Developing Countries.* New York: UNICEF, 1964.

Symposium on Law and Population, The. New York: United Nations Fund for Population Activities, 1975.

Szalai, A. (ed.). *The Use of Time: Daily Activities of Urban and Suburban Populations in Twelve Countries.* The Hague: Mouton, 1972.

Talmon, Y. *Family and Community in the Kibbutz.* Cambridge, Mass.: Harvard University Press, 1972.

Tawney, R. H. *The Acquisitive Society.* New York: Harcourt, Brace & World, 1948.

————. "Economic Virtues and Prescriptions for Poverty," in H. D. Stein and R. H. Cloward (eds.), *Social Perspectives on Behavior.* New York: Free Press, 1958.

Taylor, F. W. *The Principles of Scientific Management.* New York: Harper Bros., 1911.

Temple, W. "The State," in C. I. Schottland (ed.), *The Welfare State.* New York: Harper & Row, 1967.

TeSelle, S. (ed.). *The Rediscovery of Ethnicity: Its Implications for Culture and Politics in America.* New York: Harper & Row, 1973.

Theodorson, G. A., and A. G. Theodorson. *A Modern Dictionary of Sociology.* New York: Crowell, 1969.

Thoenes, P. *The Elite in the Welfare State.* New York: Free Press, 1966.

Thomas, M. C., and C. C. Flippen. "American Civil Religion: An Empirical Study," *Social Forces,* 51 (1972): 218–25.

Thursz, D., and J. L. Vigilante (eds.). *Meeting Human Needs,* Vol. 1: *An Overview of Nine Countries.* Beverly Hills, Calif.: Sage, 1975.

————. *Meeting Human Needs,* Vol. 2: *Additional Perspectives from Thirteen Countries.* Beverly Hills, Calif.: Sage, 1976.

Tietze, C., and M. J. Mustein. "Induced Abortion: 1975 Factbook," *Reports on Population/Family Planning,* 14 (December 1975): 1–76.

Til, J. V. "Social Inequality: How Did We Get Here Anyway?" in A. B. Shostak, J. V. Til, and S. B. V. Til, *Privilege in America: An End to Inequality?* Englewood Cliffs, N.J.: Prentice-Hall, 1973.

Titmuss, R. M. *Essays on "the Welfare State."* New Haven, Conn.: Yale University Press, 1959.

———. "The Welfare State: Images and Realities," in C. I. Schottland (ed.), *The Welfare State.* New York: Harper & Row, 1967.

———. *The Gift Relationship.* London: Allen & Unwin, 1971.

———. *Social Policy: An Introduction.* New York: Pantheon, 1974.

Towle, C. *Common Human Needs.* New York: National Association of Social Workers, 1965.

Training for Social Welfare: Fifth International Survey—New Approaches in Meeting Manpower Needs. New York: United Nations, 1971.

Trattner, W. I. *From Poor Law to Welfare State: A History of Social Welfare in America.* New York: Free Press, 1974.

Trolander, J. A. *Settlement Houses and the Great Depression.* Detroit: Wayne State University Press, 1975.

Tropp, E. "A Humanistic View of Social Group Work: Worker and Member on a Common Human Level," in *A Humanistic Foundation for Group Work Practice.* New York: Selected Academic Readings, 1969.

Tweddle, D. "What People Who Care Really Think," *CERES,* 3 (1970): 27.

Tyler, E. T. (ed.). *Birth Control: A Continuing Controversy.* Springfield, Ill.: Thomas, 1967.

Udall, M. K. "Spaceship Earth: Standing Room Only," in D. Callahan (ed.), *The American Population Debate.* Garden City, N.Y.: Doubleday, 1971.

Van den Haag, E. "Economics Is Not Enough: On the Anti-Capitalist Spirit," *Public Interest,* 45 (Fall 1976): 109–22.

Vecoli, R. J. "Ethnicity: A Neglected Dimension of American History," in M. Friedman (ed.), *Overcoming Middle Class Rage.* Philadelphia: Westminster Press, 1971.

Verba, S. *Small Groups and Political Behavior.* Princeton, N.J.: Princeton University Press, 1961.

Vigilante, J. L. "Between Values and Science: Education for the Profession During a Moral Crisis or, Is Proof Truth?" *Journal of Education for Social Work,* 10 (Fall 1974): 107–15.

———. "Back to the Old Neighborhood," *Social Service Review,* 50 (June 1976): 194.

Vroom, V. H. *Work and Motivation.* New York: Wiley, 1964.

Walinsky, A. "Keeping the Poor in Their Place: Notes on the Importance of Being One-Up," in A. B. Shostak and W. Gomberg (eds.), *New Perspectives on Poverty.* Englewood Cliffs, N.J.: Prentice-Hall, 1965.

Walz, T. H. "The Family, the Family Agency, and Postindustrial Society," *Social Casework,* 56 (January 1975): 13–20.

Ward, B. "Not Triage, but Investment in People, Food, and Water," *New York Times,* November 15, 1976, p. L31.

Warren, R. L. "Toward a Non-Utopian Normative Model of the Community," *American Sociological Review,* 35 (1970): 219.

Webb, S., and B. Webb. *The Prevention of Destitution.* London: National Committee for the Prevention of Destitution, 1911.

Weber, M. "Bureaucracy," in H. H. Gerth and C. W. Mills (eds.), *From Max Weber: Essays in Sociology.* London: Routledge & Kegan Paul, 1948.

————. *The Protestant Ethic and the Spirit of Capitalism.* New York: Scribner's, 1952.

Webster's Third New International Dictionary. Cleveland: World Book Co., 1961.

Weinberger, P. E. (ed.). *Perspectives on Social Welfare: An Introductory Anthology.* New York: Macmillan, 1974.

Weinberger, P. E., and D. Z. Weinberger. "The Jewish Religious Tradition and Social Services," in P. E. Weinberger (ed.), *Perspectives on Social Welfare: An Introductory Anthology.* New York: Macmillan, 1974.

Weingarten, M. *Life in a Kibbutz.* New York: Reconstructionist Press, 1955.

Weiss, C. H. *Evaluating Action Programs: Readings in Social Action and Education.* Boston: Allyn & Bacon, 1972.

————. *Evaluation Research: Methods of Assessing Program Effectiveness.* Englewood Cliffs, N.J.: Prentice-Hall, 1972.

Whitten, E. B. "Disability and Physical Handicap: Vocational Rehabilitation," in *Encyclopedia of Social Work.* New York: National Association of Social Workers, 1971.

Whyte, W. F. *Money and Motivation.* New York: Harper Bros., 1955.

————. *Organizational Behaviour: Theory and Application.* Homewood, Ill.: Dorsey, 1969.

————. *Organizing for Agricultural Development: Human Aspects in the Utilization of Science and Technology.* New Brunswick, N.J.: Transaction, 1975.

Wickenden, E. *Social Welfare in a Changing World: The Place of Social Welfare in the Process of Development.* Washington, D.C.: Department of Health, Education, and Welfare, 1965.

Wilensky, H. L. *The Welfare State and Equality: Structural and Ideological Roots of Public Expenditures.* Berkeley: University of California Press, 1975.

Wilensky, H. L., and C. N. Lebeaux. *Industrial Society and Social Welfare.* New York: Free Press, 1958.

Williamson, J. B., *et al. Strategies Against Poverty in America.* New York: Wiley, 1975.

Wilson, G., and G. Ryland. *Social Group Work Practice.* Cambridge, Mass.: Houghton Mifflin, 1949.

Wiltse, K. M. "The Field of Social Work: An Overview," in A. E. Fink, *The Field of Social Work.* New York: Holt, Rinehart & Winston, 1974.

Winston, E. "The Contribution of Social Welfare to Economic Growth," *The Social Welfare Forum, 1966.* New York: Columbia University Press, 1966.

————. "A National Policy on the Family," *Public Welfare,* 27 (January 1969): 54–58.

Witte, E. W. *The Development of the Social Security Act.* Madison: University of Wisconsin Press, 1962.

Wojiechowski, S. "Poland's New Priority: Human Welfare," in D. Thursz and
    J. L. Vigilante (eds.), *Meeting Human Needs,* Vol. 1: *An Overview of Nine
    Countries.* Beverly Hills, Calif.: Sage, 1975.
Woodroofe, K. *From Charity to Social Work in England and the United States.*
    Toronto: University of Toronto Press, 1962.
Work in America. Cambridge, Mass.: MIT Press, 1973.
*Workbook on the First National Affiliate Workshop on Planning and Providing
    Abortion Services.* New York: Planned Parenthood–World Population,
    1973.
World Population: Challenge to Development. New York: United Nations,
    1966.
*World Population Growth and Response: 1965–1975—A Decade of Global
    Action.* Washington, D.C.: Population Reference Bureau, 1976.
Wright, S. R., and J. D. Wright. "Income Maintenance and Work Behavior,"
    Social Policy, 6 (September-October 1975): 24–32.
Yakabe, K. *Labor Relations in Japan: Fundamental Characteristics.* Tokyo:
    International Society for Educational Information, 1974.
Yarmolinsky, A. "The Service Society," *Daedalus,* 97 (Fall 1968): 1263.
Your Social Security Earnings Record. Washington, D.C.: Department of
    Health, Education, and Welfare, 1975.
Zablocki, B. *The Joyful Community.* Baltimore: Penguin, 1971.
Zaidan, G. C. *The Costs and Benefits of Family Planning Programs.* Baltimore:
    Johns Hopkins Press, 1971.
Zald, M. N. (ed.). *Social Welfare Institutions.* New York: Wiley, 1965.
Zimmerman, C. Z. "The Future of the Family in America," *Journal of Marriage
    and the Family,* 34 (May 1972): 323.
Zimmerman, M. "Abortion Law and Practice: A Status Report," *Population
    Reports,* E (March 1976): 25–40.
"ZPG: A Fascist Movement!" in D. Callahan (ed.), *The American Population
    Debate.* Garden City, N.Y.: Doubleday, 1971.

INDEX

Index